American Civil Religion

American Civil Religion

What Americans Hold Sacred

PETER GARDELLA

OXFORD
UNIVERSITY PRESS

Oxford University Press is a department of the University of Oxford.
It furthers the University's objective of excellence in research, scholarship,
and education by publishing worldwide.

Oxford   New York
Auckland   Cape Town   Dar es Salaam   Hong Kong   Karachi
Kuala Lumpur   Madrid   Melbourne   Mexico City   Nairobi
New Delhi   Shanghai   Taipei   Toronto

With offices in
Argentina   Austria   Brazil   Chile   Czech Republic   France   Greece
Guatemala   Hungary   Italy   Japan   Poland   Portugal   Singapore
South Korea   Switzerland   Thailand   Turkey   Ukraine   Vietnam

Oxford is a registered trademark of Oxford University Press
in the UK and certain other countries.

Published in the United States of America by
Oxford University Press
198 Madison Avenue, New York, NY 10016

© Peter Gardella 2014

All rights reserved. No part of this publication may be reproduced, stored in a
retrieval system, or transmitted, in any form or by any means, without the prior
permission in writing of Oxford University Press, or as expressly permitted by law,
by license, or under terms agreed with the appropriate reproduction rights organization.
Inquiries concerning reproduction outside the scope of the above should be sent to the
Rights Department, Oxford University Press, at the address above.

You must not circulate this work in any other form
and you must impose this same condition on any acquirer.

Library of Congress Cataloging-in-Publication Data
Gardella, Peter, 1951–
American civil religion : what Americans hold sacred / Peter Gardella.
ISBN 978-0-19-530018-5 (pbk. : alk. paper)—
ISBN 978-0-19-530017-8 (hardcover : alk. paper)   1. National characteristics, American.
2. Public history—United States.   3. Symbolism—United States.
4. National monuments—Social aspects—United States.
5. Collective memory—United States.   6. Patriotism—United States.   I. Title.
E169.1. G273 2014
973—dc23
2013022355

For those who have served in the armed forces of the United States, especially during times of war.

CONTENTS

Acknowledgments   ix

1. What Is American Civil Religion?   1
2. America: The Name, the Concept, and the Word   9
3. Jamestown and Its Anniversaries   16
4. The Mayflower Compact   31
5. Plymouth Rock, the Pilgrims, and the Indians   38
6. City on a Hill: From Jesus to Winthrop, Kennedy, and Reagan   54
7. The Freedom Trail and Boston Common   61
8. The Liberty Bell, Independence Hall, and the Slave Quarters   67
9. The Flag   81
10. The Declaration of Independence   98
11. The Great Seal and the Dollar Bill   113
12. The Constitution   117
13. Washington, D.C.: The City, the Capitol, and the White House   132
14. The Star-Spangled Banner   150
15. The Washington Monument   160
16. The Battle Hymn of the Republic   168
17. Gettysburg and the Gettysburg Address   172
18. Lincoln's Second Inaugural Address   183
19. Arlington National Cemetery   191
20. The Statue of Liberty and Ellis Island   200
21. America the Beautiful   216

22. The Lincoln Memorial   225
23. Mount Rushmore in the Black Hills   232
24. God Bless America   246
25. This Land Is Your Land   252
26. The Four Freedoms   257
27. Iwo Jima: The Picture, the Monuments, and the Battle   270
28. Disney Parks   278
29. The Kennedy Inaugural   292
30. King's Speeches: The Mall (1963) and Memphis (1968)   302
31. Vietnam Veterans Memorial   317
32. Transforming the National Mall   323
33. Ground Zero, Martyrdom, and Empire   345
34. Conflict, Consensus, and the Future   359

ACKNOWLEDGMENTS

My first thanks for this book must go to Theo Calderara, my editor at Oxford University Press. More than a year after I submitted the proposal to Cynthia Read at Oxford (who did not say no, but wisely pointed out that a book like this would be "a lot of work"), Theo offered to edit it. Over the years since we signed a contract, he has suggested innumerable improvements. His contributions have ranged from alerting me to new publications in the field to urging complete reorganizations of some chapters to voting decisively in favor of including the Four Freedoms. And despite the slow pace of my work, he has never lost faith. At Oxford, I would also like to thank Cynthia Read for enabling the religion operation to flourish and Charlotte Steinhardt for helping me with the process of choosing pictures and getting permissions to print some pictures and some texts.

Among my fellow scholars, Colleen McDannell of the University of Utah and Peter Williams of Miami University of Ohio read the proposal and some early chapters and provided useful suggestions. Theresa Sanders of Georgetown University gave me ideas and support. Dr. Martin Blatt of the National Park Service corrected some errors on the Freedom Trail. The spirit of the late Sydney Ahlstrom, my thesis advisor, who was writing about a "post-Christian" American national faith in 1972, has continued to inspire my work. The late Robert Bellah, who brought the phrase "civil religion" into contemporary discourse and became its (sometimes reluctant) scholarly saint, spoke to me about his own Christian commitments.

My wife, Professor Lorrie Greenhouse Gardella of Albertus Magnus College, has discussed every choice I have made, read and re-read every chapter and revision of this book, and made many perceptive comments. Besides her editorial suggestions, she has also provided emotional support and a model of the scholarly work ethic, turning out her own successful book while mine went more slowly. My son, William Gardella, has read every chapter at least once. William also took many of the pictures that appear in the text and talked with me about civil religion on many a long drive between Connecticut and Pittsburgh, where he started and finished college and law school while the book was being written. My wife's mother and father, Annette and Milton Greenhouse, have read several chapters, and her mother has encouraged me with praise of my writing and urged me to finish the project before too many more years go by. As a veteran of World War II who tells wonderful stories of that time, Milton Greenhouse has been an example to me of the living power of American civil religion. A virtual member of the family, my old friend Charles Mulholland, has contributed technical support on a level that only someone with a degree in computer science and decades of experience in the field can supply.

Other members of my family have contributed in less direct, but still important ways. When I realized that no book on American civil religion could be complete without some account of the Disney Parks, I was fortunate enough to have a niece, Susan, who has long worked for Disney and who hosted me on a visit to Disney World. Susan is the daughter of my brother Steve, and my earliest attachment to American civil religion was inspired in part by Steve's military career, which began when I was a toddler and he was attending the US Naval Academy and extended through the Vietnam era. I visited the Epcot Center with my brother John, during a reunion with him and Steve and my third brother, Anthony. John and Anthony are also veterans, members of the last cohort of young men for whom military service was nearly universal. Graduating college in 1973, the year that the draft ended, I escaped Vietnam and never served in the armed forces.

Manhattanville College, where I have taught the history of religions since 1983, supported this project directly by allowing me to teach an honors seminar on American civil religion in the spring of 2006. My students in that course—Gustavo Gimenez, Amanda Raz, Sally Reardon, Marcos Reyes Martinez, and Susan Trolle—did research and reports based on particular topics from this book, and their work helped me decide about including or excluding some chapters. Indirectly, Manhattanville has supported me by providing a nurturing atmosphere in which to work as a scholar and teacher. Unlike some universities, Manhattanville is a safe place to take intellectual risks.

In the fall of 2009, the Rye Community Synagogue of Rye, New York, hosted me as their scholar in residence for a weekend, during which I gave three talks on American civil religion. I recall with pleasure the enthusiasm of Laura Leach, the chair of the committee that invited me, who joined in when "God Bless America" was being sung. Rabbi Daniel Gropper's agreement helped to confirm my choice of the values of freedom, democracy, peace, and tolerance as key elements of American civil religion. I also recall with gratitude the challenge raised by a woman in that congregation whose name I never learned, who insisted that American civil religion cannot really be religious. Such principled opposition can be a real help to clear thinking.

American Civil Religion

1

What Is American Civil Religion?

Around the world, people both love and hate American values and symbols. Since 1776, when the United States issued the first Declaration of Independence, more than a hundred national governments, or about half of the governments on earth, have come into being through declarations of independence. Though the American flag is frequently burned, students in China created a version of the Statue of Liberty in Tiananmen Square in 1989, and some lower caste Indians venerate a goddess of English, modeled on Lady Liberty. The US government has often tried to export values such as personal freedom and political democracy, and has always found people who hold American symbols and values to be sacred—worth living and dying and perhaps killing for. This attachment to national symbols and this missionary spirit, which goes beyond patriotism, raise basic questions about what religion is.

Still, most Americans have never heard the phrase "American civil religion," or considered what it might mean. Scholars have debated the existence of this religion and its meaning since 1967, when sociologist Robert Bellah wrote a bold and insightful article called "Civil Religion in America." Bellah wrote for a scholarly periodical named *Daedalus*, after the craftsman of ancient Greece who made the wings that his son Icarus used for his fatal flight. Perhaps mindful of the fate of Icarus, the scholarship following Bellah has demonstrated remarkable timidity and precision, arguing over issues such as whether there is more than one American civil religion and how civil religion differs from mere nationalism, or from the political religions of totalitarians like the Nazis. Bellah himself, a Christian believer and a lay preacher in the Anglican tradition, became disillusioned with American civil religion during the Vietnam era. More recently, in reaction against the wars in Iraq and Afghanistan, other scholars have declared that Americans should stop building new monuments for a decade or two, or even that the phrase "American civil religion" should be forgotten, because it inevitably signifies an oppressive, univocal ideology.

But the monuments of the National Mall in Washington—the Lincoln Memorial, the Vietnam Veterans Memorial, the Washington Monument—will not disappear. They have been joined in recent years by memorials that testify to the diversity and vitality of American civil religion, such as the Korean War Veterans Memorial, the United States Holocaust Memorial Museum, the Franklin Delano Roosevelt Memorial, the National Museum of the American Indian, the World War II Memorial, and the Martin Luther King, Jr., Memorial. These memorials are all within walking distance of the National Archives, where the words of the Constitution and the Declaration of Independence are displayed on a site that was intended by the architect of Washington, Pierre L'Enfant, for a national church. Every day, people from around the world line up—many with an attitude that resembles that of pilgrims—to visit these documents.

Outside the capital, American civil religion flourishes at many sites. Fifteen hundred miles from Washington, enormous heads carved into Mount Rushmore represent four American presidents (George Washington, Thomas Jefferson, Theodore Roosevelt, and Abraham Lincoln) as, to use the words of sculptor Gutzon Borglum, "the gods they have become." At the Alamo in Texas and at Pearl Harbor in Hawaii, Mexicans and Japanese join Americans to commemorate military martyrs. In New York harbor, the Statue of Liberty has greeted ships since 1886. She lifts her torch today next to Ellis Island, a former inspection and detention center recently turned into a sacred site, a shrine to the memory of immigrants. Both Lady Liberty and Ellis Island stand across a stretch of water from the memorial and museum at Ground Zero. In October 2012, the tip of Roosevelt Island, next to Manhattan, was dedicated as sacred to the Four Freedoms (Freedom of Speech, Freedom of Worship, Freedom from Fear, and Freedom from Want) that were proclaimed as the war aims of the United States during World War II. Those freedoms are now affirmed in the preamble to the Universal Declaration of Human Rights of the United Nations. In the seventh inning of every World Series game that has been played since 2001, the television broadcast and the fans in the stands have paused to sing Irving Berlin's "God Bless America," which has joined "The Star-Spangled Banner" (which is performed before almost all athletic contests) among a short list of national hymns.

This book argues that these monuments, texts, and images, along with the behaviors and values associated with them, amount to a real religion. The purpose of this book is to present this religion. More than forty monuments, texts, and images of American civil religion will be discussed here in the chronological order of their emergence, beginning with the name "America" and proceeding to the memorial and museum at Ground Zero and the current plans for changing the National Mall. Some chapters—such as the chapters on the development of Washington, D.C., the chapter on Gettysburg, and the chapter on military martyrdom that includes the Alamo, the memorials to Custer's Last Stand, and Pearl Harbor—deal with more than one related monument or more than one text. Each chapter will tell the story of its monuments, texts, and images from the beginning to the present.

The whole story is unified by four values—personal freedom (often called liberty), political democracy, world peace, and cultural (including religious, racial, ethnic, and gender) tolerance—that have come to dominate American civil religion. Today, these values are often advanced by political leaders and advocates who ask Americans to kill and to risk their own lives while executing policies of the US government. Questions may be raised over whether these four are the most central values. Those who have tried to identify the values of American civil religion have sometimes included the value of free enterprise or capitalism, but that may be subsumed under personal freedom or liberty whenever the freedom to make or to have money is actually held sacred. The value of capitalism for its own sake has been denied by important contributors to American civil religion, including John Winthrop, Theodore and Franklin Delano Roosevelt, John F. Kennedy, and Martin Luther King, Jr. But liberty, democracy, peace, and tolerance are denied by no one who claims to speak in the tradition of the United States, even though many Americans hold different ideas about what liberty, democracy, peace, and tolerance entail, or how far a particular set of actions undertaken in their names may be justified. In a recent textbook on American civil religion, scholar Gary Laderman claims that it makes violence a "sacred sacrament," but again this is contradicted by many in this book, such as Martin Luther King, Jr., Woody Guthrie, and Katherine Lee Bates. Although the United States is a very violent nation, and violence always raises religious issues because it touches the boundary of life and death, violence is not a value of American civil religion like liberty, democracy, peace, and tolerance.

For example, with regard to cultural tolerance, even those Americans who would deny equal rights to gays and lesbians or who would profile Muslims as potential terrorists do not dispute the general principle that tolerance of different cultures is good, or that such tolerance is a central part of the American ideal. This book will trace the roots of the current value of cultural tolerance back as far as the first decades of Jamestown and Plymouth colonies, each of which survived in part because English settlers learned to work closely with Native Americans and with those who disagreed with them on religious grounds. In 1646, a visiting Jesuit priest counted eighteen languages on the streets of the Dutch colony of New Amsterdam, a place that would eventually see riots over slavery and violence between Protestants and Catholics, but which would become the culturally tolerant city of New York. Prejudice against Jews was rampant in America for centuries, and still exists to some degree, but the United States was the first nation to allow Jews to be citizens while remaining Jews, and George Washington wrote a letter affirming tolerance to the Jews of Newport, Rhode Island. Rhode Island itself was an outlier among American colonies in practicing religious tolerance, but its example and those of the other tolerant colonies, such as New Amsterdam, Pennsylvania, Maryland, and Georgia, carried the day.

Similar stories may be told regarding liberty, democracy, and peace. The Puritans who sought liberty for themselves in Massachusetts Bay gave no freedom to others and abhorred the word "democracy," but their elections and town meetings led directly to our own. The Puritan vision of America as a city on a hill was a Messianic hope for world peace. The bell cast for the Pennsylvania statehouse was probably inscribed with "Proclaim liberty throughout all the land" as a protest against the hereditary governorship of the Penn family, but as the bell aged and cracked, it came to stand for broader causes.

The Liberty Bell took on different meanings in each of seven phases of the development of American civil religion. Cast in the (1) colonial or primal phase of civil religion, the bell had its place in the argument between legislators and the Penn family, and it rang to proclaim events in Philadelphia. During the (2) revolutionary or classical phase, it rang above the building that came to be called Independence Hall because the Declaration of Independence and the Constitution were written there, and the bell became identified with those documents. Small cracks appeared during the (3) national or continental phase, while what was normally called the State House Bell was rung for hours at a time to celebrate the visit of Lafayette in 1824 and to mourn the deaths of John Adams and Jefferson on July 4, 1826. The large, iconic crack that ended the bell's active ringing career came on February 22, 1846, when the bell was rung to commemorate Washington's Birthday. As the issue of slavery came to a head in the Civil War and led to the (4) sacrificial phase of American civil religion, the cracked bell was presented as a martyr and named the Liberty Bell on the cover of an Abolitionist magazine of the same name.

American civil religion entered its (5) imperial phase as the nation healed and embarked on overseas conquests from the end of Reconstruction through World War I. During those years, the Liberty Bell received homage as a relic at the 1876 Centennial. It was sent on seven transcontinental railroad journeys between 1885 and 1915, drawing crowds to events that unified the American South and West. In the (6) global phase of civil religion, from the 1930s through Vietnam, the Liberty Bell (or Liberty Belle) was depicted, personified as a woman, on the fuselages of several B-17 bombers.

As American civil religion moved from an age of global dominance to a more (7) multicultural era, the Liberty Bell gained its own building, across the street from its original home in Independence Hall, to accommodate visitors from around the world at the Bicentennial in 1976. The association of the bell with cultural tolerance had already increased during the last half of the twentieth century, as demonstrators from groups for African-American civil rights, for gay rights, and for the first Earth Day in 1970 held demonstrations and sit-ins around the Liberty Bell. In 2002, as another new building to display the bell was being constructed, the remains of the presidential mansion once inhabited by George Washington, who lived there when the national capital was in Philadelphia, were discovered. The slave quarters of that mansion were found next to the new building, and the names and stories of some of Washington's slaves were remembered. A memorial to those slaves, with a framework marking the presidential mansion and windows at ground level making the original foundations of the slaves' rooms visible, was built next to the Liberty Bell center. The slave memorial became a culminating symbol of the multicultural phase of American civil religion, a phase that continues at this writing. Visitors now see the slave memorial as they approach the bell and pass through a series of exhibits that highlight the role of the bell in promoting rights for all Americans, for ethnic minorities, and for women.

Unless the Liberty Bell is regarded as part of a religion, its history and the power it exerts make little sense. On my last visit to the Liberty Bell, a child protesting that she was not included as her elders joined the long line outside the visitors' center was told that there was no reason for her to wait on line to see "a cracked bell." In fact, there is nothing rational about waiting on such a line. It belongs to the essence of religion to go beyond reason, even when religion includes some rational goods. The word "religion" derives from the Latin *ligo*, which means "I bind," and religion has to do with what is binding or obligatory. Religions are not philosophies or sets of beliefs but systems of symbols, actions, and ideas that purport to bind together groups of people, or people and gods, or even the elements of nature. Religions may be explained or defended by reason, but they do not gain their power from reason any more than a piece of music or a work of visual art does.

Those accustomed to Western religions, which are centered on God or on gods, tend to think of religion as requiring some divine or supernatural element, but the broader phenomenon of religion does not demand this. Taoists, Buddhists, and Confucians often demonstrate undeniably religious behavior, including elaborate symbolism and ritual, without affirming a god. To refer to religions as "faiths," as some writers do, omits many whose religions do not consist of beliefs but of practices.

As I have defined religion elsewhere, the word designates "a system of nonrational commitments that holds life together." This does not mean that rational values are excluded. Devotion to the values of American civil religion—personal liberty, political democracy, world peace, and cultural tolerance—can be justified on rational grounds. These values might arise from a philosophy of transcendent morality or enlightened self-interest. But most Americans have not come to these values through reason. They have learned to value liberty, democracy, peace, and tolerance through the monuments, texts, and images of American civil religion. And devotion to the word "America," or to the American flag, or to the Liberty Bell does not guarantee rational consistency. Clearly, the US government that ordered the confinement of its own citizens of Japanese ancestry to internment camps in 1942, or that dropped more bombs on Vietnam than were dropped by all sides in World War II, or that enforced slavery and forbade Native Americans to practice their religions, cannot be identified with liberty, democracy, peace, and tolerance. As with any religion, behavior that contradicts American civil religion does not indicate that its values have been lost or that the religion does not exist. When most Americans salute the flag, or sing the National Anthem, or visit Arlington National Cemetery, the emotions they feel do not arise from a rational conclusion. If American civil religion works well for them, the emotions will lead to an affirmation of the values. If the religion works badly, they may feel emotions without any connection with values, just as Christians may be moved by a crucifix without absorbing any Christian love or compassion, or Jews may be moved by the Exodus narrative without gaining any passion for justice or vision of social change.

Not everyone has a religion, although most people do. There are those for whom life does not hold together. Others try to hold life together with rational calculations. But most people in the United States are powerfully influenced both by a traditional religion inherited from their families and by American civil religion.

Americans are not unique in having a civil religion. Think of the power of Lenin's tomb for Russians, of the Arc de Triomphe for the French, of Tiananmen Square for the Chinese. In the United Kingdom, the queen heads both a branch of Christianity, the Church of England, and a civil religion that extends to the Commonwealth of Nations. Each of these civil religions can move people to devotion and to sacrifice. Each can give the strength that religions give, a strength that grows from the sense that life does hold together and that individual lives are connected to a larger or more basic dimension of reality. But American civil religion may claim to be the strongest and most elaborate civil religion of the world. In part, this strength stems from a weakness. Because Americans have no natural, common culture, but use a borrowed language and live on land recently taken from other nations, the United States needs a civil religion more. Even among the other nations of the Americas, most have a more coherent ethnic, religious, and cultural heritage than the United States. Our pledges of allegiance and devotion to the flag arise in part from the need to create unity out of our diversity.

Some writers have argued that American civil religion derives from biblical faiths; others have drawn parallels between the United States and ancient Rome, where the civil religion was very strong. As Catherine Albanese has pointed out, both of these positions are correct. American civil religion employs texts, symbols, and rituals that evoke a chosen, special people under a single God, following the model of ancient Israel, and other texts and symbols and rituals that stress the unity of different ethnic and religious groups under a common and sacred state, following the model of ancient Rome. This book will argue that the Roman model has become more prevalent, especially as the American sphere of influence in the world has grown larger, but it cannot be denied that American civil religion can also be fiercely monotheistic and biblical. If one could bring an ancient Roman back to stand at the Lincoln Memorial, it would probably be difficult to convince the visitor that Americans do not worship their dead emperors; but Lincoln's genius as a theologian of the civil religion was his ability to evoke the mysterious judgments of the biblical God to call Americans away from narrow views.

To mention Israel and Rome is to suggest that the United States must face an ending, a fall of the empire or a confrontation with Babylon, an apocalypse. But even if the United States enters a time of declining power, American civil religion will continue, just as the civil religions of England, France, Russia, and Japan have survived declines in power. Even the spirits of ancient Israel and Rome have never really died, but continue to inspire the world. There is nothing in the present situation that should make anyone conclude that American civil religion will sink into irrelevance or be condemned by history. As James Russell Lowell wrote in the great Abolitionist hymn, "Once to Every Man and Nation":

> *New occasions teach new duties, time makes ancient good uncouth,*
> *They must upward still and onward, who would keep abreast of truth.*

And in the sixth verse:

> *Was the Mayflower launched by cowards, steered by men behind their time?*
> *Turned those tracks toward Past or Future that make Plymouth Rock sublime?*
> *Lo, before us gleam truth's beacons; we ourselves must Pilgrims be,*
> *Launch our Mayflower and steer boldly through the desperate winter sea.*

Let us now turn to see where previous generations have steered.

SOURCES

Albanese, Catherine, *America: Religions and Religion* (Belmont, CA: Wadsworth Publishing, 1981; 4th ed., 2006).

Armitage, David, *The Declaration of Independence: A Global History* (Cambridge, MA: Harvard University Press, 2007).

Beiner, Ronald, *Civil Religion: A Dialogue in the History of Political Philosophy* (New York: Cambridge University Press, 2011).

Bellah, Robert, "Civil Religion in America," *Daedalus* 96, no. 1 (Winter 1967), 1–21.

Bellah, Robert N., and Stephen M. Tipton, eds., *The Robert Bellah Reader* (Durham, NC: Duke University Press, 2006).
Bloom, Harold, *The American Religion: The Emergence of the Post-Christian Nation* (New York: Simon & Schuster, 1992).
Chernus, Ian, "We Need to Stop Using the Phrase, 'American Civil Religion,'" http://hnn.us/articles/we-need-stop-using-phrase-american-civil-religion (June 8, 2012).
Chidester, David, and Edward Linenthal, eds., *American Sacred Space* (Bloomington: Indiana University Press, 1995).
Gentile, Emilio, *Politics as Religion*, translated by George Staunton (Italian ed., 2001; Princeton, NJ: Princeton University Press, 2006).
Haberski, Raymond Jr., *God and War: American Civil Religion since 1945* (New Brunswick, NJ: Rutgers University Press, 2012).
Laderman, Gary, *American Civil Religion* (Minneapolis, MN: Fortress Press, 2012).
Maier, Pauline, *American Scripture: Making the Declaration of Independence* (New York: Alfred A. Knopf, 1997).
Remillard, Arthur, *Southern Civil Religions: Imagining the Good Society in the Post-Reconstruction Era* (Athens: University of Georgia Press, 2011).
Savage, Kirk, *Monument Wars: Washington, D.C., the National Mall, and the Transformation of the Memorial Landscape* (Berkeley: University of California Press, 2009).

2

America: The Name, the Concept, and the Word

"America" is the sacred name of the nation legally known as the United States of America. National hymns like *America the Beautiful* and *God Bless America*, which will be the subjects of later chapters in this book, have no rivals employing the full legal name. Phrases like "the American dream" and "the American way of life" lose their poetry if "the United States" or "US" is substituted. The word "Americans" is the most evocative way to name those living in the United States. At the same time, objections from people of other nations on the American continents (who are undeniably also Americans), from linguists seeking precision, and from dissenters against the imperialist tendencies of American civil religion cannot be discounted.

The story of how America got its name is oddly accidental and somewhat controversial, and so are the possible etymologies and meanings of that name. Amerigo Vespucci, a Florentine explorer who sailed for Spain and Portugal in the 1490s and early 1500s, was the first to conclude in print (in published letters to his patron, Lorenzo de' Medici) that the lands the Europeans had found in the Caribbean and Brazil were not part of Asia. Impressed by Vespucci's writings (one of which was apparently a forgery issued without his consent), the humanist scholar Matthias Ringmann, working on a new geography with cartographer Martin Waldseemüller, gave the name of America to what is now called South America in a book and world map published in 1507. The map became known as the "baptismal certificate of the New World," and the only known surviving copy was purchased for $10 million by the Library of Congress in 2003 (see Figure 2.1). It is now displayed in the Library of Congress, just across from the eastern side of the Capitol, in a room where the darkness needed to protect fragile documents also provides a fitting air of mystery. Although Waldseemüller made later maps that took back the honor he had given Vespucci, deferring to the claims of Columbus and calling the Americas *Terra Incognita*, or "Unknown Land," his earlier naming stuck. In 1538, Gerald Mercator's influential geography

Figure 2.1 The "America Map," or *Universalis Cosmographia*, the first map to use "America" (see lower left) Martin Waldseemüller and published in 1507. Library of Congress, Geography and Map Division.

applied the name of America to the northern continent as well. Spain came reluctantly to this usage, preferring "the New World" well into the eighteenth century, but the name of America and its derivation from Amerigo Vespucci were both irreversibly established by the time the British colonies united. Ralph Waldo Emerson blamed Vespucci for defrauding Columbus and regretted in 1835 that "broad America must bear the name of a thief." By then, however, even Emerson recognized that it was too late to change. Though Vespucci may seem to have little deserved to have two continents named for him, his hypothesis that there were new continents both to the West and to the South caused an intellectual revolution that transformed the European picture of the world. Perhaps Amerigo did deserve the fame that his name attained.

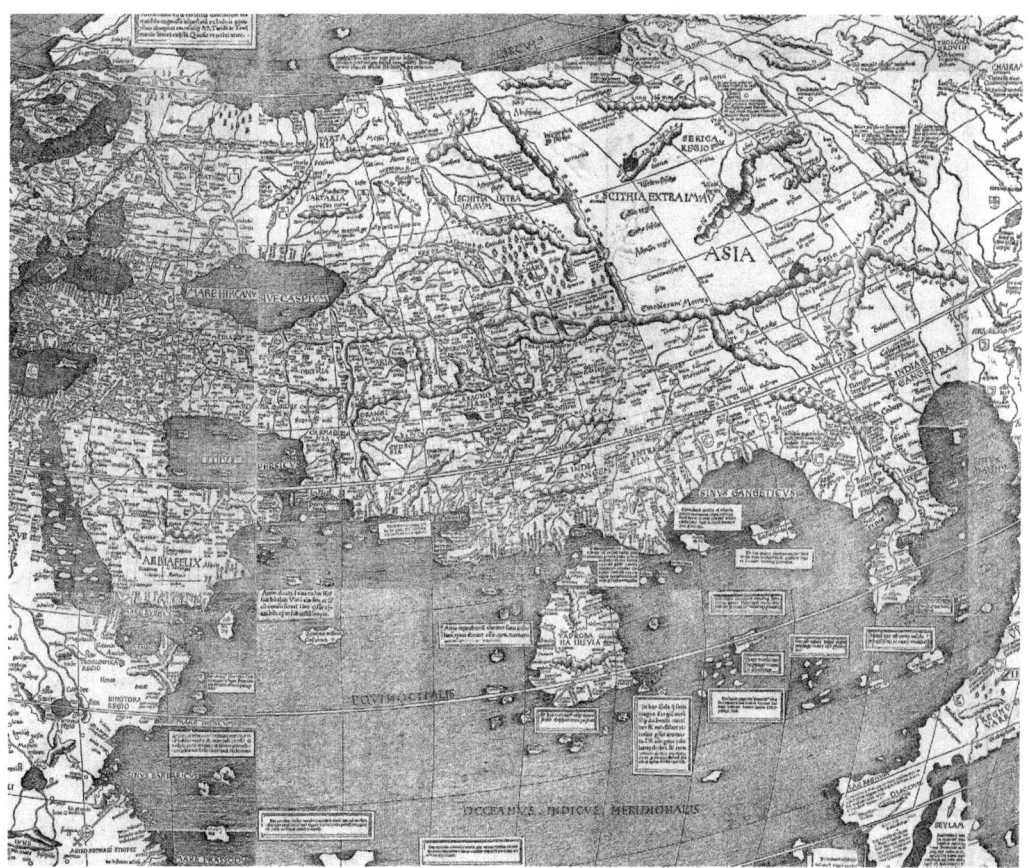

to name a continent and to show America as separate from Asia, was drawn by German cartographer

On the other hand, some (beginning with Jules Marcou, a geologist who worked at Harvard from 1848 to the 1880s) have argued for a native source for the name, trying to keep America while eliminating Vespucci. Vespucci's name, Amerigo, had been Latinized to Albericus in his book of letters, the *Mundus Novus* (or New World), and several have speculated that the prevalence of "America" over "Alberica" resulted from the influence of Carib, the language of the Mosquito Indians whom Columbus met on the coast of Nicaragua. These Indians referred to the inland parts of the continent, and particularly the mountains where they found their gold, as *Amerrique*. Spanish and Portuguese sailors may have spread this name "America" around Europe before Waldseemüller and Mercator ever published their geographies, and the common usage of the explorers may have

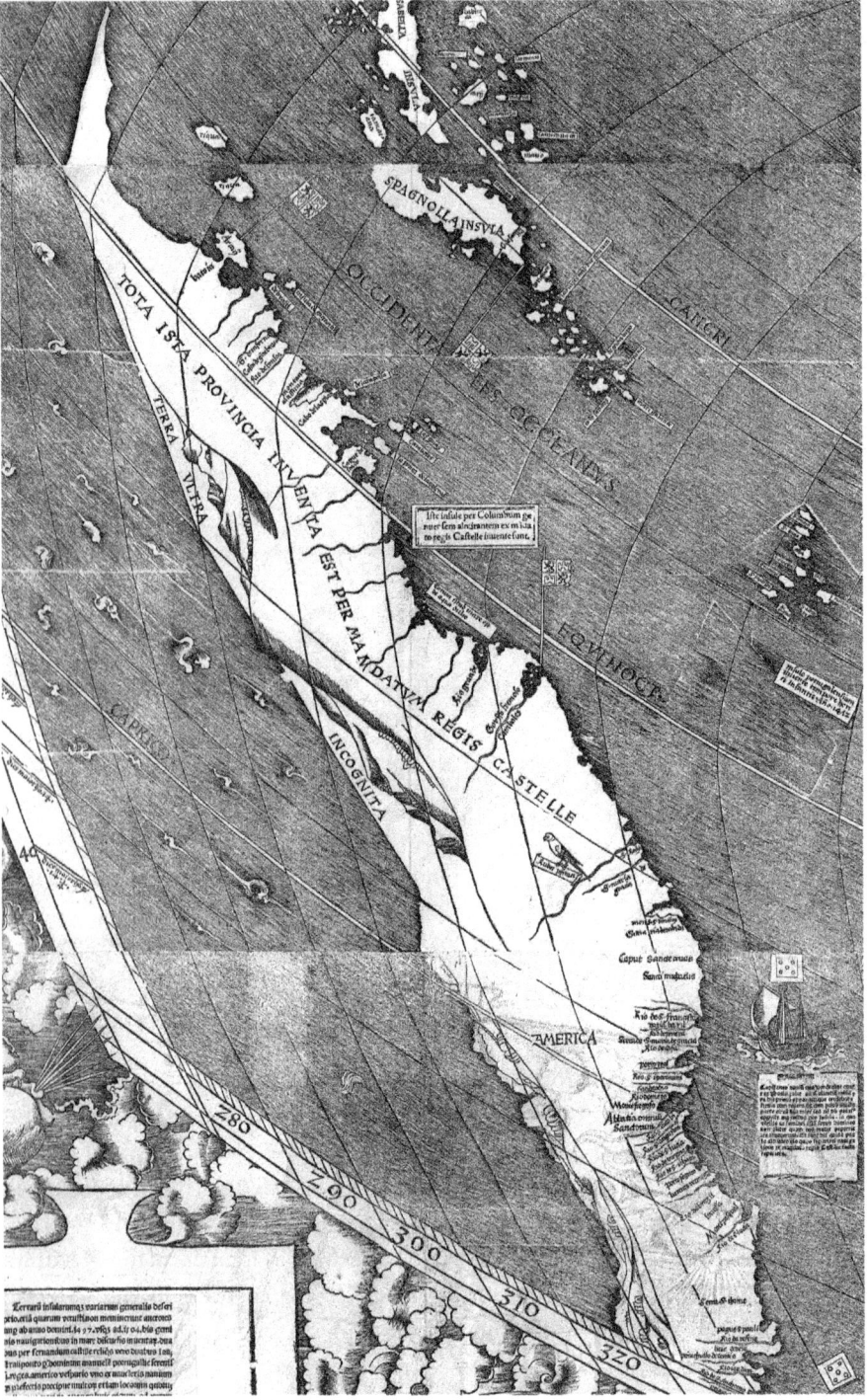

Figure 2.2 A detail from the Universalis Cosmographia of 1507 shows the first appearance of the word "America" as the name of a territory on a published map. This act of naming has been called "the birth certificate of the New World." (Library of Congress, Geography and Map Division).

influenced the cartographers, or at least made Waldseemüller's naming more acceptable among explorers. Pushing the Native American connection further, it appears that the Carib word *Amerrique* means "great, high, prominent," and it was used especially for the mountains to the west of the Mosquito seacoast lands. Connecting the name to the highest culture of Mesoamerica, novelist Jan Carew of Guyana has asserted that the root of *Amerrique* was a Mayan word for "land of strong wind" or "land of the spirit."

Other theories have attached the name of America to the Vikings and the Old Norse word *Ommerike*, meaning "farthest outland," which in turn derives from *Amalric*, or "kingdom of heaven," or to the Scandinavian *Amt*, or "district," and *Eric*, for the Viking explorer Leif Ericsson. Some English authors have argued that the name derives from Richard Ameryk, a merchant of Bristol who sponsored the journeys of John Cabot (Giovanni Caboto), the Italian who enabled England to claim Canada. Another claim invokes the Algonquian Indian word *Em-erika*. According to some members of the Church of Jesus Christ of Latter-Day Saints, their Book of Mormon contains the place names *Alameki* and *Amalickiah*, both of which connect with the Semitic *melekh*, or "king." By Mormon theory, Semitic words would have been widespread in America because the lost tribes of Israel came here long before European contact.

Even if Amerigo Vespucci is admitted as the most likely source, the meaning of the name America remains in dispute. According to some, the name Amerigo designates a master workman or assigner of tasks. Related names are the Greek Aimulos, Latin Aemilius, and Old German Amalrich or Emmerich; modern forms include the feminine Amelia and Emily and the masculine Amery and Emery. Others derive the syllable *rig* from the root for "ruler," which appears in English *bishopric* and German *Reich*, joined with *Hama* for "home" or "village" (as in *hamlet*), so that the name Amalrich or Amerigo means "ruler of the community." While etymologies from the Carib Indians and the Mayans link the word "America" with height, greatness, wind, and spirit, European sources link it with work and mastery.

In recent decades, political controversies have emerged over whether the name "America" should ever be used to designate the United States. Politically liberal publishing houses, such as the United Church of Christ's Pilgrim Press, forbid this usage in their style sheets. In books from such publishers, "United States" and "US" have begun to function as adjectives. During the July 4 holiday week of 2007, the *New York Times* published an op-ed piece by two editors of *Le Monde* urging that Americans call themselves "États-Uniens," or in English, "United Statesians," following the example of news media in Québec. The fact that two other American nations, Mexico and Brazil, also call themselves "the United States" had not influenced these French thinkers. Scholarly organizations like the Modern Language Association of America and the American Academy of

Religion have found their names under challenge from those who see the appropriation of "American" by organizations in the United States as a form of US imperialism. The scholarly field of American studies, with its national American Studies Association (ASA), has also been forced to reconsider its initial focus on the United States. For 2007, the ASA chose "América Aquí: Transhemispheric Visions and Community Connections" as the theme for its annual meeting in Philadelphia. One of the founders of the American Name Society, George R. Stewart, commented that "the makeshift establishment of the national name was the worst misfortune in our whole naming-history."

At the center of all this history and politics stands the word itself, "America," a linguistic and acoustic reality commanding a range of meanings that develops constantly through use. The relation of "America" to "the United States" is somewhat reminiscent of the relation that the word "Russia" once bore to the political "Union of Soviet Socialist Republics," but "Russia" has ties with an ethnic group and a language, which "America" does not. Immigrants to the United States become Americans, but immigrants to Russia in Soviet days did not become Russians. "America" has come to stand for the ideal of a society free from ethnicity and indifferent to cultural heritage—a culture that incorporates all others and integrates them into a new whole, as expressed in the word "Americanization" and the statement popular among many generations of immigrants, "We're all Americans now." It also stands for the natural setting of the nation, the land occupied by the political entity called the United States, the land of "purple mountain majesty" and "fruited plain" celebrated by the song "America the Beautiful."

The word "America" consists of four syllables, with three open vowel sounds, two liquid consonants, and one hard "c." In comparison to other names of great nations and empires, such as Rome (*Roma*), China (*Xianhua*), or Britain, "America" is a complex and strongly rhythmic word, amounting in itself to forty percent of a line of iambic pentameter. In songs like "America the Beautiful" and "God Bless America," or a poem like "Let America Be America Again" by Langston Hughes, the word functions as a central component of the poetry and an expression of aspiration in itself. According to Allen Walker Read, a Columbia University professor of English who served as president of the American Name Society, it was not too enthusiastic to say that "the name America is a sublime poetic inspiration" and that a name of greater "euphony, harmony, and sympathy with other continental names could not possibly be imagined."

Read hoped in 1993 that the imprecision of Americans calling themselves a name that could apply to others would eventually lead people from the United States to identify with all places in the Americas. He saw a parallel to the use of "European" for all those inhabiting the European Union, predicting that "American" would become "a benign example of a usage that benefits international relations." On the other side of the question, those who protest US policies and those who fear that the United States may turn in a less democratic direction have used the harsher, German spelling, *Amerika*, to express their criticism and their vision of dystopia. An ABC television mini-series by that title, in which the Soviet Union occupied the United States, aired in 1987. More recently, "America" has begun to appear again as a first name, as in America Ferrara, the star of the movie *Real Women Have Curves* (2002) and of the *Ugly Betty* television series, which aired from 2006 to 2010. Both transcending and crystallizing political and cultural divisions, "America" functions as the most sacred and the most contested word in the civil religion of the United States.

SOURCES

Cohen, Jonathan, "The Naming of America: Fragments We've Stored Against Ourselves," http://www.uhmc.sunysb.edu/surgery/america.html (July 7, 2007).

Fernández-Arnesto, Felipe. *Amerigo: The Man Who Gave His Name to America* (London: Weidenfeld & Nicolson, 2006).

Lester, Toby, *The Fourth Part of the World: The Race to the Ends of the Earth, and the Epic Story of the Map That Gave America Its Name* (New York: Free Press, 2009).

Read, Allen Walker, *America: Naming the Country and Its People* (Lewiston, NY: Edwin Mellen Press, 2001).

Rousseau, Martine, and Olivier Houdart, "There's a Word for People Like You," *New York Times*, July 6, 2007, p. A15.

Stewart, George R., *Names on the Land: A Historical Account of Place-Naming in the United States* (Boston: Houghton Mifflin, 1967).

3

Jamestown and Its Anniversaries

Jamestown has a great story, evocative ruins, and a rich heritage. At Jamestown, English settlers first met Native Americans and Africans. The values of personal freedom or liberty, political democracy, world peace, and cultural tolerance have all appeared in the rituals and monuments, movies and books surrounding this place.

The English mission to found an empire was passed at Jamestown from monarchists to American democrats. At the three hundredth anniversary of that transition, Theodore Roosevelt came to Jamestown in 1907 and sent a Great White Fleet of sixteen battleships to show the Stars and Stripes around the world. At the four hundredth anniversary in 2007, Queen Elizabeth II of Great Britain gave a speech that echoed the National Park Service's presentation of Jamestown as the meeting place of English, Native American, and African cultures.

To begin with the story: on May 13, 1607, a hundred and four English men (no women) landed on a swampy peninsula on the James River, off Chesapeake Bay and about thirty miles inland from the Atlantic. One of their first acts after landing was to set up a huge cross and hold services, led by the Anglican priest Robert Hunt. Immediately attacked, they built a fort of logs and attempted to trade with those they called "the naturals," about thirty groups of Algonquian-speaking Indians whose central nation was the Powhatan. These Indians had formed a confederacy, perhaps in part because they were being decimated by European diseases that had been spreading since the 1570s. The site of Jamestown had been cleared of forest and abandoned by a group called the Paspahegh, and the remaining Paspahegh paid homage to the "emperor" of the Powhatan, who was named Wahunsonacock but was often called "Powhatan" by the English.

One of the leaders of the English expedition was an adventurer in his late twenties, Captain John Smith. Smith had already fought Spaniards and Turks in Europe, been sold into slavery as a war prisoner, escaped after killing his Muslim master, and made his way back from Turkey through Russia to England. When Smith was captured by Indians and brought to Wahunsonacock, he was apparently saved from death by the king's favorite daughter, a twelve-year-old girl named Matoaka who went by her nickname, Pocahontas. The young men who were about to smash Smith's skull with clubs stopped when Pocahontas took the Englishman's head in her arms and shielded it with her own head. Historians debate whether the rescue was real and spontaneous, a political ploy by Wahunsonacock, or part of an initiation ceremony, and some have charged that Smith made the whole thing up, but all agree that Smith was released and was then regarded by the king and Pocahontas as a family member.

Pocahontas helped the English survive by bringing food to Jamestown in its first year, as disease (some related to malnutrition) reduced the number of English to thirty-eight. Smith became president of the colony, and he forced the colonists to give up searching for gold to concentrate on clearing land for agriculture. In a famous decree, he canceled the original policy of sharing all food from a common store and quoted the apostle Paul to the effect that "he who will not work, shall not eat." News that people could own the land they cleared raised the numbers of colonists to five hundred. Injured in an explosion of the gunpowder he carried on his belt (possibly because of sabotage by enemies), Smith returned to England in 1609 to seek a skilled surgeon. Relations with the Indians then deteriorated, and the English were trapped inside the fort. During the "starving time" of that winter, the number of colonists fell to sixty. In the spring of 1610, this remnant had buried its cannons and started back to England when ships arrived with fresh provisions and people.

In 1613, the English took Pocahontas hostage as she was visiting one of their ships. While she endured a year of captivity at Jamestown, Pocahontas perfected her knowledge of English and adopted Christianity, accepting the baptismal name of Rebecca. She also seems to have negotiated a truce. In 1614, Wahunsonacock sent representatives to the wedding of Pocahontas and the colonist John Rolfe, who was the first man to plant the West Indian tobacco that made Virginia a successful colony. She and Rolfe had a son, and in 1616 they took him to England, where Lady Rebecca Rolfe amazed the court of King James with her command of English dress, manners, and speech. At first regarded as the embodiment of hope that Indians would merge with the English in the New World, Pocahontas/Rebecca came to stand for the tragic outcome of those hopes when she fell ill and died, at age twenty-two, on the ship that was taking her back to Virginia. Yet in a sense she succeeded: through her son, Pocahontas was claimed as an ancestor by the heirs of important Virginia families, including Edmund Randolph (secretary of state under George Washington), President John Tyler, and Edith Bolling, the wife of President Woodrow Wilson. Celebrated in a 1995 Disney animated movie, Pocahontas exerted influence that continued through 2007, when her descendant Harrison Tyler (b. 1926) presided over many events at the four hundredth anniversary of Jamestown.

Another aspect of Jamestown's cultural heritage dates to 1619, when English pirates raiding Spanish ships captured a cargo of African slaves bound for the

Caribbean, and twenty of the Africans ended up in Jamestown—the first African slaves to arrive in the English colonies that would become the United States. Ironically, the Jamestown of 1619 also saw the birth of representative democracy in Virginia, the first meeting of the House of Burgesses. Even more ironically, that free legislature slowly transformed the temporary slavery resulting from capture in war or indentured servitude into a permanent condition, removing the means that slaves originally had to become free. Many of the first Africans in Virginia raised cattle and crops to buy their freedom, then acquired land and paid for English servants of their own, but in 1670 a law was passed against Africans owning white servants. In 1705 the practice of slaves buying their freedom was made illegal, and in 1723 the Burgesses made it illegal for owners to set slaves free except for some extraordinary service, such as helping to stop a slave revolt. By then, Virginia had become the society of white planter aristocrats that would fight for permanent African slavery in the Civil War. The English who settled Jamestown had seen themselves as opposed to slavery, in contrast with their Spanish rivals, but changes in British imperial policy and profits from plantations in America changed their minds. Despite that change, African-American families, including those named Harman, Sweet, Tucker, Mathews, Gibson, and Longo, retained their freedom by moving to other colonies and continue to flourish in the United States today.

The Indians of Virginia had already driven off two potential Spanish settlements before the English came to Jamestown, so at first they did not fear the newcomers, but by 1621 the colonists had grown to about twelve hundred, living in many separate farms and villages. Indians often came to the homes of the English, trading and visiting. Feeling comfortable enough to fulfill one of their original intentions, the Virginia Company decided to establish a college for Indian boys and to accept them as apprentices in English families. This made some Indians suspicious. Meanwhile, the father of Pocahontas had died in 1619 and been replaced as leader of the Powhatan by Opechancanough, a much less conciliatory chief. The truce begun by the marriage of Pocahontas and John Rolfe ended in a stroke of guerrilla warfare, when many of the "naturals" rose at dawn on Good Friday of 1622 and launched a simultaneous attack all over Virginia, killing about 350 settlers, more than a quarter of the English population. Jamestown itself was saved by an Indian convert who warned the English, but repercussions from the attack resulted in the dissolution of the Virginia Company of London and the takeover of the colony by the Crown. Official government policy changed from conversion to extirpation. Another concerted Indian attack in 1644 cemented the enmity of the Powhatan and the English.

In 1676, English rebels led by Nathaniel Bacon burned Jamestown in a protest against Governor Berkeley and the Burgesses for taxing the planters excessively and for not acting aggressively enough to drive the Powhatan out of Virginia.

Though the statehouse was rebuilt, the city never fully recovered, and the capital moved to Williamsburg in 1699. Since then, Jamestown has not appeared as a city on Virginia maps. Its buildings fell into ruins, and its land was used for agriculture and sometimes abandoned. On the other hand, the story of Jamestown and its location, convenient to traffic on the river, meant that the site of Jamestown was often visited, depicted in paintings and plays, and remembered.

The first organized memorial took place in 1807, when about three thousand people arrived on thirty-two boats. The occasion featured a band, eight men carrying a huge cannon ball supposed to date from the original colony, and student speakers from the College of William and Mary. Those who came to Jamestown that day celebrated the imperial mission, its transformation into democratic forms, and the ancestors.

Opening the ceremonies with prayer, the Episcopal bishop of Virginia, James Madison (a cousin of the man who would soon be President James Madison), pronounced a declaration by God that "here, shall the great work of political salvation commence; here I will strike deep the roots of an everlasting empire." The first oration, by student G. B. Baldwin, focused on the past. Beginning with praise of Pocahontas and John Smith, Baldwin extolled Britain's encouragement of free trade, the colonists' establishment of a legislature, and the devotion of the settlers to agriculture rather than gold, then urged his audience to defend republican government and freedom of the press, predicting the conversion of the world to these American standards. John Madison, an adopted son of the future president, spoke next on lessons for the present, such as the tendency of oppressive taxes to provoke revolution, the need for citizens to defend their rights, and the importance of a division of power between executive and legislative branches. Later that night, at a Williamsburg tavern, the group enjoyed and recorded fifteen toasts, including one for Pocahontas, the "benignant spirit" who "so often snatched our ancestors from famine and the sword" and who remains "in the midst of us... the guardian genius of our fathers, of our infancy, of our cradles."

In its account of the day, the *Virginia Apollo* newspaper contrasted the Jamestown story with those of Spanish colonies. The story of Jamestown featured "the majestic Powhatan... the gentle spirit of Pocahontas... and the gallant and romantic Smith," as opposed to "the destructive progress of a Pizarro and a Cortez, and the inhuman systems of civil and ecclesiastical policy" that caused the sacrifice of millions "at the shrine of bigotry and avarice." Long before the United States came into existence, the *Apollo* argued, Jamestown showed that the English in North America had a unique and noble culture that deserved to transform the world.

Dramatic and artistic affirmations of Jamestown and Pocahontas appeared throughout the antebellum years. A sensational and mildly sensual play, *The*

Indian Princess or La Belle Sauvage (The Beautiful Savage), was a hit on the stage of Philadelphia in 1808. The play was based in part on a book of purported history from 1803 that described John Smith resisting the maiden's "tumultuous extasy [sic] of love," while later Pocahontas was unable to refuse John Rolfe because of the "ardour of his caresses." Several depictions of the early 1800s featured an adult Pocahontas naked above the waist, shielding the Englishman from the war clubs (see Figure 3.1). This visual style changed as tastes became more Victorian. In 1840, *The Baptism of Pocahontas*, chastely depicted by Virginia artist John Gadsby Chapman, became one of the first paintings installed in the Capitol Rotunda at Washington.

At the 250th anniversary celebration of Jamestown in 1857, former President John Tyler spoke for two and a half hours before an audience of eight thousand. Because of the looming crisis over slavery, Tyler could not simply celebrate the American empire or the achievements of his ancestors, though he did say that "out of their ashes has arisen an empire of almost boundless extent." He

Figure 3.1 A sandstone relief of Pocahontas saving Captain John Smith, with her father, Chief Wahunsonacock, ruling over the scene, was carved by Antonio Capellano in 1825 and has stood ever since above the west door of the Capitol Rotunda. The bare breasts of Pocahontas are typical of nineteenth-century depictions. Architect of the Capitol.

had to focus on the consequences that dated from the Jamestown of 1619, with "the landing at this place of twenty negroes [sic] from Africa." Tyler tried to justify slavery in Virginia by means of historical context, pointing out the role of Northern merchants in the trade that brought slaves to the South and the "great constitutional charter" of the United States, which was largely written by Virginians like James Madison. Perhaps reflecting discomfort over racial mixing, Tyler never mentioned his own descent from Pocahontas, which his grandson would proudly recall in 2007. Third among the recorded toasts that day, however, after the toasts to Jamestown and John Smith, came "*Pocahontas*—the forest Queen of America, who stayed the uplifted war-club... Virginia will ever cherish her memory with filial fondness and veneration."

During the Civil War, the river near Jamestown became the scene for the battle of the *Monitor* and the *Merrimac* (officially renamed the *Virginia*), the first ironclad warships in the world. The Confederate Army used slaves to build an earthen wall at the site of the original settlement and placed cannon behind the wall to control traffic on the James River, but the Union Army successfully invaded and the freed slaves burned the Jamestown mansion in which they had lived. At the site today, the remains of the Confederate wall can still be seen, although some of it has been excavated to reveal the decayed logs left from Captain John Smith's fort.

The bitter aftermath of the Civil War started at Jamestown, when Union soldiers forced officers of the Confederate Army to gather at the ruins to take oaths of loyalty to the government at Washington. During the Republican, Northern supremacy of the Gilded Age, Plymouth Rock triumphed over Jamestown as the birthplace of America. Historians like Henry Adams (descendent of John and John Quincy Adams) attempted to consign the story of Pocahontas and John Smith to legendary status, and it became fashionable to contrast the virtuous Pilgrims of Massachusetts with lazy Virginia cavaliers.

Still, the three hundredth anniversary of Jamestown in 1907 produced revelatory moments and lasting consequences. Lyon Tyler, the son of President Tyler and president of the College of William and Mary, pushed for a large event, and the US Congress authorized money for a Jamestown Tercentenary Exposition, mixing the spirit of a World's Fair with a historical commemoration. There were exhibitions by states and visits from foreign naval ships as well as commercial and amusement features. A "Cairo Street" like the one that had proved so popular at the 1893 Columbian Exposition in Chicago featured belly-dancing. Among the educational exhibits were more than a hundred people from the Philippines, representing five of the native nations conquered by the United States in the Spanish-American War and a more recent guerrilla uprising, who lived all summer on display in replicas of their natural habitats. Wild West shows and a model Indian village celebrated the white American conquest of the West. In a "Negro

Building," Booker T. Washington and other African-American leaders celebrated the heritage of those twenty Africans who had come to Jamestown in 1619. The Negro Building was the only indoor exhibit open to African-Americans at the Exposition.

Race, individualism, and empire featured in speeches by President Theodore Roosevelt, opening the fair, and Woodrow Wilson, then president of Princeton, who spoke on July 4. Roosevelt began by greeting the foreign delegates, starting with England and Ireland and proceeding to the rest of Europe, Latin America, and Asia, singling out Japan. His first conclusion was that the "blood" of Americans was a special mixture, drawn from all of Europe and destined to take part in a great and peaceful union of the world.

Never mentioning Africa or slaves, Roosevelt gave an outline of US history, in which the soldiers of Robert E. Lee and Ulysses S. Grant were extolled without reference to the causes for which they fought. Indians came into Roosevelt's speech only indirectly, as he referred to "the great wooded wilderness, the Indian-haunted waste" that greeted the Jamestown settlers. Later, he described the "frontiersman" of the West facing the need "to do battle with the savage, and when the savage was vanquished" to fight "the hostile forces of soil and climate." All this fighting led to prosperity, and now the nation had to regulate conflict between the wealthy and the working poor. Roosevelt promised to fight both "sinister agitation against all property" and "the predatory classes whose anti-social power" stems from their wealth. In the end, his answer was to foster individual virtue, "the character of the average man." If Americans continued to treat "each man on his worth," refusing to let their government become the instrument of a "plutocracy" or a "mob," then Roosevelt saw "no height of triumph unattainable in this vast experiment of government by, of, and for a free people."

A few months later, Woodrow Wilson helped to celebrate July 4 at Jamestown by asking, in his address at the Exposition, whether Americans still adhered to the principles of the Declaration of Independence. His answer was yes, but only if we continue to "escape socialism" by continuing to focus our laws and our government on individuals, not corporations or other groups. In his conclusion, Wilson used the heritage of Jamestown to prove the strength of liberty. Individual freedom "ought still to linger in the very air of this place," he said. The projects of governments "never throve in America," whether planted by the French or Dutch or Danes, "but the free English energy throve like a thing bred for the wilderness." He urged Americans to recall that "[t]he future, like the past, is for individual energy and initiative; for men, not for corporations or for governments." Although Roosevelt and Wilson represented different political parties, they both saw a limitless realm of individual liberty extending from Jamestown.

This 1907 celebration created the first permanent monuments at the site. Only a cobblestone foundation remained from the church where the House of Burgesses had begun, but there was also a tower that had become an object of reverence; it was made of bricks that had formed part of a 1639 church burned in 1676, during Bacon's Rebellion, and erected again in 1690. For the Tercentenary, a new group called the Association for the Preservation of Virginia Antiquities (APVA) hired a Massachusetts architect to construct a small church connected to this tower, and he pulled down the remains of two seventeenth-century houses so that he could build with authentic-looking brick. Though the resulting structure, modeled on the St. Luke's Church built in 1632 in Isle of Wight County, Virginia, has never been consecrated for services by the Episcopal Church, it was dedicated as the Jamestown Memorial Church on May 13, 1907. Described as a combination of "demolished authenticity and ersatz verisimilitude," the church does enable visitors to stand in a building on the site where American representative government began and to see the seventeenth-century foundation through windows in the floor.

Another monument, a 103-foot obelisk of grey granite, was built with a $50,000 grant from the US Congress. Inscriptions on the four sides of the obelisk respectively commemorate the three hundredth anniversary in 1907; the Virginia Company for its role between 1607 and 1624; "representative government in America," which "began in the first House of Burgesses, assembled here July 30, 1619"; and climactically, on the south façade:

> JAMESTOWN
> THE FIRST PERMANENT
> COLONY OF THE
> ENGLISH PEOPLE
> THE BIRTHPLACE OF VIRGINIA
> AND OF
> THE UNITED STATES
> MAY 13, 1607

At the base appear two sentences from the advice of the Virginia Company to the colonists in 1606, given to them before they left England. The first urges unity among the colonists, and the second admonishes them "to serve and fear God the giver of all goodness, for every plantation which our heavenly father hath not planted shall be rooted out." These words were seized upon in 2007, as the four hundredth anniversary approached and evangelical Christians campaigned to revive consciousness of how Christian the Jamestown settlers were.

Pocahontas was remembered at the Tercentenary by the Pocahontas Association, formed in 1906 and composed largely of Virginia women who claimed descent from the daughter of Wahunsonacock. The Association hired a sculptor, William Ordway Partridge, to create a statue of their ancestor. After research at the Anthropological Bureau of the Smithsonian, Partridge unaccountably produced a Pocahontas wearing Plains Indian clothing and a feather in her hair, after the Plains fashion. He also gave the statue a long face, paying no attention to the face revealed in the contemporary engraving of Pocahontas at the court of King James. A model of the statue was displayed at the Tercentenary Exposition, and an eighteen-inch bronze replica was given by the Association to Edith Bolling Galt (a descendant of Pocahontas) when she married President Woodrow Wilson in 1915. Not until June 1922 was the life-size bronze version of the statue dedicated at Jamestown, where it still stands before the church (see Figure 3.2).

That ceremony revealed layers of irony with regard to the Indian role at Jamestown. Those dedicating the statue were proud to note the presence of a "full blooded Indian of the Rappahannock tribe [which had been part of the Powhatan confederacy] in native dress." Both the APVA and the Pocahontas

Figure 3.2 This statue of Pocahontas at Jamestown, commissioned by the Pocahontas Association for the three hundredth anniversary of 1907, inaccurately puts its subject in Plains Indian garb. Its depiction of Pocahontas warning the settlement, with her hands in the position of a goddess or saint dispensing a blessing, was accurate. Photograph by the author.

Association supported a campaign by the Rappahannock to change a Virginia law that denied them the right to vote. In her speech celebrating Pocahontas, on the other hand, a Richmond woman named Cynthia Tucker Coleman rejoiced that America was "redeemed from the dominion of the savage to yield its wealth of soil and climate to the race which should dominate the world." Surely the Rappahannock must have flinched to hear these words. Yet among other Indians, such as the Cherokee of Oklahoma, word that Virginia was remembering Pocahontas led Indian women to form Pocahontas Clubs that continue into the twenty-first century. The years around the Jamestown Tercentenary were the nadir of Native American history. The census of 1920 revealed the lowest moment of population, and anthropologists referred to Indians as "vanishing Americans" whose cultures would soon disappear; near the moment of death, however, a rebirth began. In 1924, the Indian Citizenship Act gave Native Americans the right to vote, and population has increased from 0.2% of the US total in 1920 to 0.9% in the 2010 census.

Although the statue at Jamestown does not represent Pocahontas accurately, it does represent an advance in dignity over the bare-breasted maidens of the nineteenth century, and even over the kneeling Pocahontas of the Capitol rotunda. The sculptor tried to capture a moment when Pocahontas came to warn the settlers of an Indian attack, and she is striding forward, head slightly raised, "in command of her surroundings," as one scholar has noted. There is also an archetypal quality to the posture of the statue. With both arms out slightly, palms exposed and fingers pointing down, this Pocahontas assumes the posture of the Virgin Mary dispensing blessing in countless statues and paintings from the Middle Ages and the Renaissance, and on the Miraculous Medal of Roman Catholics in modern times. Mary inherited this gesture from the Egyptian Isis, from the goddesses of Greece, and from nameless goddesses of the Stone Age; she shares it with Kwan Yin of China. The Pocahontas who stands at Jamestown is not so much warning as ruling, in the way that the goddess rules, by dispensing gifts.

At a spot overlooking the beach and the James River, probably within the original area of the fort, the celebrants of 1907 authorized a bronze statue of John Smith, which was completed in 1909. Where Pocahontas is at eye level with visitors, so that many stand beside her to have their pictures taken, John Smith has been set on a tall base of stone from which he watches the river. He wears chest armor and a sword, on which his left hand rests, so that he seems ready to fight any invader. At the same time, his right hand holds a book, recalling his role as an author, the first historian of Virginia and the man whose *Generall Historie* gave New England its name. Both Smith's face and clothing are accurate, based on a contemporary painting.

The statue also suggests deep connections across three centuries, between John Smith and Theodore Roosevelt. Roosevelt sailed to Jamestown on the presidential yacht *Mayflower* in December 1907, eight months after opening the Tercentenary, to send a Great White Fleet around the world. Both Smith and Roosevelt were adventurers, writers of history, soldiers, civilian leaders, and dramatic self-promoters, and both saw themselves as engaged in historic missions—Smith for England against other colonial powers, particularly Spain, and Roosevelt for the United States in another age of colonization, facing Europe and especially Japan.

While a fleet of sixteen battleships (and destroyer escorts) painted white with golden trim may seem better designed for public relations than for battle, Roosevelt wrote in his 1913 autobiography, "In my own judgment the most important service that I rendered to peace was the voyage of the battle fleet round the world." The fleet was his answer to a widespread fear that the United States would not be able to defend its acquisitions of Hawaii and the Philippines from the Spanish War of 1898. Though Roosevelt won the Nobel Prize for mediating an end to the Russo-Japanese war in 1905, and the American president tried to cultivate friendship with Japan, he felt a growing truculence from the Japanese. *Harper's Magazine* in 1907 warned that the dispatch of the fleet might mean war with Japan, and Roosevelt was not sure that war would not break out. He told the captains of the ships to drill the crews and to prepare constantly to be attacked. The brightly decorated ships in Yokohama Harbor had the serious purpose of announcing both to Japan and to the domestic audience that the United States intended to remain a Pacific power. In the Great White Fleet, the symbolic dimension of civil religion and the realities of military strategy came together.

No fleet of warships had ever sailed around the world in 1908. As Roosevelt told the sailors on their return, "Other nations may do what you have done, but they'll have to follow you." After the fleet came home, the replicas of governors' mansions from the thirteen colonies that had been constructed as state pavilions for the Jamestown Exposition became Admirals' Row at the Hampton Roads Naval Base, from which American sea power still projects itself to the world. America's emergence as a world power seemed to justify the statement of Lord Bryce, the British ambassador, that the settlement of Jamestown "compared in its momentous consequences with the overthrow of the Persian Empire by Alexander, with the destruction of Carthage by Rome, with the conquest of Gaul by Clovis, with the taking of Constantinople by the Turks."

By the time the three hundred fiftieth anniversary of Jamestown arrived in 1957, the United States had become the leading power in the world. Relations with the English mother country had been strained by the Suez Canal crisis of 1956, when Washington and Moscow combined to insist that the British, French, and Israelis allow President Gamal Abdel Nasser of Egypt to take control of the canal the French had built, and through which the Great White Fleet had steamed. At Jamestown, this anniversary featured physical improvements rather than ideological statements. The National Park Service had taken over the site in 1934, and now it built a Colonial Parkway linking Jamestown with Williamsburg, a bridge connecting Jamestown Island (no longer a peninsula because the river had moved) to the mainland, and a Visitor's Center. Though the British still participated in celebrating Jamestown's anniversary, even sending the young Queen Elizabeth II, the rituals were comparatively quiet and struck no original notes. President Eisenhower proclaimed May 13 as "Jamestown Day," mentioning only that "government representative of the people was transplanted to the New World" at that site. Queen Elizabeth saluted the "experiments and adventures in freedom" shared by Britain and America and anticipated the "free and sincere co-operation" of the two nations "in the search for a just and lasting peace for all mankind."

Vice President Richard M. Nixon went to Virginia for the 1957 anniversary and gave a speech that continued the emphasis on individual liberty begun by Theodore Roosevelt and Woodrow Wilson. Almost plagiarizing Wilson, Nixon stressed that America's greatness arises not from natural resources or from the greatness of her people, but from our adherence to the "principle that the primary source of a nation's wealth comes from individual rather than government enterprise." The most striking point in Nixon's speech pointed out the high mortality rates of Jamestown's first years, claiming that "no battle in which our nation has fought has taken so heavy a toll of the participants as died on the Jamestown beachhead in the years from 1607 to 1610." Perhaps Nixon had seen the presentation by Wyndham S. Blanton, a medical historian, who numbered 525 deaths among the English in the first three years and estimated that out of 7,549 people who came to the colony between 1607 and 1624, only 1,095 survived. Recalling death at such a rate lent gravity to Nixon's apocalyptic conclusion, which began when he invoked "the masters of the Kremlin" and said that America and Britain had never "faced so great a threat... as we face today." His final words promised that if Americans held fast to "freedom of individual opportunity... the lamp which was lighted at Jamestown will never fail."

Sixteen years later, as the Nixon administration suffered through Watergate, Jamestown returned to America's consciousness through a television series, *Alistair Cooke's America*. In one of the most iconic moments of that thirteen-part series (also a book that sold a million copies), the British-born, naturalized American Cooke stood with the swamps of Jamestown behind him and wryly described the hardships of the first years for settlers who had been "taken in by the promotional literature." He approvingly quoted John Smith's dictum, "He that will not work, neither shall he eat," as the source of an American aversion to welfare. Paying attention to the Indians only as enemies, Cooke never mentioned Pocahontas. African slaves came into this part of his story only as adjuncts to the success of tobacco and the plantation system, not as free planters who employed Englishmen themselves.

During and after the 1970s, the rise of ethnic and gender awareness transformed American understandings of Jamestown. Black Power and the American Indian Movement, feminism and social history all contributed. In 1995, mass media brought some of these reinterpretations into the marketplace by means of a Disney animated feature, *Pocahontas*.

Following on the success of heroines in *The Little Mermaid* and *Beauty and the Beast*, *Pocahontas* went further in the feminist direction. Unlike her predecessors, Pocahontas chose her own destiny rather than a man. The film made Pocahontas a mature young woman, not a twelve-year-old, when she met John Smith, and it repeated the almost certainly inaccurate supposition of a romance between them, but when Smith was injured and returned to England, Disney's Pocahontas chose to stay for the sake of her people. She not only remained faithful to her heritage—never converting to Christianity and getting her spiritual counsel from Grandmother Willow, a talking tree—but she converted John Smith to a kind of nature religion through the Oscar-winning song, *Colors of the Wind*. The song says that in contrast to Smith, who thinks that "the Earth is just a dead thing you can claim," the Indian woman knows that "every rock and tree and creature has a life, has a spirit, has a name." During the scenes that accompany the song, Pocahontas stops Smith from shooting a bear, hands him a cub, leads him to leap from a waterfall, and rolls with him in a meadow. The scene climaxes when Pocahontas and Smith release two eagles who fly to the top of a tree. "How high will the sycamore grow?" she asks. "If you cut it down, you will never know." As the "colors of the wind" appear on his own breastplate armor, Smith appears convinced.

With the animated film *Pocahontas*, the transformation of the daughter of Wahunsonacock from forest siren to Christian lady to virgin goddess, already evident in the 1922 statue, was complete. This goddess Pocahontas was one with the American land. "The rainstorm and the river are my brothers," she sang; "The otter and the heron are my friends." Conservation, a movement that began with hunters in the days of Theodore Roosevelt, here came together with cultural tolerance as an aspect of American civil religion, and the Indian was enlisted as one symbol of the combination. In a more realistic movie about Jamestown and Pocahontas, *The New World* (2005), director Terence Malick continued this trend. Actor Colin Farrell played John Smith as a sensitive and introspective man, dreaming of a place where humanity could begin again. Pocahontas was played by Q'orianka Kilcher, a Peruvian-German descended on one side from Incas, whose face resembled that of the Pocahontas etching and who tried to embody the New World. Meanwhile, the Disneyland of Paris (at first called EuroDisney) featured a Pocahontas Village with water slides and teepees and artificial mountains to inspire the Old World. More recently, Matthew Sharpe's post-apocalyptic novel *Jamestown* (2007), which begins with men leaving the ruins of New York to exploit Indians in Virginia, has made Pocahontas into a text-messaging, eventually telepathic teen who is (again) a spirit of the land.

By 2007, in ceremonies for the four hundredth anniversary, the meaning of Jamestown had shifted from the triumphs of individual liberty and Anglo-American empire to the birth of pluralism out of tragic cultural conflict. The most striking example came in the speech of Queen Elizabeth, who expressed a readiness to "reflect more candidly on the Jamestown legacy" than she had fifty years before. While in 1957 she had considered "the exploration of new worlds, the spread of values and of the English language, and the sacrifice of those early pioneers," Queen Elizabeth now saw Jamestown as a place "where three great civilizations came together for the first time—Western European, Native American and African." She recalled not only the "drive and idealism" of the English but also the "will of the native Powhatan people to find ways to coexist." She saw that the meeting of these peoples had "released a train of events which continues to have a profound social impact, not only in the United States, but also in the United Kingdom and Europe." Considering the impact of Jamestown had led her to reflect that "[h]uman progress rarely comes without cost." Still, at least one of the legacies of Jamestown, the "deep friendship" and "durable relationship" between the United Kingdom and the United States, seemed to her "something worth commemorating."

The world "commemoration," as opposed to "celebration," showed that the Queen was in touch with the National Park Service of the United States, which had chosen not to "celebrate" but to "commemorate" the anniversary in deference to the Powhatan. The Park Service also created a display and multimedia presentation in the Visitor's Center that presented Jamestown as the meeting place of English, Native American, and African cultures and the beginning of a multicultural United States. Large maps with Indian names appeared on the walls, and the narration of the multimedia show stressed conflict and trade, the gradual enslavement of Africans, the resistance of Indians, and the disorder of Bacon's Rebellion. Displays at the museum demonstrate, for example, that the Powhatan had obsidian arrowheads sharper than modern surgical scalpels, though they still wanted English iron because of its durability. As the show ends with triumphal music, its invitation to wander through Jamestown and to feel the spirits of the past conveys some sense of menace, a feeling that many of those ghosts might be angry.

To leave the air-conditioned, sleekly modern Visitors' Center and walk over a long wooden bridge through the swamp to the ruins of Jamestown induces the effect of a trip back in time. Swamps have a naturally ancient look, and it is easy for a visitor to imagine that the reeds and trees and water are the same that the English confronted in 1607. On the slightly higher ground of the island, a visitor first sees the obelisk from the Tercentenary, then the church with its seventeenth-century tower, and then the statue of Pocahontas in the square outside the church. After walking thirty yards farther to the beach, anyone would feel that the broad river is timeless. There John Smith stands on his pedestal, and around the site there are still active excavations.

Recent triumphs of science at the site have enabled us to see exactly where the palisades of the oldest fort stood. Because a dedicated archaeologist, William M. Kelso, began to dig Jamestown up with his own hands in 1994, we now know much more about the site than was known fifty years ago. Graves within the fort, from the days when the English worked under instructions not to let the Indians see that they could die, are being identified, with all of the tragic sense that the discovery of graves implies. A unique building called an "archaearium," built over the foundations of the old statehouse, enables visitors to see artifacts from the first settlers and to look into foundations and abandoned wells. The site of Jamestown now combines ruin, monument, museum, and active place of discovery in a way that leaves visitors with deeply positive *and* negative senses of connection to many levels of the past. In the commemorations of Jamestown, personal freedom, political democracy, world peace, and cultual tolerance have all attained their places, while the tragic sense of the past has not been obliterated. Jamestown has come to deserve its role as the primal location of American civil religion.

SOURCES

Abrams, Ann Uhry, *The Pilgrims and Pocahontas: Rival Myths of American Origins* (Boulder, CO: Westview Press, 1999).

Applebaum, Robert, and John Wood Sweet, eds., *Envisioning an English Empire: Jamestown and the Making of the North Atlantic World* (Philadelphia: University of Pennsylvania Press, 2005).

Hashaw, Tim, *The Birth of Black America* (New York: Carroll & Graf Publishers, 2007).

Horn, James, *A Land as God Made It: Jamestown and the Birth of America* (New York: Basic Books, 2005).

Kelso, William M., *Jamestown: The Buried Truth* (Charlottesville: University of Virginia Press, 2006).

Stewart, William, *The Great White Fleet: A Collection of Postcards, Medals, Photographs, and Memorabilia,* http://www.greatwhitefleet.info/index.html (February 7, 2008).

4

The Mayflower Compact

> In the name of God, Amen. We whose names are under-writen, the loyall subjects of our dread soveraigne Lord, King James, by the grace of God, of Great-Britaine, Franc, and Ireland king, defender of the faith, etc., haveing undertaken, for the glorie of God, and advancemente of the Christian faith, and honour of our king and countrie, a voyage to plant the first colonie in the Northerne parts of Virginia, doe by these presents solemnly and mutualy in the presence of God, and one of another, covenant and combine our selves togeather into a civill body politick, for our better ordering and preservation and furtherance of the ends aforesaid; and by vertue hearof to enacte, constitute, and frame such just and equall lawes, ordinances, acts, constitutions, and offices, from time to time, as shall be thought most meete and convenient for the generall good of the Colonie, unto which we promise all due submission and obedience. In witnes wherof we have hereunder subscribed our names at Cap-Codd the 11. of November, in the year of the raigne of our soveraigne lord, King James, of England, France, and Ireland the eighteenth, and of Scotland the fifty fourth. Ano: Dom. 1620.

The first agreement among European colonists to create their own government in America was signed on the *Mayflower* before the landing at the site of Plymouth, Massachusetts, in 1620. Opening with an oath, "In the name of God, Amen," the text of the Mayflower Compact was explicitly religious. It defined the purpose of the colony in religious terms: "for the glorie of God, and advancemente of the Christian faith" (see Figure 4.1).

And yet, the agreement said nothing about a church. No minister signed the instrument, because no minister accompanied these settlers. The leaders aboard the *Mayflower* saw themselves as "Separatists," too Protestant—which meant too free of images, vestments, rituals, and control by bishops—to belong to the Church of England, but many of those on the ship were not Separatists. The effect of the Compact was purely political: it bound Separatists and non-Separatists alike into a "civill body politick," able to elect a governor and to make laws. As the statement of a nondenominational government acting "in the name of God," the Mayflower Compact became a founding document of American civil religion.

Figure 4.1 The earliest painting of the signing of the Mayflower Compact, by Thomas Matteson, shows the lay elder William Brewster handing a pen to Governor John Carver, who died within months, as future governor William Bradford lifts his eyes to heaven, and soldier Miles Standish looks on from the lower left with Priscilla Mullins. Library of Congress.

Though brief and vague, this agreement of the *Mayflower* passengers (or at least of the 41 adult males who signed it) to form themselves into a government seemed critical to them as well as to later generations. The second governor of the colony, William Bradford, wrote that the need for such a compact arose because of the "discontented and mutinous speeches" that some on the *Mayflower* had "let fall," saying that "when they came a shore they would use their own libertie; for none had power to command them." Only about half of those on the *Mayflower* were members or allies of the Separatist congregation that first fled England and then Holland to secure their freedom to practice a plain form of Christian worship. Many of the 102 colonists had joined as servants or as recruits of the London investors who financed the project, hoping to make money by fishing or farming or trading. Some of these "strangers" claimed that the plans for a settlement that the investors and Separatists had made with the Virginia Company were void, because the ship reached America at a point much farther north than they had intended, in the area governed by the royal Council for New England. Since the Separatists had no patent to establish a colony so far north, these people argued that when they left the *Mayflower* it would be every man or family for themselves.

By creating a government, the men who signed the Mayflower Compact hoped to prevent anarchy, and they did. The probable author of the Compact was an elder of the Separatist congregation named William Brewster, a former official of Queen Elizabeth's government, and the only university-trained person on board. In the new system, John Carver, a member of the congregation who had negotiated for a patent with the Virginia Company, was elected governor. Captain Miles Standish, the soldier hired by the London merchants to organize defense in the colony, signed on to the agreement and used its authority to lead armed parties of exploration.

The government established by the Compact was strong enough to enforce communism, with the colonists sharing all goods as they struggled to survive, for several years. Under its godly Governor William Bradford, Plymouth turned to individual land ownership much less quickly than Jamestown had under the more military John Smith. Bradford did ascribe the later flourishing of the colony to the decision for personal property, which he saw as a concession to the fallen state of human nature.

In the centuries since 1620, the Mayflower Compact has been claimed by partisans for many aspects of American civil religion. Tories and Federalists wishing to emphasize the English origins of the United States stressed the professions of loyalty to "our dread soveraigne Lord, King James." Whig historian George Bancroft, on the other hand, wrote in 1834 that "[i]n the cabin of the *Mayflower*, humanity recovered its rights" to government by the people. Today, some Christian evangelicals quote Bancroft to argue for the Christian roots of American democracy. At a more rationalistic moment—the Forefathers' Day address of 1802—future president John Quincy Adams cast the Pilgrims as the forerunners of Locke and Rousseau. Adams claimed that the Mayflower Compact was "perhaps, the only instance in human history of that positive, original social compact, which speculative philosophers have imagined as the only legitimate source of government."

In 1820, at the bicentennial celebration of the landing at Plymouth, the young Daniel Webster added to his growing fame with a speech that became known as the Plymouth Oration. Webster celebrated the Compact as the birth of a national empire, the instrument that made America into the Pilgrims' home. "Before they reached the shore, they had established the elements of a social system.... The morning that beamed on the first night of their repose saw the Pilgrims already *at home* in their country.... Here was man...on the shore of a rude and fearful wilderness; but it was politic, intelligent, and educated man." A century later, at the tercentenary celebration in 1920, Senator Henry Cabot Lodge drew the lesson of American exceptionalism. Lodge saw "in this same small paper" a "proclamation of democracy, something which had quite faded away in Europe, and had never before been declared in the American hemisphere." Though Lodge charged Daniel Webster with an overly optimistic faith that progress was inevitable, both men placed the Compact into a narrative about progress and democracy.

Sixteen years later, in 1936, the first professional historian to give a Forefathers' Day address tried to set the record straight. "Like many of [the Pilgrims'] praiseworthy acts, the Compact has been overrated," Professor Samuel Eliot Morrison of Harvard argued. The agreement was nothing more than "a necessary result of the Pilgrims' landing outside Virginia." Because it provided no "frame of government or fundamental law," it could not really be called a constitution. It did not establish democracy, "since the signers assumed exclusive right to political power in the Colony." Armed with a thorough knowledge of Plymouth court records, Morrison pointed out that Governor Bradford exercised "almost complete discretionary power" for decades, ruling without a body of written law until 1636.

Even Morrison, however, introduced an element of sacred awe when he gave his audience a verbal picture of what might have happened on the *Mayflower* when the Compact was signed:

> Breakfast has been eaten, a psalm of praise and thanksgiving sung by all, and an extempore prayer said by Elder Brewster. The sea is smooth, the weather fair, and everyone feeling fine; it will be an hour yet before the course has to be altered and final preparations made for anchoring. So at this opportune moment the leaders summon the other men into the great cabin, read the compact which they had drafted the day before, and request everyone to sign or make his mark. After that is done, and the generalty dismissed, we may suppose a little quiet handshaking among the leaders, and a few remarks like "Thank God, Governor, that's over!" and "I never expected John Billington to sign—it must have been your prayer that brought him to it, Elder!"

This prominent historian found the meaning of his story in affirmations of faith. After making his rational argument that the Mayflower Compact had little impact on history, since the colonies at Jamestown and Boston proceeded as they would have without taking any notice of what went on in Plymouth, Morrison turned his address into a sermon. He affirmed divine providence, saying that no other cause could be found for Plymouth's survival "than the Pilgrims' profound faith in God, and God's response to their prayers." Repeating the point, he asserted that the annals of Plymouth "illustrate a great and universal spiritual law, that faith in God brings God's assistance." In drawing this conclusion, Morrison anticipated a way of seeing the Mayflower Compact that has grown more powerful over the last few decades, as evangelical Christians have sought to transform politics.

Historian R. Stephen Warner began a study of the rise of evangelicals by describing a bicentennial service from July 4, 1976, when a reading of the Mayflower Compact was held in the Presbyterian Church of Mendocino, California. The minister's sermon noted that the Compact identified the purposes of the colony with "the glory of God and the advancement of the Christian faith." Pointing out that the Pilgrims promised "all due submission and obedience" to these goals, the pastor argued that all Americans should regard themselves as inheritors of that bond. More than thirty years later, the website of a Christian group called *Vine and Fig Tree* used the Compact as proof that "Christian theocrats" founded America. Mark Ammerman, writing for the mainstream evangelical magazine *Christianity Today* in 2007, saw the Mayflower Compact as "a natural extension of the Pilgrim church covenant." This instrument of political incorporation also grew directly from personal faith, as "a reflection of the 'treasure' in their [the Pilgrims'] hearts," expressing "their understanding of the right and the ability of the covenanted man (under God) to choose his own leaders, make his own laws, and change those laws for the sake of justice and the overall good of society." Ammerman agreed with Samuel Eliot Morrison that the Mayflower Compact included "no concept of a fully democratic society," but argued that the Pilgrims who signed it were impelled toward democracy by their personal faith.

The original of the Mayflower Compact has not survived. The text appeared in *Mourt's Relation*, a collection of letters and diaries and documents from Plymouth first published in England in 1622. It was reproduced in William Bradford's *Of Plymouth Plantation*, which circulated in manuscript form, was taken to England during the American Revolution by the last colonial governor of Massachusetts, and finally printed in 1912. Reproductions of the page of Bradford's manuscript that contains the Compact are widely sold, with the handwriting conveying something of the sacred aura that belongs to an original.

If the politics of the art world had not intervened, a painting of the signing of the Mayflower Compact would now hang in the Capitol Rotunda alongside the baptism of Pocahontas, the landing of Columbus, and six other historical paintings. When Congress commissioned paintings for the Rotunda, Samuel F. B. Morse (who later invented the telegraph and Morse code) was among the leading painters in the United States and the founder of the National Academy of Design in New York. Morse wanted to paint the signing of the Compact for the Capitol, but he failed to win the commission. The artist who was selected, Robert Walter Weir, also wished to paint the signing of the Compact, but he feared Morse, who was extremely possessive of the subject. Weir eventually painted the embarkation of the Pilgrims from Holland, a picture that now hangs in the Rotunda. Decades later, in 1857, Edwin White produced a picture of the signing in which William Brewster resembles Moses receiving the commandments from God. Sunlight streams dramatically from a skylight in the cabin onto the Compact as Brewster extends his left arm upward with an open palm. This reverent image contrasted with the earliest painting of the scene, by Tompkins H. Matteson, which was painted in 1853 and reproduced earlier in this chapter. There Elder Brewster holds out a pen to soon-to-be Governor Carver, with both men and the others around the table looking like substantial merchants who have just agreed on an important contract.

Popular culture has combined the sacred and secular images of the Compact. In an MGM epic movie of 1952, *Plymouth Adventure*, which won an Academy Award for special effects for its depiction of storms at sea, the signing of the Compact was the emotional climax of the film. Having arrived at Cape Cod without a patent for settlement, the Pilgrims face rebellion from the strangers in their midst, and especially from John Billington (a non-Separatist who would be hanged for murder in 1630). "Every man can take what he pleases," Billington argues, refusing to work with others for the common good. "We starved and froze for weeks. We're free now. I'll trust my own strong back to get me my share of living." William Bradford (whose primary importance so far has been as the husband of the female lead, the beautiful Gene Tierney) quells anarchy by saying that the "greatest danger we face is that we may disagree, that we may each go grubbing in the wilderness for himself alone and so face quick destruction." Bradford offers each man a chance to sign, "irrespective of religion or former condition," and so to become a member of "one body politic."

After this plea for the practical need for government, the scene shifts toward the sacred, as the camera takes a low angle to show the table and the light from above. Elder Brewster reminds the passengers and the audience, "We are not alone in this room. God is in this room." Then Brewster connects God with human progress: "For whenever a man goes upward he takes another step toward the fulfillment of the Godhead that lies within him. What say you, gentlemen?" Even Billington takes up the offer (as the historical Billington did). The balance of power on the ship has shifted from the "strangers" and the hard-living Captain Christopher Jones (played by Spencer Tracy) to the Pilgrim leaders.

While the men sign, the young Pilgrim Edward Winslow reads their names, in effect calling a roll. Hired men like John Alden the carpenter (played by Van Johnson) seem grateful to be included; some cannot write their names, but only mark the paper with an X. Winslow sums up the meaning of the act in secular terms: "Whether they know it or not, they have laid hold of great principles hitherto unrevealed to the nations of the earth. They are about to establish just and equal laws adopted and administered by the people, a government based upon the will of the governed."

No one now recalls *Plymouth Adventure* as a classic movie. It focused on a love triangle between Captain Jones (Spencer Tracy), Mrs. William Bradford (Gene Tierney), and William Bradford (Leo Genn) that has no basis in history. In its presentation of the Mayflower Compact, however, the film expressed a cultural consensus. It combined the secular and the sacred. Both the film and the Mayflower Compact related God to individual liberty and democratic government in a way that has remained central to American civil religion.

SOURCES

Abrams, Ann Uhry, *The Pilgrims and Pocahontas: Rival Myths of American Origin* (Boulder, CO: Westview Press, 1999).

Bush, Sargent, Jr., "America's Origin Myth: Remembering Plymouth Rock," *American Literary History* 12, no. 4 (Winter, 2000), 745–756.

Hamel, Elsie, "*Plymouth Adventure* (1952)," http://www.lehigh.edu/~ineng/ewh0/ewh0-title.html (March 23, 2008).

Sargent, Mark L., "The Conservative Covenant: The Rise of the Mayflower Compact in American Myth," *The New England Quarterly* 61, no. 2 (June, 1988), 233–251.

Seelye, John, *Memory's Nation: The Place of Plymouth Rock* (Chapel Hill: University of North Carolina Press, 1998).

Warner, R. Stephen, *New Wine in Old Wineskins: Evangelicals and Liberals in a Small-Town Church* (Berkeley: University of California Press, 1990).

5

Plymouth Rock, the Pilgrims, and the Indians

Plymouth Rock is the oldest important artifact of American civil religion. Though the Rock looks small and disappointing to most visitors (Figure 5.1), a cult of the Pilgrims has grown up around it. The Rock has been moved and broken four times by *Mayflower* descendants, chipped away by Plymouth businessmen, urinated on by drunks, and buried in sand by Native Americans. The four hundredth anniversary of the Pilgrims' landing, in 2020, has already provoked a search for consensus.

Controversy starts with the identity of the Rock, because the English were living at Plymouth for more than a century after the *Mayflower* arrived in 1620 before it was marked as anything special. Geologically, it was a ten-ton piece of granite (now reduced to six, of which only three are visible), a few feet high that had been left on the beach as masses of ice retreated more than ten thousand years ago. Though the Rock may have been remembered as a marker of the place where the founders of Plymouth first came ashore on December 22, 1620, no one wrote about it. During the seventeenth century, as Plymouth Colony was overshadowed and then absorbed by Massachusetts, becoming known as the "Old Colony," the Rock on the shore attained no wider fame. One map published in 1715 did make note of a "great rock" that marked one boundary of the town.

The Rock began to be called Forefathers' Rock in 1741, after an incident that coincided with the religious revival known as the Great Awakening. For several years, outdoor meetings and traveling preachers brought new, young members into the churches of New England; at the same time, those churches were being torn apart by conflict over the emotional sensationalism of the preachers (such as George Whitefield, Jonathan Edwards, and George Tennent) who were inspiring these multitudes to seek church membership. Whenever an "itinerant" preacher came to a community, the churches would have to decide whether to allow him to use their pulpits. Often the losers in these votes were disaffected

Figure 5.1 All that remains of Plymouth Rock, in its protective cage. The original ten-ton granite boulder was never very large, but it was split during a disastrous move in 1774, chipped away for souvenirs, then split again when it was moved in 1834. Photograph by William Gardella.

enough to found another church. All over New England, towns that began with one Congregational church now had two: an "Old Light" church that disapproved of emotional preaching and a "New Light," revivalist church.

An elder of the original Plymouth Church, Thomas Faunce, started the cult of Plymouth Rock at the same time that he left his home congregation, along with other "Old Lights" who had fallen into minority status. The "New Lights" tended to be younger, more enterprising types who criticized their elders with regard to politics and economics as well as religion. Some of them wanted to build a wharf from the main street of Plymouth to the water, covering the "great rock" near the high-tide line. Disapproving of these plans, Elder Faunce (who was not only a church elder but also ninety-five years old) had himself carried in a chair to the beach to speak against the construction. He said that he had brought his children and grandchildren to the rock every year and stood them on it, recalling the story of the landing at Plymouth. Because Faunce's father had come to Plymouth in 1623 and Faunce himself had known several of the *Mayflower* passengers, his story was believed. Although construction of the wharf went forward, the top of the rock was allowed to protrude though a hole in the wood. For the next thirty years it interfered with the wheels of commerce but stood for conservative values, the good old ways in church and state.

In the following decades, tensions between old and new extended to relations between Britain and America. Those tensions increased after the British victory in the French and Indian Wars in 1763. An Old Colony Club was founded at Plymouth in 1769, a few months before British troops enforcing taxation shot five civilians in the Boston Massacre. The club had the explicit purpose of giving those who could prove descent from the first generation an alternative to mixing with newcomers in taverns. On December 22, 1769, and on that date for a few years thereafter, the Old Colony Club held a celebration of the 1620 landing, with a meal of shellfish, waterfowl, and venison to recall the diet of their ancestors. These meetings included prayer for peace and continued union with Great Britain, and they became caught up in conflict over the impending revolution.

Where Plymouth once had a majority of New Lights who cared little for the old ways in the church, it now had many Liberty Boys (or Sons of Liberty) who wanted to break from the British Empire. With the Liberty Boys stood Theophilus Cotton, the heir of Boston's first pastor and colonel of the local militia. On the other side was Edward Winslow, a Mayflower descendant who took note of Forefathers' Rock on a map of 1774 and who referred to the Sons of Liberty as "Sons of Licentiousness." During the evening of December 21, 1774—the night before the Old Colony Club dinner and a few months before hostilities began at Lexington and Concord—the Plymouth rebels decided to capture Plymouth Rock. Armed with wooden screws, they raised the rock from its bed, put chains around it, and tied the chains to many teams of oxen—thirty or forty, according to some accounts—intending to drag the rock up to the main street and place it next to an elm they had named a Liberty Tree, from which they hung effigies of tax collectors and to which they attached a Liberty Pole to fly a "Liberty or Death" flag. Forefathers' Rock was to become one more symbol of the rebel cause. Unfortunately, as they raised the rock, it broke in half. Some saw the break as a sign that the colonies would break free from Britain. Leaving the lower half of the rock where it was, the Liberty Boys brought the upper piece to the Liberty Tree. They also took over the celebrations of Forefathers' Day from the Old Colony Club, most of whose members decided to side with the Tories. After the Revolutionary War began in earnest the celebrations ceased, and they were not resumed until 1793.

It was at the revival of Forefathers' Day in 1793, under the auspices of the town government of Plymouth, that Chandler Robbins, pastor of the oldest Congregational church in town, first called the Forefathers "Pilgrims." Although the name was based on a passage from Governor William Bradford's history of Plymouth, in which Bradford said that the colonists did not complain about hardships because they "knew they were Pilgrims" on the way to Heaven,

Robbins was actually beginning a strange usage. Pilgrims are normally travelers *to* a sacred place like Jerusalem or Mecca (or Heaven), and the forefathers of Plymouth were primarily refugees *from* religious persecution, seeking escape and a place of safety. But by the time Robbins spoke, Plymouth had actually become a place of pilgrimage that centered on its Rock. The journal of James Thacher, a revolutionary soldier who passed through Plymouth in 1775, spoke of "holding converse with celestial spirits" at the site and asked, "Can we set our feet on their rock without swearing, by the spirit of our fathers, to defend it and our country?" Though the Separatists of the *Mayflower* would not have answered to the name of "Pilgrim," James Thacher had become a pilgrim to their site.

Thacher went on to write a history of Plymouth that has been reprinted many times (as recently as 1992). The name "Pilgrim" became part of a cult of Plymouth that expanded beyond clubs for the descendants of the *Mayflower*. By the two hundredth anniversary in 1820, the Old Colony Society and the town government had been replaced in running the celebrations by a Pilgrim Society that did not discriminate by ancestry, accepting anyone willing to pay dues.

During the nineteenth century, Plymouth Rock came to be seen as the foundation of an American empire. Speaking at the Forefathers' Day of 1802, the young John Quincy Adams noted that it had been less than two centuries since "the first European foot" touched the Rock and predicted that in "[t]wo centuries more...our numbers must exceed those of Europe itself." Those whom Adams called the "exalted Pilgrims" had founded an empire that would "disdain the power of human calculation" to become the "noblest empire of time."

The most vivid passages in Adams's speech contrasted the Pilgrims with other builders of empires. "The founders of your race," he assured those gathered at Plymouth, "are not handed down to you, like the fathers of the Roman people, as the sucklings of a wolf." Unlike the inheritors of Islamic empires, the descendants of the Mayflower settlers did not begin with "a nauseous compound of fanaticism and sensuality, whose only argument was a sword, and whose only paradise was a brothel." Adams rejoiced that "no Gothic scourge of God" (recalling Attila the Hun) and "no bastard Norman tyrant" (such as William the Conqueror) stood among "the worthies who first landed on the rock." Morally superior to the founders of all earlier empires, the Pilgrims demonstrated that superiority in their treatment of the Indians. "No European settlement ever formed upon this continent has been more distinguished for undeviating kindness and equity toward the savages." Not only did the Pilgrims have a right to settle where the Indians only hunted, but according to Adams they also purchased all of the land on which they settled.

Unlike at Jamestown, where the claim of descent from Pocahontas and John Rolfe distinguished the first families of Virginia, no ancestral link to the Indians kept the memories of the helpful translator, Squanto, or Chief Massasoit, with whom the Pilgrims made their first treaty, sacred in the celebrations at Plymouth. Not until the protests of 1970, when Indians buried Plymouth Rock in sand, would the descendants of Massasoit claim their place in Forefathers' Day. Meanwhile, those who extolled the empire of the Pilgrims tended to follow the example of Daniel Webster, the orator who referred to the Indians as "roving barbarians" who practiced a religion of "idolatrous sacrifice."

Webster's 1820 bicentennial address became widely known as "The Plymouth Oration." It placed Plymouth Rock at the center of a panorama of history that extended from ancient Greece to the "consummation of all things earthly, at the throne of God." Dressed in knee britches and a resplendent silk gown, with eyes that English writer Thomas Carlyle described as two pieces of burning anthracite coal, Webster spoke for three hours with legendary power.

At many points in the speech, Webster used the rock as a way to remind his audience where they were: "We have come to this Rock, to record here our homage for our Pilgrim Fathers.... Beneath us is this Rock, on which New England received the feet of the Pilgrims." Their arrival was an event comparable to the battle of Marathon, where the Greeks won the survival of their culture against the Persians, and the Pilgrim colony had grander results than the colonies of Greece or Rome. "Two thousand miles westward from the rock where their fathers landed, may now be found the sons of the Pilgrims... cherishing, we trust, the patrimonial blessings of wise institutions, of liberty, and religion. The world has seen nothing like this." Estimating that "more than a million of people, descendants of New England ancestry," were now living in regions that had been "unpenetrated forest" only sixty years before, Webster predicted that "Erelong, the sons of the Pilgrims will be on the shores of the Pacific." Three aspects of the Pilgrim way—their free system of government, based on a broad division of property; their commitment to education, from free grammar schools to universities; and their religious devotion, which he called the most potent force in history—guaranteed that the empire of America would exceed the glories of Greece, Rome, England, and Europe. Having conjured the Pilgrims from their graves at the start of his address, Webster invited their descendants from a century in the future to his conclusion. "On the morning of that day," he said, anticipating the commemoration of 1920, "the voice of acclamation and gratitude, commencing on the Rock of Plymouth, shall be transmitted through millions of the sons of the Pilgrims, till it loses itself in the murmurs of the Pacific seas."

One cloud darkened the bright horizon of Webster's vision of the future: the continuing trade in slaves from Africa. Here again he invoked Plymouth Rock, urging his hearers to "pledge ourselves here, upon the rock of Plymouth, to extirpate and destroy it." A prefiguration of secession and Civil War appeared in his insistence that "[i]t is not fit that the land of the Pilgrims should bear this shame longer," and that any place that continued to support slavery should be "set aside from the Christian world." Such associations of Plymouth Rock with the cause of abolition, and with the North in the Civil War, became common over the next decades. In James Russell Lowell's abolitionist hymn, *Once to Every Man and Nation* (1844), the author asked Americans to face the future even if it held war: "Was the *Mayflower* launched by cowards, / Steered by men behind their time? / Turned those tracks toward Past or Future / That make Plymouth Rock sublime?" During the 1840s, Plymouth was represented in Congress by John Quincy Adams, who defeated a "gag rule" against discussing slavery and came to be known as "the Representative from Plymouth Rock." During the war, a lithograph espousing the Union cause showed a Plymouth Rock of Gibraltar-like proportions, with cannons mounted on it, an underground railroad running through it, and a rebel leader hanging from it on a rope held by an eagle.

Daniel Webster himself did not maintain the anti-slavery oath he had sworn on Plymouth Rock. By the time he died in 1852, he had come to support the Missouri Compromise and to speak in the US Senate in favor of enforcing the Fugitive Slave Law. The Plymouth Oration was nevertheless so well remembered that it set the framework for the three hundredth anniversary celebrations in 1920.

In the intervening period, the memorials of Plymouth Rock developed in sometimes regrettable ways. Victorian fondness for tourism, sentiment, and the collection of souvenirs led Plymouth shops to sell egg-sized pieces of the Rock, guaranteed to "take a very fine polish," for $1.50. The French observer Alexis de Tocqueville said that he saw such pieces displayed in many American households in the 1830s. In November 2005, several of these nineteenth-century mementos were sold by electronic auction on Ebay, for prices up to $909. Pieces of the Rock were displayed in Henry Ward Beecher's Plymouth Congregational Church in Brooklyn, New York, and in the Nevada State Museum of Carson City, Nevada. More serious breakage occurred after the Pilgrim Society opened Pilgrim Hall, now the oldest museum in the United States, in 1824 to display items including the sword of Miles Standish and the crib of Peregrine White, born at sea on the *Mayflower*. When the leaders of the Society tried to have the top section of the Rock moved from the town square, where the Liberty Boys had left it, to the portico in front of their institution in 1834, the cart carrying the Rock collapsed and that piece broke into two, which were then cemented together. For nearly fifty years these parts of the Rock remained in front of Pilgrim Hall, far from the shore, surrounded by a five-foot fence; the year 1620 was painted on that portion of the Rock. Meanwhile, the base of the Rock remained closer to the shore, under the wharf originally built in 1741.

The Pilgrim Society bought the wharf, intending to reunify the rock in a better setting, in 1859, but its fund-raising and design efforts were delayed by the Civil War. By 1867, the wharf was removed and a granite dome (or *baldachino*), with an arch on each of its four sides and a scallop shell at the top recalling the early meals of the Pilgrims, was erected over the lower part of the Rock, and in 1880 the pieces of the Rock were finally brought back together and protected by iron gates under the canopy. Designed by a Mayflower descendant and illustrator of children's books named Hammatt Billings, this monument quickly proved unsatisfactory, both because it reminded people of Catholic altars and because development along the harbor meant that it left the Rock eight or nine feet above the high-tide line. In another parallel with Catholic practice, bones from the old Pilgrim cemetery on Cole's Hill were treated like relics of saints: they were dug up, certified as genuine by Dr. Oliver Wendell Holmes, and installed in a chamber at the top of the canopy, over the Rock. When the dome began to leak, the presence of these bones made people uncomfortable.

Meanwhile, the Victorian era also produced a National Monument to the Forefathers, about a mile from Plymouth Rock, with a cornerstone containing yet another piece of the Rock along with papers and maps from Pilgrim days, which was designed by Billings in 1853 and finally completed in 1889, despite the designer's death in 1874. Originally intended to soar as high as the Statue of Liberty in New York, this monument reached about half that height, eighty-one feet, and featured a massive female figure of Faith at the center, pointing to the heavens, with statues of two females and two males around the base representing Morality, Education, Law, and Liberty.

Both the canopy over the Rock and the monument expressed a dignified but sentimental spirit, with elaborate allegorical figures and very specific symbolism. The same spirit also appeared in a series of nineteenth-century paintings that have been described as "feminizing the rock," because they center on Pilgrim women coming ashore. Disputes between the descendants of John Alden and Mary Chilton, regarding which of them came ashore first, were addressed by a painting (Henry Bacon's *Landing of the Pilgrims*, 1877) that showed Alden helping Chilton onto the Rock. In Henry Wadsworth Longfellow's epic poem *The Courtship of Miles Standish* (1858), John Alden (an ancestor of Longfellow) proudly claimed that "my foot was the first that stepped on this rock at the landing," but then lamented that life had no meaning without the love of Priscilla Mullins. Although one historian has called the years from 1820 to 1920 "the Pilgrim Century," and others have noted that the Pilgrims and Plymouth Rock gained predominance in prestige over the settlers of Jamestown (and even over the Puritans of Boston) among Victorians who hated slavery and loved sentiments and female imagery, this Pilgrim victory came with great costs to the physical Rock and to the knowledge of the truth about colonial history.

New England Societies sprang up in cities across the nation during the 1800s, and each of them gathered on December 22 to celebrate the landing at Plymouth Rock. In 1881, Mark Twain spoke at one of these celebrations, before the New

England Society of Philadelphia. Ever the iconoclast, Twain urged the New Englanders of Philadelphia to "get up an auction and sell Plymouth Rock!" He said that the Pilgrims were "a simple and ignorant people," who had "never seen any good rocks before," so that they were "excusable for hopping ashore in frantic delight and clapping an iron fence around this one," but their descendants were educated and enlightened, and should know that "in the rich land of your nativity, opulent New England, overflowing with rocks, this one isn't worth at the outside, more than thirty-five cents." As usual, Mark Twain's message proved to be both countercultural and prophetic.

As Senator Henry Cabot Lodge, the featured speaker for the tercentenary celebration in 1920, noted, "Every century, apparently, has a poor opinion of its immediate predecessor." Lodge gave a speech that paralleled Webster's Plymouth Oration quite explicitly, seeking to replace the sentimentality that had intervened over a hundred years with a new, more critical sense of history. In agreement with Webster, Lodge recalled the Greek victory at Marathon and argued that the Pilgrims intended to create an empire growing from the Rock in America, which they immediately saw as their home. On the other hand, however, Lodge argued that Webster was wrong to believe that material progress implied spiritual progress, or that progress itself was a law of human history. Recalling the Great War that had just passed, the senator said that "the savage of the Neanderthal period" had shown himself to be "lurking behind the demure figure of nineteenth century respectability," only now the savage had modern weapons as well as "primitive instincts and passions." Germany fought for a materialistic, scientific philosophy of life, and the Allies had shown themselves willing to die for spiritual values like the love of liberty and justice, but the battle had not really ended. According to Lodge, those gathered at Plymouth Rock in 1920 faced "an exhausted and almost prostrate world, with suggestions in Asia of world conquest [from Japan]" while in the Soviet Union a Communist revolution "has replaced the autocracy of the Czars" and was "threatening the destruction of all civilization."

When Lodge referred to Neanderthals lurking in the nations of his own day, he revealed the transformation that separated his perspective on history from that of Daniel Webster. For Webster in 1820, the world was still six thousand years old. Lodge set his tercentenary address into the contexts of geology and evolution, observing as he began to speak that "[g]eologically and even racially three centuries are not worth computing." It was in part this vast expansion of historical scale, from a few thousand to billions of years, which made Lodge doubt any connection between time and progress. The horseshoe crab was so old that its fossils were found in coal mines, he noted, but no one celebrated the crab's anniversaries and the crab had not improved. Given how long it took for living things to change, Lodge cast doubt on hopes to improve humanity by political change and technical invention. He pointed to "the astonishing permanence of human nature and human desires" and "the racial and climactic, anatomical and physical differences among men" that must "make social development seem as slow, almost, as the operation of geologic changes in the earth's surface." The people of 1920 had come to believe in race and in racial hierarchy more than in rapid human progress, according to the Senator: "no one now imagines that by environment and education a Hottentot [one group of native South Africans] can be turned into an Englishman."

Daniel Webster had ended his Plymouth Oration by welcoming the descendants of 1920 "to the immeasurable blessings of rational existence, the immortal hope of Christianity, and the light of everlasting truth!" For Senator Lodge, who fought successfully to keep the United States out of the League of Nations and to place strict quotas on immigration to America from Southern and Eastern Europe, Africa, and Asia, no such invocation of 2020 seemed possible. The best he could recommend for a modern son of the Pilgrims was to avoid confusing "moral and economic values," to maintain the freedom of thought that developed from the Pilgrim quest for religious freedom, and to earnestly do the work before him in the "fragment of time awarded him for his existence here." Although Lodge agreed that the achievement of the Pilgrims *deserved* to be eternal—the last line of his speech said that if "the great republic is true in heart and deed to the Pilgrims of Plymouth it will take no detriment even from the hand of Time"—he both lacked and rejected Webster's assurance of eternity.

One parallel between the speeches was set up for dramatic effect. While the senator quoted three long paragraphs from Webster's conclusion, he came to Webster's line about a "voice…commencing on the Rock of Plymouth," that "shall be transmitted through millions of the sons of the Pilgrims, until it lose itself in…the Pacific seas," and at that moment a phone placed on the podium rang. The call was from Governor Stephens of California, and it was answered by Governor Calvin Coolidge of Massachusetts, who told his colleague that he was "seated in the chair of Governor Bradford at Plymouth," and that he wanted to say that "Massachusetts and Plymouth Rock greet California and the Golden Gate, and send the voice which is not to be lost in the waves and roar of the Pacific." In sight and hearing of the audience, Daniel Webster's prophecy about 1920 had been fulfilled and improved: the voice would be transmitted, but it would not be lost. By agreeing to this demonstration, Lodge undercut the pessimism of his speech.

In fact, the tercentenary celebrations literally gave the Rock a voice. "I, the rock of Plymouth, speak to you Americans" was the first line of an enormous pageant that was performed in the summer of 1921, with 1,300 actors, a chorus of three hundred, and an orchestra. Written and produced by Professor George Pierce Baker of Harvard, the playwriting teacher of Eugene O'Neill and Thomas

Wolfe, *The Pilgrim Spirit* took place at the base of Cole's Hill, where the Rock could be spotlighted when it delivered its lines. A dozen performances between July 13 and August 13 filled 10,000 seats each time, and on August 1 President Warren Harding attended, arriving in the presidential yacht *Mayflower,* accompanied by four battleships. The plot began with Norsemen approaching the Rock and being driven away by Indians, and continued through the crises of Plymouth colony to the arrival of Washington and Lincoln, who each gave brief speeches. Throughout, the Rock offered commentary, sometimes humble ("Of me the rock in the ooze, they have made a cornerstone of the Republic"), but more frequently demanding. When the Pilgrims banished one who would not keep their law, the voice of granite said, "This is your heritage, all you Americans. Do ye maintain it?" At the end of the pageant, which evoked the Great War through martial music and a procession of flags of the Allies, a spotlight shone on the *Mayflower II* in the harbor and the Rock spoke its last line: "The path of the *Mayflower* must forever be kept free."

One of the participants in the tercentenary was born in a Plymouth—although it was Plymouth, Vermont—and personally represented a peak of the Puritan heritage in the United States. Before Calvin Coolidge received the governor of California's phone call on the podium during the address of Henry Cabot Lodge, he gave the first address of the day, with words that elevated Plymouth Rock to the status of a sacrament, a material vehicle for the power of God. "Plymouth Rock does not mark a beginning or an end," Coolidge said. "It marks a revelation of that which is without beginning and without end, a purpose, shining through eternity with a resplendent light."

After Coolidge and the tercentenary, the Pilgrim Century went into a slow decline, with the symbols of Plymouth reorganized to fulfill the more modest role that Plymouth Rock plays in the civil religion today. The most elaborate plans for the tercentenary had included an enormous semicircular harbor for the yachts of visitors, with a central temple for the Rock itself, flanked by long porticoes. Scaled-down changes in the memorials included the destruction of Hammatt Billings's *baldachino* and the reunion of all pieces of the Rock at the high tide level on the beach. All of the wharves and commercial buildings around that part of the shore were taken out, as were the buildings on Cole's Hill across the street, where the seating for the pageant was placed in 1921, after which the Hill was left clear except for the sarcophagus of Pilgrim bones and a bronze statue of Massasoit. The stage was set for what became the smallest and most visited (now about one million people a year, compared to two million at Jamestown) of the state parks of Massachusetts. Unlike Jamestown, Plymouth Rock has never come under the care of the National Park Service.

Over the Rock in its new (as close as possible to the original) location, the architects McKim, Mead, and White designed a granite portico with sixteen columns. Visitors enter the portico from street level and look down to the Rock on the beach from several yards above. Iron bars, without gates, enclose the rock on all sides, so that the high tide can reach it twice a day but no one can stand on it, as James Thacher had in 1775 and Calvin Coolidge in 1920. When visitors see the fragment of a boulder that remains, with a clearly visible stripe of concrete that needed renewal in 1989 and the date "1620" carved into it, they are almost universally disappointed. A sense of exclusion produces feelings of frustration in some people that, especially when fueled by alcohol, can lead to vandalism. People commonly throw coins at the Rock, and some visitors throw litter. Tales abound in the local bars about men urinating on the rock or jumping down to take yet another piece.

On the lintel above the columns are carved words that may also convey a message of exclusion: ERECTED BY THE NATIONAL SOCIETY OF THE COLONIAL DAMES OF AMERICA TO/COMMEMORATE THE THREE HUNDREDTH ANNIVERSARY OF THE LANDING OF THE PILGRIMS. The Colonial Dames of America were founded in 1890 and are limited in membership to the descendants of people who held positions of leadership in the colonies before the American Revolution. They are one of several such organizations that, like the Old Colony Club of colonial times, have responded to immigration by banding together and promoting pride in their heritage. Although the Dames are a women's group, the temple they commissioned for Plymouth Rock has a severely masculine, Roman mood. Its columns belong to the Doric order, relatively thick and plain, with squared-off, plain capitals, and so considered suitable for gods (unlike the thin Ionic or fluted Corinthian columns, with their more elaborate capitals, suitable for goddesses and civic buildings). Perhaps Pilgrim Fathers are not gods, but the current temple for Plymouth Rock leaves an impression of ancestor worship, particularly if a visitor reads the inscription.

Across the street from the temple and the beach is Cole's Hill, where the Pilgrims buried their dead—52 of the 102 people who arrived in 1620—after the first winter. On Cole's hill there is another rock, much smaller than the one under the portico on the beach, which bears a plaque with the words "NATIONAL DAY OF MOURNING" and the following text:

> Since 1970, Native Americans have gathered at noon on Cole's Hill in Plymouth to commemorate a National Day of Mourning on the US Thanksgiving holiday. Many Native Americans do not celebrate the arrival of the Pilgrims and other European settlers. To them, Thanksgiving Day is a reminder of the genocide of millions of their people, the theft of their lands, and the relentless assault on their culture. Participants in a National Day of Mourning honor Native ancestors and the struggles of Native peoples to survive today. It is a day of

remembrance and spiritual connection as well as a protest of the racism and oppression which Native Americans continue to experience.

Under this text are the words, "Erected by the Town of Plymouth on behalf of the United American Indians of New England."

The plaque represents a struggle between the descendants of the Pilgrims and the Wampanoag Indians that began in 1970, during the three hundred fiftieth anniversary of the landing. A Wampanoag named Frank James (also known as Wamsutta, the name of Massasoit's eldest son) was invited to speak at the annual Pilgrim Progress, a Thanksgiving procession past Plymouth Rock to the graves on Cole's Hill in which Plymouth residents take the parts of those who survived the first winter. Asked to submit the text of his speech to the white authorities who ran the procession (supposedly so they could prepare a press release), James showed them a text that demanded "a more humane America, a more Indian America, where men and nature once again are important; where the Indian values of honor, truth, and brotherhood prevail." He called the decision of Massasoit, who was chief of the Wampanoag in 1620, to help the Pilgrims "our biggest mistake." He finished by hoping that the three hundred fiftieth anniversary of the landing would mark "the beginning of a new determination...to regain the position in this country that is rightfully ours."

Frank James was refused his place on the Thanksgiving podium, so he and his fellow Indians held their own demonstration, which began the National Day of Mourning. They heard his speech themselves, next to the statue of Massasoit on Cole's Hill. They then shoveled sand over Plymouth Rock, boarded the *Mayflower II*, and threw the manikin representing its captain, Christopher Jones, into the harbor.

Nearly thirty years of illegal Indian demonstrations followed, culminating in the interruption of the Pilgrim Progress of 1996 and the arrest of twenty-five demonstrators on Thanksgiving of 1997. In 1998, the city of Plymouth and the United American Indians of New England came to an agreement: the Day of Mourning would go forward without disrupting the Pilgrim Progress. Indians would not have to get a parade permit for their gathering, and the town would pay for the National Day of Mourning plaque to be installed on Cole's Hill. On Thanksgiving of 1998, the son of Frank James, Moonanum James, addressed the gathering of thousands. He celebrated the agreement that had been reached and then turned to the future, in an even more millennial vision than that of Daniel Webster.

> Some ask us: Will you ever stop protesting?...We will stop protesting when the merchants of Plymouth are no longer making millions of dollars off the blood of our slaughtered ancestors. We will stop protesting

when we can act as sovereign nations on our own land without the interference of the Bureau of Indian Affairs...When corporations stop polluting our mother, the earth. When racism has been eradicated. When the oppression of Two-Spirited people is a thing of the past. We will stop protesting when homeless people have homes and no child goes to bed hungry. When police brutality no longer exists in communities of color. We will stop protesting when Leonard Peltier and Mumia Abu Jamal and the Puerto Rican independistas and all the political prisoners are free. Until then, the struggle will continue. Today, we will correct some history...in a country that continues to glorify butchers such as Christopher Columbus, glorifies slave-owning presidents such as Washington and Jefferson and even carves their faces into the sacred Black Hills of the Lakota.

Every year since 1998, the National Day of Mourning and the Pilgrim Progress have continued side by side at Plymouth. As Plymouth has focused more on developing its tourist trade, enactments of the Pilgrim Progress have begun to occur on a Monday in June and on every Friday of August. This march is particularly objectionable to Indians because of its military symbols, the guns and swords carried by the men. Although some have suggested having the march without the guns and swords, others have replied that there would be no point in having a deliberately inaccurate historic re-enactment.

Despite the 1998 agreement, relations between whites and Indians are much less settled at Plymouth than at Jamestown. Using the national holiday of Thanksgiving, the United American Indians of New England have connected the rival rituals at Plymouth to national issues from gay rights, homelessness, and hunger to the convictions of Leonard Peltier and Mumia Abu Jamal and the role of the Bureau of Indian Affairs in granting or withholding recognition to tribes. At Jamestown, the Powhatan have insisted on and secured recognition for themselves, but they have not said they will protest until a millennium of justice arrives. At Plymouth, the Wampanoag have enlisted allies from the whole country to make Plymouth Rock the focal point of a struggle over whether or not the English settlement of North America was a good thing. It is hard to predict what may happen when the National Day of Mourning and Thanksgiving coincide during the four hundredth anniversary in 2020, but the possibilities range from chaos to a detailed account and recognition of conflict, as in the new Visitor's Center at Jamestown. Some protestors at Plymouth are seeking a national holiday celebrating Native Americans.

Meanwhile, evangelical Christians and conservatives have begun to object to the settlement that has kept the peace since 1998. Doug Phillips, writing for Dr. James Dobson's Focus on the Family, has called the current memorial

"Plymouth Crock" because of Plymouth's tolerance of the National Day of Mourning and sponsorship of the plaque that refers to "genocide" against Native Americans. Phillips reiterates the 1802 position of John Quincy Adams that the Pilgrims bought all the land they took and treated the Indians well. In the local newspaper of Plymouth, accounts show that more evangelical groups are coming to celebrate Thanksgiving there as a way of affirming the Christian roots of the United States.

Another, more unifying perspective on Plymouth Rock has arisen from advances in genealogy and genetics. According to the General Society of Mayflower Descendants, in the early twenty-first century about 35 million Americans, or about 12 percent of the nation, can probably claim descent from the English settlers of Plymouth who survived the first winter. At Thanksgiving of 2002, journalists Cokie and Steven V. Roberts wrote an article for the Sunday supplement *USA Weekend* celebrating the changing image of Mayflower descendants. They included their own grandchildren, in whom the genes of William Brewster and those of Russian Jewish socialists and Zionists have mixed. Pictures accompanying the article showed Black and Syrian and Chinese Americans who also claim Mayflower descent.

Continuing the work of Daniel Webster and Henry Cabot Lodge, Cokie and Steven Roberts celebrated individual liberty, which they detailed as religious freedom, economic freedom, and political freedom, as the heritage of Plymouth. Unlike Webster and Lodge, they did not focus their message for the future so much on the expansion of an empire of Mayflower descendants as on the need for the United States to continue to welcome newcomers. Here they cited Hilda Hernandez-Lara, an immigrant from Mexico who became a Marine supply officer and had just finished six months on an aircraft carrier, only to be assigned for a year to the naval base on Okinawa, where she would serve despite having to leave a five-year-old son in the care of others. Hernandez-Lara accepted the assignment because "It's my job," as she told the journalists. She was offered as an example of an American who knows "why we give thanks this week."

Planning for the 2020 anniversary of the landing at Plymouth Rock aspires to new levels of pluralism and inclusiveness. For a start, the town appointed the Rev. Dr. Peter J. Gomes, a man with Plymouth roots who long served as chaplain and professor at Harvard, to chair the planning committee. Gomes traced his ancestors to the Cape Verde islands, some from Portugal and some from Africa. He startled Harvard by coming out as gay in 1991, as part of his response to a student publication that cited the Bible to denounce homosexuality. His interest in Plymouth history extended back at least to 1971, when he wrote an essay that was part of a collection of writings published by the Pilgrim Society, called

"Plymouth and Some Portuguese." The essay described the Cape Verdeans who came to Plymouth to work on whaling ships and then on nearby cranberry bogs.

At the first public meeting for planning, on December 3, 2007, Sachem Randy Joseph of the Wampanoag, representatives of two societies of Mayflower descendants, a leader of the Old Colony Club that descended from the Tories, and a spokesman from the evangelical Plymouth Rock Foundation all participated. Although no one from the United American Indians of New England, the group that runs the National Day of Mourning, attended the meeting, it seemed possible that the 2020 commemoration would come closer to the broad commitment to social justice that the descendants of Wamsutta seek. An inclusive logo for the four hundredth anniversary, featuring a sailing ship surrounding the outline of an Indian, was unveiled in 2010. Unfortunately, planning meetings were disrupted when the Rev. Dr. Gomes died suddenly in February 2011, but they have resumed.

Before his death, Gomes asked Plymouth's Congressman to explore "the possibility of Plymouth's historic venues achieving national park status before 2020." The National Park Service has shown at Jamestown that it can construct an inclusive narrative. At Plymouth, it is easy to imagine that the Park Service might create a Visitor's Center that would tell the story of Squanto, who returned from English captivity to find his village destroyed by disease, and Massasoit, who had his life saved from typhus by the English, with whom he made a treaty, alongside the story of Miles Standish, who was eager to lead punitive raids on Indian villages. It seems likely that a Park Service center on the history of Plymouth would at least mention the Cape Verdean ancestors of Gomes and other immigrants such as the Italians, including Bartolomeo Vanzetti, the famous anarchist who sold fish near Plymouth Rock before he was executed in 1927.

One demand of the National Day of Mourning—that the merchants of Plymouth stop "making millions of dollars off the blood of our slaughtered ancestors"—will probably need to be modified if peace and unity are to be attained. Plymouth harbor was always shallow and therefore less useful for industry than Boston's, and Plymouth's most successful manufacturing company, the Plymouth Cordage Company, which made ropes for ships, was merged into a German conglomerate and closed in 1966. Since then, the town has been developing in what some call a "theme park" direction. It may be come the only example of a real town turned into a theme park by American civil religion. The nearby Plimoth Plantation site hosts continuous re-enactments of Pilgrim life in 1627, a year for which there is good documentation. The *Mayflower II* rides in the harbor, manned by more re-enactors employed by Plimoth Plantation. Near Plymouth Rock, the streets are lined with restaurants serving clam chowder and souvenir shops. One of these stores sells witchcraft supplies that would have made Governor William Bradford, Elder William Brewster, and Captain Miles Standish livid.

Perhaps the children of Massasoit will always disapprove of celebrating Plymouth Rock. But the story of Plymouth, from the days of Governor Bradford to the Old Colony Club, the Sons of Liberty and Daniel Webster, Henry Cabot Lodge and Calvin Coolidge, down to the Rev. Dr. Peter Gomes, is a story of the increasing commitments to personal freedom, political democracy, and cultural tolerance in American civil religion.

SOURCES

Abrams, Ann Uhry, *The Pilgrims and Pocahontas: Rival Myths of American Origin* (Boulder, CO: Westview Press, 1999).

Philbrick, Nathaniel, *Mayflower: A Voyage to War* (London: HarperPress, 2006).

Seelye, John, *Memory's Nation: The Place of Plymouth Rock* (Chapel Hill: University of North Carolina Press, 1998).

6

City on a Hill: From Jesus to Winthrop, Kennedy, and Reagan

In the image of the city on a hill, American civil religion has borrowed directly from Christianity. The metaphor began with an admonition of Jesus to his disciples, according to the Gospel of Matthew: "Ye are the light of the world. A city that is set on an hill cannot be hid.... Let your light so shine before men, that they may see your good works, and glorify your Father which is in heaven" (Matt. 5:14, 16 KJV). Sixteen hundred years later, Governor John Winthrop used the same image to admonish Puritans who were about to found a colony at Massachusetts Bay. Almost four centuries after Winthrop, Presidents John F. Kennedy and Ronald Reagan transformed the city on a hill metaphor to call the United States to new missions. Here is the famous conclusion of Winthrop's address, for a lay sermon called *A Model of Christian Charity*:

> Thus stands the cause between God and us. We are entered into covenant with Him for this work. We have taken out a commission. The Lord hath given us leave to draw our own articles. We have professed to enterprise these and those accounts, upon these and those ends. We have hereupon besought Him of favor and blessing. Now if the Lord shall please to hear us, and bring us in peace to the place we desire, then hath He ratified this covenant and sealed our commission, and will expect a strict performance of the articles contained in it; but if we shall neglect the observation of these articles which are the ends we have propounded, and, dissembling with our God, shall fall to embrace this present world and prosecute our carnal intentions, seeking great things for ourselves and our posterity, the Lord will surely break out in wrath against us, and be revenged of such a people, and make us know the price of the breach of such a covenant.
>
> Now the only way to avoid this shipwreck, and to provide for our posterity, is to follow the counsel of Micah, to do justly, to love mercy, to

walk humbly with our God. For this end, we must be knit together, in this work, as one man. We must entertain each other in brotherly affection. We must be willing to abridge ourselves of our superfluities, for the supply of others' necessities. We must uphold a familiar commerce together in all meekness, gentleness, patience and liberality. We must delight in each other; make others' conditions our own; rejoice together, mourn together, labor and suffer together, always having before our eyes our commission and community in the work, as members of the same body. So shall we keep the unity of the spirit in the bond of peace. The Lord will be our God, and delight to dwell among us, as His own people, and will command a blessing upon us in all our ways, so that we shall see much more of His wisdom, power, goodness and truth, than formerly we have been acquainted with. We shall find that the God of Israel is among us, when ten of us shall be able to resist a thousand of our enemies; when He shall make us a praise and glory that men shall say of succeeding plantations, "may the Lord make it like that of New England." For we must consider that we shall be as a city upon a hill. The eyes of all people are upon us. So that if we shall deal falsely with our God in this work we have undertaken, and so cause Him to withdraw His present help from us, we shall be made a story and a by-word through the world. We shall open the mouths of enemies to speak evil of the ways of God, and all professors for God's sake. We shall shame the faces of many of God's worthy servants, and cause their prayers to be turned into curses upon us till we be consumed out of the good land whither we are going.

According to the Rev. Dr. Peter J. Gomes, Professor of Divinity and Chaplain of Harvard College from 1974 until his death in 2011, Winthrop's *Model of Christian Charity* was the greatest sermon of the last millennium. We do not know when or where it was delivered, though it must have been sometime between Winthrop's election as governor of the Massachusetts Bay Company and his arrival at what would become Boston. It could well have been given in a church, although historians have often pictured it taking place on the *Arbella*, the flagship of the Great Migration of 1630, in which about seven hundred Puritans came to America. This was a large group compared to the parties of about one hundred that founded Jamestown and Plymouth. Whether or not the sermon was the greatest of the millennium, there is no doubt that it came at an important moment in American history and set a tone for much that followed. According to historian Edmund S. Morgan, John Winthrop was America's "first great man."

Like the authors of the *Mayflower Compact*, Governor Winthrop appears to have feared that the vast spaces and freedoms of America might lead the colonists to scatter quickly and to become selfish, or at least centered on themselves and their families rather than on the colony as a whole. He probably thought that the people of Jamestown had scattered too quickly through Virginia, leaving themselves open for the disastrous Indian attack of 1622, which killed a third of the white planters. Besides, a scattered people would not fulfill the basic purpose of the Puritan migration: to show England that the Puritan model of state and church could actually work.

Unlike the Separatists (later called "Pilgrims") of Plymouth, Winthrop's Puritans did not want to leave the Church of England but hoped to reform it. Their move to America was a strategic maneuver, not a flight, and Winthrop and the other leaders published a clear statement that they still regarded themselves as Anglicans. Of course, with an ocean separating them from the bishops and the king, and with their royal charter in their own possession in Massachusetts, they would govern themselves differently from most Anglicans, both in church and state. When Winthrop referred to "a due form of government both civil and ecclesiastical," he had very specific things in mind, many of which he could not advocate in public. The votes of shareholders in the Massachusetts Bay Company had put Winthrop in office, and he would sometimes be voted out in annual elections over the coming decades. Town meetings and meetings of church members would decide legal and moral questions. There would be no aristocrats in Massachusetts and no bishops to appoint or to discipline the pastors of churches. If issues arose that needed to be decided for all the churches, the governor would call a council. Although both lay and clerical elders elected in the churches came to these councils and commanded considerable respect, so that the system was sometimes called "a speaking aristocracy before a silent democracy," the government of Massachusetts was among the most democratic the world had ever seen. Democratic but not tolerant: because the government and the churches controlled most aspects of life, from how richly people could dress to how they worshipped, Massachusetts has been called a "totalitarian democracy." Puritan loyalty to the Crown and the Church of England was real, but based on the condition that they intended to transform the whole system, bringing it into line with what they believed to be standards drawn from Old and New Testament models.

When English Puritans rebelled against the attempts of King Charles I to impose his own vision of Anglican ritual and royal authority on Great Britain, the Puritans of America found that their "city on a hill" quickly became a sideshow. Oliver Cromwell's Puritan government cut off the head of Charles I in 1649, at the climax of the first modern revolution in the West, and the House of Commons has ever since held power over the monarch in England. Meanwhile, Massachusetts and the other English colonies grew and prospered, as Pilgrims and Puritans turned into Yankees. Although there had been no question in the 1600s that the non-separating Puritans of Boston, led by Winthrop, were far more important than the Separatists of Plymouth, by the time of the American Revolution the Pilgrims and Plymouth Rock had more prestige. Boston's history of driving dissenters like Anne Hutchinson and Roger Williams into exile, hanging Quakers on Boston Common, and holding witch trials made the persecuted Pilgrims of Plymouth appear to be more attractive ancestors. Scholars distinguished between Pilgrims and Puritans, although the Plymouth crew was just as puritanical as any, and some saw the Puritans as tyrants and the Pilgrims as progenitors of freedom. Other writers, such as H. L. Mencken, blamed all Puritans for all that was bad in American culture.

Between 1930 and the 1970s came a great reversal. Looking for roots as the United States engaged the great crises of the twentieth century, American intellectuals rediscovered the Puritans and John Winthrop. Historians like Samuel Eliot Morison, Perry Miller, Edmund S. Morgan, and Sacvan Bercovitch explored what Bercovitch called "the Puritan origins of the American self." According to Morgan, who published a classic Winthrop biography, *The Puritan Dilemma*, in 1958, the tension between being "in the world but not of it," seeking to make government pure without separating saints from sinners, as in a sect or commune, provided a basis for the American project. College and high school anthologies of American history and literature republished John Winthrop's *Model of Christian Charity*, and especially its last paragraphs, again and again. Suddenly the Pilgrims of Plymouth seemed quaint and impractical, the Puritans of Boston serious and substantial.

Ironically, President John F. Kennedy, the first (and so far only) Roman Catholic to hold the presidency, proved to be the first president to apply to himself John Winthrop's words describing America as a city on a hill. Kennedy redirected the metaphor from the people to his own government. On January 9, 1961, weeks before Kennedy went to Washington for his inauguration, he addressed the Massachusetts state legislature (still called the General Court, as it had been since Winthrop's day). His speech quoted Winthrop's "city on a hill" phrase in precisely the manner in which Winthrop used it, but as an admonition to himself as much as to his audience. Referring to the pressures on him to appoint certain people to the Cabinet and other posts in his administration—pressures that were to some extent coming from the legislators of Massachusetts to whom he spoke—Kennedy said that he would be "guided by the standard John Winthrop set before his shipmates on the flagship *Arbella* three hundred and thirty-one years ago, as they, too, faced the task of building a new government on a perilous frontier." He then quoted Winthrop: "we shall be as a city upon a hill—the eyes of all people are upon us." He told the General Court that "our governments, in every branch, at every level, national, state and local, must be as a city upon a hill—constructed and inhabited by men aware of their great trust and their great responsibilities." He said that when "the high court of history" judged how the people of his time discharged their trust, they would be seen as good only if they acted with courage, judgment, integrity, and dedication—"the historic qualities of the Bay Colony and the Bay State." About to become the first Roman Catholic president of the United States, Kennedy sought to assume and to offer his colleagues the mantle of John Winthrop.

Another Catholic, President Ronald Reagan's speechwriter Peggy Noonan, transformed Winthrop's words in 1989. In Noonan's use of the city on a hill, America became the New Jerusalem from the book of Revelation, the ultimate destination of history, as well as the successor of Winthrop's Boston and of the followers of Jesus in the gospel of Matthew. Noonan built on precedents: often Ronald Reagan had referred to the United States as a "city on a hill," or as a land singled out by God. For his farewell address, delivered on national television January 11, 1989, Noonan gave Reagan this classic piece of rhetoric:

> And that's about all I have to say tonight, except for one thing. The past few days when I've been at that window upstairs, I've thought a bit of the "shining city upon a hill." The phrase comes from John Winthrop, who wrote it to describe the America he imagined. What he imagined was important because he was an early Pilgrim, an early freedom man. He journeyed here on what today we'd call a little wooden boat; and like the other Pilgrims, he was looking for a home that would be free. I've spoken of the shining city all my political life, but I don't know if I ever quite communicated what I saw when I said it. But in my mind it was a tall, proud city built on rocks stronger than oceans, windswept, God-blessed, and teeming with people of all kinds living in harmony and peace; a city with free ports that hummed with commerce and creativity. And if there had to be city walls, the walls had doors and the doors were open to anyone with the will and the heart to get here. That's how I saw it, and see it still.
>
> And how stands the city on this winter night? More prosperous, more secure, and happier than it was eight years ago. But more than that: After two hundred years, two centuries, she still stands strong and true on the granite ridge, and her glow has held steady no matter what storm. And she's still a beacon, still a magnet for all who must have freedom, for all the pilgrims from all the lost places who are hurtling through the darkness, toward home.

Reagan was using the city on a hill not to call Americans to solidarity or common responsibility, as Winthrop and Kennedy had, but to evoke "a home that would be free." For Reagan, the image of the city validated the search for personal freedom, the most central and enduring value of American civil religion.

The values of peace and cultural tolerance appeared as well, for the city was "teeming with people of all kinds living in harmony and peace." Along with these values came a change in the role that the city on a hill played with regard to the rest of the world, and a change in the biblical source and resonance of the image.

In Reagan's farewell, the city on a hill became the destination of history, not an example. The phrase still came from Jesus, in the Gospel of Matthew's Sermon on the Mount, but the image came instead from the book of Revelation (or Apocalypse), the last book of the Christian Bible. The original version of Reagan and Noonan's city—its streets teeming with people and commerce and its gates always open, surrounded by darkness that cannot prevail against it, the destination of all who are saved—appeared in Revelation 21 and 22 as a city called the New Jerusalem. This image of the city was the source of the cliché that the streets of America are paved with gold.

> And in the spirit he [an angel] carried me away to a great, high mountain and showed me the holy city Jerusalem coming down out of heaven from God. It has the glory of God and a radiance like a very rare jewel, like jasper, clear as crystal. It has a great, high wall with twelve gates, and at the gates twelve angels... and the street of the city is pure gold, transparent as glass. I saw no temple in the city, for its temple is the Lord God the Almighty and the Lamb. And the city has no need of sun or moon to shine on it, for the glory of God is its light.... Its gates will never be shut by day—and there will be no night there. People will bring into it the glory and the honor of the nations. But nothing unclean will enter it, nor anyone who practices abomination or falsehood.... Blessed are those who wash their robes, so that they will have the right to the tree of life and may enter the city by the gates. Outside are the dogs and sorcerers and fornicators and murderers and idolaters, and everyone who loves and practices falsehood.
>
> —Rev. 21–22, NRSV

Stephen Prothero has pointed out that Reagan added the word "shining" to the phrase "city on a hill" from Matthew. By making the city on a hill shine and then lifting the New Jerusalem to stand "tall... on the granite ridge," Noonan and Reagan merged the New Jerusalem from Revelation with the city on a hill from the Sermon on the Mount. Reagan's farewell address changed the meaning of the city on a hill from an example for the world to the location of the Messianic era. All of history was moving toward the United States. All who loved freedom were "hurtling through the darkness" (a darkness that the book of Revelation filled with dogs and sorcerers and fornicators and murderers and idolaters) toward America.

Nor were Noonan and Reagan alone in their new vision of the city on a hill. From the studios of the Christian Broadcasting Network, Pat Robertson (a Yale Law School graduate and the son of a senator from Virginia) worked from the 1980s through the first decade of the twenty-first century to promulgate a theology of Christian and American "dominion." This theology affirmed the hope that the United States might remain true enough to Christianity so that, even when the Antichrist ruled the rest of the world during the times of Tribulation that were predicted in Revelation, a safe haven for Christians might be maintained in America. A variant of this theology inspired Tim La Haye and Jerry Jenkins in their best-selling *Left Behind* series of novels, which featured American Christians fighting a European Antichrist to a standoff throughout the Tribulation. According to videos posted on YouTube in 2008, Sarah Palin preached similar hopes for Alaska to a youth group in her former church. As the twentieth century turned into the twenty-first, John Winthrop's exemplary city on a hill became a mighty fortress, the ultimate refuge of the saints. For tens of millions of Americans, the idea that the United States would become a New Jerusalem, a central location in the redemption of the world, belonged both to the civil religion and to evangelical Christianity.

SOURCES

Bremer, Francis J., *John Winthrop: America's Forgotten Founding Father* (New York: Oxford University Press, 2003).

Bercovitch, Sacvan, *The Puritan Origins of the American Self* (New Haven: Yale University Press, 1975).

Morgan, Edmund S., *The Puritan dilemma: The Story of John Winthrop*. Edited by Oscar Handlin (Boston, Little, Brown, 1958).

Moseley, James G., *John Winthrop's World: History as a Story, the Story as History* (Madison: The University of Wisconsin Press, 1992).

Prothero, Stephen, *The American Bible: How Our Words Unite, Divide, and Define a Nation* (New York: HarperCollins, 2012).

Schesinger, Robert, *White House Ghosts: Presidents and Their Speechwriters* (New York: Simon and Schuster, 2008).

7

The Freedom Trail and Boston Common

Every year, 4 million Americans walk through almost four centuries of American civil religion on the Freedom Trail and Boston Common. Sites like the Bunker Hill Memorial, the *U.S.S. Constitution* ("Old Ironsides"), and the Robert Gould Shaw Memorial to the 54th Massachusetts (the first black regiment from the North in the U.S. Army) have a sacred quality that stands out against the urban traffic. At the beginning of the Freedom Trail that links these sites, the Boston Common and the Public Garden combine the categories of sacred and secular, historic and monumental and recreational space.

In one sense, the whole Common can seem sacred, at least to a visitor who enters while reflecting on its history. Its land was purchased in 1634, by contributions from every family of Boston, from an Anglican priest named William Blackstone who had arrived before the Puritans and who did not wish to live in their new colony. Almost immediately, the Common began to witness what scholar David Chidester has argued makes a place sacred—the willingness of people to fight and to die over it. Just weeks after the land was purchased, a majority of Bostonians voted at a town meeting to divide its original 44 acres (about equal to 44 football fields) among the families of the town, but they were thwarted by the refusal of Governor John Winthrop to meet with the committee to make the division. Eventually, another meeting accepted Winthrop's argument that using the land and the large pond on it as a common would encourage solidarity. Pasturing cows and sheep, doing laundry in Frog Pond, drilling the militia, quarrying stone, dumping garbage, and burying the dead were the first uses of the Common. Public executions, including those of Anne Hibbens for witchcraft in 1656, four Quakers in 1659 and 1660, and eight Indians after King Phillip's War in 1678, were held there. During the 1700s, a prison, a workhouse where the poor spun yarn, and a granary to store a public supply of food against famine stood on the Common.

Figure 7.1 The Robert Gould Shaw Memorial, by Augustus Saint-Gaudens, commemorates the Massachusetts 54th Regiment, in which African-Americans and freed slaves fought under white officers. It stands today as one of the most sacred places on the Boston Common. National Park Service.

Political and religious conflict, sometimes rising to violence, occurred on the Common—from the Antinomian Controversy of 1636 (when John Winthrop was defeated in an election that featured speeches there) to the Great Awakening of 1741 (when evangelist George Whitefield preached to 23,000 people on the Common) to the American Revolution (when a British tax collector's boat was dragged from the harbor to the Common and burned while other officials were covered in tar and feathers). In 1970, a crowd of 100,000 protestors against the Vietnam War gathered on the Common for a rally that ended in a march to Harvard Square and a riot, with burning cars and smashed storefronts and police dispersing the crowd with tear gas and clubs. Sarah Palin drew thousands to the Common for a rally of the Tea Party movement to protest taxation on April 14, 2010. If conflict engenders sacredness, the Common has seen enough to qualify.

The most renowned sacred site on the Common stands at its northeast corner, at the foot of Beacon Hill and across the street from the state capitol building. The Robert Gould Shaw Memorial (Figure 7.1), unveiled in 1897 after more than twelve years of work by sculptor Augustus Saint-Gaudens, celebrates the heroism of the white Colonel Shaw and the black soldiers of the Massachusetts 54th Regiment, who marched to the Civil War in 1863 after a rally on the

Common by the largest crowd ever gathered in Boston until that time. Shaw and most of his men died attacking Fort Wagner in South Carolina, but their conduct in that battle and before proved that soldiers of African descent, including former slaves, were capable of courage under fire and were willing to die to secure the freedom of all Americans. In Boston, which was the greatest stronghold of the Abolitionist movement, Shaw and his soldiers became objects of reverence.

Saint-Gaudens hired forty black men to model for the memorial, so that the soldiers who are marching behind and around the mounted figure of Shaw would have distinct, individual identities. Inscribed with verse by James Russell Lowell and a brief history of the regiment by Harvard president Charles W. Eliot, the memorial has inspired generations to create more art. Composer Charles Ives began his first publicly performed work, *Three Places in New England* (1930), with a brooding eight-minute tone poem called "The St. Gaudens in Boston Common." In 1942, John Berryman started his long poem *Boston Common* with the contrast of a drunk asleep near the memorial and the heroism of the sculpture. In 1960, the conflict over civil rights led Robert Lowell, a descendent of James Russell Lowell, to write in his *For the Union Dead* that the monument to black soldiers "sticks like a fishbone" in the throat of a city and a nation where black children were still trying to integrate public schools. In 1989, actor Denzel Washington won an Oscar for his role in *Glory*, a film about the 54th Massachusetts that showed its credits over footage of the Shaw Memorial. Although several other monuments—for example, the monuments to the entire Civil War, to George Washington, to abstractions like Religion and Learning, and even to the ducks (from the classic children's book *Make Way for Ducklings*)—stand on the Common and in the Public Garden, none approaches the power or the fame of the Shaw Memorial.

On every side of the Common are historic sites, but the whole area has been integrated, and made more sacred, by a line extending to the North, marked by red bricks and red granite stones, that has been known since 1951 as the Freedom Trail. The Trail began as the idea of an editor of the *Boston Herald-Traveler*, Bill Schofield, who became frustrated by trying to direct visitors to historic sites like the Old North Church, where Paul Revere's friends hung lamps to warn of the British invasion in 1775, the Old State House, where the Declaration of Independence was first read to Bostonians, and the site of the Boston Massacre, which was marked by a circle of paving stones. Schofield wrote a column in March 1951 proposing a path marked by signs and maps, which he called Freedom Way; by June, the city government and the Chamber of Commerce had decided to establish the Freedom Trail and provided brochures and signs. In 1964, a Freedom Trail Foundation was set up to improve coordination; in 1966, the first Freedom Trail Information Center was built on the Common; and in 1974, the National Park Service became involved, establishing a Boston

National Historical Park that oversees some sites on the Freedom Trail and cooperates with others. Those sites now include four churches, three cemeteries, Paul Revere's house, the Old State House, the site of the Boston Massacre, Faneuil Hall, a Benjamin Franklin statue, and the site of America's first public school, the Boston Latin School. The Freedom Trail extends across part of Boston Harbor on a bridge to the Charlestown dock of Old Ironsides and the Bunker Hill Memorial.

The birth of the Freedom Trail brought together and changed the significance of many sites that were already sacred, but for different reasons. For example, even without the Freedom Trail, the Park Street Church would appeal to tourists as worthy of attention because it is large, impressive, and old, built in 1810 at the corner of Boston Common bounded by Park and Tremont streets. Evangelical Christians might visit because the church is still just as committed to evangelical Christianity as it was when the congregation was founded, during the Second Great Awakening in 1809. But because of the Freedom Trail, the church is identified as "brimstone corner," not for the fiery sermons that are still preached there but for the gunpowder that was stored in its basement during the War of 1812. The Freedom Trail website tells visitors that this was the church where the hymn *My Country 'Tis of Thee* was first performed, and where William Lloyd Garrison gave his first major Abolitionist speech. Through the Freedom Trail, the Park Street Church sanctuary has been firmly integrated into American civil religion. The effects of the Freedom Trail exemplify the growth and increasing coherence of American civil religion during the years immediately after World War II, when the start of the Cold War against communism seemed to call for assertions that liberty and democracy were sacred.

At the extreme northern end of the Freedom Trail, over the bridge from downtown Boston to Charlestown, the Bunker Hill Memorial and the *U.S.S. Constitution* can be seen within a few blocks of each other. Bunker Hill is topped by a 221-foot granite obelisk that was erected in 1843 (Figure 7.2), an early example of the nineteenth-century American fondness for obelisks that filled cemeteries and culminated in the Washington Monument. Obelisks are originally religious symbols, derived from the Egyptian sun god, intended to represent the rays of the sun and immortality. A visitor's center that opened in 2007 tells the story of the battle on the hill, where American citizen soldiers showed for the first time that they could stand before British naval cannons and the British regular army.

In the harbor at the base of Bunker Hill, the *U.S.S. Constitution* rides at anchor. It still serves as a commissioned vessel in the US Navy and sails briefly at least once a year. The ship is called "Old Ironsides" not because it is made of metal, but because cannon balls of the War of 1812 bounced off its extremely dense and thick black hull, which is made of a live-oak wood so heavy that a plank of it

Figure 7.2 Rising from the top of a hill where British cannonballs once landed, bouncing and setting fires with their heat, the Bunker Hill Monument anchors one end of the Freedom Trail, with the other at Boston Common. National Park Service.

would not float but sink in water. Those who board Old Ironsides may at first feel no more religious than visitors to a whaling museum like Mystic Seaport, but the sign that can be seen in the officers' quarters with a list of captains that begins in 1797 and continues to the present suggests ancestor worship. The meticulous care with which the ship is maintained resembles the care that Japanese give to their wooden Shinto shrines. In whatever mood visitors board the ship, it must be difficult for them to leave the *Constitution* without some sense of reverence.

More than any other site of American civil religion, Boston Common and the Freedom Trail juxtapose secular urban life, the bustle of business and recreation, with the solemnity, historic associations, and symbolism of religion. Dogs catch Frisbees and children play near the Shaw Memorial, and the Park Street Church stands across the street from the busy Park Street subway station. The Bunker Hill Memorial obelisk rises from a small park in the midst of a crowded neighborhood of townhouses and competition for on-street parking. Contemporary pilgrims following the Freedom Trail share sidewalks with natives hurrying to work. Adequate respect is not always shown: the Civil War memorial near the center of the Common has to be cleaned of graffiti, and the sword in George Washington's hand in the Public Garden has been broken so frequently that it is now replaced with vinyl. Still, the casual atmosphere of this sacred space is more a strength than a weakness. A combination of enlightened leadership and unconscious reverence has enabled Boston to avoid what Garrett Hardin called "the tragedy of the commons," which he saw as the inevitable exploitation and decline of common space. The utilitarian place where Puritans did their laundry, hanged Quakers, and shot Indians has become a magnificent public space, sacred to liberty, democracy, and even cultural tolerance.

SOURCES

Fischer, David Hackett, "Boston Common," in Leuchtenberg, William E., ed., *American Places: Encounters with History* (New York: Oxford University Press, 2000).

Hardin, Garrett, "The Tragedy of the Commons," *Science 162* (1968) 1243–1248.

Loewen, James W., *Lies across America: What Our Historic Sites Get Wrong* (New York: The New Press, 1999).

City of Boston, "A Quick Tour Along the Freedom Trail," http://www.cityofboston.gov/freedomtrail (June 1, 2008).

Whitehill, Walter Muir, *Boston: A Topographical History* (Cambridge, MA: Harvard Univeristy Press, 1968).

8

The Liberty Bell, Independence Hall, and the Slave Quarters

Every year, more than 3 million people line up and pass through security to see the bell that hung above the building where the Declaration of Independence and the Constitution were approved and signed (Figure 8.1). The Liberty Bell Center receives several times as many visitors as Independence Hall, even though both places are free of charge and they stand across the street from each other. This disparity results in part from convenience, since Independence Hall requires a tour and the Liberty Bell Center does not, but also from one religious factor: the difference between a historic site and a relic, a remnant from a martyr or a saint. At a historic site, visitors are expected to remain outside the event that the site commemorates, but a relic invites personal confrontation.

Another dimension to what the Park Service calls Independence National Park has recently emerged, with the discovery that the quarters in which George Washington kept nine slaves stood just outside the entrance of the building where the Liberty Bell has been displayed since 2003. After many archaeological discoveries and arguments among politicians, activists, and scholars, an agreement has been reached that a memorial to the former "President's House" and the slaves who worked there should greet visitors to the Liberty Bell. Independence Hall has meanwhile become a replica of itself, stocked with reproductions of chairs and tables made to resemble those from the late eighteenth century. Visitors to Independence Hall enter a site that has been called "sacred" since the 1840s, but they experience a diorama/museum, very dependent on the skills of those who did the reproductions and of a National Park Service docent who delivers an exposition of what happened in these rooms in 1776 and 1787. Visitors to the Liberty Bell walk through a graphic display of more than 250 years of history since the Bell was cast and recast, rung and cracked, carried across the nation and reproduced, and invoked by Abolitionists and suffragettes and Martin Luther King, Jr., who used "Let Freedom Ring!" as a climax of his "I Have a Dream" speech. While Independence Hall expresses consensus history,

Figure 8.1 Visitors can approach the Liberty Bell closely enough to appreciate the strain that created its iconic crack. Photograph by the author.

the Liberty Bell inspires debate and reflection. Both contribute to the power of American civil religion, but the bell has become more and more powerful ever since it cracked and went on display, over 150 years ago.

Beginning with its birth in colonial times, the Liberty Bell has participated in civil religion in several distinct ways, in roles that corresponded with changes in the function of the bell and its degree of importance. The bell was ordered by the Pennsylvania legislature in 1751, the fiftieth year after William Penn's grant of a charter for self-government to those who lived in the colony that he owned. Stamped with a biblical quotation—"Proclaim liberty throughout all the land unto all the inhabitants thereof" (from Leviticus 25:10)—the bell has always celebrated liberty with religious overtones. The bell was meant for a steeple that was being added to the building that would become Independence Hall, which was the largest public building in the colonies and the seat of the elected assembly that William Penn had created. Though the bell was born with a great parentage—cast at the Whitechapel Bell Foundry, now the oldest manufacturer in England, in business since 1570—it cracked at its first ring in America; it was then melted down and recast twice in Philadelphia before ever being installed above the colonial capitol. For decades, it functioned to call legislators to their meetings and to announce public occasions and acts of government.

In its first role, as a herald of government, the bell was important but not always beloved. Neighbors complained in 1772 that the bell was being rung too often, for the increasing numbers of political crises, and that its loud and growling tone was "extremely dangerous and may prove fatal" for those forced to hear it frequently. It may or may not have been rung to mark the Declaration of Independence in July 1776—there is no contemporary record of it, and the steeple was in disrepair at the time. During the Revolution, the bell was a potential strategic resource, in danger of being melted down by the British for ammunition. Along with nine bells from churches, it was smuggled out of the city and hidden when the British occupied Philadelphia. It went unused for eight years, one in exile and seven in storage, before being rehung. The bell tolled in 1787 to announce that the Constitution, written in the building below, had been ratified. During the Washington and Adams administrations, Philadelphia became the nation's temporary capital, and the bell continued to serve government.

After 1800, when the US government departed for the District of Columbia and the capital of Pennsylvania also moved from Philadelphia, the bell began to be used in a purely memorial role. It rang to mark anniversaries like July 4th and the deaths of revolutionary heroes like Franklin, Washington, and Hamilton. In 1816, the state sought to sell the former State House and its bell. Fortunately, the city of Philadelphia decided to buy and to preserve the old State House, using it for courtrooms and the City Council, and the bell continued to ring. Hairline cracks, sometimes filed smooth to lessen the vibration of the edges against each other, began to appear. During Lafayette's visit to Philadelphia in 1824, the room where the Declaration of Independence and Constitution had been worked out was first called Independence Hall, a title that was gradually applied to the whole State House and that led to the bell being called the Independence Bell. In 1826, when both Thomas Jefferson and John Adams died on July 4, the fiftieth anniversary of Independence Day, a great ceremony took place in which the bell took part. By 1828, when the steeple over Independence Hall was rebuilt, the old State House Bell had become so unimportant that it was replaced by a bell twice as large, while the old bell was sold for scrap. It was spared from destruction only because the maker of the new bell, who had accepted the old as partial payment, decided that the cost of removing the old bell from its room below the steeple would exceed the proceeds from selling the metal.

Having survived into the 1830s, the bell continued to be used to mark occasions like the death of Chief Justice Marshall, when it apparently suffered another crack. A visitor to Philadelphia named R. G. Williams, writing in *The Anti-Slavery Record* for February 1835, referred to it for the first time in print as "the Liberty Bell," probably reflecting a local custom, and reported that the bell was rung every July 4 and February 22 (for Washington's birthday). Williams also remarked that the command for the bell to "Proclaim Liberty throughout all the land, and to all the inhabitants thereof" had long been "considered a sort of prophecy," but that to this point, "its peals have been a mockery, while one sixth of 'all inhabitants' are in abject slavery." Memorials of the Revolution and the Founders seemed less important as the nation faced a new crisis.

The rise of the bell to greatness began with its adoption as a symbol of liberty, and its public christening as "the Liberty Bell," by Abolitionists in the 1830s. Many Abolitionist publications and speaker's platforms at rallies featured the bell. In 1839, a picture of the old Philadelphia bell was placed on the first issue of *The Liberty Bell*, an annual anthology of writings on abolition published by the American Anti-Slavery Society. The inscription on the bell, which in its biblical context actually did refer to setting slaves free in a fifty-year Jubilee, and the traditional role of the bell in celebrating the July 4 declaration that all men are created equal, both suited the message of Abolitionists.

A disastrous crack and a fictional story helped make the Liberty Bell a much more potent symbol of liberty. In February 1846, as the bell was being rung to celebrate the birthday of George Washington, the jagged crack from the lip to the crown that marks it today appeared. The *Philadelphia Public Ledger* reported on February 26 that "[t]he old Independence Bell rang its last clear note on Monday...and now hangs in the great city steeple irreparably cracked and dumb." Inspired by this event, a Philadelphia newspaperman and popular sensational novelist named George Lippard published a story in 1847 that made the bell central to the events of July 4, 1776. According to Lippard's tale, an illiterate old bell ringer who supported American independence had asked a rich young boy to read the inscription on the bell to him, and then to tell him when the delegates in the State House had voted for independence so that he could ring the bell. Just as the old man despaired that the delegates would vote as they did, and began to think that the boy had forgotten him, he heard a voice from the street calling, "Ring, Grandfather, ring!" The story added to an emerging cult of the bell as herald, relic, and even martyr of American liberty, a symbol not yet fulfilled because the slaves were not free. Meanwhile, Independence Hall became more sacred when the bodies of John Quincy Adams, the former president who died at work in the House of Representatives in 1848, and Henry Clay, "the Great Compromiser" who died in 1852, were both laid in state there enroute to their burials.

In 1852, Philadelphia's city government brought the broken bell down from the steeple and displayed it in the room where the Declaration of Independence had been signed. Pictures were taken of the bell on a pedestal draped with American flag bunting, with a stuffed eagle perched atop its crown. By the time the Civil War began, most people in the United States would have recognized the Liberty Bell with its famous crack. When the martyred president, Abraham Lincoln, laid in state in Independence Hall in 1865, the *Evening Bulletin* of

Philadelphia noted it was fitting for "the mangled head of the most illustrious victim of slavery" to lie next to "the old bell which first sounded abroad the glad tidings of a people disenthralled." The 1876 Philadelphia Centennial Exposition, the first World's Fair held in America, drew pilgrims from across the nation and the world to see the bell of Independence Hall. Though the bell had not rung in thirty years, it had never been more powerful as a symbol of liberty.

After the Centennial, the Liberty Bell began a new role in American civil religion, that of a physical source of national unity and greatness. On seven railroad journeys between 1885, when the bell was shipped from Philadelphia to New Orleans as a gesture of national reconciliation, and 1915, when it went on a complex, 10,000-mile trip between Philadelphia and San Francisco, following a northern route out and a southern route back, the Liberty Bell reached every region of the continental United States. During these trips, the Liberty Bell became a celebrity and proved its power as a relic. Generations of Americans came out to railroad stations for one of the 376 scheduled stops it made in those thirty years, to hear speeches extolling it and to hold their children up to touch it. The former president of the Confederacy, Jefferson Davis, rose from a sickbed to give a speech welcoming the Liberty Bell on its trip to New Orleans. In 1893, John Philip Sousa wrote *The Liberty Bell March* (later used as the theme of *Monty Python's Flying Circus*) to celebrate its arrival at the World's Columbian Exhibition in Chicago. The bell went to Charleston, South Carolina, to Atlanta, to the 1904 World's Fair in St. Louis and in 1903 to Boston, where cartoons showed the Liberty Bell as a woman, dancing with a masculine Bunker Hill Monument. The Panama-Pacific Exposition at San Francisco in 1915 included a replica of Independence Hall with the actual Liberty Bell inside. In that same year, the bell made an electronic intercontinental trip, when the first telephone connection was completed across the nation, connecting Philadelphia and San Francisco. The first live sound heard on that line was the ringing of the Liberty Bell by striking it with a hammer. Listening on another line from Baltimore, Alexander Graham Bell broke in to recall his visit to the bell in Philadelphia.

During its travels, the Liberty Bell came to embody a moment of American unity and pride in which the nation took its place on the center stage of world politics, acquiring Caribbean and Pacific colonies in the Spanish American War of 1898, holding onto these lands against insurgents in the early 1900s, sending the Great White Fleet of sixteen battleships around the world, and building the Panama Canal. Sometimes, demonstrating the critical potential of religious symbols, the bell was used to question whether all actions of the United States were compatible with liberty. For example, during the Republican National Convention of 1900, the *New York Journal and Advertiser* ran an editorial cartoon depicting a plutocrat wearing a suit made of dollar signs, proudly showing the

Liberty Bell to a half-naked man in a grass skirt. The caption below read, "Ring Out and Proclaim Trust-Imperialism Throughout the Land."

After being established by its travels as what the *San Francisco Chronicle* called a "sacred relic," the Liberty Bell stayed home to serve as a universal symbol of liberty. Restrained from travel by reformers in the Philadelphia city government (who objected to the costs of sending the bell and city officials across the nation), the bell became not only an object for pilgrimage, but the reminder of a national consensus that liberty must expand. A popular song, "Liberty Bell, It's Time to Ring Again," with a picture of the bell on the sheet music, recruited American soldiers for World War I. Advocates of women's suffrage made a duplicate of the bell, carried it around the country, and finally rang it on Independence Square in 1920, on the day the Nineteenth Amendment to the Constitution, giving women the vote, went into effect. This was the first of many duplicates made to promote a cause. Campaign buttons for Alf Landon in 1936 and Wendell Willkie in 1940 featured the Liberty Bell and the phrase "Ring It Again" in their efforts to rally the nation against what Republicans saw as the tyranny of Franklin Roosevelt and his socialist New Deal. On the morning of June 6, 1944, to celebrate the D-Day invasion of Normandy, the mayor of Philadelphia struck the Liberty Bell seven times, one for each letter of "liberty," with a hammer made of dogwood from Valley Forge, and broadcast and recorded the tones. There was also a B-17 bomber named *Liberty Belle*, bearing (like many such bombers) the image of a young woman on its nose.

After the war, duplicates and images of the bell multiplied in many contexts. In 1950, every one of the states and territories of the United States received a physical duplicate bell, paid for by the Department of the Treasury, as part of a campaign to sell savings bonds for "financial independence." When *Washington Post* cartoonist Herbert Block (more commonly known as Herblock) wanted to support President Truman's acts in favor of civil rights for African-Americans, he showed Truman as "the bell ringer," ringing the Liberty Bell with the words "civil rights" printed across his chest. Anti-Communists on the National Committee for a Free Europe raised money to cast a ten-ton World Liberty Bell and to install it in Berlin. Images of the Liberty Bell began to seem ubiquitous, appearing on the Franklin half-dollar coin and in the advertising for Pennzoil Motor Oil, which still uses the bell on its website and products today. Both liberty and the Liberty Bell, it seemed, should replicate and expand across the world.

A remnant of this phase of replication and expansion continues in the *Let Freedom Ring!* ceremony, which is held at the bell at 2 P.M. every July 4th. Begun at the initiative of President John F. Kennedy, who wanted to bring bells into competition with fireworks in celebrating Independence Day, the ritual involves guards in eighteenth-century costumes and a retinue of children, descendants of signers of the Declaration of Independence, who are gathered to tap the

Liberty Bell thirteen times (one for each colony) with gloved hands. At the same moment across the country, bells are supposed to be sounded. The silence in my neighborhood indicates that *Let Freedom Ring!* has not had the same impact as other Liberty Bell events, but the Park Service continues to try.

Between 1915 and 1976, the original Liberty Bell remained at Philadelphia in the original Independence Hall, so that visitors paid simultaneous homage to the Founding Fathers who signed the Declaration of Independence and wrote the Constitution and to the bell that rang to celebrate their achievements. Possibly because the physical Declaration and Constitution – the real relics of those events – are enshrined in Washington, D.C., rather than at Independence Hall, the Philadelphia site became more and more focused on the Liberty Bell. For example, when the city celebrated the Sesquicentennial of Independence with an International Exposition in 1926, it placed an eighty-foot replica of the Liberty Bell, high enough so that cars and trucks could pass under it, at the entrance to the exposition grounds. Brochures for visitors to the hall featured the bell as the "finish line" of a tour.

In the current phase of the Liberty Bell's career, beginning in the 1950s and extending in planning beyond the present, the bell (and by extension Independence Hall) has become a focus for confrontations and demonstrations regarding liberty and oppression. Foundations for this stage were laid in 1942, when the city of Philadelphia turned over administration and maintenance of Independence Hall, including the Liberty Bell, to the National Park Service. Though the city retained ownership, plans for Independence National Park involved creating open space through the demolition of many tax-paying properties. Eventually, three blocks of buildings north of Independence Hall and another block to the south were demolished. The open space contributed to a revival of tradition from the nineteenth century, when demonstrations against immigrants, for freedom in Europe, and for labor unions often occurred in Independence Square, just behind the Hall. In 1912, the city had restricted such demonstrations by an ordinance that limited gatherings at Independence Hall to "patriotic meetings to celebrate some event in the history of the Nation, State, or City." Ethnic celebrations of the Irish, Polish, and Italians came to be allowed at the site because of connections to Revolutionary commodore John Barry, General Casimir Pulaski, and Christopher Columbus. In 1947, a federal judge ruled the city ordinance unconstitutional, and the National Park Service took a more tolerant view of free speech near Independence Hall than the city had. In 1948, black Philadelphians began to hold an annual Freedom Day at the Liberty Bell every February 1. An all-night sit-in at the Liberty Bell for civil rights took place in 1965; the Mattachine Society protested anti-sodomy laws between 1965 and 1969; and clashes between protestors for and against the Vietnam War took place in 1966 and 1969. In April 1970, the first Earth Day drew thousands who filled all three blocks of Independence Mall and signed a Declaration of Interdependence, with Ralph Nader presiding.

In preparation for the Bicentennial of the Declaration of Independence in 1976, the Park Service built a separate visitors' center for the Liberty Bell, close to but not connected with Independence Hall. Using careful research based on paintings and drawings from the era and architectural evidence from the walls of the building, the Park Service returned the hall to a state as close as possible to its condition between 1776 and 1800, when the bell would have been in the tower below the steeple and not on display in the hall itself. The restoration turned what had been for centuries a working courthouse and City Council chamber into a reproduction, frozen in time. Only a few objects in the rooms—including Washington's chair from the Constitutional Convention and a silver inkwell used in signing the Declaration of Independence—were authentic, since the British had sacked the building and the Americans used it for a hospital during the Revolution. Entrance was now restricted to guided tours, so that the numbers of visitors to the hall plunged from a peak of 1.5 million to the current level of about 800,000 per year. Meanwhile, the bell grew more popular and powerful.

After 1976, the Liberty Bell, which had long been the main attraction at Independence Hall, began to draw more than 3 million people a year to its modern building, which had large windows through which visitors could see Independence Hall as they gathered around the bell. There were protests against moving the bell from the building that had been its home since 1753, but practical considerations and showmanship overcame them. The bell was moved for Philadelphia's first Bicentennial event, at midnight on January 1, 1976. Visitors in the room where the Declaration of Independence had been signed and the Constitution debated now had to stand behind a rope to keep them from the reproductions of Windsor chairs and baize-covered tables, but visitors were still allowed to touch the Liberty Bell. Some left roses in its crack.

In the following decades, some used the accessibility of the bell to make other points. Two hundred demonstrators for abortion rights, chanting "No choice, no liberty," took over the pavilion on July 4, 1992. Supporters of Mumia Abu-Jamal, convicted for the murder of a Philadelphia police officer, occupied the building for three hours on July 3, 1999. At 9:30 A.M. on April 6, 2001, a twenty-six-year-old Nebraskan tourist named Mitchell Guillatt, wearing a T-shirt depicting a crucified Jesus and crying out "God is real," struck the bell five times with a handheld sledgehammer, knocking small chips of metal off its lip, before he was tackled by a Park Service ranger. By the time of this incident, the lines outside the pavilion had grown so annoyingly long, and the wait so disproportionate to the amount of time visitors were allowed to spend near the bell (a bit more than the span of a three-minute ranger talk), that another setting was demanded. The present visitors' center, which tells the story of the bell on a wall of displays leading to a large room where visitors can spend as much time as they like near (but no longer touching) the Liberty Bell, opened in 2003.

Over the 250 years since the bell first rang in its steeple, its career paralleled the development of American civil religion in all of its phases, as outlined in Chapter 1. Rooted in the Bible through its inscription in a colonial context, the bell gained a new dimension of meaning with the Revolution, another in the national celebrations of the Continental era, and yet another with the Abolition movement and the Civil War. The years between 1885 and 1915, when the bell went on its travels, saw a great imperial expansion of American influence and of civil religion. These were the decades when the Pledge of Allegiance was written, when John Philip Sousa began to tour with his own band, and when flags were placed in public schools. After World War I came the age of recording, film, physical reproduction, and worldwide mission for the bell, corresponding with a global mission for American civil religion. The last few decades have seen a multicultural phase, with new kinds of conflict over the values of American civil religion and over the way the Liberty Bell should be displayed.

While the visitors' center that opened in 2003 was still under construction, the most serious controversy in the history of the bell, and for that matter of the entire Independence National Park, broke out. An article written by Edward Lawler Jr. for the January 2002 issue of the *Pennsylvania Magazine of History and Biography* pointed out that the entrance of the new Liberty Bell center would be directly above the slave quarters of a mansion that had stood on the site from 1767 until 1832, and which George Washington had occupied for six years of his presidency, between 1790 and 1796. Nine of Washington's household slaves had lived on that spot. While visiting Philadelphia to give a talk about "Restoring Memory," Professor Gary B. Nash of the University of California in Los Angeles met with Park Service officials to try to get some acknowledgement of the slave quarters onto the site and into their interpretive narrative, but he was told it was too late. On a radio show, Nash charged that history was not only being "managed and manipulated," but "downright buried." Nash and Randall Miller, professor of history at St. Joseph's University in Philadelphia, wrote an op-ed piece for the *Philadelphia Inquirer*, and the newspaper's editorial board picked up on the story in sympathy. Three groups—one called Ad Hoc Historians; another called the Independence Hall Association, a white establishment group that has lobbied for Independence Park since 1942; and a coalition of black Philadelphians called Avenging the Ancestors—began to pressure the Park Service. Avenging the Ancestors began to demonstrate at the site with crowds of hundreds on every July 3rd in 2002.

In October 2003, Philadelphia mayor John T. Street provided $1.5 million in city funds to make a memorial for the slave quarters. Next the Pennsylvania delegation to Congress (particularly US Representatives Chaka Fattah and

Robert Brady) became involved, and in 2003 inserted language requiring the Park Service to develop an "appropriate commemoration" of Washington's slaves at the site into the Park Service budget. In 2005, Congress appropriated $3.6 million to implement a plan that produced a design, featuring the outline of the mansion on the ground, a modernist sculpture illustrating slavery and liberation, and the specific stories of the slaves. The slave memorial opened in December 2010.

Some of those stories that the memorial tells should, as Professor Nash has said, lead visitors to "enter the door of the pavilion in a whole new frame of mind." For example, when Washington moved to Philadelphia, he expressed concern in his journal that living in that Quaker city, and in the proximity of many free black people, would give his slaves a thirst for "compleat freedom." Oney (or Ona) Judge, who had served Martha Washington since she was ten and who was sixteen in 1790, made her escape just before the family returned to Mt. Vernon in 1796. She may have been motivated in part by a plan to give her to Washington's granddaughter as a wedding present. At any rate, she enlisted the help of Philadelphians she had come to know to get her luggage put on a ship, left the house while the family was at dinner, and sailed to New Hampshire. President Washington was extremely irritated by her leaving "with no provocation" and sent an agent to New Hampshire armed with shackles to bring Judge back. Judge offered to return to service if she could be declared legally free, but Washington refused because of the effect he thought it would have on his three hundred other slaves. He was further inconvenienced by the cook Hercules, whose expertise had produced many state dinners in the mansion, who now stole out of the house by night and hid in the woods outside Philadelphia, never to be found, leaving behind a six-year-old son. Washington then took steps to put the remaining slaves into a carriage by surprise and send them back early to Mt. Vernon. Two years later, in 1798, he sent his nephew to New Hampshire in another attempt to force Judge to return, but the man reported that the feelings of the people were so much against slavery that it would be impossible to shackle the woman and take her through the streets. After Washington died in 1799, his passing marked in Philadelphia by the muffled ringing of the Liberty Bell, his will set his slaves free, but those belonging to Martha remained in bondage.

Not everyone is thrilled with the idea of telling such stories in Independence Park. When Steven Warshawsky, a self-described conservative commentator for *American Thinker*, visited the Liberty Bell Center in 2007, he found that the theme of "freedom vs. unfreedom" was the controlling idea of the pictures and text, video and sound that lined the wall on the way to the bell. The text had been rewritten, under pressure from the Ad Hoc Historians group, after the discovery of Washington's slave quarters. For Warshawsky, the exhibit was structured "to emphasize the Liberty Bell's ties to various civil rights movements for minorities." It also implied that the bell "has little relevance to a middle-class white male like myself, except as a tool to scold me and my presumed ancestors for our wrongdoing against others."

Warshawsky's story was datelined March 18, 2007. Three days later, ground was broken for an archaeological dig that uncovered the presidential mansion with its slave quarters. As the dig progressed through that spring and summer, people were stunned by how much was left. Stone foundations of every room were visible, including the great bow window of the first Oval Office, where presidents Washington and John Adams greeted dignitaries. The slave quarters where the cook Hercules and other male slaves slept was identifiable, as was the bedroom where Oney Judge slept. The dig remained uncovered months longer than scheduled, while the Park Service debated what to do. At the end of February, a design for the President's House memorial had been selected, but it was a design for the surface of the Mall, reproducing a few architectural features and an outline of the house below. After seeing what remained from the real house, US Representative Bob Brady said, "How can you cover that up?... We need to rethink what we're doing there.... Damn! I got chills." But the costs of preserving the exposed walls, with mortar crumbling, and bringing visitors down 10 feet into the earth, would be much higher than those anticipated for the ground-level memorial. Eventually the dig was filled in, after a libation ceremony run by the Avenging the Ancestors Coalition. On July 31, 2007, they poured water and sand from the Nile on the floor of the slave quarters, while chanting blessings in languages from Ghana, Zambia, Kenya, South Africa, Zimbabwe, and the Yoruba land of Nigeria. The blessing was apparently successful, because above the buried foundations a powerful set of walls has risen on the surface, and the slaves have gained their monument.

Conservative Steven Warshawsky was not only "dispirited" by the Park Service exhibit leading up the bell, but also by the display of the bell itself. Though that room is described by the Park Service as a "shrine" in which visitors can quietly walk around the Liberty Bell, it seemed cold and unadorned to Warshawsky. There are none of the flags and eagles and other decorations that surrounded the bell in the nineteenth century. Warshawsky also objected that the bell is cordoned off to keep visitors from touching it, not with "elegant ropes or velvet cords, but with harsh steel cables." Again, the aesthetic is modernist, presenting the relic in its simplicity, unembellished.

The Liberty Bell is what former Park Service guide Jill Ogline called "the greatest relic of America's heroic age." What makes it great, first and foremost, are the words, which are clearly readable. The command to "[p]roclaim liberty throughout all the land, unto all the inhabitants thereof" derives from the rules of ancient Israel for running a Jubilee every fifty years, in which all debts were canceled, slaves were freed, and families who had sold their land to survive were given back their property. No land or person could be sold in perpetuity, because both belonged to God.

For the Quaker legislator Isaac Norris, who asked that this inscription be put on the bell, the words probably had a double meaning. Norris belonged to the anti-proprietary party in the Pennsylvania Assembly, so for him the words may have expressed a hope that the descendants of William Penn, the proprietor whose family owned Pennsylvania, would grant Pennsylvanians the right to elect their governor. In 1701, fifty years before the bell was ordered, William Penn had drawn up a Charter of Liberties that established religious toleration and gave the inhabitants of Pennsylvania the right to elect a legislature, while he retained the proprietary governorship. The legislature that ordered the bell may have been thinking of celebrating that Charter of Liberties, but Penn's descendants retained the governorship until a new constitution was decided in 1776. For Abolitionists, suffragettes, anti-Communists, antiwar demonstrators, civil rights leaders, gay rights advocates, avengers of slave ancestors, and so many others today, the words on the bell continue to have such double messages.

After the words, the visitor sees the rough, unpolished metal of the bell. Black and uneven, it has an organic texture. It looks old and worn but strong. Though originally produced by the English firm that later made Big Ben, its current form resulted from the work of two Philadelphians named John Pass and John Stow, whose names are also on the bell. They had probably never made a bell before, but learned how from a book after the original English bell cracked and the captain of the ship that had brought it refused to take the heavy (2,080-pound) cargo back. They added copper to the copper and tin mixture, hoping to make their bell less brittle, but brittleness is related to vibration and a good clear ring. There was a huge feast laid on by the city for the first bell that Pass and Stow made, but its sound was described as flat and uninspiring, like that of two heavy shovels being banged together. Then they tried again, added more tin, and made the final Liberty Bell. Its sound had become a deep and resonant E flat, with a distinctive after tone. People said that it sounded as though it "meant something."

On June 6, 2004, a Frenchman named Patrick Daudon stood on the shores of Normandy and rang a bell he had commissioned to replicate, so far as can be told, the exact metal content and shape of the Liberty Bell. Daudon did this to thank the United States for the D-Day invasion and subsequent liberation of France. (A link to a website where the sound of Daudon's replica can be heard appears among the Sources at the end of this chapter.)

Finally, and most important, the power of the Liberty Bell lies in the crack. A lightning bolt of a breach, zig-zagging from the lip to the words on the crown, is interrupted by two round bolts inserted to hold the metal together. The crack was made somewhat wider shortly after it appeared in 1846 by an attempt to file the edges to see if the bell could still be rung. There have been proposals to melt the bell down and fix the crack, once in 1876, for the Centennial, and later by the original English bellmakers after World War II, as a gesture of gratitude, but these were wisely refused. Metallurgists say that repeated melting and recasting of a bell increases its brittleness. At any rate, the crack not only resulted in the bell being brought down from the obscurity of the steeple and displayed, but also in its unique look. The symbolism of the crack has proved suggestive for generations: many have seen the crack as a symbol of the flaws of democracy, while others have seen the suffering needed to preserve it.

Mystery surrounds the crack, beginning with the bell made by the Whitechapel Bell Foundry in London. The ship that brought the bell in 1752 had a rough passage, so the bell could have been damaged in its cargo hold. Perhaps the first Americans who tested the bell held the clapper against it, causing too much vibration. As for the bell that emerged from Pass and Stow's two recastings, it also endured some rough treatment on its flight from the British occupation of Philadelphia. The cart that carried the bell to Allentown, where it spent a year in the cellar of the Zion Reformed Church, broke down in the streets of Bethlehem, Pennsylvania, and that accident gave the bell a jolt. Over nearly a hundred years in the steeple of Independence Hall, the bell also saw more hard use than we are accustomed to putting bells through today. It often rang for hours, over and over, in celebration or with a leather-wrapped clapper for mourning. Even on the day of its last clear note, it had rung well for hours before it cracked at noon.

Whatever caused the crack, it made the bell a relic of martyrdom. Religions need martyrs, to stand for commitment to the ultimate power that holds things together, and American civil religion has many martyrs: Lincoln, Kennedy, Martin Luther King, Jr., the Unknown Soldier, the thousands in graveyards at places like Gettysburg. The crack made the Liberty Bell a relic of martyrs for liberty that remains for us to visit. Efforts to surround the bell with narrative, from the stories of the slave quarters to the replicated furniture at Independence Hall, are the healthy responses of a living community to the wound that is the crack.

SOURCES

Boland, Charles Michael, *Ring in the Jubilee: The Epic of America's Liberty Bell* (Riverside, CT: The Chatham Press, 1973).
Daudon, Patrick, link to the sound of a replica of the Liberty Bell, http://www.ushistory.org/LibertyBell/more/normandybell.htm.
Fischer, David Hackett, *Liberty and Freedom: A Visual History of America's Founding Ideas* (New York: Oxford University Press, 2005).
Kammen, Michael, *Mystic Chords of Memory: The Transformation of Tradition in American History* (New York: Alfred A. Knopf, 1991).
Mires, Charlene, *Independence Hall in American Memory* (Philadelphia: University of Pennsylvania Press, 2002).
Nash, Gary B., *The Liberty Bell* (New Haven: Yale University Press, 2010).

Ogline, Jill, "'Creating Dissonance for the Visitor': The Heart of the Liberty Bell Controversy," *The Public Historian* 26, no. 3 (Summer, 2004), 49–57.
Philadelphia Inquirer, http://www.philly.com/inquirer/.
Rosewater, Victor, *The Liberty Bell: Its History and Significance* (New York: D. Appleton, 1926).
US History, http://www.ushistory.org/LibertyBell/index.html.
Warshawsky, Steven, "Visiting the Liberty Bell." from the RealClearPolitics website, http://www.realclearpolitics.com/articles/2007/03/visiting_the_liberty_bell.html (June 27, 2008).

9

The Flag

The American flag has become a sacramental object. "Sacrament" is a Christian term for rituals that use objects to transmit spiritual power. Unlike other objects that could be called sacramental—the bread and wine of Christians, the foods that Hindus offer to the gods, the tobacco of Native Americans—flags have no biological value as food or psychological effect based on ingestion. But flags do have powers that surpass those of things that can be consumed. Flags last longer, and their spiritual qualities are independent of any particular ritual. Flags are not just objects or symbols, but entities with power in themselves, like the icons of Orthodox Christians or the consecrated wafer that Catholics call "the sacrament" because it contains God. Each flag sacramentally contains the land, people, government, and spirit of the United States.

Flag rituals are the daily sacraments of American civil religion. Pledging allegiance to the flag at school and in Congress, singing "The Star-Spangled Banner" before sporting events and operas, ceremonially raising and lowering the flag, flying the flag at half staff, and folding the flag at military funerals have become familiar to everyone. Behind these flag rituals lies a consensus that cannot be understood apart from the story of political and religious conflict that this chapter will tell.

Protestors carry the flag to associate their causes with the nation, wave the flag to attract attention, or burn the flag to express contempt. In response, many are seeking a constitutional amendment to make the flag the only class of object made sacred by the laws of the United States, an exception to the constitutional right of free expression and to the common law tradition that people can do what they want with their own property. Meanwhile, American culture has come to accept casual uses of the flag that would have looked wrong to previous generations and to reject others that were once acceptable. The Native American custom of using the flag on clothing has become much closer to the norm than when the Navajo and Lakota began it in the 1870s.

Americans now see their flag everywhere. All government buildings, libraries, and schools have flags outside. Public schools have a flag in every classroom, so that students can recite the daily pledge of allegiance wherever they are, though the pledge is not required in every state. Flags appear next to the pulpits and altars of churches and in the sanctuaries of synagogues, demonstrating that the civil religion can include and be included in other religious traditions. Flags are ordinarily found in front of car dealerships, factories, and warehouses, on bumper stickers and on the cabs of trucks, as pins on the lapels of politicians and newscasters. To foreign visitors, it often seems odd that ordinary individuals, homes, businesses, and vehicles in the United States are marked by the national flag, because only a few other nations follow similar customs. Since the terrorist attacks of September 11, 2001, private citizens have commonly hung flags on public property, such as highway overpasses and bridges, ignoring rules passed by Congress in 1942 to govern the flag's display.

Military personnel were the original priests of the flag, which came to be widely used in American civil religion only after thousands fought and died to save it—literally, not figuratively. Following the Civil War battle of Antietam, for example, twenty Union soldiers received the Medal of Honor, and eight of those awards were for saving or capturing flags. Flags at that time were tools of communication in battle, marking positions and signaling advances and retreats. The flag-bearer carried no rifle, but was accompanied by a color guard of one or more soldiers who would not fire unless the flag was attacked. On the first day of the battle of Gettysburg, the 24th Michigan regiment lost nine soldiers who were carrying its flag.

Though our flag rituals have become prominent, the flag's origins are obscure. It is not known with certainty who proposed the design of thirteen stripes of red and white with thirteen white stars on a field of blue that Congress authorized on June 14, 1777. A lawyer and signer of the Declaration of Independence named Francis Hopkinson, a protégé of Benjamin Franklin, asked Congress to pay him thousands of dollars for designing the flag and some other objects, but Congress refused on the ground that many people had made suggestions. By 1777, American warships and soldiers had already used other flags, including "Don't tread on me" banners featuring a rattlesnake and a flag called the Continental Colors, which had thirteen red and white stripes and a British Union cross in the upper left field. The design approved by Congress was derived from several models. Red, white, and blue were the colors of the British flag (commonly called the Union Jack), and alternating red and white horizontal stripes appeared on the flags of the East India Company, a British authority independent of the Crown that governed India and exported tea to the colonies. George Washington marked his headquarters tent during the Revolution with an almost square flag of dark blue, bearing thirteen six-pointed stars. When Congress hired a Latin teacher named Charles Thomson to design the Great Seal of the United States in 1782, he used the colors of red, white, and blue and said that he had followed the meaning of the colors in the flag. Thomson listed those meanings as red for hardiness and valor, white for purity and innocence, and blue for vigilance, perseverance, and justice, but there was no mention of any meanings of the colors in the Congressional act authorizing the flag.

That act does say that the stars in their field of blue will have the effect of "representing a new constellation," and those words imply one (admittedly speculative) explanation for why this design has worked so well. Constellations are visible only at night, and white stars against dark blue evoke twilight or dawn. Red can be a color of the sun, as in the flag of Japan. Together, the two parts of the flag suggest both night and day, the sunlit earth and the stars. It may be fitting that six of these flags have been planted on the moon, representing an earthly nation that has sometimes claimed a destiny in space.

The design of the flag is also inherently pluralist, implying the value of tolerance in American civil religion. This pluralist design, incorporating symbols of different parts of one nation in the same flag, continued the tradition of Britain's Union Jack, which combined the red cross of St. George for England and Wales with the white cross of St. Andrew for Scotland in 1606, then added the red cross of St. Patrick for Ireland in 1801. But the Americans went further in the direction of pluralism: rather than creating one symbol, like the unified crosses of the Union Jack, for the whole country, the American flag maintained a separate stripe for each of the thirteen colonies of the revolution and a separate star for each individual state, just as each state maintained its own government. Unusually, and perhaps uniquely, among flags of the world, the American flag included a provison for change, the addition of a star for any new state joining the union. Over two centuries, as the number of stars grew from the small, often circular constellation of thirteen to the mass of fifty stars on American flags today, these additional stars have added power to the visual impact of the American flag.

A final touch in combining the red stripes from the East India Company flag with the white stars and dark blue background of Washington's headquarters flag may be ascribed to the Philadelphia flag-maker Betsy Ross, whose house is still visited by tourists as the birthplace of the flag. Though no historian now ascribes the whole design of the flag to Ross, and many have downplayed her role as a legend, Marla R. Miller has lately argued that it is plausible that Betsy Ross was responsible for the change from the six-pointed stars, with thin rays, of Washington's flag to five-pointed stars with thicker rays. Ross worked primarily as a manufacturer of upholstery, but she did become a flag-maker in 1776 and 1777, when Washington and the Continental Congress were urgently seeking a large supply of distinctive flags. As Miller argues, Ross may well have demonstrated that a thicker, five-pointed star could be more easily cut quickly out of folded fabric, so that a seamstress could even make several stars at once. Her practical suggestion may have also appealed to Washington because it created a pentagram, an element of Masonic symbolism. Both Washington and Ross's husband were Masons.

From a practical standpoint in 1777 and immediately after, the design worked well as intended—as a signaling device, primarily on ships but also in land battles. Red and blue attract the eye from opposite ends of the light color spectrum, and white light separates the extremes and includes all colors. Flag makers of the eighteenth century had good dyes for red, yellow, and blue, but yellow was the color of quarantine and green dyes tended to look muddy. Washington remarked that when Americans used the Union Jack in the left-hand field of their Continental Colors, many British soldiers saw it as a sign that the Americans desired to remain in the British Empire, but the "new constellation" of the Congressional flag contradicted any such intention. By the time the United States fought Great Britain again, in the War of 1812, the flag of the new country was firmly established, although still not guaranteed to survive. Francis Scott Key focused on the flag as he observed the British attack on Fort McHenry, and he was inspired to write "The Star-Spangled Banner" by seeing a giant flag that still flew over the fort after a night of bombardment.

Neither Key's song nor American victory in that war brought the flag anything like the popularity it later attained, however. Throughout the decades between the Revolution and the Civil War, no custom of private homes or individuals flying the flag emerged, and flags did not normally fly over American schools. *The Star-Spangled Banner* stood behind *Hail, Columbia* and *America* ("My Country, 'Tis of Thee") among the songs most often played on state occasions and holidays. Studies of antebellum magazines, newspapers, and books show more eagles and allegorical women than flags as symbols of America.

The Civil War made the flag more important, partly because flags were used for battle in so many places and partly because of the challenge to the Stars and Stripes from the Confederate Stars and Bars. When the Union army occupied New Orleans, General Benjamin Butler hanged a man for taking down the Stars and Stripes. Meanwhile, all over the nation, the war brought repeated rituals in which regiments about to depart for battle were presented with handmade flags by the women of their areas. Then came the battles themselves, with so many flag bearers playing heroic roles, often killed but sometimes surviving against great odds. Battle flags became relics, sanctified by blood. A song written by George F. Root in 1862, "Battle Cry of Freedom," sold 700,000 copies of sheet music with lyrics that began, "Oh, we'll rally round the flag, boys, we'll rally once again, shouting the battle cry of freedom." The torn flag of Fort Sumter, where the Confederacy had first attacked, was carried around the Union and auctioned repeatedly to raise money for the war effort. In 1864, poet John Greenleaf Whittier immortalized an old woman named Barbara Fritchie for (supposedly) flying the Stars and Stripes out her window as Confederate troops led by Stonewall Jackson marched through Frederick, Maryland. According to the poem, Jackson ordered his soldiers to shoot at the flag and they did, nearly causing it to fall, but Fritchie caught it, leaned from the windowsill and waved it at them. "Shoot, if you must, this old grey head / But spare your country's flag, she said," Whittier wrote. Ashamed, Jackson relented, and Barbara Fritchie became so famous that when Winston Churchill visited Frederick, Maryland, he went to her former house and recited eight lines of the poem. In Nashville, a retired Northern sea captain defied Confederate occupiers by flying the former flag of his ship, a flag that he called Old Glory. His deed gave the name of Old Glory to all versions of the Stars and Stripes. The original Old Glory, with a white anchor sewn below the stars in the blue field, is still displayed in the Smithsonian.

Three years after the war ended, in 1868, a former Union sergeant named Gilbert H. Bates took a bet with fellow veterans that he could carry an American flag on a 1400-mile walk through the South. Bates agreed to carry the flag unfurled, to travel by day, and not to employ any one to protect him. He intended to sell pictures of himself and the flag for twenty-five cents each to raise money for a fund for Civil War widows and orphans from both sides. Despite grim predictions from observers as astute as Mark Twain, who wrote that Bates would return to Washington with one leg, one eye, and one arm, Bates won his bet. The people of Vicksburg, Mississippi, escorted him with a brass band. Everywhere on his route through Georgia, the Carolinas, and Virginia, he was hailed with cannon salutes by former Confederate soldiers. At Richmond, the former capital of the Confederacy, he waved the Stars and Stripes for a crowd in a park outside the capitol building. Four years later, in 1872, Bates carried the flag in Great Britain, from Scotland's Gretna Green to London, to show that Britain held no enmity against the United States despite British support for the South in the war. Again, Bates was greeted with great enthusiasm, and the English bought thousands of American flags to hail his passage.

A new peak in the cult of the flag came in 1876, the centennial year of the Declaration of Independence. The Grand Army of the Republic (GAR), a veterans' group founded in 1866, had shrunk in the 1870s but grew again as the centennial approached, and the GAR began a long campaign to bring the flag into every public school. At the Philadelphia exposition of 1876, the first World's Fair held in the United States, a popular exhibit illustrated the history of the flag. That exhibit taught the legend of Betsy Ross and began the career of her former home as a place of pilgrimage, revered as the birthplace of the flag. The Philadelphia artist Archibald Willard, a Civil War infantryman himself, created a sensation at the fair with *The Spirit of '76* (Figure 9.1), a life-size painting of three generations of men—an old man with a drum in the middle, a grandson drumming on one side and a father playing a fife on the other—who march through a smoky battlefield with a thirteen-star flag behind them, while a wounded soldier in the

Figure 9.1 The Spirit of '76, painted by a former Civil War infantryman named Archibald Willard for the Philadelphia Centennial Exhibition of 1876, proved very popular both at that fair and in lithographs. It depicted an anachronism, since Congress did not authorize the Stars and Stripes as a national flag until 1777. Library of Congress.

foreground salutes. So many people wanted to see *The Spirit of '76* that the painting was exhibited for weeks in Boston, and then in Washington, Chicago, San Francisco, and other cities. Though the title was misleading, since Congress had not created the Stars and Stripes until 1777, lithographs of the painting could not be produced fast enough to meet demand. Through these reproductions, an image of the flag appeared on many American walls.

In the next few decades, the Grand Army of the Republic was joined by the Sons and then by the Daughters of the American Revolution in efforts to promote the flag. Inspired by a former teacher and later Chicago dentist named Bernard Cigrand, the groups campaigned for a national Flag Day on June 14, to mark the day that Congress voted to authorize the Stars and Stripes in 1777. Though Flag Day eventually succeeded, this minor holiday was overshadowed by the results of a drive to bring flags and a ritual salute of the flag into all the nation's schools. Here the GAR was joined by a national magazine, *The Youth's Companion*, which had existed since 1827 and had attained a circulation of half a million, including many adult readers, by 1890. When the magazine took up the cause of flags in schools, it brought to that cause all of the techniques of commerce. Advertisements promised free "flag certificates" that schools could sell for ten cents each, giving the buyer a share in the school flag, with which the editors said that a "school can raise money for its Flag in one day." *The Youth's Companion* took mail orders for many sizes of flags, from pocket versions with carrying cases to six-foot flags for $3.50 and nine-foot flags for $5.35. By the middle of 1892, the magazine had sold 25,000 school flags.

In the early 1890s, thousands of students in New York City and Indians attending US government schools in the West had already begun to salute the flag every morning, using a ritual invented by George T. Balch, a New York teacher and Civil War veteran who had published *Methods of Teaching Patriotism in the Public Schools* in 1889. Balch's book instructed students to face the flag and touch their foreheads and hearts while saying, "We give our Heads!—and our Hearts!—to God! and our Country!" The students then extended their right arms, palms down, toward the flag and said, "One Country! One Language! One Flag!" Eerily prophetic of the Nazi pledge to "Ein Reich, Ein Volk, Ein Fuehrer" (one Government, one People, one Leader), the Balch salute was intended to foster assimilation among the children of immigrants and Indians, who were its first practitioners.

A more generic form of flag salute was published by *The Youth's Companion* in 1892. Written by an assistant editor at the magazine, a Baptist minister and Christian socialist named Francis Bellamy, this "Pledge of Allegiance" had much less dramatic, sacrificial, and assimilationist content than Balch's. In its original form, it read, "I pledge allegiance to my Flag and the Republic for which it stands, one nation, indivisible, with liberty and justice for all." With Bellamy's evocations of "one nation, indivisible" and "liberty and justice for all," the heritage of the Civil War and the movement to abolish slavery attained a permanent place in the new salute to the flag. This pledge quickly became one of the sacred texts of the American civil religion. The first triumph of the new pledge came on Columbus Day of 1892, when *The Youth's Companion* successfully promoted a national celebration. Tens of thousands of public school children in New York, Chicago, and Washington, D.C., said the pledge at once. They also performed a prescribed physical salute that began in military fashion, with the right hand above the right eye, palm down, for the words "I pledge allegiance," then continued with the words "to my flag" as they extended their right arms toward the flag, palm up.

In 1898, the state of New York made the Bellamy pledge of allegiance mandatory for all public schools at the start of each day. Many other states followed, sometimes provoking protests in the name of freedom of religion and freedom of speech. In 1943, the Supreme Court ruled that Jehovah's Witnesses, who regard the flag as an idol, could not be expelled from school for refusing to say the pledge.

Three additions have been made to the language of Bellamy's pledge, along with one subtraction from its original ritual. After hearing thousands of students in Boston recite the words on Columbus Day of 1892, Bellamy decided that "I pledge allegiance to my flag and *to* the Republic" sounded better than his first version. A second change came after two National Flag Conferences that met in Washington, D.C., during 1923 and 1924, where delegates from more than sixty organizations (including the GAR, the American Legion, the Daughters of the American Revolution, and the Ku Klux Klan) gathered to write a Flag Code, specifying how the flag was to be displayed and treated. In the pledge that came out of these conferences, the simple "to my Flag" was replaced by "to the flag of the United States of America." Some delegates who supported the addition had objected that any citizen of any nation could say the original pledge, so that it was insufficiently American. In 1942, when Congress passed the Flag Code into law, the bill accepted the new text, but abolished the arm gestures of the Bellamy salute because they too closely resembled Fascist and Nazi salutes.

Then, in 1954, responding to Christian complaints (and a campaign by the Roman Catholic Knights of Columbus) that "little Muscovites" and Communist atheists could recite the pledge, Congress passed a law adding "under God" after the "one nation" in the pledge. President Eisenhower signed the bill on Flag Day, June 14, saying that the inclusion of "under God" would "strengthen those spiritual weapons which forever will be our country's most powerful resource, in peace or in war." Devotion to the flag, which was once an instrument of battle, had now become a weapon in itself.

The question of whether inserting "under God" into the pledge recited in public schools amounted to a government "establishment of religion," violating the First Amendment to the Constitution, did not come up in 1954. In the Cold War atmosphere, the modified pledge continued to spread. Laws to make the recitation of the pledge mandatory in public schools were enacted in about half of the states, and many more schools led their students to say the pledge without any legal requirement. In the 1988 presidential race between George H. W. Bush and Michael Dukakis, the veto of a mandatory pledge bill by Dukakis when he was governor of Massachusetts became a key issue. Then Vice President Bush visited a flag factory to underline his disagreement with Dukakis. The US House of Representatives began to open all of its meetings with the pledge in 1988, and the Senate took up the practice in 1999. In 2002, the Supreme Court reviewed a ruling by the 9th Circuit Court, based in San Francisco, that the phrase "under God" did violate the Constitution and would have to be removed. Congress expressed great outrage, affirming the pledge by a 99–0 vote in the Senate and 416–3 in the House, and lining up on the Capitol steps to recite the pledge in public. After the nation held its breath, the Court avoided the constitutional issue by ruling that the plaintiff, Michael A. Newdow, was a non-custodial parent and so had no standing in the suit he had filed on behalf of his daughter.

Ironically, but perhaps inevitably, flag desecration increased as the cult of the flag intensified. The first forms of desecration were political and commercial. In the nineteenth century, it became common for advertisers to use the white stripes of the flag for their messages, selling everything from canned hams to political candidates. Pictures of products and candidates (including Abraham Lincoln) sometimes replaced the stars in the blue field. Justice John Marshall Harlan of the Supreme Court wrote in an 1896 opinion upholding a Nebraska law against commercial use of the flag that a brewer had no "right of personal liberty" to put the flag on his bottles of beer. That same year saw a campaign for president that exploited the flag to an unprecedented degree. Political boss Mark Hanna wrapped William McKinley, the last of five Union officers from the Civil War to be elected president, in the Stars and Stripes and implied that all traitors to the flag were Democrats. On October 31, 1896, three days before the election, Hanna and the Republicans staged a massive Flag Day that gathered crowds for ceremonies across the country. The parade in New York saw flags thirty-six feet long, with the names "McKinley and Hobart," the Republican ticket, added in a strip sewn to the end. Though McKinley won, there was a reaction. Some Democrats tore down and even burned McKinley flags at rallies, and public opinion and political practice turned against the partisan use of the flag.

For example, although most members of the Daughters of the American Revolution (DAR) almost certainly supported McKinley, the president of the DAR expressed regret about the role given the flag in the 1896 campaign. During the last years of nineteenth century and the first years of the twentieth, state after state passed laws against flag desecration. Usually, such laws included verbal attacks, partisan political use, and commercial use, as well as physical desecrations like dragging the flag in the mud. The courts also moved with the times. In 1900, the Illinois Supreme Court ruled that despite Illinois law, a cigar maker had the "personal liberty" to place "harmless" pictures of the flag on his boxes of cigars. By 1907, the US Supreme Court was ready to uphold a Nebraska law that banned the use of the flag in commercial packaging and advertising. Even songwriter George M. Cohan received some criticism for his hit song *You're a Grand Old Flag*, which was performed with elaborate flag choreography in the 1906 Broadway musical *George Washington Jr*. The original lyric read, "You're a grand old rag," because Cohan was quoting a veteran of Gettysburg who had shown him an old flag from the battle and called it that. After complaints from critics and patriotic groups, Cohan changed the word. One critic still complained that Cohan "can bring himself to coin the American flag... into box-office receipts."

As the United States approached entrance into World War I, ritual uses of the flag became more prominent, and so did opportunities for desecration. Woodrow Wilson declared June 14, 1916, a national Flag Day and personally led a parade of 66,000 people in Washington. In the same year, the Reverend Bouck White, leader of the Church of Social Revolution in New York, became the first American citizen arrested and jailed for politically motivated flag desecration when he published a cartoon that showed the flag entangled in money and war, and then publicly burned a flag to protest his arrest for the cartoon. He was found guilty under the flag desecration laws of New York State, fined a hundred dollars for each offense, and sentenced to sixty days in jail. As the war went on, many states used the laws they had passed to punish even verbal desecration of the flag. In 1918, a Montana man named E. V. Starr was heard to say that the flag was "nothing but a piece of cotton" and that the Wilson administration was a corrupt tool of the British. His neighbors tried to force him to kiss the flag, but Starr refused, saying that it "might be covered with microbes." Convicted in state court and sentenced to a $500 fine and at least ten to twenty years in jail, Starr appealed. Although the federal judge who heard the appeal said that it was Starr's persecutors who had actually profaned the "sacred banner," the judge felt constrained by the 1907 Supreme Court support of states banning commercial use, so he upheld the conviction while advising Starr to seek a pardon.

The war seemed to make both Congress and state legislators unaware of First Amendment guarantees of freedom of speech and freedom of the press. In 1918, Congress passed a Sedition Act that declared it a crime to "utter or publish any disloyal language intended to cause contempt for the American form of government, or the Constitution, or the flag, or the uniform of the Army or Navy." The Montana statute under which Starr was sentenced made it a crime to utter "disloyal, profane, violent, scurrilous, contemptuous or abusive" words about the US government, soldiers, or flag. Twenty-seven states passed such laws during this time.

After "normalcy" returned in the early 1920s, an era of codification began. The Flag Conferences in Washington that added "of the United States of America" to the Pledge of Allegiance also compiled a Flag Code with twenty pages of rules on how and when and where to display American flags and how not to use them. Actual punishments for violators were not part of the Flag Code, however, even when Congress enacted it into law in 1942.

By then the tide was turning in favor of free expression. In 1931, the Supreme Court ruled in *Stromberg v. California* that the First Amendment included symbolic speech such as the display of flags. World War II, perhaps because the United States was allied with the Communist Soviet Union in a struggle against racial ideologies in Germany and Japan, did not engender as much virulent nationalism and anti-Communism as World War I had. Neither new sedition laws nor incidents of flag burning seem to have arisen.

When the next wave of flag desecration cases arose, in the late 1960s, they provoked prosecutions based on the old state laws and some new ones, including the first federal anti-desecration statute, which was signed by President Lyndon Johnson on July 4, 1968. Because many cases were not appealed, so that they went unreported in standard legal references, estimates vary widely regarding how many there were and how they were decided. A single American Civil Liberties Union (ACLU) lawyer, Burt Neuborne, claimed in 1972 that he had personally handled three hundred flag desecration cases. Many people were charged with wearing the flag disrespectfully, for example sewn onto a trouser seat, or were arrested for simply wearing the flag, as on a shirt.

According to Robert Justin Goldstein, a political scientist who has written and edited four books on flag desecration, sixty major cases were reported and adjudicated between 1966 and 1972, of which nine were for flag burning. The most noted case of burning, before two hundred thousand people at a 1967 rally against the Vietnam War in Central Park, New York, resulted in no arrests but in the passage of the federal flag desecration law. A New Yorker named Sidney Street, on the other hand, was arrested for burning the flag at an intersection on June 6, 1966, as a response to the news that civil rights leader James Meredith had been shot while attempting to walk through Mississippi. "If they let that happen to Meredith we don't need an American flag," Street told the policeman who arrested him. Three years later, in 1969, the Supreme Court overturned Street's conviction because of the possibility that his speech contributed to the conviction, without ruling on whether the New York law banning flag burning was inherently unconstitutional. Street was fortunate, because most convictions under state laws against flag burning never made it through the appeals process, and the ACLU was advising people by the mid-1970s that they could do nothing for people who burned the flag. With regard to other acts, the record was mixed. Goldstein noted that the sixty cases of flag desecration recorded in legal references between 1966 and 1972 resulted in 55 percent acquittals, while defendants tried in reported cases between 1972 and 1976 were acquitted 70 percent of the time.

Meanwhile, the culture was moving into more and more acceptance of casual use of the flag. The change is evident when one compares how people responded to a flag shirt in 1968 to their likely response decades later. The flag shirt in question belonged to Youth International Party (Yippie) leader Abbie Hoffman, one of the Chicago Seven charged with rioting at the 1968 Democratic Convention. Later that same year, Hoffman was demonstrating in Washington, outside a hearing of the House Committee on Un-American Activities, when he was arrested under the new federal anti-desecration law for wearing a shirt that had the American flag on it. He was convicted, despite his claim that the shirt was available in retail stores and that anyone wearing an Uncle Sam outfit would be just as guilty. While he appealed in the spring of 1969, Hoffman appeared on a television talk show hosted by Merv Griffin. He took off his coat during the interview and revealed that he was wearing the same shirt, throwing the CBS television network into damage control mode. The show was aired with an announcement to the effect that Hoffman was wearing something that might offend viewers, and a blue dot was imposed over the flag during the broadcast. Eventually, in 1971, a three-judge federal appeals court ruled that the shirt did not desecrate the flag.

The same nation that arrested and jailed Abbie Hoffman, and that could not stand to look at him wearing a flag shirt on a talk show, went to the movies by the millions in 1969 to see *Easy Rider*, a film in which Peter Fonda rode across the country on a motorcycle with a teardrop-shaped gas tank painted as the American flag, wearing an American flag helmet and a leather jacket with a complete American flag on the back. To add insult to injury, Fonda's character hid money and drugs in a tube inside his flag gas tank. Perhaps this proved acceptable because the character did not engage in political protest, or because at the end of the film he was shot by a Southern redneck.

It can be argued that artists and writers gradually broke down the taboo on casual use of the flag over decades. Painter Jasper Johns, who was born in 1930, painted his first *Flag* in 1954 and continued for decades to paint flags in various forms, some with newsprint showing through, some with different colors or words, making various cultural and political allusions. Poet Allen Ginsberg took to wearing an American flag top hat, and Ken Kesey, a leading exponent of LSD in the mid-1960s, painted the flag on his sneakers and had a tooth filled with a representation of the flag. In 1967, a New York gallery owner named Stephen Radich went to jail for a second-floor window display that included a flag arranged and stuffed as a cadaver, hanging from chains. When the Broadway musical *Hair* opened in April 1968, it included a scene and a song that conservative William Buckley, among others, saw as flag desecration. Cast members stood onstage and folded a flag, saying "Folding a flag is taking care of the nation. Folding a flag is putting it to bed for the night." One naked male cast member was wrapped in a flag, cradled and rocked in it. Then a panicked voice shouted: "I fell through a hole in the flag, I'm falling through a hole in the flag." Finally came the brief song: "Don't put it down / Best one around / Crazy for the red blue and white," which also defended the new generation ("'Cause I look different you think I'm subversive / Crazy for the blue white and red."). Although astronauts James A. Lovell and John L. Swigert walked out of a performance of *Hair* in 1970 in protest of the flag scene, most audiences remained. That same year saw actress

Raquel Welch wear a star-spangled bikini top and a red-and-white striped bottom while she used a dildo to rape a young man in the movie version of Gore Vidal's novel *Myra Breckinridge*.

In 1970, *Time* magazine reported in its July 6 issue both that flag manufacturers had doubled their sales in the last year and that a Manhattan clothier had shipped 36,000 flag shirts to retailers. Construction workers had taken to wearing flag decals on their hardhats, hanging flags over beams on their work sites, and using small flags to cover the pipes with which they attacked demonstrators. In the violent culture war that broke out between construction workers and anti-war protestors, both sides used the flag in ways not sanctioned by the Flag Code.

Laws governing the flag came more and more under challenge. Supreme Court rulings in 1969, 1972, and 1974 found that various parts of the flag desecration laws of New York, Massachusetts, and Washington were unconstitutional restrictions on freedom of speech. Twenty states responded by altering their flag desecration laws to focus on physical mutilation and burning. With the end of the Vietnam War, the issue faded because flag burning and other demonstrations ceased.

A single incident of flag burning in 1984 touched off a drive to protect the flag that has continued ever since. At the Republican National Convention that nominated President Ronald Reagan for a second term, a member of the Revolutionary Communist Party named Gregory Lee Johnson burned a flag, was convicted under the Texas flag desecration law, and was fined two thousand dollars and sentenced to a year in jail. When the Texas Court of Criminal Appeals reversed the conviction, citing freedom of speech, prosecutors asked the Supreme Court to review. In June 1989, the Court ruled five to four for Johnson, striking down the flag-desecration statutes of forty-eight states (Alaska and Wyoming did not have such statutes on the books), as well as the 1968 federal flag protection law. Public response was overwhelmingly negative, and Congress quickly passed a new Flag Protection Act that President George H. W. Bush signed on October 28, 1989. That law set off a wave of flag burnings in a dozen American cities. Groups of people who burned the flag in Seattle and Washington, D.C., were arrested, and by 1990 their cases were before the Supreme Court, which again voted five to four to strike down the new law. Although the court's decisions had seemed to leave room for a statute that banned flag burning in itself, any public protest while the flag was burned seemed (at least to a narrow majority of the justices) to engage the constitutional guarantee of free speech.

Now the focus of those who wanted to protect the flag shifted from statutes to a constitutional amendment. An extremely simple statement, "The Congress and the States have the power to prohibit the physical desecration of the flag of the United States," was sent by the first President Bush to Congress immediately after the Supreme Court decision in 1990. It passed both houses by large majorities, but failed to get the requisite two-thirds. The amendment came up for a vote again in 1995, in 2000, and in the summer of 2006, when it received a two-thirds vote in the House and failed by a single vote, with 66 in favor and 34 against, in the Senate. That single vote almost surely would have put the amendment into the Constitution, because a campaign by the American Legion has resulted in all fifty state legislatures sending resolutions to Congress asking that the amendment be passed. At this point, the proposed amendment is even simpler than the one proposed in 1990, because "and the States" has been eliminated in the interest of avoiding the complications that might ensue with many state laws. The amendment that failed by one vote in 2006 reads, "The Congress shall have power to prohibit the physical desecration of the flag of the United States."

What laws would be passed if the amendment succeeds is a matter of speculation. Exactly what would constitute a "flag of the United States" might raise issues over burning flag shirts, posting models of burning virtual flags on the Internet, and burning flags that have been modified by replacing the stars with other symbols or superimposing an image. What would constitute "physical desecration" would also have to be specified. The American Legion provides the service of burning worn flags to dispose of them, as recommended by the Flag Code, so a simple prohibition of burning could be awkward.

During the effort to pass a flag-protection amendment, the attacks on the World Trade Center and the Pentagon on September 11, 2001, set off one of the great flag crazes in American history. According to the largest flag manufacturer in the United States, Annin & Company, more flags were sold in the ten days following September 11 than in the whole year before. Orders became backed up until midsummer of 2002. Wal-Mart reported selling 118,000 flags in a single day. Evidence of the 2001 surge of flags still marks the American landscape. Flags hang (in violation of the Flag Code) all day and all night from highway bridges and buildings where they were never seen before, and by now most have been replaced several times. Pickup trucks with small flagpoles on the cabin or the sides of the cargo bed are still common. Cartoonist Garry Trudeau drew a comic strip in which his characters from "Doonesbury" thanked the terrorists for giving Americans back the flag as a symbol of unity, rather than a tool for political agendas.

It seems clear that the flag has gained religious power. As one man said in the 1970 *Time* article on the flag, "I see the flag as I see God: a supreme being." Evangelist Billy Graham was quoted in the same piece, calling the flag "our Queen." According to Colonel James A. Moss, who founded the United States Flag Foundation in 1924 and served as its president until his death in 1941, "the Religion of the Flag" is "a truly big and broad religion that can be embraced and practiced by everyone regardless of racial blood or dogmatic creed." Moss called the flag "our national sacramental," equal to the Cross and the Star of David, and he wrote that the stars in the flag's blue field were "remindful" of the Star of Bethlehem. Today another retired officer, Major General Patrick H. Brady, the president of the Citizens' Flag Alliance, which spearheads the drive for a flag protection amendment, calls his cause a "sacred debt" and rejoices that the 2001 attacks reminded Americans of what veterans know: "the unifying, comforting and inspirational magic of Old Glory."

Like all religious objects, the flag can appear oppressive and can be employed as a weapon to suppress critical thought. Religion always tends to hold a society together, but religion does not always promote values like love, faith, and compassion. No more stringent test should be applied to American civil religion and to its elements, including the flag, than to religions like Christianity, which has put the cross on the breastplates of Crusaders and Conquistadors. Crusader crosses, like the English Cross of St. George that now forms part of the Union Jack, were the first national flags.

Remarkably creative uses of the American flag have appeared among Native Americans and in the civil rights movement. Even while US Army cavalry were battling the Lakota, then slaughtering them at Wounded Knee, and herding the Navajo into prison camps before allowing them to return to their land, some among these first nations of the Americas admired and appropriated the American flag. They seem to have both recognized its power as a war symbol and appreciated its potential to signal a willingness to work with the European invaders. In Navajo weaving, the flag began to appear on blankets and clothing beginning in the late 1870s, and that practice has continued to this day. Lakota beadwork has put American flags on slippers, vests, shirts, and leggings, with an explosion of art in the 1890s and after.

During the second half of the twentieth century, as the dances and material exchanges of the Powwow circuit united Native Americans across the continent, the cult of the flag spread. Every Powwow today begins with the entrance of the flag, which is done with great respect. Though this may seem strange for a people who have been so mistreated by the US government, the vast majority of Native Americans have come to regard the flag as a symbol of the land itself and as a standard that belongs to warriors, and so accept the flag as a powerful object and insist on their share in it, even when they dissent from specific policies of the government.

In the movement for the civil rights of African-Americans, the American flag was not at first a positive symbol. Henry McNeal Turner, a bishop of the African Methodist Episcopal Church, described the flag at the turn of the twentieth century as "a dirty and contemptible rag." In the early 1960s, the psychologist Kenneth Clark, who was a key figure in the *Brown v. Board of Education* Supreme Court decision that desegregated public schools and universities, found African-Americans saying that the flag was "for the white man," and that the red in the flag stood for blood, particularly for the blood shed when white Americans will "lynch you, hang you, barbecue you, and fry you."

African-Americans began to use the flag after the assassination of Medgar Evers, a field secretary for the National Association for the Advancement of Colored People (NAACP) in Jackson, Mississippi, on June 12, 1963. Two days later, on the Flag Day holiday of June 14, African-American women and children marched through Jackson carrying American flags. Evers, a veteran of World War II, had suggested the idea before he was shot. Police and segregationist mobs delighted in smashing the picket signs of protestors for civil rights, but Evers thought that these white Southerners might react differently if the marchers were carrying flags. After 1963, flags became a normal presence at civil rights marches. The national revulsion against police who were enforcing segregation laws, turning their dogs and fire hoses on demonstrators, resulted in part from the fact that those demonstrators were carrying American flags.

In sports, the flag has come to dominate all ceremonies. During World War I, and subsequently on special occasions like opening day or Memorial Day, it became customary to perform *The Star-Spangled Banner* while facing the flag before baseball games. The years of World War II made that custom general, at all sports events, and it has continued ever since. Since September 11, a trend has emerged toward huge flags, some as large as football fields and supported by hundreds of people both around the edges and underneath. The people below both keep the flag from touching the ground and help to make ripples of motion to simulate a flying flag. According to a spokesman for the American Legion, the idea that a flag that touches the ground must be destroyed is "an old wives' tale," and the superflags that have lately appeared at baseball's All-Star game, the Super Bowl, college football games, and NASCAR races are not exploitative but simply "great."

But even in sports, reverence for the flag has opened the possibility of dissent. During the college basketball season of 2002–2003, just before the United States invaded Iraq, a basketball player at tiny Manhattanville College made news on all television networks, especially CNN and Fox News, because she began to turn her back to the flag when the national anthem was played before games. When Manhattanville played at the Merchant Marine Academy, the court was lined by cadets holding flags and the stands filled with fans who each had a flag. People who never would have come to Manhattanville games came to boo Toni Smith, and one ran onto the court to hold an American flag in front of her. Though the college, led by President Richard A. Berman, supported her right to protest, it also began a program called "My Soldier," which sent letters and care packages to troops, the following year.

Those who objected to Smith's protest often said that turning her back on the flag amounted to rejecting the whole country. In one sense, she accepted this analysis, saying that she could not continue to salute the flag not simply because of the impending war, but because of the government's indifference to economic inequality and an American history that included the slaughter of her black and Native American ancestors. "It was everything that the flag is built on," she said. Both for Smith and for those who vilified and attacked her, the flag was not just a symbol, but a sacrament in which the whole nation was present.

SOURCES

Corcoran, Michael, *For Which It Stands: An Anecdotal Biography of the American Flag* (New York: Simon & Schuster, 2002).

Goldstein, Robert Justin, *Saving "Old Glory": The History of the American Flag Desecration Controversy* (Boulder, CO: Westview Press, 1995).

Guenter, Scot M., *The American Flag, 1777-1924: Cultural Shifts from Creation to Codification* (Rutherford, NJ: Farleigh Dickinson Press, 1990).

Herbst, Toby and Joel Kopp, *The Flag in American Indian Art* (Seattle: University of Wahington Press, 1993).

Leepson, Marc, *Flag: An American Biography* (New York: St. Martin's Press, 2005).

Marling, Karal Ann, *Old Glory: Unfurling History* (The Library of Congress, 2004).

Masur, Louis P., *The Soiling of Old Glory: The Story of a Photograph That Shocked America* (New York: Bloomsbury Press, 2008).

Miller, Marla R., *Betsy Ross and the Making of America* (New York: Henry Holt, 2010).

Moss, James A., *The Flag of the United States: Its History and Symbolism* (Washington, DC: United States Flag Association, 1941).

Smith, Whitney, *The Flag Book of the United States* (New York: William Morrow, 1970).

10

The Declaration of Independence

The first sentences of the second paragraph of the Declaration of Independence are the most important words of American civil religion. As historian Joseph Ellis has written, this is "the seminal statement of the American creed." These words are carved on one wall of the Jefferson Memorial:

> We hold these truths to be self-evident, that all men are created equal, that they are endowed by their Creator with certain unalienable Rights, that among these are Life, Liberty and the pursuit of Happiness. That to secure these rights, Governments are instituted among Men, deriving their just powers from the consent of the governed.

The Declaration of Independence serves as both a sacred text and an icon. As text, it has been reinterpreted and claimed by parties of the revolutionary generation, by both sides of the Civil War, by those fighting for women's rights and racial and social equality, by historians, philosophers, and political scientists, and by radicals of all sorts. The Declaration's phrase "created equal" has justified social revolutions, while the prominence of "independence" has been central to political conservatism. Whether used by those on the Left or the Right of the political spectrum, the Declaration of Independence has always stood for the sacredness of liberty and democracy.

As an icon, the physical Declaration is visited by more than a million people every year. The original, signed parchment that they see was injured by a wet-press copying in 1823 that sent 201 facsimiles out into the nation. This parchment was then displayed in rooms where it was exposed to smoke from tobacco and candles and to sunlight, so that only the words written in all capitals remained easily legible. After visitors were shocked by its condition in 1876, it was hidden in darkness for decades and then displayed again in the 1920s. It was kept in Fort Knox during World War II, carried around the nation on a Freedom Train in the late 1940s, and featured as a treasure map in a very popular Disney movie in 2004. Pilgrims now view it in a marble shrine built in 1935, at the location that Pierre L'Enfant, the architect of Washington, intended for a national church.

Although revolutions rarely start at shrines, enshrinement has not blunted the revolutionary power of this text. In 2008, the National Archives building that displays the Declaration was occupied by protestors who turned the document's charges against King George into indictments of the US government. All over the world, independence movements have continued to cite the Declaration, making it the most globally significant statement of American values.

American civil religion gained worldwide influence because the Declaration's opening paragraphs, announcing the separation of a new state from an empire and advancing a political theory based on human rights, proved useful to the people of many colonies. More than a hundred states—about half of all the governments on earth—have come into being since 1776 through declarations of independence. The world has seen four waves of declarations: for half a century after 1800 in Latin America, and then for a few years after World War I in Europe, after 1945 in Africa and Asia, and after 1990 in the former Soviet empire. Most declarations have spoken to all humanity, just as the American Declaration addressed "a candid World." And the United Nations adopted several ideas from the Declaration in 1948, when it passed a Universal Declaration of Human Rights.

Written with rhythms that Thomas Jefferson (the original author, whose draft was edited by a committee and by Congress) intended to be read aloud, the text begins:

> In CONGRESS, July 4, 1776.
> The unanimous Declaration of the thirteen united States of America
> When in the Course of human events, it becomes necessary for one people to dissolve the political bands which have connected them with another, and to assume among the Powers of the earth, the separate and equal station to which the Laws of Nature and of Nature's God entitle them, a decent respect to the opinions of mankind requires that they should declare the causes which impel them to the separation.
>
> We hold these truths to be self-evident, that all men are created equal, that they are endowed by their Creator with certain unalienable Rights, that among these are Life, Liberty and the pursuit of Happiness. That to secure these rights, Governments are instituted among Men, deriving their just powers from the consent of the governed. That whenever any Form of Government becomes destructive to these ends, it is the Right of the People to alter or to abolish it, and to institute new Government, laying its foundation on such principles and organizing its powers in such form, as to them shall seem most likely to effect their Safety

and Happiness. Prudence, indeed, will dictate that Governments long established should not be changed for light and transient causes; and accordingly all experience hath shown, that mankind are more disposed to suffer, while evils are sufferable, than to right themselves by abolishing the forms to which they are accustomed. But when a long train of abuses and usurpations, pursuing invariably the same Object evinces a design to reduce them under absolute Despotism, it is their right, it is their duty, to throw off such Government, and to provide new Guards for their future security. Such has been the patient Sufferance of these Colonies; and such is now the Necessity which constrains them to alter their former Systems of Government. The History of the present King of Great-Britain is a History of repeated Injuries and Usurpations, all having in direct Object the Establishment of an absolute Tyranny over these States. To prove this, let Facts be submitted to a candid World.

A list of grievances against King George III followed. Ranging from brief statements, such as that the king consented to laws "[f]or imposing taxes on us without our Consent" to long assertions of royal plots ("He is, at this Time, transporting large Armies of foreign Mercenaries to compleat the Works of Death, Desolation, and Tyranny, already begun…"), the grievances were meant to demonstrate that King George's rule in America had become destructive of the proper ends of government and so had rendered itself illegitimate. After the list of royal misdeeds, Congress claimed that its petitions to the king and to the British people had been met with "repeated injury" or with silence. The word "independent" did not appear until the last paragraph, where independence was finally declared:

> We, therefore, the Representatives of the UNITED STATES OF AMERICA, in GENERAL CONGRESS, Assembled, appealing to the Supreme Judge of the World for the Rectitude of our Intentions, do, in the Name, and by the Authority of the good People of these Colonies, solemnly Publish and Declare, That these United Colonies are, and of Right ought to be, FREE AND INDEPENDENT STATES; that they are absolved from all Allegiance to the British Crown, and that all political Connection between them and the State of Great-Britain, is and ought to be totally dissolved: and that as FREE AND INDEPENDENT STATES, they have full power to levy War, conclude Peace, contract Alliances, establish Commerce, and to do all other Acts and Things which INDEPENDENT STATES may of right do. And for the support of this Declaration, with a firm reliance on the Protection of divine Providence, we mutually pledge to each other our Lives, our Fortunes, and our sacred Honor.

The central sentence of the paragraph, from "That these United Colonies" to "totally dissolved," came verbatim from a resolution presented to Congress by Richard Henry Lee of Virginia on June 8, 1776, and finally passed on July 2. While Lee's independence resolution was pending, Congress appointed a committee of five—including Thomas Jefferson, Benjamin Franklin, and John Adams—to draw up a declaration setting forth the reasons for independence. The list of powers of "free and independent states" came from Jefferson and the committee. Jefferson also wrote the concluding pledge of "our Lives, our Fortunes, and our sacred Honor." Meeting as a Committee of the Whole between July 2 and July 4, Congress added the two references to God to this last paragraph.

Other changes by Congress included the elimination of a long paragraph that denounced King George for encouraging the slave trade. According to Jefferson, delegates from South Carolina objected, and some from the North were uncomfortable denouncing a trade in which merchants from their colonies had long participated. Congress also eliminated a statement criticizing the people of Great Britain for electing oppressors of America to the British Parliament and another that broke relations of the colonies with Parliament.

An earlier important change took place during the deliberations of the drafting committee, when Benjamin Franklin apparently changed Jefferson's original "We hold these truths to be sacred & undeniable" to the less sanctimonious "We hold these truths to be self-evident." Details of the drafting process were preserved in part because Jefferson disliked many of the edits, and circulated his original draft and the draft that the committee submitted to Congress and to some friends asking their opinions.

Almost immediately, the document began its career as a sacred text. It was reread in public on July 4, 1777, at festivities in Philadelphia, Boston, and Charleston, South Carolina. The custom of a July 4 holiday marked by bells, cannons, firecrackers, and a reading of the Declaration spread throughout the United States in the 1780s and 1790s. For most of this time, the document was generally regarded as what John Quincy Adams called it, "merely an *occasional* state-paper" that set forth American reasons for separating from Great Britain. The political theories of the second paragraph, involving equality and rights, including the right of revolution, were rarely discussed in speeches or in print before the 1790s. Perhaps, as Jefferson intended, they expressed a consensus of "the American mind" so well that they needed no discussion.

With the emergence of political parties that called themselves Federalists (led by John Adams) and Democrats (led by Thomas Jefferson) in the 1790s, and with an added impetus from the French Declaration of the Rights of Man in 1791, contests over the Declaration began. Attention focused both on the authorship of the Declaration and on the meaning of its philosophy. Democrats held readings of the Declaration and hailed Jefferson as the author, which irritated John Adams (who had indeed contributed to the text on the drafting committee and in Congress). During Adams's presidency (1797–1801), when many in the United States feared the excesses of the French Revolution and laws like the Alien and Sedition Acts were directed against French influence, it seemed dangerous to argue that citizens could dissolve any government that denied their rights. Federalists contended that under a government like that of the United States, which ruled by consent of the governed, there could be no such right of revolution.

Events gradually restored an American consensus behind the Declaration. During the War of 1812, the Declaration was hidden in Leesburg, Virginia, where it escaped the fires set in Washington by the British. After that challenge to American independence had been met, and following the collapse of the Federalist Party in the aftermath of the war and the deaths of most Revolutionary leaders, Americans turned to the Declaration with more reverence. In 1817, Jefferson himself urged John Trumbull to paint the signing of the Declaration, and Trumbull created a painting that now hangs in the Capitol Rotunda (Figure 10.1). Trumbull made money by exhibiting the painting to large crowds before it was installed in Washington.

During the 1820s and 1830s, July 4th became an "American Sabbath," and the Declaration was its central scripture. Jefferson and Adams reconciled their

Figure 10.1 One of the murals in the Capitol Rotunda, John Trumbull's *Signing of the Declaration of Independence* was painted at the urging of Thomas Jefferson. Architect of the Capitol.

differences by letter. When both founders died on the fiftieth anniversary of the Declaration, the timing seemed providential.

Just weeks earlier, Jefferson had expressed his regrets at not being able to attend a celebration of the fiftieth anniversary of Independence in a letter in which he called the Declaration "an instrument pregnant with our own, and the fate of the world." He expressed his hope that the document would be a "signal of arousing men to burst the chains under which monkish ignorance and superstition had persuaded them to bind themselves, and to assume the blessings and security of self-government." Revolutions outside the United States were already fulfilling Jefferson's hope. The years between 1810 and 1847 saw Declarations of Independence in Colombia, Venezuela, Mexico, Argentina, Chile, Peru, Guatemala, El Salvador, Nicaragua, Costa Rica, Panama, Greece, Brazil, Nicaragua, Bolivia, Uruguay, Ecuador, Belgium, Colombia, New Zealand, Texas, California, Honduras, Paraguay, the Dominican Republic, and Liberia.

The Liberian declaration of 1847, establishing an independent state of former slaves in West Africa, reflected an American dispute over how the equality and rights supported by the original Declaration could relate to slavery. The Liberian text did not oppose any empire, but simply announced that the American Colonization Society, which had sponsored the settlement, now renounced its right to rule the African land it had purchased. It set forth a list of grievances against slaveholders in the United States, but none against the Colonization Society. Though it did recognize "in all men, certain natural and inalienable rights: among which are life, liberty, and the right to acquire, possess, enjoy and defend property," the Liberian Declaration did not say that "all men are created equal."

As the American debate over slavery heated up, the Declaration's philosophical assertions came under scrutiny. If it were true that all men are "created equal," with rights to "life, liberty, and the pursuit of happiness" that cannot be taken away, how could one man legally hold another as a slave? The argument that African slaves were captives from just wars—rebels and aggressors worthy of capital punishment who could justly be worked to death or killed—had been used since the sixteenth century and repeated by John Locke, among others, but it had lost all plausibility.

According to *Cannibals All!* (1857), one of the important writings of pro-slavery theorist George Fitzhugh, the American Revolution "had nothing more to do with philosophy than the weaning of a calf. It was the act of a people seeking national independence, not the Utopian scheme of speculative philosophers, seeking to establish human equality and social perfection." John C. Calhoun, the powerful senator from South Carolina, called the Declaration simply "a formal and solemn announcement to the world, that the colonies had ceased to be dependent communities, and had become free and independent States." For Calhoun, the equality posited by the Declaration was a "hypothetical truism" about humanity in a state of nature, not only irrelevant to any civil society but actually "poisonous" to good social order. Theories of human equality and rights had no necessary connection with the sacred cause of American independence, at least in the writings of Fitzhugh and Calhoun.

Decades before Fitzhugh's book, however, the egalitarian implications of the Declaration had already begun to influence American politics. In 1829, Abolitionist William Lloyd Garrison argued that the grievances listed in the Declaration against King George III were "pitiful" in comparison to those suffered by the slaves, and professed himself ashamed of his country for its "unmeaning declamations in praise of liberty and equality" every July 4th. In 1847, Garrison and fellow Abolitionist Wendell Phillips pitted the Declaration against the Constitution. They issued a call to every American "to devote himself to the destruction of the Union and the Constitution" in hope that a state might arise that fulfilled "the principles of the Declaration of Independence, whose promises made us once the admiration of the world."

One year later, many of Garrison's allies in the anti-slavery movement, including Lucretia Mott and former slave Frederick Douglass, joined Elizabeth Cady Stanton and other advocates of rights for women who gathered for the first women's rights convention at Seneca Falls, New York. That convention issued a "Declaration of Sentiments" that mirrored the Declaration of Independence to make its point. The first two paragraphs of the Seneca Falls declaration exactly reproduced the words of 1776, with two exceptions. The women of Seneca Falls wrote that "all men *and women* are created equal," and that it had become necessary for "one *portion of the family of man*" rather than "one people" to assume a different relation to the rest. After the theory supporting women's right to "life, liberty, and the pursuit of happiness" and to the creation of a new system of government, the Declaration of Sentiments listed grievances. It placed men in the same tyrannical position, relative to women, in which the Declaration of Independence had placed King George III.

Four years later, in 1852, the Ladies' Anti-Slavery Society of Rochester, New York, asked Frederick Douglass to address their Independence Day meeting. In a lengthy and argumentative oration entitled *What to the Slave Is the Fourth of July?*, Douglass used the Declaration to castigate white Americans. "Are the great principles of political freedom and of natural justice, embodied in that Declaration of Independence, extended to us?" he asked. He condemned the "national inconsistencies" of a people that could "declare before all the world" that all men are created equal, with inalienable rights to life, liberty, and the pursuit of happiness, and yet "hold securely, in a bondage which, according to your own Thomas Jefferson, 'is worse than ages of that which your fathers rose in rebellion to oppose,' a seventh part of the inhabitants of your country." Replying to the charge that the Constitution supported slavery, Douglass pointed out that the document never explicitly mentioned slaves. In his conclusion, he insisted on maintaining hope in the United States, "drawing encouragement from the Declaration of Independence, the great principles it contains, and the spirit of American institutions."

Many in America were moving away from the understanding of the Declaration that encouraged Frederick Douglass. As the issue of slavery grew more and more urgent, more people were prepared to dismiss the political philosophy of the Declaration as meaningless but dangerous rhetoric. In 1856, a leader of the dying Whig Party, Rufus Choate, warned the party convention that if the new Republican Party won the upcoming presidential election, the government of the United States would appear to the states of the South as an enemy government, which would take as its constitution "the glittering and sounding generalities of natural right which make up the Declaration of Independence."

Despite Choate's fears, Republicans did not win the White House in 1856. The next year brought an authoritative statement on the Declaration and slavery from Chief Justice Roger Taney of the Supreme Court in the *Dred Scott* case, which upheld laws that demanded the return of fugitive slaves. As Taney admitted, the words "all men are created equal" seemed "to embrace the whole human family," and he argued that "if they were used in a similar instrument at this day [they] would be so understood." Looking back to 1776, however, Taney saw a different intention: "it is too clear for dispute, that the enslaved African race were not intended to be included, and formed no part of the people who framed and adopted this declaration."

Abraham Lincoln made the Declaration of Independence the foundation of his political creed, and he included slaves in its assertion of equality. Although Lincoln made statements that now strike us as racist, he always kept the equality clause of the Declaration firmly in mind. He denied advocating that the slaves should be freed and made "politically and socially our equals." He said that a "physical inequality" at least of color, and possibly of moral and intellectual capacities, prevented complete integration between white and black people. But Lincoln also said, in the debates during his unsuccessful 1858 campaign against Senator Stephen Douglas, that a black man had as much right as anyone to eat the bread he had earned. As early as 1854, speaking on the law that allowed slavery to be introduced by popular vote in Kansas and Nebraska, Lincoln argued that the right of self-government could not extend to the government of others. "If the Negro is a *man*, why then my ancient faith teaches me that 'all men are created equal,' and that there can be no moral right in connection with one man's making a slave of another." In a dramatic speech on July 10, 1858, in Chicago, Lincoln reflected on Independence Day and pointed out that many in the audience were "German, Irish, French and Scandinavian," and so might have no blood connection to the Anglo-Americans of 1776. "But when they look through that old Declaration of Independence they find that those old men say that 'We hold these truths to be self-evident, that all men are created equal.'" When immigrants recognized this truth, according to Lincoln, they saw "the father of all moral principle in them, and that...they have a right to claim it as though they were blood of the blood, and flesh of the flesh of the men who wrote that Declaration, and so they are."

At the end of that Chicago speech, Lincoln warned that if the Declaration did not apply to slaves, it might not apply to others, and that to say some men were not equal led to the "arguments that kings have made for enslaving the people in all ages of the world." He challenged the audience: "If that declaration is not the truth, let us get the Statute book, in which we find it and tear it out! Who is so bold as to do it?" Someone did say, "Me!" but most cried "No, no!" Lincoln replied, "Let us stick to it then, let us stand firmly by it then." This moment has been re-enacted for millions over the last four decades in presentations of Lincoln at the Hall of Presidents in Disney World.

Lincoln's most famous words grew directly from his interpretation of the Declaration of Independence. As the Gettysburg Address, delivered at the dedication of the cemetery for soldiers who fell at Gettysburg in 1863, began: "Fourscore and seven years ago our fathers brought forth on this continent a new nation, conceived in liberty and dedicated to the proposition that all men are created equal." This very brief speech went on to say that the cause of the war was to test whether "any nation so conceived and so dedicated can long endure." According to Garry Wills, one of the Declaration's prominent interpreters, Lincoln here perpetrated a "giant (if benign) swindle," and "one of the most daring acts of open-air sleight-of-hand" in history. Wills and others have argued that Lincoln alone redefined "all men are created equal" to include slaves and sanctified the new meaning at Gettysburg. But as we have seen, before Lincoln there were Elizabeth Cady Stanton and Frederick Douglass, and after him there would be others, some accepting an expansive definition of equality and some denying it.

In the aftermath of the Civil War and Lincoln's death, during the Reconstruction years and the backlash against Reconstruction, the assertion of equality in the Declaration of Independence lost much of its power in American public discourse. Celebrations of July 4th became more focused on fireworks and band music and less on reading the Declaration as part of an "American Sabbath." Then came the centennial of the Declaration of Independence in 1876, which was celebrated in Philadelphia by a Centennial Exposition that treated the physical Declaration as an icon. The original parchment of the Declaration was brought from Washington to be displayed in the room of Independence Hall where it had been edited and adopted. Meanwhile, the Constitution, which was debated in that same room, remained in a box in a closet, and its centennial in

1887 occasioned no great festivities. Neither the egalitarian principles of the Declaration nor their implementation in the Constitution fared well during the Gilded Age.

Writing in the *Harvard Law Review* for January 1900, William F. Dana argued that the Declaration of Independence had nothing at all to do with equal rights for black people, or with the rights of American Indians (who would not be citizens until 1924) or with equality for women (who would not vote until 1920). Dana's answer came straight from John Locke, who in his *Second Treatise of Government* first established a right of revolution. For Locke, perfect equality existed in a state of nature, but ceased when people banded together in civil societies and set up governments to protect their property. The Congress that passed the Declaration knew that they did not live in a state of nature but in civil society, and they sought to justify their revolution on the basis of natural rights, as those rights had been modified by their consent to government. "These men were largely men of the English race, and they had the traits of character that have given that race predominance in the world," Dana wrote. "They built on facts.... They had no love of failure, or intangible ideals, or disorder, or confusion." Their unquestionable unwillingness to grant equal rights to slaves, or Indians, or women was not hypocrisy, but evidence of their wisdom in knowing "that that government is best, which, not in purpose only, but in fact, brings the greatest good to the greatest number." For this legal scholar, equality in nature clearly did not extend into society.

Physical threats to the Declaration of Independence began in the summer of 1776 and continued for about two centuries. During the Revolution, the turning tides of battle sent the US Congress and its declaration out of Philadelphia (which was occupied for some time by the British) to many places, including Baltimore, Maryland; Lancaster and York, Pennsylvania; and Princeton, New Jersey. After the Treaty of Paris ended the war in 1783, the Declaration moved several times with Congress before settling in Philadelphia for ten years, until the new capital at Washington, D.C., was built. The War of 1812 sent the Declaration into hiding in Virginia while the capital was burned. When the Declaration returned to Washington, it was safe from enemy armies but not from smoke and sunlight. The next move because of war came on December 23, 1941, sixteen days after the Japanese attack on Pearl Harbor, when both the Declaration and the Constitution were removed from their shrine at the Library of Congress in Washington. They were sent by train to Fort Knox, Kentucky, where the United States kept the gold that supported its paper currency. In 1944, they were returned to Washington.

This did not end the Declaration's travels, however. As the Cold War began, President Truman's attorney general, Tom Clark, conceived the idea of sending the Declaration, the Constitution, and other items sacred to American civil religion across the nation on a "Freedom Train." Truman loved trains and campaigned on them from one "whistle stop" to another, and he endorsed the idea. With twenty-nine Marines serving as guards and interpretive guides, the Train traveled from September 1947 to January 1949, making 326 stops, reaching every state then in the Union, and receiving more than three and a half million visitors. Although the Declaration was the unquestioned star of this show, there were 127 documents on board, including one of the original copies of the Constitution, the Emancipation Proclamation, the Gettysburg Address, and the German and Japanese surrender treaties from World War II. Six historic flags, including the flag raised over Iwo Jima, also rode the Train. At stops along the route, "rededication ceremonies" were held, in which citizens pledged allegiance to the nation in the presence of these sacred documents and objects.

Having been carried through the land like a sacred relic or icon, the Declaration next found its sanctuary. The National Archives building was constructed in 1935 and decorated in 1936 with huge murals depicting fictional scenes in which Jefferson handed the Declaration of Independence to John Hancock and James Madison handed the Constitution to Washington, while dozens of other founding fathers looked on, but it had not yet housed either document. On December 13, 1952, as fighting in Korea belied the term "Cold War" and a month after the United States detonated its first hydrogen bomb, the Declaration was brought from the Library of Congress into a specially designed Rotunda for the Charters of Freedom in the National Archives. The move was made in part because the new location was thought to be the closest thing to a bomb-proof building in Washington. The trip was both highly ceremonial and heavily military. Twelve members of the Armed Forces Special Police carried the Declaration and the Constitution out of the Library in helium-filled glass cases encased in wooden crates, then placed the crates on mattresses in an armored personnel carrier. Two light tanks, a motorcycle escort, and four guards armed with submachine guns accompanied the personnel carrier down Pennsylvania and Constitution Avenues from the Library to the Archives building, with Army, Navy, Air Force, Marine, and Coast Guard personnel lining the entire route. Two days later, on December 15, the Rotunda was officially dedicated and opened to the public. President Truman gave a speech, hoping visitors would find that "the sight of these symbols will lift up their hearts, so they will go out of this building helped and strengthened and inspired."

Not everyone has. In *American Scripture*, a scholarly history of the Declaration, Pauline Maier wrote that in her visit to the Rotunda, "the spectacle had the air of a state funeral." Guards at the shrine seemed to her to exude a sense of "suppressed deep emotion," breaking silence only when they needed to ask the line of visitors to keep moving. The architecture of the shrine reminded her of "the awesome, gilded, pre-Vatican II altars" of her Roman Catholic childhood. Noting that every night when the visitors leave, the containers with their documents are lowered into a massive vault of concrete and steel twenty-two feet deep, Maier concluded that the message of the site arose from an era when American values were under threat and embodied "an assurance to the fearful that those values could not be destroyed." In a living democracy, she complained, "The symbolism is all wrong; it suggests a tradition locked in a glorious but dead past, reinforces the instincts of an anti-political age." She urged Americans not to simply "file by...reverentially," looking at a "mummified" document "lying in state at the Archives," but to discuss the implications of the Declaration of Independence for politics in their own day.

Shrines imply mystery as well as death, however. In *National Treasure*, one of the top-grossing movies of 2004–2005, the Declaration served as the key to the secret heritage (or at least the wealth) of Western civilization. According to this story, the Masons who founded the United States were heirs of the Knights Templar, and these Knights/Masons brought a vast treasure of ancient loot, including scrolls from the library at Alexandria and gold from Egypt and Babylon, to America to keep it safe from disorder in Europe. On the back of the Declaration of Independence they inscribed a treasure map, viewable only with an optical device made by Benjamin Franklin. In a succession of action-packed sequences, the Declaration is stolen from the National Archives, the optical device is found near Independence Hall, and the treasure itself is located under New York's Trinity Church, near Wall Street. The movie does give its viewers a vivid tour of some historic places, including side trips to Boston and the Intrepid Museum on the Hudson in New York. It also evokes some aspects of real history, such as the role of the Masons in Revolutionary times and figures like Franklin and Charles Carroll, who was really the last surviving signer of the Declaration of Independence. On the other hand, the movie's plot tends to reduce the Declaration's meaning to that of a treasure map, and so to reduce American civil religion to a kind of magic.

If real sacredness depends on contestation, as in the Middle Ages when monks and bishops fought over the possession of relics, the Declaration—even in its shrine—still has some power. Students in American high schools and colleges focus more and more on the hypocrisy of the Declaration's claim that slave owners have the right to build their own government on the basis of human equality. Some notice the additional hypocrisy of the Declaration's complaint that King George unleashed "the merciless Indian savages, whose known rule of warfare, is an undistinguished destruction of all ages, sexes, and conditions" on English colonists, when it was the English colonists who actually used that rule of war on Indians. Yet the Declaration's assertion of human equality continues to advance that cause by serving as the spark that ignites such arguments.

Meanwhile, the central purpose of the Declaration, to declare the independence of the United States, retains its influence at a moment when the value of independence can seem vital and at the same time dangerous. The Declaration emerged in the midst of a great age of nationalism, during which independent nations were recognized as basic units of human life. When the age of nationalism led to the World Wars of the twentieth century, the international organizations that sought to ensure world peace, the League of Nations and the United Nations, continued to take the independent nation as their basic unit. In the Universal Declaration of Human Rights adopted by the United Nations in 1948, Article 15 linked nationalism with individual rights by asserting that "[e]veryone has the right to a nationality," and that "[n]o one shall be arbitrarily deprived of his nationality nor denied the right to change his nationality." This last statement implies that individuals are also independent, with "inalienable rights" to align themselves with independent nations.

Independence itself became a sacred value in the United States and across the world. This was a new phenomenon. For most of history, families have been taken as natural, and nations have been regarded as the extensions of families. People were born into families, usually in villages where the family had lived for many generations, and the idea that they were born independent and able to choose their basic affiliations never arose. With the Declaration of Independence, however, and the experience of 50 million immigrants to the United States (the largest human migration in history until the recent movement from country to city in China), independence became a moral norm. As early as 1848, Marx and Engels wrote in the *Communist Manifesto* that the working classes had no families, because everyone worked in the factories of early capitalism. As capitalist development progressed into the twenty-first century, the middle and upper classes also sent their women to work in the marketplace and expected their children to leave the families of their birth and strike out on their own. Elders did not want to be cared for by their children but to retain their independence. Independence gained a moral value that arguably surpassed the values of community, loyalty, harmony, and even love.

At the same time, global developments led to increasing interdependence, and some thinkers and political actors began to recognize this. On March 22, 1944, philosopher Will Durant, Nobel laureate novelist Thomas Mann, and other luminaries meeting at the Hollywood Roosevelt Hotel issued a Declaration of Interdependence, which was read at a Concert of Americans at the Hollywood Bowl on July 4th and was entered into the Congressional Record in 1945. This declaration was primarily concerned with racial harmony, in reaction to the Nazi and Japanese imperial ideologies that had just been defeated in World War II and to the racial tensions that beset the United States. The "evident truths" listed by the Declaration began, "That differences or race, color and creed are natural, and that diverse groups, institutions, and ideas are stimulating factors in the development of man." It urged all to "united action" in several ways, such as "[t]o strive in concert with others to discourage all animosities arising from these differences, and to unite all groups in the fair play of civilized life."

In the moment of internationalism that followed World War II, the new United Nations also drew on the Declaration of Independence to formulate its basic principles. The Universal Declaration of Human Rights that the UN passed in 1948, with leadership from Eleanor Roosevelt, used the argument for revolution in the American Declaration to support its position that "if man is not to have recourse, as a last resort, to rebellion against tyranny and oppression," then human rights must have protection within the rule of law. The UN Declaration also began its first article, "All human beings are born free and equal in dignity and rights," a clear echo of Jefferson's prose. Article three, which said that "[e]veryone has the right to life, liberty, and security of person," also echoed Jefferson (and Locke), though it did not follow Jefferson into the positive "pursuit of happiness."

This last and most comprehensive of the Declaration's "inalienable rights" has come into conflict, in the last few decades, with those who want to underline the interdependence of humanity. Beginning in 1969, the Earth Day movement—a celebration of the natural world at or near the Vernal Equinox—has provoked several declarations of interdependence. Ecological activists have called into question whether people have an inalienable right to pursue their own happiness, at least without explicit regard for the health of the world.

Meanwhile, the oldest arguments for independence still have revolutionary force. On March 19, 2008, about a hundred members of Iraq Veterans Against the War arrived in vans at the National Archives and occupied the building for ninety minutes, handing out pamphlets and making speeches before dispersing peacefully. Their literature cited two of the Declaration's complaints against King George. The first, that the king was "transporting large Armies of foreign Mercenaries" to America "to compleat the works of death, destruction, and tyranny," was applied by the veterans to the mercenary armies of Blackwater, the Armour Group, and "Afrikaner mercs running around with AKs in Datsun pickups" who serve the United States in Iraq. The second charge, that King George "has affected to render the Military independent of and superior to the Civil Power," they connected with the claim that the president is not bound by Congress when he acts as commander-in-chief of the military. Although the occupation of the Archives received remarkably little press coverage and was mocked by some as a misdirected protest against a non-political government agency, it showed that people still care about what the Declaration of Independence says.

From another place on the political spectrum, Federalist legal theorist Donald S. Lutz has claimed the Declaration as a "national compact," the revolutionary era's version of the Mayflower Compact. This would make the Declaration a necessary document, by which America became one nation rather than thirteen separate colonies, prior to the Articles of Confederation and to the Constitution. Because the Declaration evokes God as the source of natural rights and asks God to bless the new nation, Lutz argues that its position in American law shows that God is basic to the government of the United States.

Whether or not the Declaration of Independence is our national compact, the document holds a central place in the American civil religion. From Jefferson to Lincoln to Martin Luther King, its assertion that people are "created equal" has been the dynamite that has destroyed walls of privilege and injustice. The value of independence for the founding generation has extended to personal independence and informed the lasting values of liberty and democracy. The American quest for independence has inspired revolutions on the side of ethnic and individual rights for more than two hundred years. Even when those who proclaim interdependence seem to disagree with the Declaration, their acts of declaration and many of their words echo what the men of Philadelphia declared in 1776.

SOURCES

Armitage, David, *The Declaration of Independence: A Global History* (Cambridge, MA: Harvard University Press, 2007).

Becker, Carl L., *The Declaration of Independence: A Study in the History of Political Ideas* (New York: Vintage Books, 1922).

Detwiler, Philip F., "The Changing Reputation of the Declaration of Independence: The First Fifty Years," *The William and Mary Quarterly*, Third Series, *19*, no. 4 (October, 1962), 557–574.

Gibson, Alan, *Understanding the Founding: The Crucial Questions* (Lawrence: The University Press of Kansas, 2007).

Glendon, Mary Ann, *A World Made New: Eleanor Roosevelt and the Universal Declaration of Human Rights* (New York: Random House, 2001).

Lutz, Donald S., "The Declaration of Independence as Part of an American National Compact," *Publius 19*, no. 1 (Winter, 1989), 41–58.

Maier, Pauline, *American Scripture: Making the Declaration of Independence* (New York: Alfred A. Knopf, 1997).

Wills, Garry, *Inventing America: Jefferson's Declaration of Independence* (New York: Doubleday & Company, 1978).

11

The Great Seal and the Dollar Bill

The United States has very serious, even solemn, paper money. Its color is matched in sobriety by the notes of Great Britain; but British money features the living, reigning monarch, who in the case of Queen Elizabeth II has been mocked by the Beatles, the Sex Pistols, and BBC comedians. Though the Queen is beloved by millions, she is also actively resented by many, and her place in history remains vulnerable to events. The dead white men who appear on American bills—George Washington on the dollar, Abraham Lincoln on the five, Alexander Hamilton on the ten, Andrew Jackson on the twenty, Ulysses S. Grant on the fifty, and Benjamin Franklin on the hundred-dollar bill—may also appear in advertisements and comedy skits, but their historical status is unassailable. All of them live in the American popular imagination as demigods, heroes who founded and preserved the nation, whatever their flaws. French money once featured bright colors and artists like Hector Berlioz, and the Euro now displays abstract symbols and numbers, but US currency enshrines the honored dead.

Among the paper bills of the United States, none is so sacred as the dollar, from which the phrase "almighty dollar" is derived and applied to all money. The current design of the dollar dates from 1935, when it replaced much less elaborate and coherent designs that lacked the Great Seal on the back. On the dollar of the last eight decades, Washington looks out from the front, in a Gilbert Stuart portrait that scarcely seems human, when examined closely—his demeanor is so calm, his dress and pose so formal, as to approach divinity. On the back of the bill, many religious symbols and statements balance each other. Above the large "ONE" in the white space at the center stands IN GOD WE TRUST in all caps. This was added to every US bill by act of Congress in 1957. All coins had borne In God We Trust since the Civil War, but a 1956 law made this phrase the official motto of the United States as part of the same expansion of civil religion, inspired by the struggle with godless communism, that added under God to the Pledge of Allegiance in 1954.

The most powerful religious symbols on the dollar appear in the Great Seal of the United States, the front side (or obverse) of which is printed to the right of the ONE and the back (or reverse) on the left. The symbols in these circles arose from a long process that began on July 4, 1776, when the Continental Congress appointed Thomas Jefferson, Benjamin Franklin, and John Adams as a committee to design a seal for the United States. Franklin proposed an image of Moses leading Israel across the Red Sea. Adams wanted Hercules choosing between the flowery path of pleasure and the stony path of duty. Jefferson supported the children of Israel in the wilderness on one side and Hengist and Horsa, legendary ancestors of the Anglo-Saxons in Britain, on the other. The eventual Seal included two elements recommended by this committee: an eye within a triangle with rays of blessing for the new country, and the motto E pluribus unum ("Out of many, one) written on a scroll. Unable to reach consensus, Congress appointed a second committee in 1780; among its proposals were a shield with thirteen red and white stripes, a constellation of thirteen stars, and a set of arrows. Finally, in 1782, as the colonies and Great Britain began to negotiate a peace to end the Revolutionary War, the still unsatisfied Congress appointed a third committee to create a seal. They recommended an unfinished pyramid, topped by the shining eye, specified the number of arrows as thirteen, and added an eagle, though not as a central feature. The eagle had already caused dispute among the founders: Franklin disliked eagles because of their nature as scavengers and thieves and their historic ties to Europe, to Rome, and to monarchy. He joked that the turkey, a useful American bird, would be more appropriate.

In July 1782, Congress appointed an individual, Charles Thompson, to combine the committee reports into the Great Seal that now appears on the dollar bill. A Latin teacher from Philadelphia who had served eight years as secretary of the Continental Congress, Thompson added the mottoes *ANNUIT COEPTIS* (He has favored the beginnings) and *NOVUS ORDO SECLORUM* (A new order of the ages) to the Seal; he also placed the eagle on the front and the pyramid on the back. Thompson was helped in making drawings of his conception by William Barton, a Philadelphia lawyer and artist who had originally suggested the eagle.

After Thompson and Barton's work of synthesis, the Great Seal (and the dollar bill that incorporated it) embodied a rich and novel set of religious symbols (Figure 11.1). The eye within the triangle, hovering over the unfinished pyramid, referred to God, but not in the Jewish or Christian sense. The eye was and is a prominent symbol of God for the Masons, a rationalist and republican fraternal society that rose to prominence in the French Revolution and among elites of the United States. Washington, Jefferson, Madison, and Monroe all were Masons. An unfinished pyramid represents the future of the nation, but also continues the Masonic reference, because Masons understand themselves as heirs of the skilled workmen who designed and built the pyramids. Even for those who know nothing of the Masons, a pyramid is a religious symbol, evoking

Figure 11.1 The reverse of the Great Seal makes several religious statements, from the eye of God and pyramid from Masonic tradition to the Latin mottoes *ANNUIT COEPTIS* (He has favored the beginnings) and *NOVUS ORDO SECLORUM* (A new order of the ages), which describe Jupiter and the founding of Rome in Virgil's *Aeneid*. Department of State. © Pandapaw/Shutterstock.

power and endurance and meant by the Egyptians to ensure immortality; but a pyramid is neither Jewish (except perhaps in a negative sense, as a reminder of bondage) nor Christian. In combination, the eye and the pyramid refer to a God independent of the Bible. That symbol of God, rather than the images of Moses and Israel proposed by earlier committees and rejected, stands at the center of American civil religion.

By putting the Latin *NOVUS ORDO SECLORUM* on a scroll under the pyramid and printing the Roman numerals MDCCLXXVI (1776) along the pyramid's base, Thompson expressed a claim that 1776 began a new era of history, a "year one," or the first year of a Messianic age, just as French revolutionaries would claim in 1789. Above the pyramid, the motto *ANNUIT COEPITS*, or He/She/It has favored the beginnings/undertakings, indicates in the most general way that what began in 1776 is favored by whatever powers exist. Both mottoes derived from the Roman poet Virgil, who wrote them in celebration of the birth of a new order with the Emperor Augustus.

More hints of exactly what powers favor the United States appear on the other side from the pyramid and the eye—the front side of the Great Seal—where an eagle hovers with its wings upraised, clutching olive branches in its right talons, toward which his head is turned, and thirteen arrows in the left. Above the eagle's head float thirteen stars in a field of glory; over the eagle's chest stands a shield with thirteen stars and thirteen vertical stripes. Thompson made a point of depicting the shield with no visible support, to represent the independence of the United States. Two other symbols of union—a field of thirteen stars in a cloud of glory, above the eagle's head, and a scroll reading *E PLURIBUS UNUM*, or Out of many, one—drive home the point that this union itself has great, and perhaps divine, dignity. But the greatest clue to which God we trust is the eagle. The Hebrew and Christian Scriptures make the dove the emblem of divinity: Noah sends a dove to find evidence that the Flood has receded; doves are sacrificed in the Temple; and a dove descends from heaven when Jesus is baptized. On the other hand, the eagle is the sacred bird of Zeus, and the God of American civil religion bears a strong resemblance to Zeus, or the more dignified and domestic Roman Jupiter, whose name derives from *eu + pater*, good father. Like Jupiter, the God of American civil religion stands for order, hates those who break their oaths (or treaties), throws thunderbolts (or missiles) on miscreants, supports justice more than compassion, and favors the rich and successful. God can safely be invoked by any American leader; but the God of Israel or the Savior (Jesus) cannot. The symbols of American currency imply that the "almighty" dollar belongs to a god like Jupiter.

To understand how this God relates to the rest of American civil religion, it helps to recall the first designs for the Great Seal. Franklin wanted Moses at the Red Sea, and Jefferson wanted the Israelites in the desert—both images of liberty, but of biblical liberty, which entailed obedience to a covenant with God. Jupiter, on the other hand, had no Ten Commandments and no chosen people. However often American preachers have called the United States "God's New Israel," the Great Seal that appears on the dollar bill suggests that the liberty that Americans hold sacred is not biblical but is more like Roman liberty—the more absolute freedom of citizens in the Roman republic.

SOURCES

Kammen, Michael, *From Liberty to Prosperity: Reflections on the Role of Revolutionary Iconography in National Tradition* (Worcester, MA: American Antiquarian Society, 1977).

MacArthur, John D., <http://www.greatseal.com>, copyright (1998–2004).

Ovason, David, *The Secret Symbols of the Dollar Bill* (New York: HarperCollins, 2004).

Patterson, Richard S., and Richardson Dougall, *The Eagle and the Shield* (Washington, DC: US Government Printing Office, 1978).

US Department of State, Bureau of Public Affairs, "The Great Seal of the United States" (Washington, DC: US Government Printing Office, 2003).

Wilson, Leonard, *The Coat of Arms, Crest and Great Seal of the United States of America* (San Diego, CA: N. Francis Maw, 1928).

12

The Constitution

> We the People of the United States, in Order to form a more perfect Union, establish Justice, insure domestic Tranquility, provide for the common defense, promote the general Welfare, and secure the Blessings of Liberty to ourselves and our Posterity, do ordain and establish this Constitution for the United States of America.

The primary field in which the Constitution's holiness is felt is verbal. Phrases like "We the People," "the Blessings of Liberty," "freedom of speech, or of the press," "to keep and bear Arms," "cruel and unusual punishments," and "due process of law" have echoed through the public discourse, attaining a power equal to that of prayers or the invocations of gods. "Constitutional" and "unconstitutional" have become the equivalents of clean and unclean, kosher and *trayfe*, saved and damned.

Exactly how the distinction between constitutional and unconstitutional is made reveals four basic values of American civil religion. The most basic value, personal freedom or liberty, appears often in the Constitution. Concern for liberty was a large factor in determining the form of government—three branches with separate powers—that the Constitution set forth. The second value, political democracy, was explicitly included by Article IV, Section 4, which gives the federal government the obligation to intervene to insure a "Republican Form of Government" in the states. Democracy also figures indirectly in many other clauses. The value of peace, which would become world peace, appeared in the statements that the new government would "insure domestic Tranquility" and "provide for the common defense." The value of cultural tolerance was implied by "We the People," the first phrase of the Constitution, which stands among the most revered phrases of the American civil religion, surpassed only by some from the Declaration of Independence.

Like the Declaration, the Constitution functions both as sacred text and as icon. It has been less powerful as an icon than the Declaration, but more important as a text. To examine how the Constitution functions in American civil religion, it is not necessary to deal with the entire history of the Constitution and its interpretation. Instead, this chapter will attempt to explain what aspects and phrases of the Constitution express values that have been regarded as sacred by Americans, then will turn to the enshrinement of the physical document and the religious aura that has come to surround the Constitution as a whole.

The basic form of government that the Constitution set forth—three branches with separate powers, including a legislature with an upper and lower house, an executive, and an independent judiciary—derived in part from the branches of government (King, Lords, and Commons) in the unwritten constitution of England. During the English Civil Wars of the 1640s and 1650s and the Glorious Revolution of 1688-1689, relations between these branches had been contested. A theory of a government divided into branches was advanced by authors like John Locke, Baron de Montesquieu, and John Adams, whose 1776 *Thoughts on Government* had suggested a three-branch arrangement to the colonies that were then becoming states. Arguing for ratification of the American Constitution in *The Federalist*, Number 51 (1788), James Madison made a religious argument for a government with separate branches. "If men were angels," or "[i]f angels were to govern men," Madison wrote, power could safely be concentrated, but in the current state of human nature, "[a]mbition must be made to counteract ambition." This reasoning reflected a common Protestant understanding that humans were corrupted by original sin to such a degree that they could not be trusted with power. Despite all of the history and theory behind it, however, the strong but divided federal government of the Constitution did not come into being easily in the United States.

The founding generation had a hard time deciding whether the federal government should express the will of a single people or the consensus of many sovereign states. In the original draft of the Constitution, a group called the Committee of Detail expected the phrase "We the People" to be followed by the names of the ratifying states, as in "We the People of Delaware, New Jersey, Connecticut" and so on. The states were eliminated from the text because Gouverneur Morris, a member of the Committee of Style that polished the draft eventually sent to the states for ratification, realized that the Constitution would take effect after nine states ratified, but could not predict which states would ratify or in what order.

As historian Joseph Ellis has pointed out, the choice between a national government and a federation was never completely decided, but rather consigned to a framework for endless debate that continued up to and beyond the Civil War. In phrases from the Preamble like "to form a more perfect Union" and "to promote the general Welfare," the goal of a strong central government seemed clear. On the other hand, "to secure the Blessings of Liberty" demanded, at least according to many at the Constitutional Convention, that the government's power be limited and that many spheres of action be reserved to the people and the states. This was especially true with regard to the limits of federal involvement with one form of property, the slaves who were scattered throughout the country but concentrated on the plantations of the South.

In a civil religion that made "liberty" a sacred word, slavery was always anomalous. It was the allowances made for slavery that led Abolitionist William Lloyd Garrison to reject the Constitution as a "covenant with Hell" and to burn it in a public ritual in 1854. Slavery affected four different provisions of the original Constitution and two of the Amendments, but was never mentioned by name until it was abolished by the Thirteenth Amendment in 1865. It arose first in Article I, Section 2, where the Constitution described how it would be decided how many representatives each state would have in the House of Representatives. If the slaves were counted, those states with many slaves would get more representatives. Although citizens of all states still held slaves in 1787, six states had already passed laws to abolish slavery at some point in the future, and those that had fewer slaves wanted not to count slaves at all. The compromise that made each slave count as three-fifths of a free person was expressed in a most remarkable circumlocution, using the phrase "of all other Persons" to avoid the word "slaves."

> Representatives and direct Taxes shall be apportioned among the several States which may be included within this Union, according to their respective Numbers, which shall be determined by adding to the whole Number of free Persons, including those bound to Service for a Term of Years, and excluding Indians not taxed, three fifths of all other Persons.

No slaves, but only "other Persons" were named. The same principle governed the phrasing of a compromise on the slave trade, allowing the states to continue it until the year 1808, or twenty years after the Constitution went into effect. According to Article II, Section 9, slaves were "such Persons" who might be imported:

> The Migration or Importation of such Persons as any of the States now existing shall think proper to admit, shall not be prohibited by the Congress prior to the Year one thousand eight hundred and eight, but a tax or duty may be imposed on such Importation, not exceeding ten dollars for each Person.

Finally, within the body of the original Constitution, the slavery established in one state was guaranteed not to be annulled by another state's laws, again without using the words "slave" or "slavery." The issue arose in Article IV, on the powers and obligations of the states, Section 2:

> No Person held to Service or Labour in one State, under the Laws thereof, escaping into another, shall, in Consequence of any Law or Regulation therein, be discharged from such Service or Labour, But shall be delivered up on Claim of the Party to whom such Service or Labour may be due.

It could be argued that it was not necessary to name slaves here, because this article applied equally to slaves and to indentured servants, the people "bound to service for a term of years" who counted fully toward representation and taxes under Article I. On the other hand, the cumulative effect of the omissions of the word "slave" in these three provisions, each of which was crucial to obtaining the consent of slaveholders to the Constitution, provides strong evidence of the shame that Americans felt regarding slavery. During and after the Revolutionary War, British critics of America frequently pointed out that the "sons of liberty" who felt justified in deserting their mother country because they had to be free also felt justified in holding slaves. The Atlantic slave trade reached its peak during the 1780s, the same decade in which the Revolution was won and the Constitution written. The circumlocutions that kept the word "slave" out of the Constitution were examples of the old maxim that hypocrisy is the tribute that vice pays to virtue. These labored references to "such Persons" also showed, indirectly, that the American civil religion was opposed in spirit, if not yet in fact, to slavery from the beginning of the United States. No less an authority than Frederick Douglass, the escaped slave who became an Abolitionist leader, used this omission to argue that the Constitution never supported slavery.

Explicit rejection of slavery came at last in the Thirteenth Amendment, ratified on December 6, 1865:

> 1. Neither slavery nor involuntary servitude, except as a punishment for crime whereof the party shall have been duly convicted, shall exist within the United States, or any place subject to their jurisdiction.
>
> 2. Congress shall have power to enforce this article by appropriate legislation.

In the Fifteenth Amendment, ratified on December 3, 1870, the right of former slaves to vote was established:

> 1. The right of citizens of the United States to vote shall not be denied or abridged by the United States or any State on account of race, color, or previous condition of servitude.

> 2. The Congress shall have power to enforce this article by appropriate legislation.

Although the "appropriate legislation" needed to secure an effective right to vote for former slaves and their descendants was not passed until the Voting Rights Act of 1964, and the use of a poll tax to prevent poor people from voting remained legal until the Twenty-fourth Amendment, also in 1964, the Constitution eventually embodied a conviction that slavery was wrong and that its effects should be as far as possible obliterated. The aim of securing the value of personal freedom, or the "Blessings of Liberty" mentioned in the Preamble, has been sporadically extended throughout the history of the Constitution.

"Sporadically" remains a key concept, however, because the protections of the Constitution have meant what the Supreme Court has held them to mean. The Court has reflected the political consensus that produced the presidents who have appointed the justices and the senators who have confirmed them. For example, the Fourteenth Amendment, ratified in 1868, attempted to make all citizens equal in law.

> 1. All persons born or naturalized in the United States, and subject to the jurisdiction thereof, are citizens of the United States and of the State wherein they reside. No State shall make or enforce any law which shall abridge the privileges or immunities of citizens of the United States; nor shall any State deprive any person of life, liberty, or property, without due process of law; nor deny to any person within its jurisdiction the equal protection of the laws.

Despite this Amendment, and the statement that Congress had the power to enforce it "by appropriate legislation," the Supreme Court decided that the Civil Rights Act of 1875, guaranteeing the rights of all citizens to use places of public accommodation such as hotels and restaurants, was unconstitutional, because the laws establishing segregation were entirely local. The Court also ruled in 1875 that women could be "citizens" under the Fourteenth Amendment and still be denied the right to vote by state law. In 1884, the Court ruled that American Indians had no rights under the Fourteenth Amendment because they were not born "subject to the jurisdiction" of the United States.

Meanwhile, several specific liberties and rights were protected in the Constitution, even before the Bill of Rights (the first ten Amendments) was ratified in 1791. Under Article I, Section 9, the Constitution limited the powers of government to hold citizens in custody and to convict them outside normal court procedures:

> The privilege of the Writ of Habeas Corpus shall not be suspended, unless when in Cases of Rebellion or Invasion the public Safety may require it.
>
> No Bill of Attainder or ex post facto law shall be passed.

Regarding those held in custody, the first of these provisions insured that a court could demand that prisoners not simply be held by the government, but must be brought before a judge. This right of *habeas corpus*, deriving from the Latin for "You shall have the body," was enshrined in English law by the Magna Carta in 1215. The American Constitution also forbade Congress to place anyone under arrest, to seize their property, or to deprive them of political rights by passing a specific law to that effect (a "bill of attainder"). In the English Revolution of the 1640s, Parliament had used bills of attainder effectively to arrest and eventually to execute powerful ministers of the king. King Charles I himself was put to death in 1649 in part by means of acts of Parliament that declared some of his actions treason after the fact, or ex post facto. Such Parliamentary acts had promoted the cause of democracy, but the framers of the US Constitution feared that Congress might use bills of attainder and ex post facto laws to curtail critics or opponents of its actions. Through these provisions of the Constitution, Americans expressed their conviction that individual rights should be held more sacred in the United States than they were in Britain.

During the Civil War, President Abraham Lincoln used the exception for "rebellion" in the clause protecting *habeas corpus* to suspend that right for Confederates and their supporters. During the War on Terror following the September 11, 2001, attacks, the right to *habeas corpus* has been suspended for those suspected as terrorists, and some might argue that the clause prohibiting ex post facto laws has been ignored with regard to those called "enemy combatants" under the Patriot Act. Still, Section 9 of Article I demonstrates the centrality of individual rights in the American civil religion. In an exception to the usual tendency of the Constitution to allow states to make their own laws, the states are also forbidden to "pass any Bill of Attainder, or ex post facto law," in Article I, Section 10.

More evidence for this commitment to individual rights, or the value of personal freedom in American civil religion, can be found in Article III, on the judicial branch of government. Article III, Section 2 assures to persons accused of crimes the right of trial by jury, within the state where the crime took place. Section 3 defines treason with a clear attempt to narrow the definition, so that political opponents could not be tried as traitors, and forbids the ancient practice of confiscating the estates of traitors.

> Treason against the United States shall consist only in levying War against them, or in adhering to their Enemies, giving them Aid and

Comfort. No Person shall be convicted of Treason unless on the testimony of two witnesses to the same overt Act, or on Confession in open Court.

Congress shall have power to declare the Punishment of Treason, but no Attainder of Treason shall work Corruption of Blood, or Forfeiture except during the Life of the Person Attainted.

Two further examples of the sacredness of individual rights in the Constitution prior to the Bill of Rights appeared in Articles II and VI, which specified the oath to be taken by the president and by all members of Congress and other government officials. On the oath of the president, Article II concluded:

Before he enter on the Execution of his Office, he shall take the following Oath or Affirmation:
"I do solemnly swear (or affirm) that I will faithfully execute the Office of President of the United States, and will to the best of my Ability, preserve, protect and defend the Constitution of the United States."

With regard to American civil religion and individual rights, it is significant that no reference to God was made in this oath and that new president was given to the option of swearing or affirming. There were (and are) religious groups, such as the Quakers and some Baptists, who regard swearing oaths as forbidden by Jesus in Matthew 5:34–37, which states that one should not swear by heaven or earth, by Jerusalem or by one's own head, but simply say yes or no, and that "anything more than this comes from evil." Despite these words, most Christians have been swearing oaths on the Bible throughout history, and George Washington set a famous precedent when he brought his Bible to take the oath of office and added "So help me God" to the words prescribed by the Constitution.

As Article VI specifies, however, neither the Bible nor the reference to God could be required:

The Senators and Representatives before mentioned, and the Members of the several State Legislatures, and all executive and judicial Officers, both of the United States and of the several States, shall be bound by Oath or Affirmation, to support this Constitution; but no religious Test shall ever be required as a Qualification to any Office or public Trust under the United States.

At the time this was written, eleven of the thirteen states had religious qualifications for voting, let alone holding office. Even tolerant, Quaker Pennsylvania required an oath that office holders accepted the Old and New Testaments as the word of God. Led by the Virginian James Madison and the New Yorker Alexander Hamilton, whose states had abandoned religious tests, the Constitutional Convention here took a bold step toward the separation of church and state, long before the First Amendment.

An intimate connection between religious freedom and other liberties became evident in the First Amendment to the Constitution, approved along with nine others as part of the Bill of Rights in 1791. Calls for a Bill of Rights had begun during the ratification process. Although Madison and other authors of the Constitution at first opposed the idea, thinking that they had adequately protected individual rights in the document produced by the Convention and fearful that specifying rights might lead the government to claim that everything not specified could be regulated, political necessity and second thoughts convinced them. The first Congress wrote ten Amendments, with Madison's full participation. The First Amendment is particularly dense, packed with what at first can seem an odd assortment of different rights:

> Congress shall make no law respecting an establishment of religion, or prohibiting the free exercise thereof; or abridging the freedom of speech, or of the press; or the right of the people peaceably to assemble, and to petition the Government for a redress of grievances.

In this single sentence, six rights were specified: the right to be free of a state religion; the right to practice one's own religion; the right to speak freely; the right to publish one's thoughts in written form; the right to assemble with others; and the right to petition the government. Their conjunction grew out of colonial experience, especially the experience of James Madison when the Anglican Church was established in Virginia. According to Steven Waldman in *Founding Faith* (2008), Madison witnessed Baptist preachers being arrested, beaten, jailed, and tormented in prison for refusing to obey commands to stop preaching and to stop writing to promulgate their message. Modern evangelicals who lament the absence of prayer in schools or who seek to increase the presence of religion in the "public square" might reflect that the most committed advocates of separating church and state in the 1780s were not Deists or liberals or agnostics but evangelicals, who fervently supported both Madison and Thomas Jefferson in their efforts to eliminate any connection between the Virginia government and the church.

Although it is often cited that Benjamin Franklin urged the Constitutional Convention to begin each meeting with a prayer, it is less often noted that Franklin's motion failed quickly and overwhelmingly. The Constitution itself never mentions God. On the other hand, both Washington's Continental Army and Congress from their beginnings had paid chaplains, despite protests from some. The Founders were divided (sometimes even within themselves) about how to settle the issue of church and state, and some state establishments of religion survived the Constitution, which was regarded as binding only on the federal government until the Fourteenth Amendment was passed after the Civil War. Lincoln began the practice of declaring an annual national holiday for Thanksgiving, which suggested at least an establishment of theism.

Within the Constitution, however, a godless civil religion has prevailed. Many attempts to amend the Preamble to include some mention of God have failed. With regard to the oaths taken by officeholders, the Constitution itself stood in the place of God as the object to which officeholders were required to swear. The Constitution was in that sense defined by its own language as a sacred document, the focus of an unconditional religious commitment that held political life together. No one could hold office in the United States without pledging allegiance to the Constitution.

Next among sacred things, after the liberties of individuals, the liberties of states, and the Constitution itself, came the gun. Although the right of individuals to own guns was not officially recognized by the Supreme Court until a five-to-four decision in 2008 (*District of Columbia v. Heller*), the Second Amendment has in effect made the gun a sacred object of American civil religion, by associating it with the primary sacred value of personal freedom or liberty. According to the words of the Second Amendment:

> A well regulated Militia, being necessary to the security of a free State, the right of the people to keep and bear Arms, shall not be infringed.

The importance of this Amendment can be seen in its position, second only to the cluster of personal freedoms in the First Amendment; but its meaning has changed over the centuries. Like the "right to privacy" that grew from the Fourth and Fifth and Fourteenth Amendments, the right of individuals to own guns grew only gradually from the Second. The founding generation regarded standing armies with great suspicion, took pride in the performance of militias throughout colonial history and against the British Redcoats during the Revolution, and feared that a central government bent on tyranny would move in that direction by disarming the people, making it impossible for militias to form. For much of American history, such a general disarmament was impossible for practical reasons. The need for guns to hold land taken from Indians, to defend against wild animals on farms, and to intimidate slaves created a cult of the gun. There was no thought of a separation between individual gun ownership and the potential to form a militia—or for that matter, a posse or a lynching party.

With urbanization and the rise of organized crime, conditions changed. In 1939, the Supreme Court found in *United States v. Miller* that a law banning sales of sawed-off shotguns did not violate Second Amendment rights, because such weapons had no likely role in a militia. Advocates for gun control, such as Garry Wills, have argued in recent decades that the Amendment created no personal right to own guns, but only a right of "the people" of a state to have an armed militia. Meanwhile, many other writers, and groups such as the National Rifle Association, have argued that no militia could be possible without the right of non-professional soldiers to have guns in their homes and to "bear" them outside. In 2008, the Court decided its first Second Amendment case in nearly fifty years, *District of Columbia v. Heller*, and by a five-to-four majority struck down a District of Columbia law that effectively banned handguns in the District and required that any guns kept at home be unassembled and unloaded. As part of this decision, the Court held that the Second Amendment did create an individual right to own guns, subject to restrictions with regard to mental condition, felony convictions, and other circumstances.

The gun has come to stand for the inviolability of liberty and of the individual person, which was enshrined in many provisions of the Bill of Rights. The Fourth Amendment attempted to insure against arbitrary searches:

> The right of the people to be secure in their persons, houses, papers, and effects, against unreasonable searches and seizures, shall not be violated, and no Warrants shall issue, but upon a probable cause, supported by Oath or affirmation, and particularly describing the place to be searched, and the persons or things to be seized.

Even if a person was arrested, the Fifth Amendment forbade the government from putting that person on trial for a serious crime without an indictment by fellow citizens. In addition, the Fifth Amendment protected people accused of crimes against double jeopardy (being tried more than once for the same crime) and against being required to testify against themselves. During aggressive investigations of communists and gangsters in the middle of the twentieth century, "taking the Fifth" became shorthand for invoking the right not to be forced to incriminate oneself. Property was also associated with personal liberty by the Fifth Amendment, and protected against seizure in criminal cases without court proceedings and against being arbitrarily taken for public use.

> No person shall be held to answer for a capital, or otherwise infamous crime, unless on a presentment or indictment of a Grand Jury, except in cases arising in the land or naval forces, or in the Militia, when in actual service in time of War or public danger; nor shall any person be

subject for the same offense to be twice put in jeopardy of life or limb; nor shall be compelled in any criminal case to be a witness against himself, nor be deprived of life, liberty, or property, without due process of law; nor shall private property be taken for public use, without just compensation.

The Fourth and Fifth Amendments together have been held (since *Griswold v. Connecticut*, 1965) to establish a constitutional "right of privacy." As the provisions of the Bill of Rights have been more and more applied to the states through the "due process" and "equal protection" clauses of the Fourteenth Amendment (already quoted earlier in this chapter), the right of privacy arising from the Fourth and Fifth Amendments has been used to strike down state laws banning contraception, abortion, and sodomy between consenting adults. This process has been slow, and it remains controversial. The Fourteenth Amendment was passed in 1868, as an effort to ensure that slaves were not brought back into bondage by state law, but Connecticut was still prosecuting private conversations between doctors and patients about birth control in 1965, and sodomy between married heterosexuals was still illegal in Texas until 2003. The Court had upheld a Georgia sodomy law in 1986. Nonetheless, it seems that what Justice William O. Douglas (in *Griswold*) called a "penumbra" of protection for personal privacy has emerged from the specific protections against unwarranted search and self-incrimination in the Bill of Rights. Personal privacy has taken its place as an essential aspect of the liberty that is held sacred in American civil religion.

Much earlier than privacy, at the same time as political rights, the Constitution also established that the physical integrity of the person was a sacred value. Here, the American civil religion of 1791 could be said to have advanced a new understanding of personal liberty, generally accepted in the West today, which was not accepted by Christian governments at the time or in countries practicing Muslim *shariah* law today. According to the Eighth Amendment:

> Excessive bail shall not be required, nor excessive fines imposed, nor cruel and unusual punishments inflicted.

By "cruel and unusual," the members of Congress meant the mutilations that had been inflicted on religious and political dissenters and on those convicted of treason in England and America. Those who spoke publicly against the king in the 1600s were commonly punished by having their tongue bored through with a hot iron and their ears cut off. In Massachusetts, such punishment had been inflicted on Quakers in 1657 and 1658. Traitors faced the more serious fate of being "drawn and quartered," or hanged to the point of death, then cut down and dismembered before they were killed. Convicted traitors and spies were still being punished in this way in England in the eighteenth century, and the laws requiring it remained on the books until 1814. Even today, some nations (such as Iran and Saudi Arabia, and the northern provinces of Nigeria) that practice Islamic law still cut off the right hands of thieves and stone adulterers to death. By forbidding such practices, the Eighth Amendment made the sacredness of the body a fundamental aspect of American liberty.

Concern for the body may have gone too far on January 16, 1919, when an Eighteenth Amendment to the Constitution was ratified banning alcohol from the United States.

> After one year from the ratification of this article the manufacture, sale, or transportation of intoxicating liquors within, the importation thereof into, or the exportation thereof from the United States and all territory subject to the jurisdiction thereof for beverage purposes is hereby prohibited.

Here the Constitution came to reflect, at least for the fourteen years until this Amendment was repealed, the religious views of groups such as Methodists, Baptists, and the Women's Christian Temperance Union. It seems safe to say that only in the United States, among all nations dominated by Christians and Jews at least, would the prohibition of alcohol have ever been attempted. The fact that the Amendment passed, and that it remained in effect from 1920 until 1933, testifies to a powerful association of the physical with the moral and spiritual in American civil religion.

Though the Eighteenth Amendment was repealed, the questions it raised about personal freedom or liberty within American civil religion still remain alive. Under laws passed during the "War on Drugs" proclaimed by President Nixon in 1971, about a million people are arrested for drug use every year, and as one result of mandatory sentencing laws, about a quarter of the 2.2 million people in prison in the United States are there for using and/or selling drugs. The United States has never been able to develop a harm-reduction strategy for alcohol, for marijuana and cocaine, for hallucinogens and heroin, or even for prescription pain relievers, stimulants, and depressants, which had become the most widely abused drugs by teenagers by 2008. In the moral universe of American civil religion, the options regarding substance use and abuse have been dualistic: medicinal or illegal, prescribed or punished. Medical marijuana laws and decriminalization measures passed by several states have recently posed a new challenge to the constitutional primacy of the national government. The right of privacy and the right to religious freedom have both been cited in defense of a right to use mood-altering substances. In this area, as with the issue of gay marriage, it appears that American civil religion now holds different concepts of personal freedom sacred in different states.

Similar differences have affected American values regarding adult status and responsibility. The age of consent to sexual intercourse, for example, was set by English common law tradition at ten in most states into the 1880s, before a Purity Crusade by women's groups succeeded in raising it to a range between fourteen and twenty-one, depending on state laws and circumstances including parental consent and the age of the sexual partner. During the years of the Vietnam War, when it was national policy to draft eighteen-year-olds first, as opposed to the older focus of the draft from World War II, the contrast between liability to be drafted and lack of political rights led to a movement to lower the voting age, which succeeded in passing the Twenty-Sixth Amendment in 1971:

> The rights of citizens of the United States, who are eighteen years of age or older, to vote should not be denied or abridged by the United States or by any State on account of age.

Most religions have standards for adulthood, often marked by rituals, but in recent years the standards for adulthood in American law have been moving both younger and older. As of 1984, twenty-three states set the minimum age for alcohol purchase and consumption at twenty-one, and a majority of twenty-seven set the age younger. President Reagan initiated a policy under which states that did not enact laws raising the age to twenty-one would not receive federal highway funds, and Congress passed a law to that effect. Although Wyoming held out until 1998, the fifty states now all have laws against citizens under twenty-one buying or consuming alcohol. At the same time, state laws and court cases seem to be settling on eighteen as the line for abortion without parental consent, and several categories of girls or women (emancipated minors, and those who could prove a medical emergency or parental abuse) can have abortions without consent or notification at younger ages. The involvement of young people in the campaign of Barack Obama for the presidency gave additional impetus to a movement to lower the voting age to sixteen.

Because the legal standards were so varied and so much emotion was evoked by these issues, the definition of an adult in America seemed more and more a matter of religious conviction. The Constitution had from the beginning set varying standards for holders of varying federal offices, with a minimum age of twenty-five for members of the House of Representatives, thirty for members of the Senate (a word derived from *senex*, the Latin for "old"), and thirty-five for the presidency. In this area, as in many others, the Constitution determined that American civil religion would be flexible and broad.

Perhaps in part because of this flexibility and breadth, the Constitution as an object has neither evoked reverence nor inspired rituals to the extent that the Declaration of Independence has. The Declaration was a decisive act, completed at once, expressed in a rhetoric of affirmation and argument that contained its own accomplishment in itself, while the Constitution provided a framework for deciding questions. The Centennial of the Declatation, in 1876, and the Bicentennial in 1976 have occasioned great fairs and celebrations, and July 4 punctuates the summer every year with a reminder of the Declaration. On the other hand, Constitution Day (September 17), commemorating the signing of the document by members of the Convention in 1787, is noted in passing, but is not celebrated with school closings or parades and fireworks.

In 1883, historian J. Franklin Jameson found the original, signed copy of the Constitution folded inside a tin box at the bottom of a closet in the building housing the State, War, and Navy departments, close to the room where the Declaration was proudly displayed. The physical Constitution has gained much ground since. It and the Declaration were moved together to the Library of Congress in 1921. A National Archives building was constructed in the form of a temple, in part for the purpose of displaying both documents, in 1935. During World War II, both the Declaration and the Constitution were taken together to Fort Knox, and they were installed together in the Rotunda for the Charters of Freedom at the Archives building in 1952. Today, visitors stream through that Rotunda every day, like pilgrims seeking proximity to holy relics or icons.

Surveys reveal that many of these visitors have almost as little knowledge of what the Constitution says as the distant descendants of humans who featured in an episode of the original *Star Trek* series from 1968. In that science fiction scenario, Captain James Kirk of the U.S.S. Enterprise intervened in a war between Yangs (Yanks) and Coms (Communists) on a planet settled by humans centuries before. When the Yangs showed Kirk their holy things, he was shocked to find an American flag and a document the Yang chief called the "Ee pleb nista." The camera revealed the familiar, large calligraphy of "We the People" on a facsimile of the Constitution, which Captain Kirk apparently knew well. Reverently holding the document, Kirk read the entire Preamble aloud. He interpreted it for the Yangs, emphasizing that "We the People" meant all the people, not only chiefs or priests, and not only Yangs but Coms as well. Stunned, the ignorant but good-hearted leader of the Yangs assured the starship captain that in the future, the holy words would be followed.

According to cultural historian Michael Kammen, a religious attitude that he named "constitutionalism" has inspired Americans to protect the Constitution from attempts to destroy it, as in the Civil War, or to seriously alter its operation, as in the proposal by President Franklin Roosevelt to make the Supreme Court less independent by adding members. Documenting the effects of "constitutionalism," Kammen pointed out the remarkable durability of the US Constitution, noting that out of 160 national constitutions in existence when he was writing in 1983, 101 had been written after 1970. It could also be said that the modern great powers, nations like France and Britain, Germany and Japan, Russia and China each have had multiple constitutions, or in Britain's case constitutional revolutions, since the United States ratified its Constitution in 1788. Frustrations over the Electoral College, particularly in the wake of the 2000 and 2004 presidential elections, over the conservative effects of a Senate that does not represent the population, and over a Supreme Court that waxes liberal or conservative according to the undemocratic decisions of lifetime judges, have led to some commentators calling the Constitution outmoded, but no call for basic change seems likely to gain traction. Religions are naturally conservative, and the Constitution has become a sacred scripture of American civil religion.

Weaknesses do arise from the Constitution's status as sacred scripture. Scriptures may be revered without being effective law. Just as the laws of the Hebrew Scriptures about keeping the Sabbath and the words of Jesus about nonviolence have been honored by Jews and Christians mainly in the breach, so the Constitution of the United States has frequently been breached by those who profess to honor it. Congress passed the Smith Act in 1940, making it a crime to advocate overthrowing the government of the United States by "force or violence," despite the freedom of speech promised in the First Amendment, and Congress and the Supreme Court have ratified that choice. In October of 2001, the U.S.A. Patriot Act passed by Congress authorized the government to listen to phone calls and to intercept e-mails to a degree that seemed opposed to the rights against searches without warrants and self-incrimination promised by the Fourth and Fifth Amendments. However ineffective constitutional protections of some rights may be, the Constitution remains the primary document defining the values of personal freedom and political democracy that American civil religion holds sacred.

SOURCES

Ellis, Joseph, *American Creation: Triumphs and Tragedies at the Founding of the Republic* (New York: Alfred A. Knopf, 2007).

Kammen, Michael, *A Machine That Would Go of Itself: The Constitution in American Culture* (New York: Alfred A. Knopf, 1986).

Nisbet, Lee, *The Gun Control Debate: You Decide* (Amherst, NY: Prometheus Books, 2001). Articles by Richard Hofstadter, Joyce Lee Malcolm, and Garry Wills.

Waldman, Steven, *Founding Faith: Providence, Politics, and the Birth of Religious Freedom in America* (New York: Random House, 2008).

13

Washington, D.C.: The City, the Capitol, and the White House

A city of breathtaking vistas and tedious walks, Washington was intended to provoke awe. As the nation's capital, Washington is home to many sacred places of American civil religion. Other chapters deal with places within Washington, such as the Lincoln Memorial, the Vietnam Veterans Memorial, and recent additions to the National Mall. This chapter describes how the design of the District of Columbia, and especially the first buildings called for by that design, the Capitol and the White House, created sacred space. It also discusses how the sacred quality of the District has been affected by centuries of contention over race, gender, class, and politics.

Among the powers granted to Congress in Article I, Section 8 of the Constitution is the right to "exclusive legislation" over a District, "not exceeding ten miles square," that may be granted by individual states as the capital of the new United States. The choice of a location for this District at the border of Maryland and Virginia had much to do with George Washington, who always favored a place near his home at Mt. Vernon, Virginia. It also represented a compromise between the Northern states, which had the largest cities and the earliest national capitals, at Philadelphia and New York, and the South, which had the larger territory, plantation wealth to pay off the national debt from the Revolutionary War, and better connections with the West. The shape of the district grew from a roughly triangular intersection between two rivers, the Potomac on the west and the Anacostia on the east, flowing together and on to Chesapeake Bay. Following these rivers, the borders of the District were drawn as a diamond, or a square with sides ten miles long, sitting on its southernmost point.

The streets of Washington became a network of triangles, traffic circles, squares, and open rectangles because of Pierre L'Enfant, the young Franco-American architect and engineer who was hired by George Washington (himself a professional surveyor) to lay out the Federal District. Although Thomas Jefferson (who as secretary of state and amateur architect exerted much

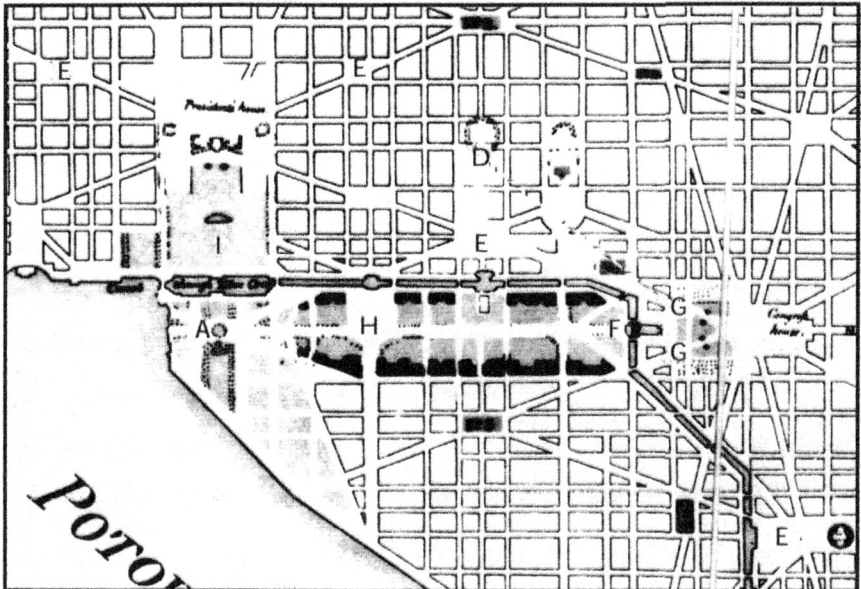

Figure 13.1 The plan of the capital by Pierre L'Enfant. The triangle of a President's House and a House of Congress, connected by Pennsylvania Avenue, with the Washington Monument at the angle, remains. The Mall extends on landfill a mile to the left, and the White House is smaller than L'Enfant intended. Library of Congress, National Park Service.

influence) suggested a compact, square grid at the center of the District for government buildings, L'Enfant projected an enormous pattern of streets (see Figure 13.1), larger than London or Paris and many times larger than the area for government in Jefferson's plan. In L'Enfant's concept, the north-south grid of streets that form square blocks was broken by angled avenues connecting major points, beginning with the Capitol and the president's house. L'Enfant's streets and avenues were incredibly wide (160 feet, more than 50 yards), and he also included a National Mall at the center. The Capitol building would divide the city into triangular quadrants—northeast, northwest, southwest, southeast. On a map, which would have been a mere abstraction in the 1790s, the whole district would be a diamond, with each point facing one of the four cardinal directions. But even at ground level in the modern city, because of the angled avenues breaking through square blocks of streets and the division into quadrants, the District is experienced as a triangular space that claims to be the center of the world, the place where all roads meet. A problem arises because two competing centers, the original at the Capitol and another at the White House, have evolved in the city. A star at the center of the Capitol Crypt marks the place where the quadrants of the District come together, while the Zero Milestone measuring the distance from Washington for all US roads stands not near the Capitol but on the Ellipse in front of the South Lawn of the White House. The effect of angles converging on a center remains powerful, but disorienting.

The shapes of Washington perform many functions and bear many messages. From a practical standpoint, the angled avenues were intended by L'Enfant to facilitate rapid travel between important buildings and unimpeded vistas from one of these buildings to another. In Europe, planners also favored such avenues to enable smooth movements of the troops that might be needed to control the capital, and L'Enfant may have considered such a function without writing about it. During the last six months of 1783, Congress had been chased from Philadelphia to Princeton, then to Trenton, and finally to Annapolis by Revolutionary War veterans demanding pay.

With regard to symbolism, the shapes of the two triangles suggested pyramids, an important shape in the Masonic tradition to which Washington, Jefferson, Franklin, and many others (probably including L'Enfant) of the founding generation belonged. Masons claimed that their traditions originated with the builders of the pyramids. The diamond shape of the District also echoed another symbol of Masonry, a compass and square brought together with the compass on top. Normally, the angle of the compass in Masonic symbols is acute, but on the Masonic apron that Lafayette gave to George Washington in 1784 the compass is set at ninety degrees, so that it forms a diamond in combination with the square. Conspiracy theorists have seen a Masonic plot, and sometimes even an attempt to control the government through magic, embedded in the layout of the District. Such speculations are not needed to support the argument that the triangles and squares of the District would have been pleasing and familiar to Masons like George Washington.

The history of religions offers other parallels. As a city set on a north-south axis, with its most important official living in a house on the northern end of a vast public mall, the District repeats the shape of Chinese capital cities, where the emperor sat in a palace at the north and faced the public to the south. As a city of many square blocks with a central garden, Washington echoes the pattern of the New Jerusalem that comes down from Heaven to be the habitation of the saints in Revelation 21.

The Capitol building, especially the Capitol dome, forms part of Washington's most powerful vistas. The dome ranks alongside the Statue of Liberty and the White House among the most recognizable architectural symbols of the United States. Begun only in 1859, after parts of the Capitol building had already been in use for almost sixty years, with a humbler dome for thirty of those years, the present dome rises from the highest hill in the area laid out for government buildings, an 88-foot elevation that L'Enfant described as a "pediment waiting for a monument." The Capitol dome's proportions follow those of the domes of St. Peter's Basilica in Rome (1590), St. Paul's Cathedral in London (1708), the Church of Sainte Geneviève, now called the Panthéon, in Paris (1789), and the dome of St. Isaac's Cathedral in St. Petersburg, the imperial capital of Russia (begun 1818, completed 1858). All of these domes share an elongated shape, an aspiration toward the sky that differentiates them from the more spherical domes of ancient Rome and of mosques. From the Vatican to London to Paris to St. Petersburg to Washington, tall domes mark the capitals of modern powers that have aspired to worldwide dominion.

When the Capitol was first built, beginning with the Senate wing in 1800 and completed by 1829 (with an interruption because of its near destruction by the British in the War of 1812), its dome was much lower and more classical, designed by Charles Bulfinch with proportions reproducing the dome of the Roman Pantheon (96 feet in diameter and 96 feet tall), a shape that is repeated in the dome of the Jefferson Memorial and many other Washington buildings. Jefferson himself asked L'Enfant for a building modeled on a Roman temple, and Washington favored a dome, so that even during the contest that was held for designs, it was expected that the Capitol would be the first domed building in the United States. Neither the original architect of the building, William Thornton, nor the second, Benjamin Latrobe, was able to complete the central section and the dome, but these were always essential to their concepts. In Jefferson's intention, the Capitol building would not only furnish meeting rooms for the houses of Congress, but also provide the United States with a Rotunda that Jefferson called "the Hall of the People," where inaugurations, impeachment trials, and religious ceremonies would take place. The present, soaring dome of the Capitol (still 96 feet wide, but now 300 feet high, and uniquely constructed of iron painted to resemble marble) was designed by architect Thomas Walter and completed in its exterior in 1863, during the Civil War administration of Abraham Lincoln, at the same time that the federal government was attaining the increased coercive power it has held ever since. It is easy to argue that Jefferson would have disapproved of the grandeur and height of the current Capitol dome, but harder to imagine that he could deny its effectiveness in projecting power.

Freedom both gained and lost a symbol at the top of the dome, where a statue of Freedom was projected as part of the design (see Figure 13.2). In 1855, sculptor Thomas Crawford made a plaster cast of the statue in Rome and sent it to Washington, where its hat provoked the ire of Jefferson Davis, then secretary of war and soon to be president of the Confederacy. The statue, nineteen and a half feet tall, wore on her head a *pileus*, the soft cap worn by freed slaves in the ceremony of manumission in ancient Rome and made famous again in the French Revolution. No doubt disapproving of the message this might send to American slaves and Abolitionists, Davis protested that such a symbol was inappropriate for the freedom of people like United States citizens, who had never been

Figure 13.2 Atop the Capitol dome stands a statue of Freedom, nineteen and half feet tall. Freedom was designed by sculptor Thomas Crawford wearing a *pileus*, the soft cap of liberated Roman slaves, but the objections of Jefferson Davis (secretary of war in 1855) led to the cap's replacement by a helmet with eagle feathers. Architect of the Capitol.

enslaved. Political pressure resulted in the cap being replaced by a helmet with eagle feathers, which is now described in the Capitol Visitors' Center as a gesture "in homage to the American Indian." Ironically, this edited symbol of freedom was translated from its plaster model, cast in bronze, and assembled primarily by a slave, Philip Reid, one of the few out of the hundreds of slaves who worked on the Capitol who was paid directly for his work. Reid worked in the studio of an Onondaga (Iroquois) Indian sculptor named Clark Mills.

If Congress had succeeded in fulfilling its early intentions, the Capitol dome and Rotunda would also have been a mausoleum for George Washington. Congress sought to have Washington's body interred in a crypt below the Rotunda, but the Washington family refused, citing the first president's clearly expressed wishes to be buried at Mt. Vernon. Even without the body, however, the Rotunda became to some degree a temple to Washington because of a fresco, *The Apotheosis of Washington*, which Constantino Brumidi was assigned to paint inside the dome during the Civil War and which he completed after the war was over, in 1865.

At the center of the Rotunda's ceiling, which was constructed under the dome about fifteen stories (180 feet) from the floor, the painted Washington looks down from the heavens, surrounded by angelic females who represent Liberty, Victory, and the thirteen states of his time. A circle of clouds makes it clear that the father of the United States is in the highest heaven. Around the edges of the ceiling below those clouds, the Roman divinities Ceres, goddess of grain; Neptune, god of the sea; Venus, goddess of love; Minerva, goddess of wisdom; Vulcan, god of the forge; and Mercury, god of commerce interact with famous Americans like Robert Fulton, inventor of the steam boat, and Samuel F. B. Morse, inventor of the telegraph. A depiction of the goddess of Freedom, resembling the statue of Freedom atop the dome and brandishing a sword, pursues figures such as Tyranny, Kingly Power, Anger, and Discord. It has been both asserted and denied that some of these enemies of Freedom are painted to resemble Confederate leaders, including Jefferson Davis and General Robert E. Lee. The whole world of the painting is so fantastic that it is easy to see why Mark Twain called Brumidi's fresco "the *delirium tremens* of art." On the other hand, the fresco gives clear evidence that within seventy years of George Washington's death, it seemed fitting to Americans to depict him as a god, sitting in the posture of Jupiter above the other powers of heaven. *The Apotheosis of Washington* still soars over what writer Jesse Holland calls "the most awe-inspiring room visitors will encounter in the Washington, D.C., area."

The eight enormous (each 12 by 18 feet) murals on the walls of the Rotunda also feature revered ancestors, but not in the company of gods and angels. Viewed on the horizontal plane rather than by spectators lifting their eyes toward heaven, these murals show some of the more human, democratic values of the American civil religion in historical events rather than mythical allegories. This is especially true of the four painted by John Trumbull and installed in the 1820s. Trumbull's murals depict the Declaration of Independence, the American victory at Saratoga, the surrender of the British at Yorktown, and Washington's resignation of his commission as commander in chief. As Trumbull explicitly intended, the subject of the whole series is the birth and securing of American democracy. Following the norms of epic, historical painting that had just been invented by artists like Trumbull's teacher Benjamin West and by Jean-Louis David, the painter of the French Revolution whom Trumbull met in Paris, Trumbull strove to combine realism with an illustration of the meaning of events. Most of the figures in each mural were painted from life. Though the groupings were invented and the interior backgrounds were more elaborately decorated than the actual rooms, the artist visited the places he depicted. Trumbull chose and composed the scenes to show democratic heroes interacting with each other on the basis of equality, behaving politely to defeated enemies, and renouncing any drive toward personal power or eminence.

As the first paintings ever commissioned by Congress, John Trumbull's murals actually saved the Rotunda itself in the 1820s, when architect Charles

Bulfinch was being pressured to find more space for offices and meeting rooms for Congressional committees. Bulfinch offered Trumbull, already hard at work on the murals, an alternative place to display them in a gallery above new meeting rooms, but the artist persuaded the architect that the paintings were specifically designed for this Rotunda and this lighting. Convinced, Bulfinch created meeting rooms below the South wing of the Capitol, where the ground fell off more steeply, and the Rotunda survived.

Many have noted the contrast between Trumbull's humanistic celebrations of the American Revolution and the other four murals of the Rotunda, which were added between 1840 and 1855. These are both more Christian in content and more concerned with the conquest of the continent and its native peoples. The later murals are *The Baptism of Pocahontas*, by John Gadsby Chapman (1840); *The Embarkation of the Pilgrims*, by Robert Weir (1844); *The Landing of Columbus*, by John Vanderlyn (1847); and *The Discovery of the Mississippi*, by William H. Powell (1855). In the Pocahontas and Pilgrim paintings, the competing claims of Jamestown and Plymouth Rock as birthplaces of English America are balanced. Columbus and Hernando DeSoto (discoverer of the Mississippi) balance the stories of East and West. Three of the four paintings show Native Americans as spectators to the action, generally watching from postures of fear, rejection, or incomprehension. All four of these later murals feature Christian symbols such as a cross, a crucifix, Bibles, and clergy in prayer.

Around the wall of the Rotunda between the murals and the fresco on the dome, about 60 feet above the floor, there was a blank space 9 feet high below a balcony. Thomas Walter and his collaborator, Captain Montgomery C. Meigs of the Army Corps of Engineers, intended to fill the space with a carved frieze modeled on the Parthenon of Athens, telling the story of American history with three hundred feet of marble sculpture, but the money for this marble frieze was never appropriated. Constantino Brumidi proposed a painted fresco with a dark background, to give the effect of a frieze, and he was finally commissioned to paint one in 1877. As a letter written by Meigs in 1855 said, the intention was to show the "gradual progress of a continent from the depths of barbarism to the height of civilization." The result enshrined a concept of Manifest Destiny and extended that dream to both continents of the Americas, following a model that had been set forth in histories by George Bancroft, Francis Parkman, and William H. Prescott.

Brumidi projected sixteen scenes, which together represented a sacred history of the United States. The series began with a female "America" wearing a Liberty cap, accompanied by an eagle holding fasces in its talons. It continued through Columbus descending from his ship to a group of Indians; Cortez at the capital of Montezuma; Pizarro leading his men to Peru; DeSoto being buried in the Mississippi; John Smith being saved by Pocahontas; the landing of the Pilgrims;

William Penn making a treaty with the Indians of Pennsylvania; New England being cultivated and settled; James Oglethorpe making a treaty with the Indians of Georgia; the Battle of Lexington; the Declaration of Independence being read in public; the surrender of Cornwallis; the death in battle of Tecumseh, who had tried to unify Native Americans; the US Army entering Mexico City; and the discovery of gold in California. Unfortunately, the process of getting approval for the paintings took eighteen years, and Brumidi died before he could complete his plan. Another Italian-American artist, Filippo Costaggini, continued the work in the midst of the eighth panel, in the figure of William Penn, who wears one shoe painted by each artist. When all sixteen panels of the original project were done, thirty-one feet of the circumference of the Rotunda remained unpainted, because the original width of panels 9 feet tall had been reduced in proportion to the fact that less visible space was available under the balcony than Brumidi had expected. Various scenes were proposed to fill the gap, and one called the "Spirit of 1917" was actually completed, but this scene was so disliked that it was painted over. Nothing was thought satisfactory until 1952, when painter Allyn Cox was commissioned to add three more scenes: Union and Confederate soldiers shaking hands at the end of the Civil War; a naval gun crew with its cannon in the Spanish-American War; and the Birth of Aviation, which shows the Wright brothers taking off and an American eagle flying with an olive branch.

Out of nineteen scenes in the frieze, eleven commemorate white people expanding their territory at the expense of Native Americans and Mexicans; eight represent battles and wars; and none acknowledges or depicts slavery or African-Americans. The overall message celebrates the conquest of two continents. Conquest is also celebrated in relief busts of explorers in niches over the murals and in relief panels above the four entrances to the Rotunda. The busts represent Columbus, Sir Walter Raleigh, John Cabot, and Sieur de La Salle. The relief panels are entitled *Conflict of Daniel Boone and the Indians; Landing of the Pilgrims; Preservation of Captain Smith by Pocahontas;* and *William Penn's Treaty with the Indians.* Shortly after these reliefs were completed, according to a Washington gossip named Benjamin Perley Poore, a Menominee Indian chief supposedly read their content with revealing directness. Pointing out the Indian holding corn in *Landing of the Pilgrims,* the chief said, "There Indians give hungry white man corn." Then he commented on Penn's treaty, "There Indians give white man land." Looking at the Pocahontas panel, he said, "There Indian saves white man's life." Finally, after examining the panel that shows Daniel Boone stabbing one Indian while stepping on the body of another, the chief observed, "And there white man kills Indian."

Although the paintings of the Rotunda have changed little since the late nineteenth century, the statuary in this central sanctuary of the Capitol reflects more recent history and continuing political currents. Unlike frescoes and murals, freestanding statues can be moved. Nothing is lightly moved into the Rotunda, of course. Powerful currents in American politics and revolutions of values have brought the statues that currently stand between the large murals into their places. In choosing which statues to have within the central shrine of American democracy, where ten dead presidents have lain in state, Congress decides which ancestors will be honored in the space intended as the pantheon of American civil religion.

The only women represented by sculpture in the Rotunda, for example, have reached their present position, next to Trumbull's mural of the surrender of the British at Yorktown, through an arduous process. In 1921, as part of the celebration of the Nineteenth Amendment giving women the vote, the National Women's Party presented Congress with a monument. This was the creation of Adelaide Johnson (1859–1955), who had carved the heads and shoulders of Elizabeth Cady Stanton, Susan B. Anthony, and Lucretia Mott, three founders of the movement for women's suffrage, emerging from an unfinished eight-ton block of white marble, to symbolize the constraints still holding women. Some have derided the monument as "Three Ladies in a Bathtub." Officially called *The Portrait Monument*, the work was unveiled in the Rotunda on February 15, 1921, the one hundred first anniversary of Susan B. Anthony's birth. Two days later, it was moved into the Crypt below the Rotunda, a place that was not open to the public. Bills proposed in 1928, 1932, and 1950 to bring the monument back to the Rotunda failed to pass. Even after the crypt was opened to visitors in 1963, supporters of the monument still thought its position was demeaning. During the 1990s, Speaker Newt Gingrich rejected a petition by seventy House members to raise the monument. As chair of the Capitol Preservation Commission, Gingrich controlled a fund of $23 million in privately raised money to maintain the Capitol, but he refused to spend any of it on moving the monument. Finally, in 1996, a private group raised $75,000 to cover the costs of moving, and Congress passed a resolution authorizing the move, which was accomplished in 1997.

A stranger story involving both gender and sex surrounds a statue commissioned by Congress, a white Carrara marble depicting Abraham Lincoln holding a scroll that represents the Emancipation Proclamation. Installed in the Rotunda in 1871, this statue of Lincoln was created by a woman named Lavinia (always called Vinnie) Ream, who was eighteen years old when she received the Congressional commission, in 1866. Ream had been working for two years with Clark Mills, the Native American sculptor who had his studio (as several other sculptors did) in the basement of the Capitol itself. At that time, politicians commonly ordered portrait busts of themselves, and Mills developed good political connections. Some of his political friends were from the South, and Mills was evicted from the Capitol on suspicion of sympathy with the Confederacy, leaving Ream to take over his studio. She made a bust of Lincoln, perhaps from personal visits at the White House or perhaps from a life mask that Mills had obtained, and used this bust as the basis for her application to do the Lincoln statue, though she had never done a statue before. In support of her case, she presented a testimonial signed by 178 prominent men, including President Andrew Johnson, General Ulysses S. Grant, members of the Cabinet and of Congress, and some artists.

How Vinnie Ream obtained such support became a subject of controversy. In August 1866, journalist Jane Grey Swisshelm, who had published in the feminist and anti-slavery press, wrote an assault on Ream's character that began by noting that Ream "had some busts on exhibition in the Capitol, including her own, minus clothing to the waist." Swisshelm described Ream as sitting in the Congressional galleries "in her most bewitching dress" during the discussion of the commission, and wrote that she "nods and smiles as a member rises and delivers his opinion on the merits of the case, with the air of a man sitting for his picture." For Swisshelm, it seemed a scandal that this "girl," as she called Ream, "carries the day" over sculptors like Hiram Powers, Thomas Crawford, and Harriet Hosmer. On the positive side, the magazine *Harper's Bazaar* found Ream enchanting, reporting after a visit to her studio that "she flitted about among the countless busts and faultless likenesses of Senators and Representatives, and the colossal plaster cast of the statue of Lincoln, like a bird herself." When the Lincoln statue was unveiled in 1871, the *Daily National Democrat* reported that Ream had kept the work in progress "decorated with flowers" as she worked, and that "their fragrance rising up to her seemed to inspire her when modeling the dead man's face, and has helped her to bring out in it all the true goodness of his character."

Ream and other female sculptors, such as Emma Stebbins and Alice Rideout, took part in a Victorian artistic revolution that was later derided or forgotten by historians and critics, but her reputation has recovered in the first years of the twenty-first century. A comment on the Lincoln statue published in 2004 echoed what was generally said when it was unveiled in 1871: that it took a female artist to show that "values like tenderness and humility...have a legitimate place in public life." By imagining a Lincoln who looks down with a fatherly expression, Vinnie Ream is said to have added a new perspective on one of the most iconic figures of American civil religion.

On January 16, 1986, one day after the fifty-seventh anniversary of the birth of Dr. Martin Luther King, Jr., a bust of King was placed in the Rotunda. This testified to another revolution in American values, bringing the first and only sculpture of an African-American into the Capitol, which was built by African-American slaves. The bust was authorized by Congress in 1982, about a year before the signing of legislation creating a national holiday on Martin Luther King Day.

The other sculptures in the Rotunda (as of August 2012) represent presidents George Washington, Thomas Jefferson, Andrew Jackson, Ulysses S. Grant, James Garfield, Dwight D. Eisenhower, and Ronald Reagan. The statues of Presidents Washington, Jackson, Garfield, Eisenhower, and Reagan were placed in the Rotunda by an act of Congress and will remain indefinitely, or until another act removes them. Alexander Hamilton, the first secretary of the treasury and the moving force behind the Constitution, also has a seven-foot marble statue in this American Pantheon. Although few Americans could identify much of the art of the Rotunda, about 4 million people come to see it every year, which is about twice as many as go to Lourdes or to Mecca. While the exterior of the Dome appears on television every day, as a casual background for stories from Washington or about the federal government, the most devoted followers of American civil religion make a pilgrimage into the Rotunda.

For most of its history, the Capitol was surrounded by housing, including many tenements and alleys that housed servants (see Figure 13.3). The National Mall, which now stretches for miles south of Capitol Hill to the Washington and Lincoln monuments, with museums and government offices on either side, long held a railroad station, grazing cattle, and commercial activity, including slave markets. The Chinatown of the District once began at the southwestern foot of the Hill, where the National Museum of the American Indian now stands on the Mall. But, beginning with the McMillan Commission of 1901, and continuing

Figure 13.3 This photograph of the dome's construction, taken in 1858, also shows the condition of Washington's streets, which remained unpaved well into the 1880s and dominated by commerce into the 1960s. Note the iron ribs of the dome, which is made of iron painted to resemble marble. Architect of the Capitol.

through a Supreme Court ruling of 1954 that property could be taken by eminent domain even for purely aesthetic reasons, non-governmental buildings and lower-class housing have been swept from the Hill and the Mall. Daniel Burnham, the architect who made the White City for the Chicago World's Fair of 1893, was hired to recreate it in Washington. The 1920s brought the Lincoln Memorial at the far end of the Mall. The 1930s saw the construction of the National Archives, with its shrine for the Constitution and the Declaration of Independence, at the place on the Mall that L'Enfant had intended for a national church. In 1935, the Supreme Court finally left the Capitol and moved into its own building, built in the style of a temple on a level with the Capitol at its north side.

Approximately 1.6 miles from the Capitol stands the White House, which was the other anchor of L'Enfant's plan for the District. In the original plan, a foundation for which was laid before the designer's clashes with local landowners resulted in his being fired, the building he called a "presidential palace" was to be 696 feet wide, more than two football fields, a breadth not attained by the Capitol itself until massive new wings were added during the Civil War. The residence that was actually erected was 170 feet wide, with two stories above ground rather than three. Some critics say that the building is too small for its site, and wings to the West and East have been added in the twentieth century to accommodate offices. Still, it was probably the largest house in the United States until the mansions built in the Gilded Age.

The most emotionally charged aspects of the White House are its whiteness and the regularity of its exterior. Made of stone at George Washington's insistence, rather than the brick that Jefferson recommended, the walls were whitewashed from the beginning, and then covered with thick white paint to disguise charring after the British burned the house in 1814. One night during the Civil War, Walt Whitman "took a long look at the President's house" lit by a "lustrous flooding moon" and gaslights, and marveled: "everything so white, so marbly pure and dazzling, yet soft." The basic façade resembles that of Leinster House, the residence of an Irish duke built in the eighteenth century near the birthplace of the White House architect, James Hoban, but the addition of a projecting portico (also designed by Hoban, just before he died) in 1829 gave the president's house more resemblance to a temple. Though "the White House" was a common name for the building from the beginning, it did not become the official name of the building until the administration of Theodore Roosevelt.

Washington took a strong personal interest in the house, although he knew that he would never live there. He personally marked off the site, within L'Enfant's enormous foundations, where the actual house would be built. His experiences of entertaining at the president's houses in Philadelphia and at Mt. Vernon had convinced him of the need for a large residence and particularly for a large room, now called the East Room, for receptions. After a clash with

Congress, Washington succeeded in getting the Treasury and War departments located next to the president's house rather than near the Capitol.

The most emblematic room in the White House, the Oval Office, takes its shape indirectly from Washington's practice of greeting visitors at formal receptions, which were called levées following the custom of the British monarchy, in the president's house at Philadelphia. Once a week, Washington would have the doors of the house opened at 3 P.M. and stand before a fireplace. As each caller entered, he would be announced by a servant, approach the president, and bow, saying nothing, then take his place in a circle of visitors around the room. When the circle was complete, Washington would walk around it, bowing but not shaking hands, greeting each man and saying something, possibly political though not confidential. After the guests had been addressed, Washington would return to his place. Each visitor would approach again, one by one, bow and depart. In a democratic change from the practice of royal levées, the guests were allowed to turn their backs to Washington as they left the room, rather than exiting walking backward as they would when leaving a king. The oval Blue Room of the White House was designed as a setting for these levées, which John Adams continued but Jefferson dropped. Still, the Blue Room retained its prominence because of its centrality and its striking view onto the South Lawn and the national Mall, with a perspective that eventually included the Jefferson and Washington monuments. As one historian wrote, "In Washington's bow can be found the seed of the oval shape of the Blue Room." Another scholar noted that, "[i]n a wonderful migration of symbols," the Blue Room gave rise to the room that has become "the most common representation of the presidency itself." The Oval Office was not part of the original house, but was foreshadowed by the Blue Room and built first under William Howard Taft, as part of a West Wing extension in 1909. That extension burned in the 1920s. The present Oval Office dates from Franklin Delano Roosevelt. If those who visit the president sometimes complain that the office was deliberately made in an oval shape to disorient them, it could be that they are sensing the atmosphere of the formal, presidential levées that lay behind the shape.

Most rooms of the White House are stately but not sacred, functioning as spaces in a living museum rather than as a temple like the Capitol Rotunda. Even the East Room, where the bodies of Lincoln and John F. Kennedy were laid out before being moved to the Capitol, is basically a reception hall where Tad Lincoln once rode a cart pulled by goats, Theodore Roosevelt held wrestling matches, and Amy Carter scarred the floor with her roller skates. One object in the room has the status of an icon: the oldest thing in the White House other than the exterior walls, a full-length portrait of Washington, painted by Gilbert Stuart in 1797, which Dolly Madison had removed from its frame and rolled up just before she fled the British, who burned the house in 1814. Because the pose of Washington in the painting resembles a statue of the Emperor Augustus, it has sometimes been criticized as imperial.

Upstairs, the room now called the Lincoln Bedroom, which contains a bed in which Lincoln did sleep (though he disapproved of its cost), was actually Lincoln's office. It still holds furnishings from his time, and so exudes some sense of sanctity. However, no interior wall or floor of the White House actually dates from any time before 1948, when President Truman found the building so unsound that he had to have it completely gutted and remade in steel and concrete. Problems arose because, in the rebuilding after the 1814 fire, James Hoban had to save time and money by using wooden floors and supports where he had first used stone and brick. Even in Lincoln's day, the floor of the East Room was held up by logs moved in to prevent collapse.

Outside, the White House projects very different feelings to the north and south. At the north side, where the square North Portico marks the front door, the boundary fence is one block from the portico and on the same level as the house. Demonstrators gather constantly. Some hold signs that might actually be read from the house; some give speeches to crowds; some wear costumes, such as prison jumpsuits. Guardhouses to check the credentials of those who have business in the house stand next to driveways. Meanwhile, on the south side, the South Lawn extends down a hill for more than two blocks. Those who gather here do not protest, but look up at the rounded South Portico over a fountain and see only the center of the house, because rows of trees on either side of the South Lawn hide the wings. People take pictures of each other and of the building in silence, with the attitude of worshippers or of people approaching royalty. At the north, the city can be seen and felt around the White House, but at the south, a park of four square blocks called the Ellipse links directly to the Mall, and anyone who turns away from the house sees the Washington Monument and the Jefferson Memorial in the distance. President Truman added the Truman Balcony, at the second floor level of the South Portico, so that the president, the president's family, and their guests could enjoy this sacred landscape in privacy.

As the most important sites of the District have become larger and better developed, they have also become more distant from the people, and Washington has come more and more to resemble what commentator Sam Smith called it in 1974, "democracy's Disneyland." Residents of the city and visitors have both been affected. Tides in American race relations have washed over Washington and changed its native landscape, while political power and violence have shaped the history and spirit of the capital city.

Until the middle of the twentieth century, the federal district consistently held a population that was about 30 percent African-American. One provision of the Compromise of 1850, which allowed California to enter the Union as a free state, while New Mexico and Utah chose their status by vote, ended the slave trade (though not slavery itself) in Washington. During the Civil War, the District became a Mecca for slaves fleeing the South, and with Lincoln's assassination, radical Republicans wanted to make its government an example. Voter registration was opened to all in 1867, and for about ten years the District became "the colored man's paradise," in the words of Mary Church Terrell, author of *Colored Woman in a White World*. Congress permitted an elected city council, and the council not only included some black citizens but also passed ordinances forbidding racial discrimination in hotels, restaurants, bars, and theaters. Frederick Douglass founded a black newspaper, the *New Era*, Howard University gave former slaves a college education, the District's public schools were supported equally in black and white neighborhoods, and the federal government hired black men for all sorts of office work. An African-American named James Wormley ran the best hotel in the city, and at the ball celebrating Ulysses S. Grant's second inauguration in 1873, the races mixed on the dance floor. White political bosses used thousands of black workers in public works projects that accomplished major goals, such as channeling the polluted river that once ran near the White House into an underground course and paving Pennsylvania Avenue.

Shocked by the fiscal crash of 1873 and by disclosures of enormous spending on public works in Washington, Congress passed a temporary measure in 1874 that put the government of the District under a panel appointed by the president. The end of Reconstruction in 1876 brought an end to home rule in the District and to racial equality. In 1878, an Organic Act made the appointed governing panel permanent, and citizens of the District would not vote for local officials again for ninety years. Then the Supreme Court ruled that segregation in private business could be legal. By the time Frederick Douglass died, in 1895, even he would not have been served at a white restaurant in Washington. Still, Howard University continued its work, the Dunbar High School offered a college preparatory course within the black school system, and black businessmen dominated catering and continued to run hotels and even a bank. The paradoxes of race in Washington were well illustrated at the dedication of the Lincoln Memorial in 1922, when the president of the Tuskegee Institute, Robert Russa Moten, was a featured speaker, but had to walk to the platform across a road that separated the black seating area from the white. Because white Southerners had so much power in Congress, and Congress ran the District, the direction of change through the 1930s was not toward equality.

The increase in government employment because of World War II brought the District to the largest population it has ever known, 802,000 in the 1950 census. The war also caused new reflection on racial ideologies, which resulted in a scathing report on *Segregation in Washington* (1947), commissioned by the Julius Rosenwald Foundation and prepared by Professor Joseph Lohman of the University of Chicago. While resistance to segregation had never entirely ceased—the Negro Alliance boycotted A & P food stores and People's Drug Stores in the 1930s—now action had more chance of success. In 1953, the Supreme Court ruled that the ordinances passed by District city councils during Reconstruction should still be enforced against a restaurant that refused service to African-Americans. The next year brought *Brown v. Board of Education*, the landmark school desegregation case.

After *Brown* made school segregation illegal, whites began to flee urban school districts across the country, and the District was no exception. The 1960 census was the first to show a black majority, 411,737 to 345,263, making Washington the first large majority-black city in the United States. Total population had fallen by about forty thousand in ten years. These trends continued through the 1960s, with the additional impetus of a serious riot by blacks in the summer of 1968, and the population reached a 76 percent black majority in 1970. President Nixon called the District the "crime capital of the world" as he campaigned for re-election in 1972. Washington quickly became the most heavily policed city in the nation. District police, Capitol police, National Park police, Executive Services police, and thousands of other law enforcement officers from the military and from government agencies began to crack down. Urban renewal programs moved thousands of poor people, almost all black, out of the Southwest and Foggy Bottom areas near the Mall and government buildings and into Southeast area projects, across the Anacostia River and far from the tourists and officials. By 1980, trends had begun to reverse, with the black population falling far faster than the white. The total population of the District went down to 638,000 in 1980, 606,000 in 1990, and 572,000 in 2000, then rose again to 601,723 in 2010 and an estimated 632,323 in 2012. Almost all of the losses of population were among blacks. White population held steady, and so rose in percentage to 42.9 percent by 2012, with blacks at 50.9 percent.

In the late twentieth and early twenty-first centuries, concerns about security and the power of money made minorities, tourists, and natives of the District less visible around sacred places such as the Capitol, the White House, and even the Mall. The Oklahoma City truck bombing of 1995, the worst terrorist attack in American history before 2001, led to the closing of Pennsylvania Avenue to vehicular traffic on the block occupied by the White House. The aftermath of the September 11, 2001, attacks on the World Trade Center and the Pentagon accelerated the process. Streets approaching the Capitol were blocked, so that private citizens could no longer drive their cars to the Capitol steps. For most Americans, tours of the Capitol and the White House became impossible without passes from the offices of their Representatives, which took time— anywhere from one month to six months—to obtain. A new Visitors' Center opened in the Capitol in 2008, with speeches that included Senate Majority

Leader Harry Reid giving thanks (in a speech that embarrassed many) that the visitors he could once smell coming into the Rotunda would now be brought in gradually, through an air-conditioned space underground. Tours of the Capitol, which once routinely included the meeting rooms of the House and Senate, were limited to a few minutes at one station in the Rotunda, a few minutes in the Statuary Hall, and a moment in the Crypt. Visitors to the White House were restricted to a Visitors' Center across the street, except for those who obtained passes from their Representative months in advance. Meanwhile, gentrification near the Capitol turned blocks that had been middle-class housing into exclusive neighborhoods; urban renewal turned blocks of housing into convention centers; and the combination of Smithsonian and government money built a solid wall of museums and offices all around the Mall.

In a classic text of 1961, *The City in History*, philosopher Lewis Mumford lamented that the immediate area around the Capitol was still "spotted by an outbreak of urban eczema that a baroque architect would at least have been able to hide behind a wall, if the patron lacked sufficient authority to demolish the buildings themselves." Beginning in the 1960s and continuing for decades, the federal government took that authority to demolish and to rebuild. All of the avenues around the Mall were lined with massive edifices, horizontal skyscrapers, making up in bulk for the height they were denied by a law that limits the height of buildings relative to the breadth of streets, in effect ensuring that the Washington Monument will remain the tallest structure in the District. Two centuries after L'Enfant made his plan, the avenues he drew finally gained what Mumford wrote about the ideal avenues of baroque European capitals: buildings that "stand on each side, stiff and uniform, like soldiers at attention," so that the citizens may be "duly awed and intimidated," watching soldiers and statesmen move down the avenue, their parades resembling "a classical building in motion."

This gain in grandeur may have accompanied a loss for democracy. By 2007, according to James H. S. McGregor, the Capitol, the White House, the Supreme Court building, and many other sites in the original plan of the federal District demonstrated an "apparently necessary but markedly undemocratic exclusiveness." The major power centers of the District, McGregor concluded, had become "[w]ary of the public but open to persons with influence" and "fixed in their own histories," so that they seemed unlikely to change. On the other hand, Jeffrey F. Meyer claimed in 2001 that the "iconography" of the District, and especially of the Capitol and the Mall, "is clearly composed of a more malleable material and always open to new interpretations." Meyer pointed out that "previously excluded groups" had succeeded in claiming "the symbolic power of the national capital," and that other appropriations might be expected in the future.

There is much to recommend both the optimistic and the pessimistic views of what the developing landscape of the capital says about the development of American civil religion. Surely it is a gain to have a National Museum of the American Indian at the foot of Capitol Hill, where Chinatown once began. The museum provides some reparation for the scenes of white men killing and displacing Indians that decorate the Capitol Rotunda. Although the Mall may resemble the processional ways of imperial Babylon, Rome, Beijing, or the Champs-Élysées after which it was modeled, it has also been used for democratic ends, from the bonus marchers of the Depression through Martin Luther King, Jr., and the activists who covered some of it with an AIDS quilt. Though the Capitol Visitors' Center has displaced the building itself for most tourists, the Center displays sacred relics and icons that previous pilgrims could not see, such as the catafalque that held the bodies of Lincoln and John Kennedy, and the Masonic trowel and mallet used by George Washington to lay the cornerstone. Walking through or driving on the miles of avenues that Pierre L'Enfant planned, it is more impossible in the twenty-first century than ever before to deny that, both for good and for evil, the District of Columbia is a sacred landscape.

SOURCES

Buckley, Christoper, *Washington Schlepped Here: Walking in the Nation's Capital* (New York: Crown Publishers, 2003).

Holland, Jesse, *Black Men Built the Capitol: Discovering African-American History In and Around Washington, D.C.* (Guilford, CT: The Globe Pequot Press, 2007).

Kennon, Donald R., and Thomas P. Somma, eds., *American Pantheon: Sculptural and Artistic Decoration of the United States Capitol* (Athens: Ohio University Press, 2004).

Lewis, David L., *District of Columbia: A Bicentennial History* (New York: W. W. Norton, 1976).

McGregor, James H. S., *Washington From the Ground Up* (Cambridge, MA: Harvard University Press, 2007).

Meyer, Jeffrey F., *Myths in Stone: Religious Dimensions of Washington, D.C.* (Berkeley: University of California Press, 2001).

Moeller, G. Martin, Jr., *AIA Guide to the Architecture of Washington, D.C.* (Baltimore, MD: The Johns Hopkins University Press, 4th ed., 2006).

Mumford, Lewis, *The City in History: Its Origins, Its Transformations, and Its Prospects* (New York: Harcourt, Brace, 1961).

Seale, William, *The President's House: A History* (Baltimore, MD: The Johns Hopkins University Press, 1986; rev. ed., 2008).

Smith, Sam, *Captive Capital: Colonial Life in Modern Washington* (Bloomington: Indiana University Press, 1974).

Wolanin, Barbara A., ed., *Constantino Brumidi: Artist of the Capitol* (Washington, DC: US Government Printing Office, 1998).

14

The Star-Spangled Banner

Oh, say can you see, by the dawn's early light,
What so proudly we hailed at the twilight's last gleaming?
Whose broad stripes and bright stars, through the perilous fight,
O'er the ramparts we watched, were so gallantly streaming?
And the rockets' red glare, the bombs bursting in air,
Gave proof through the night that our flag was still there.
O say, does that star-spangled banner yet wave
O'er the land of the free and the home of the brave?

On the shore, dimly seen through the mists of the deep,
Where the foe's haughty host in dread silence reposes,
What is that which the breeze, o'er the towering steep,
As it fitfully blows, now conceals, now discloses?
Now it catches the gleam of the morning's first beam,
In full glory reflected now shines on the stream:
'Tis the star-spangled banner! O long may it wave
O'er the land of the free and the home of the brave.

And where is that band who so vauntingly swore
That the havoc of war and the battle's confusion
A home and a country should leave us no more?
Their blood has wiped out their foul footsteps' pollution.
No refuge could save the hireling and slave
From the terror of flight, or the gloom of the grave:
And the star-spangled banner in triumph doth wave
O'er the land of the free and the home of the brave.

Oh! thus be it ever, when freemen shall stand
Between their loved homes and the war's desolation!
Blest with victory and peace, may the heaven-rescued land
Praise the Power that hath made and preserved us a nation.
Then conquer we must, for our cause it is just,
And this be our motto: "In God is our trust."

> And the star-spangled banner forever shall wave
> O'er the land of the free and the home of the brave!
>
> Francis Scott Key, 1814

Americans stand up for this song, which was made the national anthem by law in 1931. As the only official hymn of American civil religion, "The Star-Spangled Banner" stresses the primary value of freedom. Before sporting events on every level from professional to high school, men take off their hats and everyone faces the flag, often holding their hands over their hearts, while the first verse is played and sung. The same ritual takes place on many other occasions, such as graduations, at the beginning of every day in some schools, and on the first night of the season at the Metropolitan Opera of New York. The entire song focuses on the sacramental symbol of the flag.

"The Star-Spangled Banner" was printed and sold on the day it was written and attained instant fame, because it celebrated a victory that Americans desperately needed. First entitled "The Defence of Fort McHenry," the song described an attack on the fort defending Baltimore (Figure 14.1). British troops had burned Washington, D.C., three weeks before. If Fort McHenry and Baltimore had fallen, the War of 1812 might have ended American hope for growth. The British wanted a treaty (which was already being negotiated) in which the United States would renounce expansion into Ohio, Indiana, and Michigan and agree to treat the Mississippi River as an international waterway. Because the fort stood, the attack failed, and the terms of the treaty changed. It is not too much to say that on the night of that battle, America's future hung in the balance.

The flag praised in "The Star-Spangled Banner" had proportions equal to its heroic role. Thirty feet tall and forty-two feet wide, with stars and stripes each two feet across, it was a garrison flag, meant to fly from a pole 90 feet high and to be visible from great distances. It was equal in area to about one-fourth of a basketball court and far larger than modern garrison flags, which measure 20 by 38 feet. Since the bombardment of the fort coincided with a rainstorm, this enormous flag had not been the one "gallantly streaming" through the night; a 17 by 25–foot storm flag had served that purpose. At sunrise, however, when the storm was over and the battle was clearly won, Major George Armistead ordered the larger flag raised while the men shot their guns and a band played "Yankee Doodle," the national song of the day. On a boat anchored eight miles down the Patapsco River toward Chesapeake Bay, a lawyer, militia officer, and poet named Francis Scott Key saw the flag and began to write "The Star-Spangled Banner."

Figure 14.1 An aerial view of Fort McHenry, the fort protecting Baltimore over which British rockets and bombs exploded in the 1814 battle immortalized by "The Star-Spangled Banner." National Park Service. Tom Darden, Maryland Governor's Office.

Key witnessed the entire attack because he was being held by the British until the battle was decided. He and John S. Skinner, another lawyer who represented the US government in negotiating prisoner exchanges, had sailed to the British fleet to seek the release of an elderly doctor, William Beanes, who had fallen foul of the British by detaining six of their soldiers as prisoners in his house. The British were threatening to try Beanes for treason, arguing that he had been born in Scotland and was still a British subject. Luckily, Key and Skinner brought with them letters from British prisoners who testified that they had received good medical treatment from the doctor. Over supper, the British officers agreed to release Dr. Beanes; however, no Americans could leave the fleet with the knowledge of the British plans for Baltimore that Key and Skinner had acquired in the course of their visit. They had to wait with the enemy through the day and night of storm and assault.

As the violent words of the song attest, the attack was spectacular. The British fleet included five rocket boats, equipped with mortars launching rockets that could fly more than two miles and explode above a fort or ship, raining hot shrapnel down on whatever was below. They also used naval cannons, and they fired about 1,800 rockets and shells in the twenty-four hours from dawn on September 13th until dawn on the 14th. The American cannons had ranges far shorter than those of the British mortars and guns, so the 1,000 soldiers in Fort

McHenry could do nothing but take shelter, hoping that the bombardment did not destroy their building or their weapons, and remain ready to fire when the British fleet approached to land troops in the harbor or to bombard the city. Four hundred shells and rockets hit the fort, destroying several of its buildings and one cannon. Major Armistead had the barrels of gunpowder taken outside the fort to avoid a disastrous explosion, and his account gives thanks that only four of the defenders were killed and twenty-four wounded. In the rain and fog of September 13 and the darkness of that night, lit by the "bombs bursting in air," Key and the British used telescopes to try to see what was happening. British Admiral Alexander Cochrane hoped he had done enough damage to bring several ships past the fort by the afternoon, but the walls of the fort had held, almost all of the guns remained usable, and the few British ships that came into range were forced to retreat. The members of a landing party that rowed with muffled oars past the fort during the night became separated from each other and failed to penetrate the city. Meanwhile, an attack by British troops south of Baltimore failed and General Robert Ross, the officer who had led the attack on Washington, was killed by an American sniper. By dawn on the 14th, when the huge flag was raised, the Americans had won the battle of Baltimore.

Key's experiences as a prisoner of the fleet appeared in the first, second, and third verses of the song. Not only had he watched the "rockets' red glare," he had also thrilled to see the flag catch "the gleam of the morning's first beam." His reference in the third verse to the "band who so vauntingly swore" that their attack would leave no country or home for Americans apparently reflected what he heard at dinner with the British officers. Though Key originally opposed the war, both as a serious Christian and as a sympathizer with Great Britain in its wars against Napoleon, he had volunteered for the militia when the invasion came. After the battle, he wrote that he was "disappointed...as to the character of British officers," who had proved to be "illiberal, ignorant, and vulgar," and "filled with a spirit of malignity against everything American." Key still maintained enough Christian charity to reflect that he had seen the officers under "unfavorable circumstances."

Before he became a lawyer, Francis Scott Key had considered the Episcopal ministry, and the fourth verse of "The Star-Spangled Banner" is filled with explicitly religious language. The battle revealed the United States as a "heaven-rescued land," so Key advised that the American people should praise God, the Power who "hath made and preserved us a nation." As we "conquer," not as imperialists but in the just cause of defending ourselves, we should take "In God is our trust" as our motto. On July 30, 1956, President Eisenhower signed a law making "In God we trust" the official motto of the United States.

Another religious dimension appeared in the tune that Key had in mind as he wrote. That tune first came to America under the title of "To Anacreon in

Heaven," which was written by British composer John Stafford Smith, with lyrics by Ralph Tomlinson, and published around 1779; it served as the theme song of the Anacreontic Club of London. The club tried to carry on the spirit of the ancient Greek poet Anacreon (c. 582–485 B.C.E.), whose surviving poems celebrate both the goddess of love and the god of wine. According to the words of "To Anacreon in Heaven," the fatherly ruler of the gods, Zeus, objected to the attempt of Anacreon's followers "to entwine / The myrtle of Venus and Bacchus' vine." The lyrics tell a story in which Apollo, the god of music, and Momus, the masked god of comedy, helped humans to evade the lightning of Zeus and eventually win his blessing. As the last chorus concludes:

> And long may the Sons
> Of Anacreon intwine
> The Myrtle of Venus
> with Bacchus's Vine.

Although "To Anacreon in Heaven" is often dismissed as a "drinking song," it was more than that. The song had an explicit message—that love and wine should be celebrated together—and a subtext of resistance to tyranny. "Old Thunder" Jove objects to the combination of love and wine, but Apollo the god of music defends his votaries. Momus, wearing his comic mask (or "risible Phiz," for laughter-provoking physiognomy) joins Apollo, and Jove is convinced. The rebels of earth win a victory over the stern father of Heaven, and the song affirms human power to resist gods. In the revolutionary America of the 1780s and after, it became very popular; several patriotic songs involving Jefferson and John Adams were written for the tune.

Tom Paine, the pamphleteer famous for *Common Sense*, used the tune for a song called "Adams and Liberty," written to celebrate July 4, 1798, which included the following verse:

> Ye sons of Columbia, who bravely have fought
> For those rights which unstained from your sires have descended,
> May you long taste the blessings your valor has bought,
> And your sons reap the soil which their fathers defended.
> Mid the reign of mild peace,
> May your nation increase,
> With the glory of Rome and the wisdom of Greece;
> And ne'er shall the sons of Columbia be slaves,
> While the earth bears a plant, or the sea rolls its waves.

According to one scholar, Paine had written "the most popular political song ever sung in America," and it was surely known to Francis Scott Key. In the winter of

1804, ten years before the battle of Baltimore, Key himself was inspired by the victory of Stephen Decatur against the Barbary pirates in the harbor of Tripoli to write a song to the Anacreon tune that concluded:

> Then welcome the warrior returned from afar
> To the home and the country he nobly defended;
> Let the thanks due to valor now gladden his ear,
> And loud be the joy that his perils are ended.
> In the full tide of song,
> Let his fame roll along;
> To the feast-flowing board let us gratefully throng,
> Where, mixed with the olive, the laurel shall wave,
> And form a bright wreath for the brows of the brave.

Clearly, an association between the tune of "To Anacreon in Heaven" and the idea of eternal victory for freedom, expressed in images of waving seas and vines and in certain rhymes, filled the atmosphere when Key wrote "The Star-Spangled Banner" and when the people of the United States first heard and sang it. The emphasis on rockets and bombs in Key's 1814 words paralleled the theme of avoiding the thunderbolts of Zeus in the original lyrics.

Buoyed by the familiarity of the tune and its themes and the welcome news of the battle, "The Star-Spangled Banner" quickly gained popularity. Every man in Fort McHenry was given a copy of a handbill with the song on the day of the victory, and it spread into the taverns. The stagecoach between Baltimore and Philadelphia had been halted by the expected fall of Baltimore, but travel now resumed, and the song spread with word of the victory. It was sung and performed by a military band in New Orleans within two weeks, and within a month, newspapers in Georgia and Massachusetts were printing the song and selling reprints. Meanwhile, the whole country was breathing a sigh of relief, having snatched victory from near defeat. The guns of Fort McHenry were fired in celebration on September 18, when news of the Navy's victory on Lake Champlain reached Baltimore. By Christmas of 1814, the Treaty of Ghent was signed, and the United States emerged from the war without losing territory or the right to expand. In January, because word of the peace had not reached New Orleans, Americans under Andrew Jackson won a final great victory, successfully defending that city while killing hundreds of British soldiers and officers. Many historians have called the War of 1812 a second Revolution, in which the United States confirmed that it could unite to defend itself and for the first time won respect from the powers of Europe. "The Star-Spangled Banner" was the song of that war.

Before it became the national anthem, however, Key's song had to displace a rival, the now obscure "Hail, Columbia," a march with a jaunty rhythm that was written for the inauguration of George Washington in 1789. Abraham Lincoln once said that he knew only two tunes: "Hail, Columbia," the song he had to stand up for, and another tune (probably "The Star-Spangled Banner" or "Yankee Doodle") that he did not have to stand for. Gradually, the simple and solemn rhythm that John Stafford Smith had written for "To Anacreon in Heaven" won over military bands. Key's words, vividly portraying the battle of Fort McHenry, also had more military appeal than the words that Joseph Hopkinson supplied for Philip Phile's music in "Hail, Columbia":

> Hail Columbia, happy land!
> Hail, ye heroes, heav'n-born band,
> Who fought and bled in freedom's cause,
> Who fought and bled in freedom's cause,
> And when the storm of war was gone
> Enjoy'd the peace your valor won.
> Let independence be our boast,
> Ever mindful what it cost;
> Ever grateful for the prize,
> Let its altar reach the skies.

In 1889, Secretary of the Navy Benjamin F. Tracy decreed that "The Star-Spangled Banner" would be the official tune played when the flag was raised on American warships and naval bases. President Woodrow Wilson ordered it played in the entire US military in 1916, as the nation geared up for World War I. Meanwhile, the song was also making headway at baseball games: it was regularly played at New York's Polo Grounds, then home of the Giants, from 1898 on, and during the seventh-inning stretch of games in the 1918 World Series. In 1929, when Robert Ripley featured the statement, "Believe it or not, America has no national anthem," in his popular *Believe it or Not!* syndicated cartoon, a movement was building to recognize "The Star-Spangled Banner." According to a major supporter, the march composer and conductor John Philip Sousa, both "the spirit of the music that inspires" and Key's "soul-stirring words" supported the choice. The Veterans of Foreign Wars (VFW) also joined the movement. J. Charles Linthicum, who represented Baltimore in Congress, sponsored the bill that President Hoover signed into law on March 3, 1931. There were many opponents, including the editors of the *New York Herald Tribune*, who said that the song had "words that nobody can remember to a tune that nobody can sing." Professors at Columbia University's School of Education said that it was wrong to have children sing such a warlike song, especially in times of peace. Many advocated then, as they do now, for "America the Beautiful" as a more appropriate anthem for a peaceful nation. Still, the military and the marching bands carried the day. At one hearing in the House of Representatives, two sopranos sang "The Star-Spangled Banner" with the Navy Band playing the tune and members of the VFW in attendance wearing their medals. The victory of the song can be seen as a step by which American civil religion became more militant. After the United States entered World War II, the custom of beginning games with the anthem became universal in major league baseball and spread to other sports.

Like the flag, the song has provoked some extremely protective responses. Those who perform the song have often found little tolerance for variation. In 1941, the great composer Igor Stravinsky wrote a revised arrangement, changing the rhythm slightly and adding some solemn dissonance, then had his music bound in gold and sent to President Roosevelt, who gave it to the Smithsonian. When Stravinsky conducted his arrangement with the Boston Symphony, the audience reacted with stony silence. The next day, Boston police entered Symphony Hall and seized the music to prevent a second performance; they were enforcing a Massachusetts law against playing the anthem in any manner other than as written. When Jose Feliciano sang a slow, blues version at the 1968 baseball World Series, he set off storms of protest that resulted in a boycott of his records by many radio stations. Comedienne Roseanne Barr did serious damage to her reputation by performing the song as a parody before a baseball game in 1990, screeching the words off key, then spitting and grabbing her crotch in imitation of baseball players. Errors are also remembered: Broadway and Las Vegas singer Robert Goulet never lived down his failure to get through the lyrics before the championship fight between Muhammad Ali and Sonny Liston in 1965.

There have been at least two exceptions to the rule against variations: Marvin Gaye was cheered for his rhythm and blues performance before the NBA All-Star game in 1983, and the electric guitar version by Jimi Hendrix at the end of Woodstock in 1969 became something of a classic. The Hendrix version was incorporated into a television ad promoting voting in 1972. It should be noted that Gaye and Hendrix both had very friendly audiences, and any later negative effects were blunted by their deaths in the year after they performed the anthem.

A particularly bitter critique of the song appeared in the Broadway epic of the 1990s, *Angels in America, Part Two: Perestroika*, Act 4, Scene 3, where the former drag queen and nurse Belize cited it as one reason why he hated the United States. "The white cracker who wrote the national anthem knew what he was doing," said Belize. "He set the word 'free' to a note so high nobody could reach it. That was deliberate. Nothing on earth sounds less like freedom to me."

In the first years of the twenty-first century, some still argue for changing the national anthem, but they seem unlikely to succeed. There are also efforts to promulgate "The Star-Spangled Banner" in more effective forms. Garrison Keillor, host of the radio show *A Prairie Home Companion*, has been campaigning for years to have the song performed in its original key of G rather than A-flat or B-flat, so that more people could sing the range of notes that it demands. This would contradict the decision made by a National Anthem Committee of music educators in 1942, which sanctioned A-flat as the preferable key for mass singing and allowed singing in B-flat "for treble voices." Between 2005 and July of 2007, a National Anthem Project sponsored by many commercial organizations, including Jeep and the International Music Products Association, with First Lady Laura Bush as honorary chairwoman and many congressmen on the masthead, tried to increase awareness and knowledge of the anthem among Americans. The website of this project included music for mariachi band and steel drum versions of "The Star-Spangled Banner," signaling the increasing value of multicultural tolerance in American civil religion. Ringtone clips of *The Star-Spangled Banner* for cellphones were also supplied by the National Anthem Project.

During the furor of anti-immigration street demonstrations in 2006, several Latin pop stars came together to sing and to release a Spanish version of the anthem, called "Nuestro Himno." Asked for a reaction, President George W. Bush said that immigrants should learn the anthem in English. This Spanish version had actually been produced by the US Bureau of Education in 1919; the lyrics appeared on the website of the US Department of State, with a reproduction of the original sheet music on the website of the Library of Congress. In the midst of the dispute about immigration, however, many Latin broadcasters and others questioned the wisdom of distributing the national anthem in Spanish.

However warlike its lyrics or unsingable its tune, there can be no question that "The Star-Spangled Banner" has acquired a sacred quality within the American civil religion. The tune has power. Its first notes, the solemn fall and rise of its opening arpeggios, cause automatic emotional responses, both positive and negative, in the generations raised since 1931.

The song arose from an English tavern, but taverns and coffeehouses were the seedbeds of revolution in the eighteenth century, when the values of personal freedom and political democracy were first integrated into American civil religion. Our version of the tune was born at the moment when our nation survived an invasion, and it became the national song during the wars that gradually made the United States the world's leading military power. The history of the song relates directly to the rise of military leadership in America. That same history also corresponds with the emergence of world peace among the values that Americans were called to hold sacred.

Through its title and subject, "The Star-Spangled Banner" is connected to the most sacred object of American civil religion, the flag. It can be argued that American civil religion has several superior hymns, including "The Battle Hymn of the Republic," "America the Beautiful," and perhaps even "God Bless

America." Still, the solemn militancy of "The Star-Spangled Banner" has won the title of national anthem and the charisma associated with this status.

SOURCES

Borneman, Walter R., *1812: The War That Forged a Nation* (New York: HarperCollins, 2004).
Lord, Walter, *The Dawn's Early Light* (New York: Dutton, 1972).
Molotsky, Irwin, *The Flag, the Poet, and the Song: The Story of the Star-Spangled Banner* (New York: Dutton, 2001).
Weybright, Victor, *Spangled Banner: The Story of Francis Scott Key* (New York: Farrar & Rinehart, 1935).

15

The Washington Monument

The monument to George Washington soars above the capital that bears his name. Because of a law relating the heights of buildings to the widths of streets, no building in the District of Columbia comes closer than 225 feet to the monument's height of 555 feet, five and one-eighth inches (about fifty stories). From a distance, the marble obelisk looks slender, connecting the earth with the sky. Its shape derives from Egyptian representations of the sun's rays. From street level, it seems enormous, with each side at the base more than 55 feet wide. Still the tallest stone structure in the world, the monument has a simple power that suggests the godlike status of Washington in American civil religion.

Other ways of commemorating Washington were attempted before this monument came to be. When Pierre L'Enfant laid out the streets of the federal district, he planned for an equestrian statue of Washington at the right angle of a triangle between the Capitol and the White House. L'Enfant was locating a monument that Congress had unanimously approved in a resolution of 1783, long before the final site of the nation's capital was known. The execution of all plans in the new district went very slowly, however, and nothing had been done for a memorial when the centennial of Washington's birth arrived, in 1832. In that year, Congress commissioned a statue of Washington, to be placed in the Rotunda under the Capitol dome. Horatio Greenough, who has been called by one biographer the first American sculptor, won the job.

Today, it is difficult to look at the statue Greenough made without laughing. Washington sits partly wrapped in a toga, his torso entirely exposed, in a pose derived from Zeus, pointing to heaven with his right hand. Greenough had taken the classical traditions of sculpture, which served him well in representing angels, too literally. After less than a year in the Rotunda, the twenty-ton statue was moved outside to the Capitol grounds, and eventually to a place in the Smithsonian Museum of American History, a museum sometimes called "the nation's attic."

Meanwhile, a group led by George Watterston, a former Librarian of Congress, historian Peter Force, and Chief Justice John Marshall organized

Figure 15.1 The original design for the Washington Monument (at left), by Robert Mills, surrounded the base of the obelisk with a circular portico, with Washington driving a chariot on the roof. At right, the Washington Monument as it appears today. Library of Congress, National Park Service.

the Washington National Monument Society to raise private money for the fulfillment of L'Enfant's original concept, a large monument on the National Mall that would be visible from the Capitol and the White House. After twelve years of slow fund-raising, in 1845 the Society held a design competition, thinking that having a definite design would attract contributions. The winning entry, by Robert Mills, again put Washington in a toga, this time driving a chariot, and included other classical elements. The chariot stood on the roof of a circular temple, 200 feet in diameter and 100 feet high, which would contain statues of thirty heroes of the Revolutionary generation. From the center of the temple rose an obelisk, something like the current monument but with a flat top, 600 feet in height (see Figure 15.1). The design was described by one critic as "an ill-assorted blend of Greek, Babylonian, and Egyptian architecture."

Whatever the defects of the Mills design, by offering lithographs of it, sometimes autographed by presidents and senators, the Washington National Monument Society did make a little money. By 1848, the Society had raised the first $87,000 of the projected $1.2 million cost, and decided that it would further spur donations if they actually started to build. Congress passed a joint resolution granting the Society thirty acres on the Mall. A slight problem arose from swampy conditions at the exact place where direct lines from the Capitol and the White House came together, so that the actual site had to be somewhat south of the Capitol axis and east of the White House axis, but the monument would still be visible from both places.

Fortunately for later generations, the architect decided to begin with the central obelisk rather than with the surrounding temple or with Washington driving a chariot. On July 4, 1848, the cornerstone was laid, in a Masonic ritual using the same ceremonial trowel and mallet Washington had used in laying the cornerstone of the Capitol. All the notables of the capital, including President Polk and Abraham Lincoln, then an Illinois congressman, attended.

Since the marble obelisk was to have a staircase inside to bring visitors to the top, an opportunity for fund-raising appeared. Every state in the Union was invited to contribute money and a stone, engraved with its name and whatever other message it wished to convey, for the inner walls. When word of this offer went out, organizations like cities, lodges of Masons and Odd Fellows and Sons of Temperance, fire companies, Indian nations like the Cherokee and the Tuscarora, school teachers from Buffalo, New York, Sabbath School children, and several foreign nations also sent stones, but very little money.

Although some of the state stones, such as Maine's, are as simple as a slab of granite bearing a carved "MAINE" in all caps, most have a more verbose message, and many of the messages reveal the state's position on the crisis of the Union that would lead to civil war. Northern states tended to make absolute declarations, such as: "Iowa. Her affections, like the rivers of her borders, flow to an inseparable union." Indiana sent a stone asserting that it "knows no North, no South, nothing but the Union." On the other hand, Southern states seemed more conditional, as in Georgia's "The Union as it was—the Constitution as it is," or Alabama's "A Union of Equality, as adjusted by the Constitution." South Carolina sent a marble stone without a verbal message, decorated with the state's coat of arms, a male and female figure, and an angel flying above, but in the 1850s parts of the angel and the man were broken off the stone by vandals, possibly offended by the role South Carolina was playing in the sectional crisis.

The memorial stones reveal how some of the many conflicts of American history have been at least partially reconciled in American civil religion. For example, in 1853 the Mormons, who had been driven by persecution across the country to what is now the state of Utah, sent a stone from the place they called Deseret. Carved in the stone was a beehive, the symbol of their industry and unity, inscribed with the words "Holiness to the Lord." According to the missionaries who brought the stone to Washington, it took a "drearisome trip of three months...principally by ox team" to accomplish their task. In 1951, the old stone was joined by one recalling that "Deseret Means Honey Bee" and commemorating Utah's ascension to statehood in 1896.

To see a stone from the Cherokee, sent less than twenty years after President Andrew Jackson had them driven from Georgia to Oklahoma on the Trail of

Tears, evokes a sense of how strong loyalty to the nation can be. The Indians who once owned the land of the District of Columbia and who still lived there contributed a stone through a fraternal organization, the Improved Order of Red Men. The Muskogee also made a stone, but never managed to ship it east from Oklahoma, and it remains there on display.

The stone sent by Pope Pius IX in 1854 sparked an anti-Catholic reaction that nearly ended construction of the monument. This pope had been hailed by Robert C. Winthrop of Massachusetts, the Speaker of the House, in his keynote address at the laying of the cornerstone in 1848. As revolutions in favor of democracy convulsed Europe, Winthrop said, Pius IX had "led the way" to reform and earned "a cordial tribute of respect and admiration" from Americans. By 1854, however, the revolutions had been crushed and Pius IX restored to leadership in Rome by French bayonets. In the United States, a party called the United Americans (commonly called "Know-Nothings" because of their use of secret conspiracies, about which they would claim to know nothing, to rig elections) had organized to oppose Roman Catholic influence and had taken control of state governments in Massachusetts and Ohio, as well as the mayoralty of Washington itself. News that the pope had sent a stone to Washington led to a Know-Nothing raid on the site under cover of darkness. The stone sent by Pius IX disappeared. Not until 1892, during the construction of a bridge over the Potomac, were the larger pieces of this stone found, though smaller pieces had been displayed by the Know-Nothings in Washington's city hall. A replacement donated by a Roman Catholic priest, the Rev. Fr. James E. Grant, and inscribed *A Roma Americae*, or "From Rome to America," replicating the inscription on the stone of Pius IX, was installed in 1982.

After the pope's stone vanished, contributions dried up, in part because of the bad national and international publicity. The Washington National Monument Society had brought the monument to 152 feet, or about a quarter of the projected height, but had also run out of money. In 1854, it appealed to Congress, which appropriated $200,000 to continue, but now the Know-Nothings struck again. Some United Americans joined the Monument Society, and they quickly called a meeting and packed it with party members, complained that the Society employed too many immigrant workers, and elected a new board of directors. Congress responded by repealing its appropriation. For four years the Know-Nothings controlled the Society and the monument, adding 26 feet of marble by using stone that earlier builders had rejected and that later had to be removed. Architect Robert Mills died in 1855. From 1858, when the Know-Nothings returned control to the original Society board, until 1878, construction ceased, and the fifteen-story obelisk stood looking, as Mark Twain wrote, like "a factory chimney with the top broken off."

The centennial of the Declaration of Independence, in 1876, brought a revival of interest in the monument and a sense of shame that it had never been completed. In August of that year, Congress passed an appropriation to continue the work and created a Joint Commission, including an officer of the old Society and adding representatives of the Army Corps of Engineers, the president of the United States, and the architects of the Treasury Department and the Capitol, to supervise construction. Four years of controversy ensued, in which radical plans to change the monument were advanced (see Figure 15.2). Most had become convinced that the circular temple with Washington driving a chariot that Mills had proposed would never be built, and the unadorned obelisk affronted Victorian tastes. Among the most seriously considered alternatives was a design by American sculptor William Wetmore Story, who proposed encasing the marble stump in a larger, ornate tower with windows, modeled on the campanile

Figure 15.2 These alternative, Victorian designs for completing the Washington Monument, which were developed after the obelisk had already been half erected, show how lucky the nation was that a lack of funds resulted in a more austere structure. Library of Congress, National Park Service.

that stands next to the cathedral of Florence, topped by a marble pyramid and a small statue of Fame. Others went beyond Story to suggest that the existing tower be torn down and replaced from scratch.

Questions were meanwhile raised about how much the tower had settled and whether the foundation would prove adequate for the completed monument. While arguments about design played themselves out, the commission permitted Lieutenant Colonel Thomas Casey of the Army Corps of Engineers to begin work on improving the foundation in 1878. Gradually, proponents of the simple shaft of marble won their battle. A committee of engineers from the Army Corps wrote that "a great, bare obelisk, plain to severity" was a "conception most suitable to symbolize the great character it would commemorate." Former House Speaker Winthrop, who had spoken when the cornerstone was laid in 1848, argued that generations had contributed to the monument, so that to destroy it would be abhorrent, and that the intention was not "to illustrate the fine arts of any period, but to commemorate the foremost man of all the ages." For that purpose, "a simple, sublime shaft...rising nearer to the skies than any known monument on earth," seemed appropriate. A final piece of design advice came from the US ambassador to Italy, George Perkins Marsh, who discovered that the rule for the height of ancient obelisks was that they should be 10 times as tall as the length of one side of the base. Since the base of the existing shaft was 55 feet, the whole monument did not need to be 600 feet tall, as projected by Mills. March also learned that the marble pyramidion at the top should be as tall as the base was wide, which resulted in a much more pointed obelisk than the one that Mills had designed.

Construction of the spire resumed in 1880, and finally concluded with the setting of the capstone and an apex, made of aluminum to attract and diffuse lightning, on December 6, 1884. The 100-ounce apex had names and dates of the construction process inscribed on the north, west, and south sides. The east side bore two Latin words, "Laus Deo," or "Praise God," a fact that contemporary American evangelicals love to note. When the monument was opened to the public, in 1886, it was the tallest structure yet made by human beings. In 1889, the Eiffel Tower in Paris nearly doubled its height, but the white stone of the Washington Monument retained its unique power.

As an obelisk, the monument has power that derives from its shape and from history. Obelisks, or single pieces of granite hewn from the stones of Aswan, had formed part of Egyptian religious symbolism since about 2700 B.C.E. They were often set up in pairs near temples. They honored Re, the sun god, by representing a ray of the sun, and connected earthly rule with the power of Re. Like most of Egyptian religion, the obelisk also celebrated immortality. Hatshepsut, the only female pharaoh, was a great builder of obelisks. Thutmose III made seven obelisks, and Ramses II, the likely pharaoh of the Exodus who ruled for sixty-six years, dedicated at least twenty-five obelisks, some by simply inscribing his own name on already standing stones and some by having new stones hewn out and set up.

Immediately after Rome conquered Egypt, the obelisk conquered Rome. Emperors from Augustus through Constantine had obelisks carried in special, triple-hulled ships across the Mediterranean. In the Renaissance, Pope Sixtus V had the obelisk in front of St. Peter's Basilica baptized, to eliminate its pagan past, and set others up at the major intersections of the city. The obelisk became an essential symbol of a Western capital of empire. After the French, under Napoleon, conquered Egypt, they brought an obelisk to Paris. The British installed an obelisk in London, and soon after the Americans brought one of the obelisks called "Cleopatra's needles," made by the queen of Egypt, to New York's Central Park. Obelisks featured prominently in tombs and mausoleums of Victorian cemeteries, and the Bunker Hill Monument in Charlestown, Massachusetts, included one that was more than 200 feet high. The completion of the Washington Monument brought this long obsession with the obelisk to its apex.

Ironically, that apex came with a structure that was not a true obelisk, for the Washington Monument was not a single piece of stone carried with heroic ingenuity to its place, but rather a composite of many blocks of stone. At the dedication ceremony in 1885, Robert C. Winthrop made this departure from the monolithic norm into a virtue, saying that "America is certainly at liberty to present new models in art as well as government," and that an obelisk made of many blocks embodied "the idea of our cherished National motto, E PLURIBUS UNUM." Forty years later, Calvin Coolidge used the same point to celebrate the setting of a memorial stone from New Mexico into the monument.

The sheer, simple presence of the Washington Monument continues to impress visitors today. The addition of the Lincoln Memorial in 1922, extending the Mall as far to the west as the Capitol is to the east, made the Washington Monument into the center of sacred space in the District, exerting power even on those who do not approach it. Freudian interpreters may mock it as a phallus, but unlike most other monuments in the American civil religion, it has resisted appropriation for any cause beyond itself. It has avoided change by addition or subtraction. Transcending even George Washington himself, the monument comes as close as anything material can come to representing the absolute. The history of the monument, with all of its conflicts and resolutions, demonstrates the American commitment to democratic government. With this monument, American civil religion laid claim to immortality.

SOURCES

Curran, Brian A., Anthony Grafton, Pamela O. Long, and Benjamin Weiss, *Obelisk: A History* (Cambridge, MA: Burndy Library, 2009).

Jacob, Judith M., *The Washington Monument: A Technical History and Catalog of the Commemorative Stones* (Washington, DC: National Park Service, 2005).

Meyer, Jeffrey F., *Myths in Stone: Religious Dimensions of Washington, D.C.* (Berkeley: University of California Press, 2001).

Torres, Louis, *"To the Immortal Name and Memory of George Washington:" The United States Army Corps of Engineers and the Construction of the Washington Monument* (Washington, DC: U.S. Army Corps of Engineers, 1984).

16

The Battle Hymn of the Republic

Mine eyes have seen the glory of the coming of the Lord:
He is trampling out the vintage where the grapes of wrath are stored;
He hath loosed the fateful lightning of His terrible swift sword.
His truth is marching on.
[CHORUS] Glory, glory, Hallelujah!
Glory, glory, Hallelujah!
Glory, glory, Hallelujah!
His truth is marching on.
I have seen Him in the watch-fires of a hundred circling camps;
They have builded Him an altar in the evening dews and damps;
I can read His righteous sentence by the dim and flaring lamps;
His day is marching on. [CHORUS]
I have read a fiery gospel writ in burnished rows of steel:
"As ye deal with my contemners, so with you my grace shall deal;"
Let the Hero, born of woman, crush the serpent with his heel,
Since God is marching on. [CHORUS]
He has sounded forth the trumpet that shall never call retreat;
He is sifting out the hearts of men before His judgment-seat:
Oh, be swift, my soul, to answer Him! Be jubilant, my feet!
Our God is marching on. [CHORUS]
In the beauty of the lilies Christ was born across the sea,
With a glory in his bosom that transfigures you and me:
As he died to make men holy, let us die to make men free,
While God is marching on. [CHORUS]
    Julia Ward Howe, 1861; *Atlantic Monthly*, IX (1862), 145

The combination of relentless rhythm with solemn, yet militant, lyrics has made "The Battle Hymn of the Republic" a sacred song of American civil religion. By stressing the elements of cosmic battle and the ancient Hebrew and mythic roots of Christianity, it evokes the universal quest for peace through victory over evil.

Despite its partisan origins on the Union side of the Civil War, the Battle Hymn has attained national, even international, acceptance. All five verses were sung at the end of the memorial service for September 11 at the National Cathedral on September 14, 2001. President Lyndon Johnson, although a Texan, had it sung by the Mormon Tabernacle Choir at his inauguration in 1965; ten days later, it was played by request of Winston Churchill at his funeral. By then, it had already become a favorite selection of the Soviet Union's Red Army Chorus, which sang the English words. Leonard Bernstein and the New York Philharmonic performed it in St. Patrick's Cathedral at the funeral of Robert F. Kennedy in 1968. Earlier in that same year, Martin Luther King, Jr., concluded his last public speech, hours before he was shot, with the words, "Mine eyes have seen the glory of the coming of the Lord!"

Julia Ward Howe (1819–1910), who wrote the words of the *Battle Hymn*, represented a movement of crusading religious liberalism that flourished in New York and Boston during the nineteenth century. The daughter of a devoutly Calvinist Episcopalian, the New York banker Samuel Ward, she absorbed Unitarian and Transcendentalist principles from William Ellery Channing, Ralph Waldo Emerson, and Margaret Fuller. After 1839, when her father died and left her wealthy, she worked as a poet, literary critic, writer, editor, and organizer for the causes of women's rights, abolition of slavery, and educational reform. In 1843, she married the doctor Samuel Gridley Howe, a political activist and pioneer in education for the blind and deaf who was named to lead the Sanitary Commission to safeguard the health of Union soldiers as the Civil War broke out. Accompanying her husband to Washington on an inspection of the Army of the Potomac in 1861, Julia Ward Howe saw the encampments around the capital, which became the "hundred circling camps" of the Battle Hymn; she saw soldiers at revival services, with preachers reading their Bibles by "dim and flaring lamps." Caught up in a Confederate attack, the Howes' carriage was surrounded by retreating Union troops, and those in the carriage began to sing *John Brown's Body*, to the same tune that later became the *Battle Hymn*.

> Old John Brown's body lies a-moldering in the grave,
> While weep the sons of bondage whom he ventured all to save;
> But though he lost his life in struggling for the slave,
> His truth is marching on.
> He captured Harper's Ferry with his nineteen men so few,
> And he frightened 'Old Virginny' till she trembled through and through,
> They hung him for a traitor, themselves a traitor crew,
> But his truth is marching on.

The troops cheered the singing, but James Freeman Clarke, a prominent Unitarian and Abolitionist who was also the Howes' pastor in Boston, suggested that a poet like Mrs. Howe could write better lyrics for the tune. That night in Willard's Hotel in Washington, writing in the dark so as not to wake her children, Howe wrote the words that were first published in the *Atlantic* magazine of February 1862, and that quickly became the anthem of the North.

Those who resonate with the song's affirmations of "glory" and of "marching on" often do not notice that the lyrics describe the last judgment. Not only does the "coming of the Lord" imply the end of this world, but "trampling out the vintage where the grapes of wrath are stored" refers to biblical images of judgment that occur first in Isaiah 63:3 and then in Revelation 14:19 and 19:15. Isaiah quotes God promising to trample nations of enemies like grapes in a wine press, so that their blood stains all His garments. Revelation expands this threat into a vision of "the wine press of God's wrath," from which blood overflows and fills the streets to the height of a horse's bridle for sixteen hundred stadia, or about two hundred square miles. A hundred and twenty years before Julia Ward Howe, the same horrific image inspired the evangelist Jonathan Edwards, who used it in the classic sermon "Sinners in the Hands of an Angry God"; in the twentieth century, novelist John Steinbeck alluded to the same prophecy in the title of *The Grapes of Wrath*. The "terrible swift sword" of the Battle Hymn recalls the sword that issues from the mouth of Jesus to smite the nations at Armageddon, in Revelation 19:15.

Alongside blood and judgment, the Battle Hymn offers triumph and consolation. "I have read a fiery gospel writ in burnished rows of steel" begins the third verse, reflecting Howe's experience of riding in a carriage among ranks of infantry armed with rifles and bayonets. That verse ends with the image of a "Hero, born of woman" who will "crush the serpent with his heel." The triumph may appear in specifically Christian terms, as in the fifth verse: "As He died to make men holy, let us die to make men free"; yet the triumph of the Battle Hymn seems universal, celebrating a cosmic victory of good over evil. In this, Howe's lyrics could not have been more unlike those of "John Brown's Body," which specifically referred to the conflict of North and South. The Battle Hymn never mentions North, South, slavery, or Union.

Such universalism enabled Howe to transcend Christian imagery even as she employed evangelical language. Howe was certainly aware of widespread myths of heroes, from Thor to Hercules, who conquered serpents, and of gods like Adonis and Dionysus who died in order to be reborn. She belonged to the first generation of Americans who heard the message of Transcendentalism, which translated texts from Hinduism and other religions, merging Christian faith with what she called "the religion of humanity." One of her pastors in Boston, Theodore Parker, wrote a famous essay on "The Transient and Permanent in

Christianity," in which he consigned most of traditional orthodoxy to transience. In later years, Howe attended meetings of the Radical Club, where she discussed Kant and Spinoza, Comte and Swedenborg with the best intellects of the United States. In her eighty-fourth year, she addressed the World Parliament of Relgions, where she made dramatic claims for Christ while sharing them with the founders of other faiths. Even the most Christian lines of the Battle Hymn, those claiming that Christ "was born across the sea / With a glory in His bosom that transfigures you and me," end with a humanistic note of equality with Jesus: "As he died to make men holy, let us die to make men free."

Before "John Brown's Body," the rhythm of the Battle Hymn appeared in a Methodist camp meeting song, "Say, Brothers, Will You Meet Us," by William Steffe, which was published in 1858. Probably derived from a slave spiritual or work song, "Say, Brothers" had very simple words:

> Say, brothers, will you meet us (three times)
> On Canaan's happy shore.
> Glory, glory, hallelujah (three times)
> For ever, evermore!

Later verses continued, "By the grace of God we'll meet you / Where parting is no more," and "Jesus lives and reigns forever / On Canaan's happy shore."

In a sense, "John Brown's Body" brought this simple Methodist expression of hope down into a world of war, corpses, and slavery, while Howe in the Battle Hymn returned the tune to heavenly concerns. Today the Battle Hymn stands alongside "Amazing Grace" among songs that link evangelical Christianity with American civil religion, functioning both in church and in civil contexts despite their Christian themes. But because the Battle Hymn is "of the Republic" and is firmly associated with war and the struggle to advance the cause of freedom, it belongs more to American civil religion than to Christianity. And strangely enough, through the magic of millennial thinking, this militant hymn ultimately supports the value of world peace.

SOURCES

Claghorn, Charles Eugene, *Battle Hymn: The Story Behind The Battle Hymn of the Republic* (New York: The Hymn Society of America, 1974).

Goodwin, Joan, "Julia Ward Howe," Dictionary of Unitarian & Universalist Biography, <http://www.uua.org/uuhs/duub/articles/juliawardhowe.html> (September 5, 2004).

Hall, Florence Howe Hall, *The Story of the Battle Hymn of the Republic* (New York: Harper & Brothers, 1916).

Ziegler, Valarie H., *Diva Julia: The Public Romance and Private Agony of Julia Ward Howe* (Harrisburg, PA: Trinity Press International, 2003).

17

Gettysburg and the Gettysburg Address

> Fourscore and seven years ago our Fathers brought forth upon this Continent a new nation, conceived in liberty and dedicated to the proposition that all men are created equal. Now we are engaged in a great civil war, testing whether that nation, or any nation so conceived and so dedicated, can long endure. We are met on a great battle-field of that war. We are met to dedicate a portion of it as the final resting-place of those who gave their lives that the nation might live. It is altogether fitting and proper that we should do this. But in a larger sense we cannot dedicate. We cannot consecrate, we cannot hallow this ground. The brave men, living and dead, who struggled here have consecrated it far above our power to add or detract. The world will little note nor long remember, what we say here, but it can never forget what they did here. It is for us, the living, rather to be dedicated here to the unfinished work that they have so nobly carried on. It is rather for us to be here dedicated to the great task remaining before us, that from these honored dead we take increased devotion to that cause for which they here gave the last full measure of devotion; that we here highly resolve that the dead shall not have died in vain; that the Nation shall under God have a new birth of freedom, and that Government of the people, by the people, and for the people, shall not perish from the earth.

"We cannot consecrate, we cannot hallow this ground," President Abraham Lincoln said at the ceremony dedicating the national cemetery at Gettysburg. The men who fought and died there had already made the site sacred. Each year, 2 million people, two-thirds the number that go to Mecca and about the same number that go to Lourdes, prove Lincoln right by coming to Gettysburg to learn about the battle and to honor those who fought it.

Yet Lincoln was wrong in the next sentence, when he said, "The world will little note, nor long remember what we say here, but it can never forget what they did here." Actually, the world continues to note what the Union and Confederate armies did at Gettysburg on the first three days of July 1863 in large measure because of what Lincoln said in three minutes on November 19. Many also remember what was said without knowing what was done: they have learned the language of the Gettysburg Address although they know little about the battle of Gettysburg. For example, Israeli prime minister Menachem Begin recited the address from memory in 1978, while on a tour of Gettysburg with President Jimmy Carter and President Anwar Sadat of Egypt, but Begin did not know any details of the battle. President Sadat had dominated the conversation up to that point, because he had studied the battle in military school. People focus on Gettysburg for many different reasons.

Meanwhile, disputes remain about what Lincoln meant by words like "a new birth of freedom," and how those words were heard when he spoke them. Both the battle and the speech clearly connected with the values of personal freedom and political democracy, two of the central values of Amercian civil religion. But both the site of Gettysburg and the text of the Gettysburg Address raise basic questions about orthodoxy and truth, legend and meaning, and how cultural tolerance came to include rebels against the United States whose government stood for the right to hold slaves.

More than any other site of American civil religion, Gettysburg demonstrates how the sacred can arise from the coalescence of word and deed, and also of history and nature. The battlefield itself, ten square miles of rolling farmland and small rugged hills, has become a place where people find power in rocks, fields, and trees and see the sublime in landscapes and perspectives (see Figure 17.1).

Figure 17.1 The landscape where the battle of Gettysburg was fought now contains hundreds of monuments, which themselves reflect long struggles over the story and the meaning of the battle. National Park Service.

Beginning immediately after the battle, there have been continuing struggles over how to handle the dead, what monuments to build, and to what extent to preserve the battlefield. The cemetery at Gettysburg began a cult of war dead in the United States that has continued in Arlington National Cemetery, in other cemeteries, and on Memorial Days. Through narratives of the battle, told at the Visitors' Center and in many books and movies, Americans make connections to their sacred history, a narrative of national survival and (for some) salvation.

The underlying facts are striking enough to make dramatic results understandable. About 168,000 men fired rifles and cannons and struck each other with bayonets and swords at Gettysburg, making it the largest battle ever fought in the Western Hemisphere. Deaths are estimated at anywhere from 7,000 to 11,000 (depending on how one counts people who died from wounds weeks later or simply disappeared) and another 29,000 were wounded and lived, many with one or more amputations. Adding about 10,000 soldiers captured, the total of 50,000 casualties was approximately ten times as many as the American casualties on D-Day in World War II. And more important than the scale of the battle and the carnage were the perilous course of the fighting, the stakes, and the result. At three different moments, one on each of the three days of Gettysburg, the Army of Northern Virginia under Robert E. Lee might have shattered the Army of the Potomac and won the battle, in which case the Confederate forces could have cut the Union capital of Washington off from the rest of the North and won the war. After Gettysburg, though the war went on for almost two more years, Lee never again threatened to take Washington. Gettysburg proved to be the turning point of the war.

At the center of a network of eight roads and a railroad, the small (population about 2,400) town of Gettysburg was well-suited to serve as a turning point. It was surrounded then, as now, by prosperous orchards and farms. As Lee's army felt its way from Virginia and Maryland into Pennsylvania, the area provided good opportunities to take provisions. The Army of the Potomac was under orders to keep itself between Lee and Washington, and the two armies circled each other so that Lee came to the battle from the north and the west while General George Meade and the Union army came from the south. Though a large battle was inevitable, the exact location was not so much planned as caused by the conjunction of roads.

Visitors today feel especially close to the battle at three places, corresponding to the three days of fighting and to the narrative in the Visitors' Center. On McPherson Ridge, due west of the town of Gettysburg, they can stand where Union cavalry first met the Confederate infantry that were advancing in force. The land there is flat and the vistas long. A short stone obelisk, one of more than 1,300 monuments on the battlefield, marks where Major General John Reynolds was shot on his horse as he directed the Union defense. By the end of that first day's fighting, the Union forces had been driven back through the streets of Gettysburg, where thousands were killed or captured. Under attack both from the west and the north, the Union army regrouped in a position centered on Cemetery Hill, south of the town. With many elements of both armies not yet arrived on the scene, the Union force was outnumbered, and by five P.M. about 9,000 Union men had been killed, captured, or wounded. When Robert E. Lee arrived at Gettysburg and assessed the situation, he left it up to General Ewell, whose two divisions faced Cemetery Hill, whether to press the attack. Years later, Lee would say that if Stonewall Jackson had survived to command those troops at that moment, the South would have won the battle, and possibly the war. Ewell decided, perhaps rightly, that his troops were too exhausted and the Union position too difficult to take, but the question of this lost chance continues to provoke debate.

To understand the battle on the second day, visitors drive south and slightly west of the town, to a landscape of exposed granite, scattered with boulders and dominated by two small hills called Round Top and Little Round Top. On July 2, Union troops were surrounded on three sides, but were holding the higher ground, with reinforcements arriving from the south to give them a slight numerical advantage. Late in the day, a crisis arose when the amateur Union General Daniel Sickles, who had no military training but earned his position by raising four brigades of soldiers, advanced too far to the west and left Little Round Top unoccupied except by a few Union signalmen. An attack by Texas and Alabama infantry nearly took the hill, from which the center of the Union position could have been shelled by cannons. The attack was held off by a rapid deployment of troops from Pennsylvania and by the heroic stand of the 20th Maine Volunteer Regiment, which ran out of ammunition and carried the day with a desperate bayonet charge, led by classics professor Joshua Chamberlain of Bowdoin College, who won the Medal of Honor. In the PBS documentary *The Civil War*, Ken Burns noted that Gettysburg was almost exactly halfway between the homes of the men from Alabama and from Maine who fought on Little Round Top.

The third and final day of the battle is best appreciated on Hancock Road, due south of the town, looking west across a shallow, flat valley of farmland about a mile wide, between Cemetery Ridge and Seminary Ridge. There, on the afternoon of July 3, more than 12,000 men from North Carolina and Virginia, led by General George Pickett, marched out of the cover of trees on Seminary Ridge and across the field in an attempt to take the center of the Union position, held by about 7,000 men, by a direct assault. Hours of artillery fire preceded this attack, which has gone down in history as "Pickett's Charge." A charge by Lee's Virginians had always succeeded in breaking the Union infantry before, and Lee may have hoped that a direct assault from the west could be followed by a flanking attack, but this time Lee's aggressive tactics failed. The artillery fire was badly aimed, perhaps because the South was using a new manufacturer of shells and could not accurately estimate their range. The shells went too far, and their explosions did not seriously disrupt the Union line of infantry or the Union artillery, though they did destroy some homes in Gettysburg. Union cannons held their fire until the charge began. About 600 cannons were engaged on the two sides at Gettysburg, and the sound of cannons was heard as far away as Pittsburgh, 180 miles to the west, and Baltimore, 54 miles to the south.

Pickett's Charge proved suicidal, exposing infantry to concentrated fire by rifles and cannons. Nevertheless, the Confederate troops did charge at a run for the last few hundred yards and breached the Union line, at a place remembered and identified by a stone monument as "The High Water Mark" of the Confederacy. The relatively few soldiers who crossed the stone wall into the Union ranks, including one mounted general named Lewis Armistead who got his hand on a Union cannon, were almost all killed or captured. When the survivors straggled back to the Confederate lines on Seminary Ridge, the battle was over.

This account leaves out many important parts of the struggle, such as the fight for Culp's Hill on the second day and the cavalry action in which thousands of horse soldiers under George Armstrong Custer kept J.E.B. Stuart from attacking the Union from the rear before Pickett's Charge. The battlefield was large, with action on three and four fronts, but the three actions highlighted here were moments when the outcome hung in the balance. They were emphasized for decades in the Visitors' Center at Gettysburg, using an electric map with lights to designate the positions of troops, which was later supplanted by a video that tells the same essential story. This canonical account of the battle was dramatized and personalized in a best-selling novel of 1974, *The Killer Angels* by Michael Shaara, which became the feature film *Gettysburg* (1993) and a mini-series for Turner Broadcasting.

Because the official narrative is so evenhanded, it tends to excite sympathy for the South. Though Union heroes like Joshua Chamberlain are celebrated, the pathos of Pickett's Charge and Lee's retreat to Virginia, trailing two miles of wagons carrying the wounded, excite more sympathy. The story in the Visitors' Center leaves out the Confederate plunder of farms and households around Gettysburg and the disappearance of hundreds of African-Americans, many of whom were captured and sent south into slavery. Concentration on military history tends to obscure the ultimate aims of the opposing sides in the war.

After the retreats of July 4, 1863, the people of Gettysburg were left in a scene that surpassed any vision of Hell in Dante or Brueghel. Union commanding General George Meade went in slow pursuit of Lee, still staying between the Confederates and Washington, and reported that "I cannot delay to pick up the debris of the battlefield," by which he meant his dead and wounded troops. At least 8,000 human bodies remained on the field, along with 3,000 carcasses of horses and mules. One widow in the center of town had fifteen dead horses on her front lawn. The stench was pervasive, and people feared that typhus or some other plague fueled by the decay would sweep away the living. A town of 2,400, without a hospital, had to deal with the care of 21,000 wounded. As Army Surgeon General William A. Hammond later noted, conditions at Gettysburg in 1863 were still "medieval," because doctors operated without knowledge of germ theory or anesthesia. The wounded filled the churches, so that no religious services were held in those buildings for weeks.

Organized religion did help in some ways. The efforts of nurses and doctors from the US Sanitary Commission were joined by volunteers from the Christian Commission. The Sisters of Mercy had a convent nearby, at Emmitsburg, and the nuns came to help. In an era when religious prejudice had fueled violence in many American cities, with anti-Catholic political parties winning statewide elections in Massachusetts and Ohio in the 1850s, the actions around Gettysburg displayed a remarkable spirit of ecumenism. Father William Corby offered a general absolution to all members of the 88th Regiment of New York, including many non-Catholics, before it entered a desperate battle in The Wheatfield, near Little Round Top, on the second day. Rabbi Michael Allen, the Jewish chaplain of a Pennsylvania regiment, held prayer services for anyone from the Army of the Potomac on Sunday mornings. Although the value of cultural tolerance had not yet been named at Gettysburg, it was already part of American civil religion.

But no religious rituals could hold back the tide of death. The American Civil War has been called the first fully industrial war. Its numerous and efficient rifles and cannons, railroads to move troops and supplies, and enormous armies brought death on a greater scale than had been seen before. At Gettysburg in the days after the battle, human life seemed cheap and futile.

The response of the people was to make every effort to identify the dead, to mark the burials, and to establish a cemetery. Congress had already authorized the president, in 1862, to acquire land for national cemeteries. Union generals had begun the process at Chattanooga, Stone River, and Knoxville. Gettysburg was the first Northern site of a major battle, and its cemetery began with efforts by local people and spread to the governments of Northern states. A local attorney name David Wills acquired the first land, near the private Evergreen Cemetery for which Cemetery Ridge had been named. Wills also hired William Saunders, the landscape architect who had designed Mount Auburn Cemetery in Cambridge, Massachusetts, which is generally thought to be the first suburban cemetery that exemplified the new attitudes of the nineteenth century toward death. In Mount Auburn, Saunders had created a suburb of the dead, with landscaping for elaborate marble tombs, sculptures, and mausoleums.

Here, in a military setting, he had a different, but equally compelling inspiration. He installed stones of granite, flat to the grass, arranged in semicircular rows by regiments, which in turn reflected the states that had sent the soldiers. Mount Auburn's decorations distinguished between families and social classes, but at Gettysburg officers and men would lie together, as they had fought and fallen.

Long before Saunders's work was done, entrepreneurs of death descended on Gettysburg, selling metal coffins and other means guaranteed to preserve bodies for a long trip home. Embalming first became common during the Civil War, and embalmers set up tents at Gettysburg. To identify and to preserve the bodies of the dead served as compensation for the incredible level of carnage. Ensuring that soldiers were buried properly, and if possible near their homes, also became an important emphasis. In the immediate aftermath of the battle, the corpses of Southern soldiers were left in the fields or in mass graves, but by the 1870s more than 3,000 bodies had been shipped south from Gettysburg, with 2,935 going to Hollywood Cemetery in Richmond.

The Gettysburg National Cemetery would eventually hold 3,512 Union dead from the battle, most from Pennsylvania, with 979 unknown. Later additions brought war dead from the Spanish-American War, World Wars I and II, Korea, and Vietnam, extending down the road from the original cemetery. It has now run out of space and is closed to further burials.

When the Gettysburg Cemetery opened in November 1863, it was a new kind of place that deserved an important ritual. No other scene of death on that scale had happened in the North. The dedication was a major event, drawing about 15,000 people, including many governors and other politicians. Edward Everett, the former Harvard president who was selected to give the keynote address at the ceremony, had been recognized as the nation's greatest orator after the death of Daniel Webster. Though today, many ridicule Everett for giving a speech nearly two hours long—in comparison to Lincoln's, which can be read in two minutes—this length of performance was exactly what was expected. Everett tried to tell the story of the battle, making the scene come alive, just as the video in the Visitors' Center does today. He also set forth an argument against the whole theory of secession, claiming that states and the citizens of states swore loyalty to the federal government under the Constitution, a conclusion that earned him warm thanks from Lincoln. By all accounts at the time, the oration was a success.

Lincoln's role as president was to say a few words of dedication, a sort of secular prayer. Just by his presence, he was marking out a new attitude of the government toward its war dead, a position of responsibility that was not evident after the Revolution, the War of 1812, the Mexican War, or the many Indian wars that still raged. The pressure of war made him uncertain that he could participate until the day before, when he apparently wrote more than half of the speech in the White House, on a piece of stationery with the "Executive Mansion" heading. The last sentences were probably written in the home of attorney David Wills, the founder of the cemetery, where Lincoln and Everett both stayed on the night before the dedication.

The few—depending on punctuation, nine to eleven—sentences of Lincoln's address are immortal. Along with his Second Inaugural, they are carved in marble on the walls of the Lincoln Memorial. On the day after, November 20, 1863, the speech was printed in full in the *New York Times*, complete with notes of where the speech was broken by applause. The *Times* account indicated that the speech was interrupted by applause five times, the first time after the clause, "that all men are created equal," and the fifth time after Lincoln urged his audience to "resolve that the dead shall not have died in vain." After the speech ended, according to the bracketed note in the *Times*, there was "Long continued applause."

Some accounts, including that of Ken Burns in *The Civil War* documentary, have said that the speech was a failure. Burns quotes Shelby Foote, the author of a huge history of the Civil War, to picture Lincoln being greeted by silence from the crowd and returning to his seat. But in fact, most contemporary newspaper stories noted that the speech was very well received. Some attacked the content of the speech, but none said that it provoked only silence.

The myth of silence began decades after the address, with Ward Hill Lamon, a friend of Lincoln's from Illinois who came with him to Washington. Lamon became marshal of the District of Columbia and traveled with Lincoln to Gettysburg to take charge of the president's security, a serious task in time of war. When the glorification of Lincoln took flight after his assassination, Lamon resisted. He stressed the common side of Lincoln in a book that sold badly. In 1885, Lamon was quoted as saying that he remembered no "hearty demonstrations" after the Gettysburg speech and recalled that the address "fell on the vast audience like a wet blanket." None of these statements amounts to an affirmation that the speech was received in silence, however. The effect of a "wet blanket" could have arisen from the contrast between Lincoln's solemn imagery of death and rebirth and Edward Everett's far more triumphal description of the victory, which ended with references to the "noble achievements of the War" and "the glorious annals of our common country." Everett moved some in the crowd to tears, where Lincoln only provoked applause.

In a best-selling short novel of 1906, *The Perfect Tribute* by Mary Shipman Andrews, the myth of silence attained an enduring place in the apocrypha of American civil religion. Andrews was a sentimental writer, born in Alabama and raised in Kentucky, who later moved to Syracuse, New York. Her story began with Lincoln feeling despondent that his speech had failed, but on the next day in Washington running into a child in the street who was desperately seeking a lawyer to make a will for his older brother, who was dying. Responding to the plea, Lincoln found that the brother was a Confederate soldier. He made the will, for a Southern aristocrat (of the "Hampton Court Blairs") whose eyes were bandaged, and who asked the strange lawyer named Lincoln to sit with him a moment after they had finished their business. The soldier wished to know if he was any relation to the president, and if he had read the speech that the president gave at Gettysburg. Explaining that his sister knew a senator who had attended the service, and that she had read him the speech that morning, the dying soldier extolled President Lincoln's words as one of the greatest speeches in history. The soldier said that the silence afterward came out of reverence: "One might as well applaud the Lord's Prayer—it would have been sacrilege." Only silence was "the perfect tribute."

He then put the speech into a new historical context, as part of the healing of the breach that caused the war: "Other men have spoken stirring words, for the North and for the South, but never before, I think, with the love of both breathing through them." Though he admitted that from his point of view, the thought behind the speech was wrong, he said that he would like to shake President Lincoln's hand. Then he reached out in the spasm of death, shook the hand of the unknown lawyer, and died.

To explain why the American public was ready to believe this myth of silence, it is useful to note that the Gettysburg Address was on one level an extremely partisan speech. The dying soldier of Andrews's story said, "It is only the greatest who can be a partisan without bitterness," and Lincoln succeeded in that. Garry Wills, in his Pulitzer Prize–winning book *Lincoln at Gettysburg*, compared Lincoln to a pickpocket who worked the crowd gathered to dedicate a cemetery, so that the crowd "departed with a new thing in its ideological luggage, that new constitution Lincoln had substituted for the one they brought with them." Legal historian George P. Fletcher made this point more specific, arguing that the Gettysburg Address became the preamble of a "second constitution" that displaced the values of individual liberty and voluntary association in favor of nationalism, equality, and political democracy. By beginning with the statement that the Founding Fathers intended that all men were created equal, then asserting that the war was fought to sustain that proposition, Lincoln certainly did support the most advanced positions of radical Republicanism and Abolitionism. The applause for "all men are created equal" at the end of the first sentence was probably not universal throughout the crowd, but instead represented a response of Lincoln's "base" to this political red meat. The *Chicago Times*, which had supported Stephen Douglas and other compromisers over slavery, complained that Lincoln had "dared" to mock the dead of Gettysburg while misstating "the cause for which they died," and libeling "the statesmen who founded the government."

For those closer to the middle of the political spectrum than the *Chicago Times*, Lincoln did have an uncanny knack for taking partisan positions without being divisive. The Gettysburg Address never mentioned slavery or its abolition. On the first day of January 1863, more than nine months before giving the address, Lincoln had issued the Emancipation Proclamation, which in effect abolished slavery while at the same time freeing no slaves. That proclamation declared that slaves in areas *held by the rebels* were now free, which meant that it could not be enforced where it applied, and did not apply where it could be enforced. Nonetheless, Lincoln was staking his claim to history, marking himself as the president who *would* abolish slavery, if he could only win the war and be re-elected in 1864. The Gettysburg Address was Lincoln's first public speech since his First Inaugural Address in 1861—a remarkable fact in this day of weekly presidential messages—and it was also the opening speech of his re-election campaign, for a second term in which he hoped to reunite the nation.

Unlike Edward Everett and most Northern speakers, Lincoln never mentioned the rebellion of the South. Everett's oration at Gettysburg called what the South was doing a "rebellion" and a "crime." Everett went on to say that secession was demonic: "an imitation on earth of that first foul revolt of 'the Infernal Serpent,' which emptied Heaven of one third part of its sons." But Lincoln's rhetoric about "the brave men, living and dead, who struggled here" would open a way for the next generation to interpret him as including Confederates who fought to destroy the United States among those "who gave their lives that the nation might live." As the dying Confederate officer in *The Perfect Tribute* said, "what we're all fighting for, the best of us, is the right of our country as it is given to us to see it."

The power of Lincoln's language, which his allies called too general and his enemies too partisan, grew from his use of religious imagery, which has contributed to the sense that his address is sacred scripture. As the poet Robert Lowell pointed out, the Gettysburg Address is filled with images of birth: "brought forth," "conceived," "created," and "a new birth of freedom." This new birth sprang from death, and particularly from the deaths of those from whom "we take increased devotion to that cause for which they here gave the last full measure of devotion." Death and resurrection is the controlling image of the Gettysburg Address. By appropriating the deepest image of hope from Christian (as well as Jewish and Muslim) religion, Lincoln lifted American civil religion to a place beyond politics. His language established one dogma: that all those who died for their country, no matter what they understood as their purpose, would be recognized.

But Lincoln also advanced two other propositions, now central to the American civil religion, to be fulfilled in the future. The assertions that "all men are created equal," quoted from the Decleration of Independence, and that "government of the people, for the people, and by the people" (a trinity paraphrased from Daniel Webster's famous *Reply to Hayne*) "shall not perish from the earth" quickly became sacred words in American civil religion. The Gettysburg Address was memorized by generations of students and reprinted in dozens of anthologies. The values of personal freedom or liberty, political democracy, and cultural tolerance were all represented in the Gettysburg Address, and all extended to both sides in the Civil War.

Anniversaries, reunions, and re-enactments have institutionalized this broad message of Gettysburg. In 1913, a fiftieth reunion of Union and Confederate veterans brought thousands to a Tent City at Gettysburg, where they were addressed by President Woodrow Wilson. President Franklin Delano Roosevelt hosted a 75th reunion, with slightly fewer than 3,000 veterans attending, in 1938, when an eternal flame for world peace was installed and lighted near the place where the first shots were fired. In 1968, the "tribal love-rock musical" *Hair* used a version of Lincoln's first sentence ("conceived in liberty, and dedicated to the one I love") to assert universal equality (as the song emphasized, "I say *all* men, are created *equal*"), and the same musical was revived in 2009 with great success. At the 150th anniversary of the battle in July of 2013, about 10,000 people from all over the world gathered in Gettysburg to camp out in uniform for three days and to re-enact the battle. At Gettysburg today there is a new Visitors' Center, offering high-quality video and extensive displays, which opened in 2009. The city still hosts a college and a Lutheran seminary, as it did in 1863, and is still surrounded by farms and orchards, but the main industry today is tourism. The National Park Service has long attempted to keep the landscape as nearly as possible in its condition on the day before the battle, and it has an ambitious program of tree removal and orchard planting to further that goal.

While other Civil War battlefields, such as Fredericksburg, Antietam, and Chattanooga, also have cemeteries and are also visited by pilgrims, Gettysburg remains the center of Civil War memorials. Only Gettysburg has a sacred text. Only Gettysburg both saved and transformed the Union.

SOURCES

Boritt, Gabor, *The Gettysburg Gospel: The Lincoln Speech That Nobody Knows* (New York: Simon & Schuster, 2006).

Desjardin, Thomas A., *These Honored Dead: How the Story of Gettysburg Shaped American Memory* (Cambridge, MA: Da Capo Press, 2003).

Faust, Drew Gilpin, *This Republic of Suffering: Death and the American Civil War* (New York: Alfred A. Knopf, 2008).

Fletcher, George P., *Our Secret Constitution: How Lincoln Redefined American Democracy* (New York: Oxford University Press, 2001).

Laderman, Gary, *The Sacred Remains: American Attitudes Toward Death, 1799–1883* (New Haven, CT: Yale University Press, 1996).

Linenthal, Edward Tabor, *Sacred Ground: Americans and Their Battlefields* (Chicago: University of Illinois Press, 1991).

McPherson, James M., *Hallowed Ground: A Walk at Gettysburg* (New York: Random House, 2003).

Wills, Garry, *Lincoln at Gettysburg: The Words That Remade America* (New York: Simon & Schuster, 1992).

18

Lincoln's Second Inaugural Address

The text of this speech is inscribed in marble on the walls of the Lincoln Memorial, on the side opposite the Gettysburg Address. After the Declaration of Independence and the Constitution, Lincoln's Second Inaugural has been regarded by many as the most sacred text of American civil religion, and some have seen it as the most profound work of theology ever written by an American. It raises basic questions about how American civil religion differs from Jewish and Christian religion. It affirms the value of world peace. Let us begin with a slow reading of Lincoln's 700 words, which Lincoln himself read slowly, taking about seven minutes on March 4, 1865. The Civil War would end on April 9, and the life of Abraham Lincoln on April 14.

> Fellow Countrymen:
> At this second appearing to take the oath of the presidential office, there is less occasion for an extended address than there was at the first. Then a statement, somewhat in detail, of a course to be pursued, seemed fitting and proper. Now, at the expiration of four years, during which public declarations have been constantly called forth on every point and phase of the great conflict which still absorbs the attention, and engrosses the energies of the nation, little that is new could be presented. The progress of our arms, upon which all else chiefly depends, is as well known to the public as to myself; and it is, I trust, reasonably satisfactory and encouraging to all. With high hope for the future, no prediction in regard to it is ventured.
> On the occasion corresponding with this four years ago, all thoughts were anxiously directed to an impending civil war. All dreaded it—all sought to avert it. While the inaugural address was being delivered from this place, devoted altogether to saving the Union without war, insurgent agents were in the city seeking to destroy it without war—seeking to dissolve the Union, and divide effects, by negotiation. Both parties deprecated war; but one of them would make war rather than let the

nation survive; and the other would accept war rather than let it perish. And the war came.

One eighth of the whole population were colored slaves, not distributed generally over the Union, but localized in the Southern part of it. These slaves constituted a peculiar and powerful interest. All knew that this interest was, somehow, the cause of the war. To strengthen, perpetuate, and extend this interest was the object for which the insurgents would rend the Union, even by war; while the government claimed no right to do more than to restrict the territorial enlargement of it. Neither party expected for the war, the magnitude, or the duration, which it has already attained. Neither anticipated that the cause of the conflict might cease with, or even before, the conflict itself should cease. Each looked for an easier triumph, and a result less fundamental and astounding. Both read the same Bible, and pray to the same God; and each invokes His aid against the other. It may seem strange that any men should seek a just God's assistance in wringing their bread from the sweat of other men's faces; but let us judge not that we be not judged. The prayers of both could not be answered; that of neither has been answered fully.

The Almighty has His own purposes. "Woe unto the world because of offenses! For it must needs be that offenses come; but woe to the man by whom the offense cometh!" If we shall suppose that American slavery is one of those offenses which, in the providence of God, must needs come, but which, having continued through His appointed time, He now wills to remove, and that He gives to both North and South, this terrible war, as the woe due to those by whom the offence came, shall we discern therein any departure from those divine attributes which the believers in a Living God always ascribe to Him? Fondly do we hope—fervently do we pray—that this mighty scourge of war may speedily pass away. Yet, if God wills that it continue, until all the wealth piled by the bondman's two hundred and fifty years of unrequited toil shall be sunk, and until every drop of blood drawn with the lash, shall be paid by another drawn with the sword, as was said three thousand years ago, so still it must be said, "the judgments of the Lord, are true and righteous altogether."

With malice toward none; with charity for all; with firmness in the right, as God gives us to see the right, let us strive on to finish the work we are in; to bind up the nation's wounds; to care for him who shall have borne the battle, and for his widow, and his orphan—to do all which may achieve and cherish a just, and a lasting peace, among ourselves, and with all nations.

Behind these words lay four decades of Abraham Lincoln's grappling with ultimate questions, and four years in the White House, when his first answers to those questions were challenged and deepened by new confrontations with death and defeat. The young Lincoln, bereft of his mother at nine years of age, was raised in a Baptist church that preached predestination and limited baptism to those who had come to believe that they were among those chosen to be saved. Since he was never baptized, Lincoln clearly never made the claim that God had given him a saving faith. As a young man, he read rationalists like Thomas Paine who challenged the creeds of all churches and the status of the Bible as revealed truth. Yet he also read the Bible often and memorized many passages.

Lincoln's skepticism became so well-known that, during his one successful race for Congress in 1846, he had to answer charges that he was an atheist. Lincoln had a handbill printed, on which he said that although he belonged to no church, he had never "denied the truth of the Scriptures." He admitted having sometimes argued against free will, and while he did not reaffirm that position, he did contend that a similar doctrine was taught by "several of the Christian denominations." When a heckler called out from a crowd, asking whether Lincoln was going to heaven or hell, the candidate responded, "I'm going to Congress." He often said that he would join a church if there were any that would limit its creed to the commands to love God and one's fellow man.

When Lincoln was president, his wife, Mary Todd Lincoln, joined the New York Avenue Presbyterian Church, and Lincoln often accompanied her to services. He expressed satisfaction that the minister there, the Rev. Phineas Gurley, did not preach on politics, which Lincoln said he got enough of during the week. As an orthodox Presbyterian, Gurley did preach a great deal on predestination, which many Protestants since John Calvin had thought of as the essential doctrine to support belief in the sovereignty of God and the human need for grace.

Here Lincoln could not agree, although he had once believed that every human act was determined, and still believed that God ruled history. The notion that God had made large numbers of people for eternal punishment in hell—including all unbelievers and believers in false religions, and so the vast majority of people, in the view of most Calvinists—repelled him. The contradiction between a God who predestined all things and yet condemned people for what He had caused offended Lincoln's sense of reason. Eventually, he would come to combine belief in God's sovereignty and punishment of sin with affirmation of human free will and hope for universal salvation.

What Lincoln said about God's punishment of both sides in the Civil War was related to this argument. "Woe unto the world because of offenses! For it must needs be that offenses come; but woe to that man by whom the offence cometh!" Quoting Jesus in Matthew 18:7, Lincoln seems to invoke predestination as well as punishment. If American slavery is a predestined offense "which, in the providence of God, must needs come," this did not mean that no one would be punished for it. By detailing the punishments of war, which fell on both sides—that all the wealth made by the slaves could be destroyed, and all the blood shed by the slaves matched by the blood of soldiers—Lincoln established that both North and South were being punished. This even-handed perspective was unique to Lincoln in his time, when pulpits on both sides rang with assurances that God favored the Union or the Confederacy, slavery or abolition. For a wartime leader to tell his nearly victorious people that they also bore some guilt for the war was an unprecedented and unrepeated act of courage. It attained a depth of analysis, a recognition of the paradox that God may work through human sin and still afflict the human instruments through whom providence works, that was sometimes seen in the Hebrew Psalms and Prophets, but rarely among Jewish, Christian, or Muslim rulers.

Lincoln first came to the conclusion that God was prolonging the war as a punishment on both sides as he privately reflected on Union defeats in battle. After Lincoln died, one of his young secretaries, John Hay, found a note dated September 2, 1862, during the Second Battle of Bull Run. It was a day when Attorney General Edward Bates reported the president saying that "he felt almost ready to hang himself." Lincoln had left a cabinet meeting and written a note: "The will of God prevails.... In great contests each party claims to act in accordance with the will of God. Both *may* be, and one *must* be wrong." He pronounced himself "almost ready to say this is probably true—that God wills this contest, and wills that it shall not end yet." Almost two years later, another precursor to the Second Inaugural appeared in Lincoln's letter to a delegation from Kentucky that had come to Washington in April 1864 to protest the enlistment of former slaves in the Union Army. There Lincoln said, "I claim not to have controlled events, but confess plainly that events have controlled me." He wrote that "the nation's condition" was not what anyone expected, but that "God alone can claim it," and concluded that "[i]f God now wills the removal of a great wrong, and wills also that we of the North as well as you of the South, will pay fairly for our complicity in that wrong," there will be nothing to say but to "attest and revere the justice and goodness of God."

In the year and a half between the decisive victory at Gettysburg and the elections of 1864, Lincoln had many reasons to believe that God was prolonging the war. Bitterly disappointed that General Meade did not pursue Lee after the victory at Gettysburg, Lincoln faced a series of Union defeats in the summer that brought Confederate troops to within five miles of Washington and cost hundreds of thousands of lives. If General Sherman had not taken Atlanta on September 2, 1864, the Democrats would probably have elected General McClellan to the presidency in November, on the platform of making a peace that preserved slavery. By the time the Second Inaugural Address was given in March, the war had destroyed so many lives and so much of the fabric of Southern life that no return to the antebellum world was possible. So many escaped slaves and black Union soldiers came to Washington to hear the speech that a reporter from the *Times* of London wrote that "at least half the multitude were colored people." In Lincoln's view, it was now clear that God had used the length and severity of the war to end slavery in the United States.

Like the extremely clever lawyer that he was, Lincoln employed the Calvinist beliefs of many Americans to convince them of this point. He made his case by stating a hypothetical in the form that lawyers call *arguendo*, "for the sake of argument." It was not necessary to assert absolutely that slavery was sinful or that God was using the war to root it out. Rather, "[i]f we shall suppose that American slavery is one of those offenses," and that God has given "to both North and South, this terrible war, as the woe due to those by whom the offense came," *then*, Lincoln asked, would we see "any departure from those divine attributes which the believers [note, not "we believers"] in a living God always ascribe to Him?" In a letter to a friend named Thurlow Weed shortly afterward, Lincoln reflected that the implication of his argument would force those who tried to disagree to deny that God governed the world.

But the God invoked by Lincoln for American civil religion was more than a judge who meted out justice and punishment for sin. The closing of the Second Inaugural asked the audience to imitate the God who, according to Matthew 5:45, gave the sun and the rain even to his enemies. As Lincoln scholar Ronald C. White has written, "Instead of rallying his supporters, in the name of God, to support the war, he asked his listeners, quietly, to imitate the ways of God." After the crushing statement that God would still be just if the war destroyed all that had been built with slave labor, and took as much blood from white Americans as had been taken from the slaves, Lincoln turned toward healing actions: "With malice toward none; with charity for all; with firmness in the right, as God gives us to see the right, let us strive on to finish the work we are in; to bind up the nation's wounds; to care for him who shall have borne the battle, and for his widow, and his orphan—to do all which may achieve and cherish a just, and a lasting peace, among ourselves, and with all nations."

This extraordinary call to peace and forgiveness before the war had even concluded reflected a unique form of faith that Lincoln had developed, and that contributed to one of the most characteristic attitudes of American civil religion, its universalism. The assumption that all can participate in American civil religion relates to belief in universal salvation. Universalism underlies the values of world peace and cultural tolerance, and in the Second Inaugural it arises directly from the contemplation of death. Haunted by death all of his life, beginning with the death of his mother and continuing through his older sister's death in childbirth in 1828, when Lincoln was nineteen, through the sudden death from typhoid of his friend (and perhaps first love), Ann Rutledge, in 1835, to the death of his son Edward from tuberculosis in 1850 and of his son Willie from bronchial pneumonia in 1862, Lincoln often reflected on the biblical promises of an afterlife. He became a provisional, uncertain believer in universal salvation, a doctrine that was represented by a Universalist Church during the nineteenth century. Unlike most Universalists, however, Lincoln did not ground his hope on divine forgiveness or on the death of Jesus. He apparently concluded that universal salvation would come through punishment for every sin, which God would enforce in this life or the next. After this "terrible war," then, the whole nation would have the chance for new life in a kingdom of God. After all of the American wars of the twentieth and twenty-first centuries, and especially after World War II, the United States has demonstrated an unusual willingness not only to forgive but to build up its former enemies. Universalist hope became the unofficial norm of many forms of American Christianity and Judaism, as well as of American civil religion, in the twentieth century.

Those who received this message of hope in 1865 were not very demonstrative. A few cheered when Lincoln said that "All knew that this interest [slavery] was, somehow, the cause of the war." A few more laughed at Lincoln's remark that it may seem strange for people to pray to God for "assistance in wringing their bread from the sweat of other men's faces." From some African-Americans came a steady chorus of "Bless the Lord" after almost every sentence. But there was no widespread applause or other response for any line that came after Lincoln's moment of satirizing the prayers of the South. This lack of enthusiasm was not surprising. Unlike the Gettysburg Address, a war speech that was given at a cemetery in view of a battlefield, the Second Inaugural was about peace and the meaning of history, and it criticized the very audience that heard it, attempting to lead them to see that "the Almighty has his own purposes."

In the immediate aftermath of the speech, reactions showed a remarkable range. Frederick Douglass, the escaped slave and anti-slavery orator, was nearly barred from the evening celebrations at the White House because he was black, but called out to Lincoln as the guards seized him. When Lincoln insisted that Douglass tell him what he thought of the address, the Abolitionist answered: "Mr. Lincoln, that was a sacred effort." According to Charles Francis Adams, Jr., a descendant of John and John Quincy Adams and a young colonel who had fought at Antietam and Gettysburg, in a letter to his father, the ambassador to Great Britain, the Second Inaugural was "in its grand simplicity and directness...for all time the historical keynote of this war." On the other hand, the reliably Republican *New York Times* was disappointed: "He [Lincoln] does not reexpound the principles of the war; does not redeclare the worth of the Union; does not reproclaim that absolute submission to the Constitution is the only peace." The *New York Herald* reported that "[t]here was a leaden stillness about the crowd" hearing the speech, and argued that the intention to see slavery destroyed "contradicts Abraham Lincoln's call to 'charity for all.'" From the Confederate side, the *Richmond Examiner* said that the speech "reads like the tail of some old sermon, and seems to have no particular meaning of any kind, at least, if any meaning lurks in it we fail to perceive it." Lincoln himself was prepared for mixed early reviews. He wrote to Thurlow Weed that people "are not flattered" to be told that there might be a difference of purpose between themselves and God, but that he thought in the end the speech would "wear as well—perhaps better than anything I have produced."

More recent reactions have shown how right Lincoln was. The decision to inscribe the whole text of the speech on the north wall of the Lincoln Memorial, which was dedicated in 1922, showed the status that the Second Inaugural had attained by then. In a 1965 article for *Christian Century*, theologian Reinhold Niebuhr made an argument, drawn largely from the Second Inaugural, that Lincoln had affirmed "the historical dynamism of Western culture" while avoiding the "evil by-product" of that dynamism: "a fanaticism which confused partial meanings and contingent purposes with the ultimate meaning of life itself."

For Niebuhr and the generations of neo-orthodox theologians who have dominated the elite circles of American Protestantism from the 1930s through the present day, Lincoln's Second Inaugural became the ultimate statement of realism combined with hope. Other scholars have echoed this judgment. As literary critic Alfred Kazin wrote in his last book, *God and the American Writer* (1997), Lincoln presided over "the one chapter in American life that brings us back to biblical history." In a commemorative volume issued by Penguin Books after the Obama inauguration in 2009, President Obama's inaugural address was printed with four other documents, in this order: Lincoln's Second Inaugural, the Gettysburg Address, Lincoln's First Inaugural, and Ralph Waldo Emerson's lecture on Self-Reliance. The Second Inaugural is clearly considered first among speeches sacred to the American civil religion.

But does Lincoln's theological speech really belong to American civil religion, or does it belong to Christianity? Lincoln used the Bible four times in this brief address, not only in the long quote from Matthew on offenses, but also when he alluded to slaveholders taking their bread "from the sweat of other men's faces" (an echo of the curse on Adam in Genesis 3:19); in the admonition to "judge not" (Jesus in Luke 6:37); and in the conclusion that "the judgments of the Lord are true and righteous altogether" (Psalms 19:9). Both friends like Frederick Douglass and critics like the *Richmond Examiner* called the speech a "sermon." Legal historian George P. Fletcher argued that the Second Inaugural was an example of the new emphasis on divine mission that entered American constitutional thinking after the Civil War. There is support here for the arguments of scholars like Will

Herberg, Harold Bloom, and David Gelernter that "Americanism" is really a biblical religion, a derivative or new form of Abrahamic monotheism.

Yet there is also something very unbiblical about the Second Inaugural, unless we take the pessimistic uncertainty of Ecclesiastes as the biblical norm. Lincoln did not believe that God spoke to him or that he knew the will of God, and the Second Inaugural Address works as a statement of civil religion even if God remains hidden, or entirely absent. "The Almighty has his own purposes." Though the destruction brought by war can be seen as a judgment of God, Lincoln offered that view as a hypothesis, a way for believers in the biblical God to see it. Whatever believers thought, the actual judgment had not been wreaked by God's angels or by fire from heaven but by cannons and rifles fired by men. American civil religion can include monotheism, but in Lincoln's version it is finally trans-theistic, affirming a power behind the cosmos that may not be personal or biblical. Most of the speech is couched in deeply impersonal language, describing conditions and actions without personal pronouns, using the passive voice, until the final call to action. The work to which Lincoln calls his audience at the end is not divine but human work, "to bind up the nation's wounds." When he asks for firmness in the right, "as God gives us to see the right," he implies that God will not give everyone the same vision.

The salvation Lincoln urges Americans to seek is a "just and lasting peace, among ourselves, and with all nations." This peace does not belong to God or to Eden or to Paradise, but to this nation and this world. It is the peace enshrined in American civil religion.

SOURCES

Carwardine, Richard, "Lincoln's Religion," in Eric Foner, ed., *Our Lincoln: New Perspectives on Lincoln and His World* (New York: W. W. Norton, 2008).
Delbanco, Andrew, "Lincoln's Sacramental Language," in Eric Foner, ed., *Our Lincoln: New Perspectives on Lincoln and His World* (New York: W. W. Norton, 2008).
Fletcher, George P., *Our Secret Constitution: How Lincoln Redefined American Democracy* (New York: Oxford University Press, 2001).
Jayne, Allen, *Lincoln and the American Manifesto* (Amherst, NY: Prometheus Books, 2007).
Kazin, Alfred, *God and the American Writer* (New York: Alfred A. Knopf, 1997).
Waugh, John C., *One Man Great Enough: Abraham Lincoln's Road to Civil War* (Orlando: Harcourt, 2007).
White, Ronald C., *Lincoln's Greatest Speech: The Second Inaugural* (New York: Simon & Schuster, 2002).
Wolf, William J., *The Religion of Abraham Lincoln* (New York: Seabury Press, 1963).

19

Arlington National Cemetery

The sign at the entrance to Arlington National Cemetery (Figure 19.1) tells visitors that they are entering "hallowed grounds." Hallowed first by nature and then by history: this is an intensely beautiful site, where George Washington's grandson George Washington Custis built Arlington House on an estate with a commanding view of the capital district. Visitors still share the view from that house where Lafayette stayed, where six of Robert E. Lee's children were born, and where Abraham Lincoln visited Union troops.

But ultimately, Arlington was hallowed by death. For ancient Romans, land became part of the *patria*, or fatherland, when ancestors were buried there. The burials, within sight of the capital, of more than 320,000 people who died in wars of the United States or in service to their country have made Arlington the center of the American *patria*. Perhaps more than any other place, Arlington Cemetery shows how patriotism becomes a civil religion.

What makes Arlington sacred today began as an act of desecration. The Union Army seized this place, the home of Custis's daughter, who had married Robert E. Lee, almost immediately after the Civil War began. This occupation was a practical step, because these heights could have been used to bombard Washington, and the fort that Union soldiers built here proved essential after the first Battle of Bull Run. But the next step was not required by military necessity—it was motivated by revenge. The man in charge of providing burial space for Union dead, Quartermaster General Montgomery Meigs, needing to create a new cemetery in July 1864, chose to begin by burying soldiers next to Lee's house, and then created a mass grave at the center of Mary Custis Lee's rose garden. He apparently intended to ensure that no one could live in the house again. As Mrs. Lee wrote, graves were "planted up to the door without any regard to common decency." Meigs came from Georgia, and he had served under Lee, whom he regarded as a traitor for choosing the Confederate side. His hatred for Lee increased when his son was killed in the war, in October 1864, and came to be buried in one of the first elaborate tombs at Arlington, again very close to Arlington House.

Figure 19.1 Stones in some sections of Arlington are not uniform, but vary with rank and cost. Members of the Supreme Court are grouped together, and some elaborate memorials exist. Photograph by the author.

By the end of the Civil War, thousands were interred around the former home. Neither Mary Custis Lee nor her husband set foot in the mansion again. However, ownership of the property was not clear. The US government had taken legal possession with a claim for $94 in taxes on land held by rebels, which Mary Custis Lee had tried but failed to pay because the law required that payment be made in person. A son of the Lee family brought suit, and the Supreme Court ruled in 1882 that he owned the land and that those buried in it would have to be removed. The dilemma was solved in 1883, when he agreed to sell the property to the government for $150,000.

Behind the acts of desecration and dedication that made Arlington a sacred place lie some of the deepest mysteries of religion. Religion treats death as both impure and sacred. As Rudolf Otto wrote in *The Idea of the Holy* (1917), phenomena that people call holy are both dangerous and fascinating, and dead bodies are commonly treated as holy. For Jews, the dead body is unclean, although it is a *mitzvah* (a good deed and a religious duty) to clean the body and to prepare it for burial. Dead bodies in Judaism have a polluting effect. Those returning from a funeral must wash their hands before entering a home, and the Torah must never be carried into a cemetery. Similarly, Roman Catholic priests walk around the coffin and sprinkle it with holy water at the funeral Mass. Theravada Buddhists have a traditional corpse meditation, which involves confronting impermanence by sitting before a corpse for as long as ten days. Japanese Shinto priests find corpses too unclean to handle and leave funerals to the Buddhists. As Western cultures have become more modern, they have tended to put more distance between life and death. Death takes place in hospitals more often than at home, and businesses have replaced homes as locations for funerals. In the nineteenth century, cemeteries were moved away from churches and cities to become suburban parks, and Arlington is one example of that trend. Spatially removed from daily life, these cemeteries were dedicated for solemn visits and ceremonies. Cemeteries became peripheral to function but central to meaning.

For example, Memorial Day began within cemeteries in 1868, when General John A. Logan, commander of a veterans' organization known as the Grand Army of the Republic (GAR), issued an order that GAR members decorate the graves of Union dead on May 30. The ceremonies at Arlington received national press. They were attended by Generals Ulysses Grant and James Garfield, both future presidents, and featured a reading of Lincoln's Gettysburg Address and the singing of hymns at the monument in Mrs. Lee's former garden, where 2,111 unidentified survivors of Bull Run were interred. Decoration Day became a habit in the United States. It turned into the day that American civil religion sets aside for acknowledging all of the nation's war dead when Congress created a legal holiday named Memorial Day in 1888.

Since 1921, Memorial Day at Arlington has centered on the Tomb of the Unknown Soldier (Figure 19.2). About half a mile to the south from Arlington House, with almost as good a view of the capital, the tomb brings some to tears with its inscription: "HERE RESTS IN HONORED GLORY AN AMERICAN SOLDIER KNOWN BUT TO GOD." On each Memorial Day, the president comes to the grave to lay a wreath and to give a speech in the amphitheater next door.

The tomb is not uniquely American, but takes part in a cult of the Unknown Soldier that began after World War I. In one sense it seems strange, because Arlington already contained thousands of unknown dead when this tomb was established, yet this unknown has been singled out. The idea offered a symbolic compensation for the industrial-scale slaughter of World War I. The number of infantry deaths brought about by machine guns, artillery, and gas in that war was unprecedented, and left many unidentifiable remains. Mass graves were insufficient as focal points for mourning.

In England's Westminster Abbey and under the Arc de Triomphe in Paris, tombs commemorating a single unknown soldier were consecrated at the same moment in 1920. To select an unknown soldier for the American site, a veteran of the Western Front walked around four coffins of unidentified remains,

Figure 19.2 The Tomb of the Unknown Soldier of World War I, joined by unknown dead from World War II, Korea, and Vietnam, overlooks Washington. Photograph by the author.

then said he heard a voice telling him that a particular coffin contained a friend. Today, there are tombs for the Unknown of World War I as far away from Europe as India and New Zealand. As the carnage of the twentieth century increased, the cult of the Unknown continued to spread. A legend of a German Unknown Soldier coming to life and seeking revenge formed part of Nazi mythology in the 1930s. In America, a superhero Unknown Soldier appeared in Ace Comics during the early 1940s. After World War II, new tombs appeared in Moscow and Eastern Europe. During the Vietnam War, Jim Morrison and the Doors sang an anti-war ballad called *Unknown Soldier*. From 1966 until 1982, DC Comics published a series under that title about an American spy, a master of disguise, who had lost his face in battle during World War II but then used his lack of identity to destroy America's enemies.

Meanwhile, the ceremonies at the Arlington tomb grew more and more precise and elaborate. For the first few years, only a civilian watchman attended the tomb, but in 1926 the military took over during the day, standing guard when the cemetery was open to the public. Since 1937, the guard has walked 24 hours a day, and a special Tomb Guard Badge demanding serious training was established in 1958. Now the guard is drawn from members of the Third Brigade, called the Old Guard, who take meticulous care of their wool uniforms, worn even in Washington's fierce summer heat, and obvious pride in the precision of their walk. The "Sentinel's Creed" that they memorize begins, "My dedication to this sacred duty is total and wholehearted." For Tomb Guards, and for at least some of the millions of visitors who fall silent as they watch the changing of the guard, a religious dimension of non-rational commitment has been added to military discipline.

In 1958, when unknown soldiers from World War II and Korea were interred beside the Unknown from World War I, Arlington was already the unquestioned center for recalling dead heroes in American civil religion. There are 144 national cemeteries in the United States, and Gettysburg preceded Arlington as the most eminent "hallowed ground," but the beauty of Arlington's site and its proximity to Washington made certain that it would surpass all others. The national unity evoked by the Spanish-American War led to two decisive steps: the creation of a memorial to the unknown dead from the U.S.S. *Maine* and the decision to create a separate section for Confederate war dead.

Both the *Maine* memorial and the Confederate section feature hundreds of gravestones facing a central focus, rather than the normal rows of stones. At the entrance of the *Maine* memorial stands a mast from the ship, on a base that lists the names and ranks of the dead, while the Confederate graves are grouped in a circle around an enormous column of sculpture by Moses Ezekiel, a Confederate veteran, in which a female representing the South holds out a wreath toward the southern side of the cemetery. A relief around the base of the monument includes a figure of Athena, goddess of defensive war, with a shield labeled The Constitution. Such female symbolism was especially appropriate, since the memorial was paid for by the Daughters of the Confederacy, a group of women, descended from Confederate soldiers, who cared for graves in the cemeteries of the South.

For years, the *Maine* memorial and the Confederate memorial were the most prominent features at Arlington, other than the Custis-Lee mansion. Together, they stood for a United States that had overcome the division of the Civil War to become a unified international power. The inclusion of Confederate dead and the pagan and female symbolism of Athena demonstrated the value of cultural tolerance, a value that would become increasingly prominent in the future of the cemetery. In 1914, the area near these two features was marked by construction of a marble Memorial Amphitheater, large enough to hold 5,000 people. Around the outside of the amphitheater were listed America's battles, beginning with Lexington and ending with Santiago de Cuba. By the time the amphitheater was dedicated in 1920, its completion had been delayed for years by World War I, and the list of battles was out of date. The Tomb of the Unknown Soldier was soon joined to the front of the amphitheater.

When the first Unknown Soldier was entombed in 1921, President Warren Harding gave a eulogy that insisted, "There must be, there shall be, the commanding voice of a conscious civilization against armed warfare." This pacifist hope did not prove prophetic. In 1958, on the ship bearing Unknown Soldiers from World War II and Korea across the Pacific, Rear Admiral Lewis Parks was less pacifistic: "These men did not fail us when the chips were down and we must not fail them in the days and years ahead when communist forces will press ever harder to drive the free world into slavery."

With the large and lengthy wars of the twentieth century, the cemetery inevitably grew. Arlington held fewer than 50,000 graves in 1941, but had more than 100,000 by 1959. The large numbers who fought in World War II, Korea, and Vietnam meant that the number of dead buried there would more than triple by 2009. As the United States transformed its military into a professional organization after the 1970s (in response to the experience of Vietnam), burial at Arlington became more popular. One in ten of the dead from the Iraq War have come to Arlington, a higher percentage than from any previous conflict. By the end of the twenty-first century, according to some projections, the number of dead in the cemetery will exceed the living population of the District of Columbia.

Arlington has, meanwhile, gradually gone beyond its original status as a beautiful, bucolic resting place for Civil War dead to become a memorial for all who have died serving a nation that has frequently been at war. Steps in that direction began as early as 1892, when the bodies of Revolutionary War veterans and veterans of the War of 1812 were brought to Arlington from graves elsewhere in the District of Columbia. This was deliberately done to create a place that enshrined the dead from all the nation's wars.

One of the most transformative moments in Arlington's history came with the burial of President John F. Kennedy, in 1963. Kennedy was a veteran of World War II with a heroic record, the captain of a patrol boat who rescued Marines trapped on an island, and who later swam for miles to save his crew and himself when the boat was torpedoed. On the day of the Kennedy assassination, it was taken for granted that he would be buried in the family gravesite at Brookline, Massachusetts, next to his son Patrick, who had died as a prematurely born infant a few months before. The decision against this seems to have come from a consideration that the grave should be open to the American people. Arlington was chosen at the combined urging of Sargent Shriver, the president's brother-in-law and director of the Peace Corps, Robert McNamara, the secretary of Defense, and Robert Kennedy, the president's brother and attorney general, who actually selected the site just below the Custis-Lee mansion and obtained Mrs. Kennedy's consent. A Park Service employee recalled that, on a visit to Arlington in March, President Kennedy had looked at the view from the mansion and said that he could stay there forever. The idea for an eternal flame on the grave came from Mrs. Kennedy.

Stunning numbers of visitors, about 3,000 per hour and 50,000 on each weekend day, came to Kennedy's grave in the first year after his burial. The design of the gravesite proved so inadequate to accommodate the crowds that a new site, slightly down the hill from the original, had to be built in 1967, and the body transferred. The gravesite is now composed of New England granite and plants that could occur in a granite field. Facing south, on a plateau partially ringed by a low wall, visitors can read six passages from Kennedy's Inaugural Address with the Capitol and the rest of Washington as background. Turning north, they face the eternal flame and the flat markers for the graves of President Kennedy, his wife, and their two infant children (Patrick and another, a daughter, who was stillborn and therefore not named in 1956). No monument for any other individual at Arlington takes so much space, but few if any begrudge the space to John Fitzgerald Kennedy.

The Kennedy grave contributed to the increasing popularity of being buried in Arlington, and the Vietnam conflict resulted in the deaths of many soldiers. During the 1960s and 1970s, Arlington averaged 30 to 37 burials per day, with a peak of 47 funerals on one day in 1968. In that fateful year, John F. Kennedy was joined in Arlington by his brother Robert. Shot on the night when he won the California primary and was seemingly destined to be president, Robert Kennedy had the only night funeral in the history of Arlington. It was scheduled for the day, but the train that brought the body to Washington from New York took eight and a half hours to make the 225-mile trip because of crowds milling along the track to see the casket, which was displayed on an open car. Now Robert Kennedy's gravesite is next to that of his brother. It has a quiet fountain and a curved wall with excerpts from two speeches on the side facing Washington, and on the other side a small marble stone, flat in the grass, that says simply "Robert Francis Kennedy." A few feet behind the stone is a plain wooden cross, painted white, which must have to be changed very frequently to keep it fresh. Though the humility of the site is striking, it could also be called an ostentatious humility. On August 29, 2009, another white wooden cross was set up, between the graves of President Kennedy and of Robert Kennedy, for their youngest brother, Senator Edward Kennedy.

Over the last decades of the twentieth century and the first decade of the twenty-first, Arlington gained hundreds of thousands of remains, not only because of Vietnam but also because of the aging of the generation that fought World War II and filled the large armed services of the Cold War. A huge Columbarium, built to hold inurnments of ashes rather than internments, expanded the cemetery's capacity. New rules restricted spouses and dependent children to a single plot, with coffins stacked. Eligibility for Arlington was restricted to those who died on active duty, those who served long enough to receive a military pension, and those who served briefly but also attained high office in national government. At times this resulted in statements such as that on the headstone of Supreme Court Justice William O. Douglas, which reads "WILLIAM O. DOUGLAS, PRIVATE, UNITED STATES ARMY," on the front, and only refers to his years as a Justice on the back.

The Douglas headstone illustrates another principle. Despite the many sections filled with rows of identical white headstones, provided at no cost by the government for those who are eligible, Arlington is not an egalitarian site like Gettysburg. Douglas lies in Section 5 with many other Supreme Court Justices, and the other Justices have their own individual, larger stones, which are allowed if other large stones are in the section. Generals and Admirals tend to be near each other in such sections.

As Arlington became more a national site than a simple cemetery, many more group memorials joined the monuments for the *Maine* and the Confederacy. Monuments for Pan Am flight 103, blown up over Lockerbie, Scotland in 1988; for the Challenger and Columbia shuttle crews, killed in 1986 and 2003; for the Marines killed in their Beirut, Lebanon barracks in 1983; and for those who died at the Pentagon on September 11, 2001, have lately been added. A large building called the Women in Military Service to America Memorial was dedicated in 1997. As one superintendent of the cemetery has said, Arlington has become American history written in stone.

When history is written in the stone of a cemetery, the law that the medium is the message has particular effects. The basic message of Arlington is inscribed on the Memorial Amphitheater, near the Unknown Soldier: *Dulce et decorum est pro patria mori*. This is a line from the *Odes* (iii.2.13) of the Roman poet Horace, which could be translated "It is sweet and fitting to die for the fatherland." During the carnage of World War I, the British poet Wilfrid Owen made bitter use of this line in a denunciation of war, just before he was himself killed. But in the beauty of Arlington, it is hard to believe that it might not be sweet and fitting to die for one's country.

It is easy to see at Arlington how completely the United States has absorbed and transformed the attitudes of Roman Stoicism. The prevailing mood is a cool, dedicated perfectionism, in which American Tomb Guards are the equal of any Stoic. Former Supreme Court Justice Oliver Wendell Holmes, who was wounded in three battles of the Civil War, is buried here, and it was Holmes's address on "The Soldier's Faith"—a Stoic reflection on the duty to keep walking forward in battle despite not understanding the cause, and despite the line of falling soldiers and the line of approaching bullets—that led President Theodore Roosevelt to appoint him to the court. But at Arlington, Americans show themselves to be more open to reconciliation with enemies, to admitting sentiment, and to incorporating differences of religion, sex, and race than the Romans were. One true parallel between American and Roman civil religions appears in the ways that both cultures have allowed religious tolerance in their monuments. Just as the Romans brought many gods of other peoples into their Pantheon, Arlington has thirty-nine authorized religious symbols for headstones, including two Muslim symbols, a Wiccan pentacle in a circle, and an atom for atheists. This is cultural tolerance brought to a high degree.

Many of the simple white stones tell a story about US history that Americans rarely admit: the story of just how often the nation has gone to war. Many stones list a name and several wars, as in "World War I, World War II, Korea," and very commonly, "World War II, Korea, Vietnam," or in the case of one colonel born in 1879, "SPAM (Spanish-American War), Philippine Insurrection, World War I, World War II." Of course, all of these wars are not seen at Arlington as contradictions of the value of world peace in American civil religion; rather, the wars were fought in pursuit of peace. Though the United States often represents itself as a nation of citizen soldiers, with no deep military tradition in the sense of the Spartans or Prussians or Japanese *samurai*, Arlington shows otherwise. Arlington also shows that at least some of the military now serve alongside the guides of the National Park Service as clergy of American civil religion.

SOURCES

Bigler, Philip, *In Honored Glory: Arlington National Cemetery, the Final Post* (St. Petersburg, FL: Vandamere Press, 1986; 4th ed., 2005).
Krowl, Michelle, "In the Spirit of Fraternity: The United States Government and the Burial of Confederate Dead at Arlington National Cemetery, 1864–1914," *The Virginia Magazine of History and Biography* 111, no. 2 (2003), 151–186.
National Geographic Society, *Where Valor Rests: Arlington National Cemetery* (Washington, DC: National Geographic, 2007).
Otto, Rudolph, *The Idea of the Holy*, translated by John W. Harvey (1917; New York: Oxford University Press, 1958).

20

The Statue of Liberty and Ellis Island

Next to the flag, the Statue of Liberty may be more emblematic of the United States than any other symbol. It was created to celebrate the most basic value of American civil religion, the personal freedom that is also called liberty. That original meaning has been subject to change and to challenge because of the statue's location in New York harbor, a major site for immigration and for other social, cultural, and political pressures.

The Statue of Liberty is also the most physically fragile of monuments. Made from copper sheets an eighth of an inch thick and exposed to wind and water, the Statue needs constant maintenance and occasional overhauls. Her symbolic power and attractiveness to pilgrims have proved almost too compelling. As experts at the National Park Service have correctly pointed out, those who made the Statue intended her to be viewed from ships and from the shore, not to have the public come onto the island and climb inside, but Americans and foreign tourists have insisted on touching the embodiment of liberty and have done so for decades. Crises of war and weather have also threatened the Statue. After the World Trade Center, just across the harbor, was destroyed in the terror attack of 2001, the Statue was closed to visitors for years. A long campaign by the New York *Daily News* publisher Mort Zuckerman and then-Congressman Anthony Weiner succeeded in getting her crown reopened in 2009. Hurricane Sandy, in October of 2012, then closed Liberty Island to visitors until July 4, 2013.

About a thousand feet from Liberty Island, where the Statue stands, sits Ellis Island, the primary destination of immigrants to the United States in the great era of immigration that lasted from 1892 until 1924. This coincidence was not intended when the Statue was conceived or dedicated, but it has shaped the meaning of the Statue for more than a century. Although Ellis Island closed as a naturalization site in 1954, and most immigrants now arrive by air, the island's historic role and its adoption by the Park Service has made it a symbol for the whole movement of people to the United States, or at least for those who came voluntarily rather than as slaves. Originally a place where immigrants were screened, and sometimes sent back to their homelands, Ellis Island has become a museum that teaches the value of cultural tolerance.

Ellis Island began as a brutally functional site, but it has become sacred. It is now visited by about 17,000 people on peak days, far more than the 11,000 immigrants per day who arrived there during its busiest times. Part of its sacredness comes from family nostalgia—it has been estimated that half of all Americans are descended from the 60 million who came through Ellis Island. But part of the holiness of Ellis Island must also be an effect of the Goddess of Liberty who stands close by.

In its original conception, the Statue of Liberty had nothing to do with immigration. It began as the dream of a French professor and political activist, Edouard-René Lefebvre de Laboulaye. This dream was first memorably expressed in 1865 at Laboulaye's estate, during an after-dinner discussion that included two relatives of Lafayette and a brother of Alexis de Tocqueville. One of the guests was contending that there could be no such thing as gratitude between nations, but Laboulaye disagreed, citing the feelings of the American and French people for each other. While Americans were grateful to France for help in gaining their freedom from Britain, Labouleye argued, the French were grateful to America for opposing British power afterward. Praising the United States also provided a way for Laboulaye to advocate for liberal government in France without directly offending kings and emperors. Laboulaye and many in his circle had fought in vain to keep the government of Emperor Napoleon III on the side of the Union in the Civil War. Now that the war was over, Laboulaye proposed that the time was right for a monument to liberty to be built by both nations, symbolizing their lasting gratitude to each other. Among the younger guests at the 1865 dinner was Frédéric-Auguste Bartholdi, a sculptor already known for his twelve-foot monument to one of Napoleon's generals. Bartholdi dreamed of equaling the Colossus of Rhodes, the ancient lighthouse large enough for ships to sail between its legs.

Laboulaye and his friends had very specific hopes about how monuments might influence French politics. As advocates of republican government, they wanted more democracy in what was then the Second Empire of France. On the other hand, they were not extreme democrats but educated men and minor aristocrats, admirers of the way that the United States seemed to embody both liberty and order. For them, liberty meant primarily freedom from slavery, which they already had, and economic freedom, freedom of religion, and freedom of the press, which they hoped to attain. They dreaded the unchecked democracy or mob rule that they associated with the French Revolutions of 1789, 1830, or 1848. When French defeat in the Franco-Prussian War of 1870 led to yet another extreme expression of democracy, the Paris Commune, Laboulaye supported the alliance between monarchists and republicans that slaughtered

30,000 Parisians who supported the communists (or *communards*, as they were known in France). Meanwhile, the sculptor Bartholdi had failed in his attempt to get support for a gigantic statue of a robed woman holding a torch, called *Progress Bringing the Light to Asia*, to mark the French triumph in constructing the Suez Canal in Egypt. In 1871, when the Commune had already been crushed but the French Third Republic was still unstable, Bartholdi wrote to Laboulaye about his intentions to visit the United States and recalled their 1865 discussion about a monument to be built by French and American efforts.

By then Laboulaye was the world-famous author of a history of the United States and a treatise on the limits of state power, and he was able to provide Bartholdi with letters of introduction to President Grant, Civil War generals Sheridan and Meade, poet Henry Wadsworth Longfellow, Senator Charles Sumner, iron magnate Peter Cooper, and retail entrepreneur Cyrus Field. Bartholdi met with American leaders at Union League Club dinners in New York and Philadelphia. The monument to liberty that he proposed at these meetings would celebrate and consolidate the triumphs both of the Northern establishment in the United States and of the moderate republicans in France.

Laboulaye illustrated the original, establishmentarian meaning of the Statue of Liberty by comparing her to another female personification of liberty, the woman at the center of an epic painting that immortalized the 1830 revolution in France, *Liberty Leading the People* by Eugène Delacroix. In that painting, the female Liberty wears a red cap, the *pileus* that was given to Roman slaves when they were freed. Her breasts have been bared by the falling away of her robes, and she strides forward, holding a Tricolor flag (the flag of the French Revolution) in her right hand and a musket with a bayonet in her left. Corpses lie before her, and her next steps will lead her to walk on them. In a fund-raising speech for the Statue of Liberty at the Paris Opera in 1876, Laboulaye exalted the chaste and sober woman designed by Bartholdi over "the one wearing the red bonnet on her head... [who] walks on corpses." In contrast, the Statue of Liberty hides her breasts under multiple layers, for she wears not only a toga but also a *palla*, a shawl draped over her left shoulder. She carries no battle flag or weapon, but a torch in her right hand and a tablet, reminiscent of the laws of Moses, in her left.

Though Bartholdi's Statue is walking, her motion is solemn, detectable only when viewed from the right (Figure 20.1). From the front or the left, the Statue of Liberty appears to be still, concentrating on holding the torch rather than advancing. Her official title also contrasts with that of the Delacroix painting. Instead of *Liberty Leading the People*, the statue of New York harbor is called *Liberty Enlightening the World*.

When the Statue was finally dedicated, in 1886, its message of ordered liberty was joined by a related theme, the triumphs of industrial power, engineering, and mass marketing. The Statue was for a moment the tallest structure in

Figure 20.1 Seen from the right, the Statue of Liberty appears to be walking. National Park Service.

New York. As Bartholdi designed the statue, he first consulted with architect Eugène Viollet-le-Duc, a noted restorer of cathedrals and other medieval structures. Viollet-le-Duc was planning a solid masonry interior, but when he died in 1879, Bartholdi turned to Gustave Eiffel. Already known for his iron bridges, and soon to be made immortal by his eponymous Tower, Eiffel designed a modern scaffolding of iron to hold up the thin copper panels. Meanwhile, construction of the outer shell proceeded by a slow and amazingly painstaking process, which involved making successively larger models of each part and hanging plumb lines from key points, then measuring the distances between the lines and making a larger scale model, until the final, full-sized part could be made of copper. The right wrist, hand, and torch were ready to be displayed in Philadelphia, among other marvels of modern industry, at the 1876 Centennial Fair. Americans paid fees to climb a ladder and to stand on the balcony around the torch, and so contributed to the construction fund. After the Fair closed, the torch stood on display at Madison Square in New York City from 1876 to 1880.

Fund-raising for the Statue quickly became as modern as its iron frame. When large donors proved insufficiently generous, Bartholdi advertised the Statue as the "future emblem of American liberty" and induced French and American commercial firms to use her image on billboards and labels for their products.

He also contracted with Emilie Gaget, the metal entrepreneur whose factory was making the copper plates, to turn out six-inch replicas of the Statue for sale.

In 1884, when the Statue was finally ready to go from Paris to New York, funds for the pedestal, which was supposed to be the contribution of the United States, had yet to be raised. Substantial steps had been taken: the pedestal had been designed by Richard Morris Hunt, an heir of New England and the first American graduate of the École des Beaux-Arts in Paris, and an engineer named Charles Pomeroy Stone had supervised the largest single pour of concrete in history for the pedestal's foundation, but the American Committee for the Statue of Liberty did not have Bartholdi's gift for fund-raising. A cornerstone for the pedestal was laid in a Masonic ceremony on August 5, 1884, but work had to be stopped for lack of money on March 10, 1885. A mocking editorial cartoon showed the Statue growing old as she sat waiting for her pedestal.

This added another layer to the Statue's meaning. Already a symbol of ordered liberty, of friendship between America and France, of industrial progress, and of the power of commerce, she would now begin to acquire her populist and multicultural affiliations. A Hungarian Jewish immigrant named Joseph Pulitzer, who had become the publisher of the New York *World*, initiated this transformation. For two years, since 1883, he had been criticizing the upper classes for not raising money for the pedestal, and now that work was halted he pulled out all the stops. "Let us not wait for the millionaires to give this money," Pulitzer pleaded. "It is not a gift from the millionaires of France to the millionaires of America, but a gift of the whole people of France to the whole people of America. Take this appeal to yourself personally," he begged each of his readers. He promised to publish the name of everyone who contributed, however little. By August 1885, Pulitzer and the *World* had raised $101,191—slightly more than the $100,000 needed to complete the pedestal—from 120,000 individual gifts. Pulitzer wrote that the gifts of the people had made the Statue "not only an ideal of Liberty—but an attestation of Liberty in every stone." The appropriation of the Statue by the immigrant community had begun.

During those same years, a fund-raising effort by the official Committee also contributed to the immigrant identity of the Statue. One of the Committee members, William M. Evarts, had met Emma Lazarus, the daughter of a wealthy New York sugar refiner named Moses Lazarus, who was well connected to the emerging Jewish aristocracy of New York. After the pogroms of 1881, when the assassination of Czar Alexander II was blamed on the Jews, Emma Lazarus had her first contacts with poor Jewish refugees from Russia who were living in temporary barracks set up by charities. Lazarus wrote articles on behalf of these refugees, quoting a speech by Evarts to the effect that they should be helped not as victims of "the oppression of Jews by Russians," but as "men and women" who were being oppressed "by men and women," in recognition that *we are men and women.*

In the autumn of 1883, Evarts asked Lazarus to contribute a poem to a literary auction that the Committee was running to raise money for the pedestal. Walt Whitman, Mark Twain, and Bret Harte had all agreed to take part. Though Lazarus at first replied that she hated to write "on order," she did submit a sonnet for the contest. The event did not raise much money, but in time Lazurus's poem became, through the power of her verse, indelibly associated with the Statue. Lazarus gave an enduring literary form to the association of the Statue with immigration.

> Not like the brazen giant of Greek fame,
> With conquering limbs astride from land to land;
> Here at our sea-washed, sunset gates shall stand
> A mighty woman with a torch, whose flame
> Is the imprisoned lightning, and her name
> Mother of Exiles. From her beacon-hand
> Glows world-wide welcome; her mild eyes command
> The air-bridged harbor that twin cities frame.
> "Keep, ancient lands, your storied pomp!" cries she
> With silent lips. "Give me your tired, your poor,
> Your huddled masses yearning to breathe free,
> The wretched refuse of your teeming shore.
> Send these, the homeless, tempest-tost to me.
> I lift my lamp beside the golden door!"

In response, poet James Russell Lowell wrote to Lazarus to say that he "liked your sonnet about the Statue much better than I like the Statue itself," because the poem "gives its subject a *raison d'être* which it wanted quite as much as it wanted a pedestal." Lazarus left America in 1885, for a long stay in England and France, and saw the completed Statue for the first time when she returned to New York in July 1887, less than four months before she died of Hodgkin's disease at the age of thirty-eight. Her poem did not do as much as Pulitzer's advocacy to build the pedestal, but it did win the contest to which it was submitted. The poem continued to be remembered in many editorial cartoons and other expressions of popular culture. It was inscribed on a bronze plaque in 1902 and the plaque was placed inside the pedestal, where it remains today.

The Statue was first unveiled on October 28, 1886, and immigrants ever since have testified that their first sight of her fulfilled all the hopes of Emma Lazarus for a "Mother of Exiles" who "lifts her lamp beside the golden door." According to an elderly Ukrainian who was quoted by scholar Rudolf Vecoli in 1994, "When you see that Liberty Statue ... it's the greatest feeling. It's like going to heaven and God accepts you." In the words of Cuban revolutionary José Marti, who lived in

New York for fourteen years, "Irishmen, Poles, Italians, Czechs, Germans freed from tyranny or want—all hail the monument of Liberty because to them it seems to incarnate their own uplifting."

Though the Statue appeared as an accepting divinity, the policies of the United States with regard to immigrants were tightening in the years just before it was erected. A federal immigration law passed in 1882 excluded any "convict, lunatic, idiot, or person unable to take care of himself." In that same year, Congress passed a law excluding Chinese from ever becoming citizens of the United States. An article published in 1885 by a Chinese immigrant, Saum Song Bo, commented that the Statue "represents Liberty holding a torch which lights the passage of those of all nations who come into this country. But are the Chinese allowed to come?"

The dedication of the Statue occurred amid one of the most hostile climates for immigrants in American history. A few months before the dedication, police in Chicago attempted to break up a protest in Haymarket Square against police killing and wounding of strikers at the McCormick Reaper Works. As the police advanced a bomb went off, killing three policemen, and four more police died in the ensuing struggle. Eight men were arrested in the wake of what came to be called the Haymarket Riots. They were charged not with actually throwing the bomb, but with inciting violence. Seven of the eight, six of them immigrants, were sentenced to death, and four were actually put to death by hanging. At the ceremony dedicating the Statue of Liberty, the main speaker, Chauncey Depew of the New York Central Railroad, welcomed "the poor and the persecuted," but took another line with the discontented. Depew declared that "there is room and brotherhood for all who will support our institutions," but that "those who come to disturb our peace and dethrone our laws are aliens and enemies forever." The number of immigrants would fall from a high of nearly 789,000 in 1882 to lows of about 230,000 in 1897 and 1898. An Immigration Restriction League, supported largely by Boston Yankees, was founded in 1894.

On the other hand, the federal government was becoming increasingly involved and efficient with regard to immigrants. Only in 1891 did Congress recognize federal responsibility for inspecting and admitting those who arrived in the United States (a task that had belonged to individual states), and on January 2, 1892, the new federal facility at Ellis Island was opened. However Americans felt about immigrants, there was now a dedicated place in New York harbor to receive them, and that place stood almost literally in the shadow of the Statue of Liberty.

Ellis Island was at first furnished with a wooden building, but after a fire in 1897 it gained one of the most massive brick structures in New York, with four impressive towers, one at each corner, and an enormous reception hall with a tiled ceiling that still needed remarkably little repair when the building was renovated in the 1980s. The island was named for a Revolutionary War–era owner who had used it to harvest oysters. Now it became the legendary place where immigrants were evaluated, accepted, or rejected and sent back on the steamships that had brought them. The years after the Spanish-American War witnessed economic expansion, which spurred immigration beyond any previous highs, until 1907 became the busiest year in Ellis Island's history. Although it operated at full capacity for only two decades before the immigration restriction laws of 1921 and 1924 closed the "golden door" to most from Eastern and Southern Europe and made it less relevant, Ellis Island became emblematic of the whole European immigration to the United States.

But to be an emblem of immigration in those years was not always a position of honor, either for Ellis Island or for the Statue of Liberty. One editorial cartoon showed the Lady in the Harbor picking up her skirts and looking disgusted as a garbage scow brought piles of people labeled "wretched refuse" (quoting the poem by Emma Lazarus) to her feet. In a story by O. Henry, imagining a dialogue between the Statue and the Goddess Diana, Liberty said that when she took "a peep down at Ellis Island" to see the immigrants whom she was supposed to enlighten, she was tempted to kill them all: "to blow the gas out and let the coroner write the naturalization papers." To be fair to O. Henry, he then gave Diana some reassuring lines, telling Liberty that in Heaven she had seen many former immigrants who had made more of themselves than the Ellis Island officials who had once pushed them around. In fact, the people of the United States have always had conflicting feelings, interests, and policies regarding immigration. When Emma Lazarus wrote her poem in 1883, anti-immigrant feeling was rising, but the young poet herself showed that there were some who felt that welcoming immigrants was part of the American civil religion. In 1902, when the poem was installed in bronze inside the pedestal of the Statue, there was a moment of confidence about "Americanization" under Theodore Roosevelt—who was nevertheless ambivalent himself, since he was among those who favored stricter standards, including a literacy test, for admission.

If being the Mother of Immigrants was a thankless job, Liberty's decreasing physical glamour reflected that fact. As she approached her thirtieth birthday, ominous reports about corrosion within indicated that the statue was in danger of falling down. In the first decades of the twentieth century, the taller buildings of Lower Manhattan began to make the Statue look insignificant, especially to the one-third of all immigrants who became disillusioned with America, or had made enough money, or were deported, and went home. Aleksandra Kollontai, a departing Russian Bolshevik, wrote that the "symbol which caused the hearts of our European fathers and grandfathers to beat with triumphant happiness and exultation" had become "so tiny...against the soaring skyscrapers of the Wall Street banks," that she was a "pitiful, shrunken, green statue that seems to be

Figure 20.2 During World War I, the Statue of Liberty appeared on many war bond posters, including this one directed at immigrants. The spacious deck pictured here would indicate immigrants of a class too high to go through Ellis Island. Library of Congress.

embarrassed." Attitude surely affected perception here, but Kollontai was right to note that the Statue was in decline.

The Statue of Liberty did not attain her full status until World War I. At first, her torch was very weakly lit; sculptor Bartholdi described it on the first night as "a glowworm." She was at last lit at night, and provided with an adequate torch, in 1916, in a ceremony for the thirtieth anniversary of her dedication that featured President Woodrow Wilson. After turning on the floodlights, Wilson said, "Throughout the last two years there has come more and more into my heart the conviction that peace is going to come to the world only with Liberty." He was preparing the nation for the war it entered the next year.

World War I made the Statue into the equal or superior of Uncle Sam. While Sam had the iconic "I Want You" poster for the Army, she was the star of Liberty Bonds, which were named for her. Financiers since Crassus in ancient Rome had loaned money (or had their money confiscated) to fund military campaigns, but now the United States funded its war effort by selling bonds to as many of its citizens as had extra money to buy them, and it was the Goddess who sold these bonds. "YOU buy a Liberty Bond, Lest I Perish," she said on one poster, with her eyes wide as she pointed at the viewer in the manner of Uncle Sam. For the poster of the Fourth Liberty Loan, she stood against a sky of flame, orange and yellow, coloring even the waters around her, above the paraphrase of Lincoln, "THAT LIBERTY SHALL NOT PERISH FROM THE EARTH—BUY LIBERTY BONDS." Immigrants were already being directly targeted in the second bond drive, in 1917, with a picture of people on a suspiciously uncrowded deck (possibly second class, though they were dressed for steerage), and the words "Remember Your First Thrill of AMERICAN LIBERTY" above them, and "YOUR DUTY—*Buy* United States Government *Bonds*" below the picture (Figure 20.2). When the war ended, Miss Liberty appeared with a friendly expression, head back and smiling, in a relaxed pose wearing a slightly *décolleté* tunic of blue with white stars and a red and white striped underskirt, a red cape flowing back from one shoulder and a sword held downward in her left hand, with the words "VICTORY LOAN" behind her head, and smaller capital letters that said "THE SAFEST INVESTMENT IN THE WORLD" under her feet.

In the posters for Liberty Bonds, the Statue took on the roles of Athena, the chaste defender of Athens, and Hera, the mother of gods who stood on a blazing battlefield in the *Iliad*, and Aphrodite the lover, who also fought in the war before Troy. From World War II through the present, the Statue has had her own momentum as an archetype, developing in many forms through American culture and the culture of the world. When Henry Adams, the descendant of presidents who became a historian, wrote in 1907 that in comparison to the medieval Virgin, "an American Virgin would never dare command; an American Venus would never dare exist," he was not anticipating how the Statue that the French had given to his country would grow in the next ten years. Adams was also failing to appreciate the ancient symbolism that Bartholdi had built into the Statue. Lady Liberty's left foots crushes a chain, the symbol of slavery, which resembles the Serpent that Genesis 3:15 (in the Latin Vulgate version) says that the seed of the Woman will crush. Roman Catholic statues of Mary commonly show her crushing a snake under her left foot. Meanwhile, the Statue's crown displays another archetypal pattern: its seven rays correspond to the symbols of Helios, god of the sun, and to Masonic costumes and symbols of the sun.

In the harbor next to Liberty, the fortunes of Ellis Island improved until World War I, then went into a long decline. The peak year for immigration through Ellis Island was 1907. Indeed, that was the peak year for all immigration to the United States until 1990, when a much larger population would absorb a slightly larger number of immigrants. From 1907 until 1914, when World War I curtailed ship traffic across the Atlantic, more than a million people a year crossed from Europe to the United States. There was always some resistance. For example, Congress passed literacy tests for admission twice in 1913, only to see the bills vetoed by Presidents William Howard Taft and Woodrow Wilson, before obtaining enough votes to override Wilson's veto in 1917. Eventually, in 1924, the gates narrowed when Congress imposed a quota system by nationality, based on the percentages of those born in particular nations in the census of 1910, with the exception of people from Asian nations, who were totally excluded. With slight modifications, such as an allowance during World War II of 105 Chinese per year, this system remained in place until 1965. A symbolic low point came in 1936, when President Franklin Roosevelt celebrated the fiftieth anniversary of the Statue of Liberty with a speech in which he dismissed any need for immigration, because the human materials for perfecting American democracy were now already present. During the next few years, the refusal of the United States to alter its quotas to include Russian and Polish Jews would contribute to millions of deaths in the Holocaust. Ellis Island remained in business, as a detention site for enemy aliens during World War II and then as a place of admission for Cold War refugees until 1954, when it was abandoned. The Eisenhower administration tried to sell the island and its buildings in 1956, but failed to find a buyer.

Clearly, Ellis Island was not yet a holy site in American civil religion, but there were a few who saw it that way. As early as 1903, photographer and author Jacob Riis called it "the nation's gateway to the promised land," and in 1905 the Boston Transcript ran an article contending that Ellis Island was "the Twentieth Century Plymouth Rock." A Russian Jewish immigrant named Mary Antin wrote, in *They Who Knock at Our Gates: A Complete Gospel of Immigration* (1914), that "the ghost of the Mayflower pilots every immigrant ship, and Ellis Island is another name for Plymouth Rock." In the 1930s and 1940s, a prominent political writer who came to America from Slovenia, Louis Adamic, advocated for national "unity within diversity" in a speech that he repeated all over the United States, called "Plymouth Rock and Ellis Island."

The political process that made Ellis Island officially sacred began in 1965, when Congress belatedly responded to an initiative of the Kennedy administration and passed a new immigration law, eliminating national quotas in favor of family affinities and skills. Not only did President Lyndon Johnson go to Liberty Island to sign the law; he also used his presidential power to place Ellis Island under the jurisdiction of the National Park Service. As Johnson said, "today we can all believe that the lamp of this grand old lady is brighter and the golden door that she guards gleams more brilliantly."

Immediately, the new immigration law began to transform the population of the United States, particularly with regard to Asian immigrants. The Hindu temples that began to appear in the late 1970s and that now multiply in many American cities and suburbs attest to this change. Mexicans, Chinese, Thais, Nigerians, Syrians, Lebanese, and people from many other nationalities previously limited in their access to the United States began to flow into the country.

For decades, however, the symbols of immigration, the Statue of Liberty and Ellis Island, fell further into disrepair. Occasionally, the Park Service brought groups of experts to see Ellis Island, but they visited a ruin. The Statue stood, and even hosted in her pedestal a small American Museum of Immigration that was established in the 1970s, but holes in her copper skin were appearing where rivets had been lost, and the connections between the copper and her iron skeleton were rusting.

What now made Ellis Island into sacred ground and saved the Statue of Liberty from decay was the conjunction of the Statue's centennial in 1986 with the nationalism of the Reagan administration and the popularity of Lee Iacocca. Iacocca was a child of Ellis Island immigrants who rose to develop the Ford Mustang and to save Chrysler (with its first federal bailout, and a number of television ads featuring himself). As the head of the Statue of Liberty–Ellis Island Foundation, Iacocca raised $350 million to renovate the Statue and to transform Ellis Island from a ruin into a tourist destination, complete with cafeteria and gift shop and commemorative souvenirs and videos. He used methods that were denounced as crass, such as selling to Coca-Cola, *USA Today*, Stroh's Brewery, Chrysler, Kodak, Nestle, Oscar Meyer, and U.S. Tobacco the exclusive right (among their competitors) to use the Statue of Liberty in advertising. Journalists and scholars often questioned the concept of a "public-private partnership" such as that between the Ellis Island Foundation and the National Park Service. Recalling the roles that Bartholdi's sales of advertising rights and Joseph Pulitzer's New York *World* played in getting the Statue of Liberty and its pedestal built, however, it seems that public-private partnership had been the rule from the start.

A dramatic climax of this partnership came on the weekend of July 4, 1986, when the Statue was rededicated with an elaborate televised show—the largest fireworks display ever seen in New York, with forty-two barges of rockets (in contrast to the normal July 4 complement of three). The Chief Justice of the Supreme Court, Warren Burger, swore in 2,000 new citizens, including Russian dancer and choreographer Mikhail Baryshnikov, on Ellis Island, while 38,000 more new citizens participated by video connection. There was an enormous concert, with many artists donating their talents. At the end of the weekend, the Statue of Liberty opened for visitors in a renovated state.

Meanwhile, on Ellis Island, the government's neglect had allowed a beautiful main building, as well as all of its surrounding buildings, to decay. The Foundation raised the money, and the Park Service worked with historians and architects to restore the structures of the island and present their meaning to the public. The Ellis Island Museum opened in September 1990.

For Lino Anthony (Lee) Iacocca, there was no question that Ellis Island was a sacred place. It was the place where, according to family legend, Iacocca's father had convinced immigration inspectors to let his wife into the country despite her typhoid fever, saying that she was just seasick. Iacocca said that the Great Hall was "a cathedral, a churchlike setting, a place to pray." Though the Statue of

Liberty had been the focus of fund-raising, and there was no doubt she was more popular than Ellis Island with the public, Ellis Island meant more to Iacocca. As he said, the Statue was "a beautiful symbol of what it means to be free," but Ellis Island was "the reality." Years later, in 2001, New York City mayor Rudolph Guiliani would say that "Ellis Island is a wonderful place, it's a sacred place, and it's hallowed ground in American history." Giuliani was responding to what the Park Service had made of the ruin.

Far more than most museums, and somewhat in the manner of the US Holocaust Memorial Museum or the Gettysburg Visitors' Center, the Ellis Island Museum attempts to involve visitors in the experiences of the people it memorializes. Arriving on a usually packed tour boat, visitors enter the room where immigrants left their luggage, to find a gigantic pile of old luggage with photos of immigrants above and around it. They are invited to climb steep stairs to the Great Hall or Reception Hall, although elevators are available, to experience the test by which the fitness of immigrants was once judged before they lined up for what was known as the "six-second inspection." On the same floor as the Great Hall are the fourteen rooms of the "Through America's Gate" display, the very rooms where more detailed inspections and interviews took place. Now photos, videos, recorded voices, and texts describe the steps and tests through which those at Ellis Island would pass before they were deemed to have proven themselves worthy to land. If they were found unworthy (for example because of poverty, mental or physical handicap, disease, or illiteracy) they were excluded, and the steamship company that brought them would be obligated to take them back. The excluded were entitled to a hearing, and this part of the museum includes an original, renovated Hearing Room where visitors can be enrolled as judges or watch while actors portraying immigrants and government workers present cases, drawn from actual files, in an event called "Decide an Immigrant's Fate," which takes place several times a day.

Other sections of the museum are less interactive, but sometimes more compelling. At the other side of the Great Hall from "Through America's Gate" is an exhibit called "Peak Immigration Years: Immigration to the U.S., 1880–1924." Beginning with the forces that impelled immigrants to leave many places, from Norway to Jamaica to Ireland, and continuing through how they came and the work they did in America, this exhibit does not allow sentiment to blur the harshness of the immigrant experience. According to historian Mike Wallace, it offers "a panoramic perspective on the making of the American working class," from child labor and union organization to upward mobility. "Peak Immigration Years" ends with sections on how immigrants maintained their cultures, and finally on how advocates for immigration restriction, including the Ku Klux Klan and eugenic racial theorists, succeeded in closing the doors of the United States, at least until 1965.

Out of all the features of the Ellis Island Museum, a less critical display on the third floor, called "Treasures from Home," has proved to be the most popular destination. It features items from the home countries of immigrants, with explanations of provenance and significance. Also on the third floor are "Ellis Island Chronicles," a set of displays covering the history of the island from Native American times until the immigration station closed in 1954, and "Silent Voices," with glass cases of items and photographs from the years when the island was abandoned.

The most scientifically significant but least personal exhibit is back on the first floor, next to the Baggage Room where visitors enter. This area, The Peopling of America Center, takes visitors back to Native American times and forward through the decades after Ellis Island closed. It includes in its charts and graphs African slaves and Asians and others who did not pass through Ellis Island, and it sets American immigration into the context of world history. At first a small display area, The Peopling of America Center was expanded with a $20 million addition that opened in the fall of 2011.

Despite the popularity of the Ellis Island National Monument, which caused an increase of visitors to Ellis Island and the Statue of Liberty by more than 2 million people (from about 3 million in 1990 to more than 4.3 million in 1991, reaching a peak of 5.5 million in the year 2000), both the museum and the Statue have continued to generate controversy. John Seelye, a historian of Plymouth Rock, argued that Plymouth remains a more universal symbol for the nation that grew from the English colonies. As Seelye wrote of Ellis Island, "The descendants of Pilgrims do not have to be told that this is a society to which they need not apply." Historian Mike Wallace, though he praised the museum for its depiction of the working class, also noted that it obscures the class distinctions among immigrants, because anyone who could afford a first or second-class steamship ticket did not have to go through Ellis Island, but went straight into Manhattan. Gender studies and art history professor Erica Rand entitled her book *The Ellis Island Snow Globe*, after an item sold in the souvenir shop and made in China, which she analyzed as an exemplar of all that is prescribed and proscribed by the choices made at the park. After Rand recounted the case of immigrant Frank Woodhull, who was suspected of having tuberculosis, subjected to a more detailed physical examination, discovered to be a biological woman, yet allowed to enter the United States under his male identity, she wondered why this case is not one of those dramatized in the "Decide an Immigrant's Fate" skits. Rand found that sex and gender have largely been erased with regard to Ellis Island and to the Statue. In an effort to combat this erasure, she asserted that "[t]he Statue of Liberty is a hot butch."

Long before President Ronald Reagan said that "[t]he Statue of Liberty is everybody's gal," in his speech at the rededication in 1986, gender issues have been flourishing around the sites of Liberty Island and Ellis Island. As far back as 1886, the dedication of the Statue was protested by feminists who circled the island on a boat, calling attention to the absence of women at this ceremony for a symbolic woman, and complaining that if Liberty came to life in America, she could not vote. Many commentators one hundred years later, in the preparations for the rededication, wrote that Miss Liberty was being sold to corporate interests or prostituted by Lee Iacocca and his Foundation, or alternatively that she was in danger and needed to be saved by powerful males like Iacocca. In 1976, art historian Marvin Trachtenberg had denied the relevance of gender studies to the Statue, arguing that what nineteenth-century people would have imagined under her robes was a traditional "academic nude," which he illustrated by an 1859 painting called *Truth*, in which an undeniably rounded, long-haired, nude woman holds aloft a torch as her right knee bends and her hips displace to the left. Given the severity of the Statue's body, which some have said was based on sculptor Bartholdi's mother, and of her face, which has been compared to the face of a Greek god and to the French philosopher Laboulaye, Trachtenberg's comparison looks mistaken, and Rand's categorization of Liberty as "butch" seems less outlandish. In 1949, an all-star team of composer Irving Berlin, writer Robert E. Sherwood, and producer Moss Hart tried to give the Statue a feminine allure in the Broadway play *Miss Liberty*, which involved the supposed model for the Statue being introduced to New York society and falling in love with an American reporter. Perhaps tellingly, the play failed badly. Some posters advertising Tony Kushner's play of the 1990s, *Angels in America*, went in another direction: they showed the Statue opening its robes to reveal a hard-muscled male body.

As scholar Marina Warner has written, "Liberty appears as a thunderbolt judge of stern unrelenting character, upright and unmerciful." This certainly fit the greatest appearance that the Statue has made in film, in the chilling climax of Alfred Hitchcock's *Saboteur* (1942), in which a villain fleeing from the scene of sabotage at the Brooklyn Navy Yard is pursued to the torch of the Statue, falls off the platform, and hangs for several precarious minutes on the Statue's hand before falling to his death. This judgmental image also suited the role that the Statue played in *Planet of the Apes* (1970), in which the discovery of its head causes Charlton Heston to realize that the planet of his exile is the future Earth, and so to fall to his knees and curse those who blew up human civilization. In *Ghostbusters II* (1989), the heroic team of the title use spectral energy to animate the Statue and to walk her through the streets of Manhattan, where she fights a demon that has barricaded itself in an art museum.

Negative and positive images of the Statue abound around the world, demonstrating the global reach of American civil religion. Ever since the Iranian Revolution of 1979, a demonic version of the Statue, with a skeleton skull and prominent teeth, has appeared against the background of an American flag on the wall of the former US Embassy in Teheran. But ten years later, Chinese rebels paid tribute to the Statue in Tiananmen Square, where the demonstrators of 1989 hailed a Goddess of Democracy, holding a torch with both hands and clearly revealing a Chinese face and a thin body under her robes. Another version of that figure, more closely resembling the American Statue, was created and confiscated by authorities at the City University of Hong Kong in 2010. At the same time in India, members of the Dalit or Untouchable caste began to spread the cult of a Goddess of English, an exact replica of Lady Liberty but wearing a hat and holding a pen instead of a torch. Now everyone in the world knows Lady Liberty, and all parties use her for their own purposes, as living religious symbols tend to be used.

Meanwhile, for many Americans, Ellis Island has definitely become, as Vincent J. Cannato, a professor of history at the University of Massachusetts (Boston) has argued, "the new Plymouth Rock." In the creation story of American civil religion, Ellis Island has become a third Eden, beside Jamestown and Plymouth. As time passes and the generations that came to Ellis Island recede from memory, the museum may become less important than it is today, but as long as immortal Lady Liberty stands beside her, Ellis Island should remain a sacred place. Together, they stand for the oldest value of American civil religion, individual liberty, and the newest, multicultural tolerance.

SOURCES

Blanchet, Christian, and Bernard Dard, *Statue of Liberty: The First Hundred Years*, translated by Bernard A. Weisberger (New York: American Heritage Press, 1985).
Boime, Albert, *The Unveiling of the National Icons: A Plea for Patriotic Iconoclasm in a Nationalist Era* (Cambridge: Cambridge University Press, 1998).
Cannato, Vincent J., *American Passage: The History of Ellis Island* (New York: HarperCollins, 2009).
Dillon, Wilton S., and Neil G. Kotler, eds., *The Statue of Liberty Revisited* (Washington, DC: Smithsonian Institution Press, 1994). Chapters include: Barbara Babcock and John J. Macaloon, "Everybody's Gal: Women, Boundaries, and Monuments"; Tsao Hsingyuan and Fang Li Zhi, "Chinese Perspectives: A Beijing Chronicle and Chinese Views of Liberty, Democracy, and the Pursuit of Scientific Knowledge"; and Rudolph J. Vecoli, "The Lady and the Huddled Masses: The Statue of Liberty as a Symbol of Immigration."
Holland, F. Ross, *Idealists, Scoundrels, and the Lady: An Insider's View of the Statue of Liberty–Ellis Island Project* (Urbana: University of Illinois Press, 1993).
Rand, Erica, *The Ellis Island Snow Globe* (Durham, NC: Duke University Press, 2005).
Trachtenberg, Marvin, *The Statue of Liberty* (New York: Penguin Books, rev. ed., 1986).
Wallace, Mike, "The Ellis Island Immigration Museum," *The Journal of American History* 78, no. 3 (Dec. 1991), 1023–1032.
Warner, Marina, *Monuments and Maidens: The Allegory of Female Form* (New York: Atheneum, 1985).

21

America the Beautiful

> O beautiful for spacious skies,
> For amber waves of grain,
> For purple mountain majesties
> Above the fruited plain!
> America! America!
> God shed His grace on thee
> And crown thy good with brotherhood
> From sea to shining sea!

This song was written by a lifelong New Englander, a poet and college professor of English, who was responding to her only trip across the Great Plains and her only ascent of an American mountain, from July 3 to 5, 1893. Katharine Lee Bates never glimpsed one of the "shining seas," the Pacific, but she crossed the Atlantic to Europe many times. Emerging from a world very different from ours, her words still inspire Americans today with thoughts of tolerance, freedom, peace, and thankfulness for beauty.

Born in 1859, Bates had a childhood memory of Lincoln's assassination and lived long enough to feel wonder before the radio. In some ways, she experienced a personal freedom and a level of cultural tolerance that anticipated the values of later Americans. She could not vote until she was past sixty, but she shared twenty-five years with her great love, a female colleague at Wellesley College with whom she traveled by rail from Chicago to Colorado and saw the view from Pike's Peak, and she suffered for her love no controversy at all. The two women bought a house together, and Katharine Lee Bates brought classes of female students to that house for weekly seminars without fear of being fired or arrested or receiving poisonous student evaluations because of her private life or public living arrangements. On the other hand, her job did once depend upon her religious faith.

The poem that she called "America the Beautiful," published in the July 4th issue of a denominational journal called *The Congregationalist* in 1895, caused an immediate sensation and elicited many reactions, but its original first verse had very different words from those above. The first version had a more classical emphasis: "O beautiful for halcyon skies," Bates wrote, using an ancient term for the calm seas around the winter solstice in the Mediterranean—a reference that resonated with few Americans then and fewer now. In the original poem the words, "Above the enameled plain!" suggested a multicolored surface to Bates, who knew how artisans since the Middle Ages had made surfaces beautiful with differently colored chips of material, but again the reference was lost on most readers. The original verse also ended differently, with an emphasis on individuals rather than the nation: "Till souls wax fair as earth and air / And music-hearted sea!" Readers of the magazine loved the poem, but responded with constructive criticisms and suggestions, and Bates revised her work in two more published versions, in 1904 and 1911. The first verse that we now sing, including the "spacious" skies, the "fruited" plain, and "from sea to shining sea," was complete by 1904. It stands as a testament to the good effects of democracy on art.

In her second verse, Bates paid homage to her New England heritage. The combination of reverence and militancy in the first four lines probably appealed to many readers of *The Congregationalist*:

> O beautiful for pilgrim feet,
> Whose stern, impassioned stress
> A thoroughfare for freedom beat
> Across the wilderness!
> America! America!
> God mend thine every flaw,
> Confirm thy soul in self-control,
> Thy liberty in law!

Bates's father, who died when she was one month old, was a Congregational minister, one of the successors of Pilgrim and Puritan pastors, with a church in Falmouth, Massachusetts, a town at the beginning of Cape Cod and very close to Plymouth Rock. Today, most Americans feel at least a little guilt about the consequences for Native Americans of the "stern impassioned stress" of Puritans and their children across Indian country, and a little ambiguity about the "thoroughfares" we have paved across the wilderness. Bates was also aware that her America was not perfect, as one can see in the prayer that God should "mend her every flaw," but she still found the English conquest of the continent to be a thrilling story.

The last lines of the verse had a more specific meaning for Bates in 1893 than they do for most today. Originally, she repeated "God shed his grace on thee" instead of "mend thine every flaw," and then moved in a more abstract, intellectual direction: "Till paths be wrought through wilds of thought / By pilgrim foot and knee!" She was probably thinking about the religious and philosophical confusion of her time, in which which she was personally involved.

Although she was the daughter of a minister, Bates herself never joined any church. She was a lifelong seeker who often wrote about her "God-craving" and climbed one of the Horns of Hattim, the traditional site of the Sermon on the Mount, to read the Beatitudes where they were first pronounced. Her college became more evangelical while she was on the faculty, and this was cause for worry when her appointment as a tenured professor came up, during the academic year of 1890–1891. In that year, the Wellesley trustees considered adding a bylaw to the effect that every member of the faculty should hold membership in an "Evangelical church," which would have excluded Roman Catholics and Christian Scientists, as well as nonmembers like Bates. They also considered requiring evidence of "sympathy with Evangelical views as commonly held by Protestant churches," which again would have excluded Bates. In the end, the bylaws were amended to demand that faculty demonstrate a "decided Christian character and influence," and this Bates could fulfill. She always believed in Christ, but found few Christian doctrines to be convincing, in an age that grappled with evolution and biblical criticism, among other new ideas. She found the words of Jesus on the cross, "Father forgive them, for they know not what they do" a "supreme proof" that the New Testament was not myth, because "What mythmaker could invent them?" In her later life, she sometimes took communion at Episcopal services and attended Roman Catholic Mass, enjoying the beauty of the churches and the rituals. Her original verses about "pilgrim foot and knee" expressed her hope that further work and prayer might make clear paths through the "wilds of thought."

By the second version in 1904, Bates had come to a decision that hope was enough for her, even if the wilds of thought were never cleared. Her new words for "America the Beautiful" turned toward civil religion, the soul of the nation. Asking God to give America "self-control" and to confirm our liberty in law pointed to a hope, common around the turn of the twentieth century, that a social utopia would soon come to pass. Bates was never a social activist, but her friend and housemate Katharine Coman, who taught history and economics, was a friend of Jane Addams and a founder of the settlement house movement. When Bates heard Woodrow Wilson speak as president of Princeton, she made a bet with a colleague that he would someday lead the nation, and she shared Wilson's dream of international law. She disapproved of American imperialism after the Spanish-American War, and this probably informed her wish for "self-control," but she was not a pacifist with regard to fighting tyranny or combating aggression. During World War I, the US Navy named a Liberty Ship for her.

When the great blues singer Ray Charles made "America the Beautiful" his own, beginning with the album *A Message From the People* in 1972 and continuing through countless live performances until his death in 2004, he began with the third verse:

> O beautiful for heroes proved
> In liberating strife,
> Who more than self their country loved,
> And mercy more than life!
> America! America!
> May God thy gold refine
> Till all success be nobleness
> And every gain divine!

These unfamiliar words got the attention of an audience polarized by Vietnam and the rise of the counterculture. Having made the point that people should actually hear the words, Charles then spoke an introduction, "And you know when I was at school we used to sing it something like this," and moved back into the first verse.

The two parts of the third verse address the issues of war and wealth. In the original of 1893, Bates was more specific. She wrote not of "heroes proved" but of the "glory-tale," a sacred history of "liberating strife," referring to the American Revolution and the Civil War: "When once and twice, for man's avail, / Men lavished precious life!" To continue this after 1898 would have been to ignore or to disown the Spanish war, which did liberate Cuba and the Philippines from an old empire, even if only to subject them to a new one. Bates traveled through Spain and wrote a book about her impressions after the war. Taking Spanish lessons with a nun from the Philippines, who was indignant about the United States taking away her country's islands, Bates wrote that she "did not try to explain our new imperialism in Spanish" and confessed that "[i]t troubles me not a little to understand it in English." She still believed, however, that to give one's life in war for the freedom of others was a pure form of mercy, so she approved of those who gave their lives to fight the Spanish.

With regard to money, the years between 1893 and 1911 were more conflicted than our own. Bates had socialist friends with whom she argued, and the communist movement had yet to gain power anywhere. In 1893, there was a financial panic worse than any until the Great Depression, bankrupting 15,000 businesses and 600 banks in the United States and throwing 2.5 million people, the equivalent of 12 million today, out of work. The original words were more critical of the drive for wealth, repeating "God shed his grace on thee" and asking for the result, "Till selfish gain no longer stain / The banner of the free!" In the 1904 and 1911 versions, there is more hope for capitalism, as Bates asks God to refine America's gold and to bring about a state of society in which success may be noble and "every gain divine."

Ambivalence about war and mercy, gold and righteousness informs the New Testament, and the words of "America the Beautiful" bring that ambivalence into American civil religion. Though Jesus tells his followers to turn the other cheek, eschewing violence even in self-defense, he also appears in Matthew's Gospel as a judge sending the damned into everlasting fire, and in the book of Revelation as a horseman, wielding a two-edged sword at the head of an army of angels. The Gospels picture Jesus telling a rich young man to sell all his possessions and give the money to the poor, and say that no one can serve God and wealth, but also contain parables that favor servants who increase their master's store of silver and an embezzling steward who makes friends by writing off his master's debts. In the New Jerusalem, the city that comes down from heaven in Revelation 21, the streets are paved with gold.

This last image, the city of God at the end of time, controls the fourth verse of "America the Beautiful":

> O beautiful for patriot dream
> That sees beyond the years
> Thine alabaster cities gleam
> Undimmed by human tears!
> America! America!
> God shed His grace on thee
> And crown thy good with brotherhood
> From sea to shining sea!

According to Revelation 21:4, in the city where God makes his habitation with the people, "God shall wipe away all tears from their eyes; and there shall be no more death, neither sorrow, nor crying." This was surely the source of the city "undimmed by human tears."

The "alabaster" of the cities has caused some confusion. "What, I say to myself, are alabaster cities?" a man from New Hampshire wrote to Bates, and a hymnbook editor from Rochester, New York, requested that she replace "alabaster" with "some word or phrase more clearly significant of American ideals." Since neither the color white nor this white, calcite mineral, a favorite of sculptors since ancient Egypt, are mentioned in Revelation, the vision of the New Jerusalem was not a source in this case. What lay behind the cities of America's future in their description by Bates was the White City, the central exhibit halls and meeting places of the 1893 Columbian Exposition at Chicago, which Bates and Katharine Coman visited before they boarded the train for Colorado. In the White City, buildings really were made of alabaster, mined in Michigan. That fair was a wonder of the modern world, introducing the zipper and the Ferris wheel, among other things, and provoking events as diverse as the first World's Parliament of Religions and the spread of belly dancing from the Middle East to America. In a very direct sense, the White City was the origin of the Washington, D.C., that Americans know today, because the architect of the White City, Daniel Burnham, was hired by the McMillan Commission to redesign Washington, where Burnham tried with some success to reproduce the effect of the White City. It was the dignified part of the fair, home to the industrial and artistic exhibits, as opposed to the Midway, where Little Egypt danced and the Ferris wheel turned. The White City and Burnham's Washington were both meant to inspire the hope for the future that appears in the "alabaster cities" of "America the Beautiful."

The religious and millennial meanings of this verse were more explicit in the last two lines of the 1893 original: "Till nobler men keep once again / Thy whiter jubilee!" The Jubilee was a holiday held every fifty years in ancient Israel, when slaves were set free and debts forgiven. The "whiter Jubilee" suggested the white robes of the saved in Revelation 4:4 and 7:9, and the white throne judgment of Revelation 20:11. This final evocation of apocalypse and resurrection was really redundant, however, since that hope already appears in the white cities without tears. After the first verse was improved by the addition of the words "crown thy good with brotherhood / From sea to shining sea," it made sense to make the poem symmetrical by repeating those words in the fourth verse, eliminating the whole Jubilee allusion. Between the first publication in 1895 and the final version of 1911, in the book *America the Beautiful and Other Poems*, most changes improved the poem by making the words less scholarly, less self-consciously literary, and more generally accessible in their language and meaning. For many years now at Wellesley, students and faculty have been substituting "sisterhood" for "brotherhood," a change that probably would have amused Katharine Lee Bates.

How the poem became a song is another aspect of the story. Already in 1904, the *Boston Evening Transcript* said that "Professor Katharine Lee Bates of Wellesley has written the American national hymn," calling its lyrics "well-nigh perfect as poetry, and in the most exalted strain as politics," but lamented the lack of music suited to the words. Bates was always a very lyrical writer. One of her Wellesley colleagues marveled at the degree to which her head was constantly filled with melody. It was partly because people began to sing the poem that Bates substituted "spacious" for "halcyon" and "fruited" for "enameled" in the first verse, to make it easier to sing. People at first sang the words to the tune of "Auld Lang Syne," and to an Irish tune from "The Harp That Once Through Tara's Halls." A composer named Silas G. Pratt wrote a musical setting in 1895 and included it in his book, *Famous Songs*, and a colleague of Bates in the Wellesley Music Department, Clarence C. Hamilton, wrote music that was used for decades at the college. In Portland, Maine, the hometown of Katharine's brother Arthur Bates, a "municipal organist" named Will MacFarlane wrote a tune that involved repeating the "America! America!" refrain at the end of each verse, and this was described as a "family favorite." But it was a tune written for other words in 1882, for a hymn that began "O mother dear, Jerusalem! When shall I come to thee?" with words and music by Samuel Ward, organist of the Grace Episcopal Church of Newark, New Jersey, that finally won the day.

Hymnbooks often include a Metrical Index of Tunes, so that people can match tunes with the number of syllables in each line of lyrics, and the tune that Ward wrote and called "Materna," for his hymn to "Mother Jerusalem," was listed under 8, 6, 8, 6, 8, 6, 8, 6, or common meter double (with 8, 6, 8, 6, or the meter of "Amazing Grace," being called common meter). In Rochester, New York, a Baptist clergyman named Clarence Barbour and his wife, who was a musician, searched the metrical index of their hymnal for tunes that would suit "America the Beautiful" and came upon "Materna," which they joined with Bates's words in services at their church in 1904. In 1910, Barbour was working for the YMCA, and he edited a book called *Fellowship Hymns* that included the first published version of "America the Beautiful" paired with Samuel Ward's "Materna."

Despite the popularity that singing the song to "Materna" immediately gained, there were those who felt that it was unworthy to have music written for other words associated with such an important poem. The National Federation of Music Clubs ran a contest in 1926, offering $500 to any "American-born composer" who provided "a truly adequate setting" for the words, with music that "expresses the love, loyalty and majesty" found in the words. The need for an "American-born composer" seems especially strange in retrospect, since Samuel Ward, who wrote "Materna," was a descendant of the colonial Yankee founders of Newark. At any rate, 961 people submitted tunes, but the four music critics who judged the contest decided that none of them were better than "Materna," and so no prize was awarded, and the musical fate of the song was sealed.

Meanwhile, a competition broke out between partisans of "America the Beautiful" and "The Star-Spangled Banner" regarding which should be recognized as the national anthem of the United States. Over the decades since it was written in 1814, "The Star-Spangled Banner" had gradually displaced "Hail, Columbia!" as a song that was played on state occasions. But then a significant momentum began to build behind "America the Beautiful." In 1926, the National Hymn Society petitioned Congress to make it the national anthem. In 1930, experts from Columbia University's School of Education criticized

"The Star-Spangled Banner" as too warlike, requiring "a feeling of danger" to be sung properly, while they pointed out that "America the Beautiful" set forth broader ideals. On March 4, 1930, the decision was made by Congress and signed into law by President Herbert Hoover: the national anthem would be "The Star-Spangled Banner." Bates had been dead for almost a year, but she had always refused to take part in any efforts on behalf of her song or to criticize the other, always standing for "The Star-Spangled Banner" and saying that she was "more than content with the heart-warming reception" that "America the Beautiful" had evoked. In recent decades, Ray Charles weighed in on making it the new national anthem, asking, "Honestly, wouldn't you rather sing about the beauty of America?" Barring some new cultural crisis, however, such a change seems unlikely.

In recent decades, scholars have speculated about what, if any, relevance the sexual orientation of Katherine Lee Bates might have to the interpretation of "America the Beautiful." The fact that Bates had a supreme love for another woman, Katharine Coman, was never denied by anyone in their lifetimes or immediately after. As Bates once wrote to Coman, in a letter quoted in a biography written by her niece, "Your love is a proof of God. How does love come, unless Love is?" Her last book, only privately published (although Bates was by then a best-selling author), was called *Yellow Clover: A Book of Remembrance*, and was filled with poems to Comer. Stories about them are vividly affectionate, recalling how they startled their hosts by sitting in one chair and singing on a trip to England, or how on one walk they had "two hands in one pocket," or how they began to give each other presents of yellow clover, watered with the "strange dew" of tears. Just before she died of breast cancer, in 1914, Coman wrote a note to Bates while her nurse was away, "I have no fear, Dear Heart, for Life and Death are one, and God is all in all. My only real concern to remain in this body is to spare you pain and grief and loneliness."

Such personal details can help to show us the emotional sources from which "America the Beautiful" drew. The rich emotional life of Katherine Lee Bates helped her to write a song that added specific elements to American civil religion, including nature mysticism, a more sacrificial sense of military virtue than that which stresses victory and empire, some skepticism about success and wealth, and a gentle hope for fulfillment in a future without tears. To call Katharine Lee Bates and Katharine Coman "lesbians," however, or to claim, as some have, that "America the Beautiful" was written by a lesbian, would be to commit an anachronism. We can say that Bates lived in a world that flourished for about a century between the 1830s and the 1930s and gradually disappeared in the 1950s and 1960s, a world in which American women lived together and worked together, without any public regard to sexual activity or gender identification. Of course, that world was not totally open. The personal freedom and cultural tolerance that Bates and Coman enjoyed was especially prevalent among academics and in certain places, as the use of the phrase "Boston marriage" to describe relations like that between Bates and Coman indicates. To point out the existence of that lost world is not original; feminist scholars like Carroll Smith-Rosenberg did this in the 1970s. To understand the values of American civil religion, it does seem important to note that "America the Beautiful" comes to Americans today as a product of that world of women, which is therefore not entirely vanished.

Katharine Lee Bates belonged to the mainstream of American civil religion in the sense that extraordinary thinkers like Jefferson and Lincoln did. Like them, she was seriously engaged with Christianity but able to commit far more wholeheartedly to the United States than to any Christian church. Her deepest faith was anchored in America, and that faith was most perfectly expressed in her greatest poem.

SOURCES

Burgess, Dorothy, *Dream and Deed: The Story of Katharine Lee Bates* (Norman: University of Oklahoma Press, 1952).

Guild, Marion Pelton, *Selected Poems of Katharine Lee Bates* (Boston: Houghton Mifflin Company, 1930).

Sherr, Lynn, *America the Beautiful: The Stirring True Story Behind Our Nation's Favorite Song* (New York: Public Affairs, 2001).

Schwartz, Judith, "Yellow Clover: Katharine Lee Bates and Katharine Coman," *Frontiers: A Journal of Women's Studies* 4, no. 1 (Spring 1979), 59–67.

Smith-Rosenberg, Carroll, "The Female World of Love and Ritual: Relations between Women in Nineteenth-Century America," Signs: Journal of Women in Culture and Society 1, no. 1 (Autumn, 1975), 1–29.

22

The Lincoln Memorial

Of all the monuments in the United States, the Lincoln Memorial (Figure 22.1) comes closest to functioning as a temple, a place where a god lives and receives worship. Ceremonies are actually held and wreaths laid before the statue of Abraham Lincoln every year on his birthday, February 12. Every day and night (the memorial is open 24 hours, floodlit after dark, and attended by Park Rangers until 11:30 P.M.), visitors confront the statue and sense a living presence. In Frank Capra's movie, *Mr. Smith Goes to Washington* (1939), actor Jimmy Stewart described the experience: "Mr. Lincoln, there he is. He's just lookin' straight at ya as you come up those steps. Just, just sitting there like he was waiting for somebody to come along" (Figure 22.2). As the first chapter of this book speculated, it would probably be difficult to convince an ancient Roman, if one could be brought back to stand at the Lincoln Memorial, that people in the United States do not follow the Roman custom of granting divinity to the greatest of their deceased rulers. The words engraved on the wall behind the statue call the memorial Lincoln's temple:

> IN THIS TEMPLE
> AS IN THE HEARTS OF THE PEOPLE
> FOR WHOM HE SAVED THE UNION
> THE MEMORY OF ABRAHAM LINCOLN
> IS ENSHRINED FOREVER

Temples imply authority and order. The wealthy Republicans who controlled the construction of the Lincoln Memorial intended to evoke triumph and solemnity, the victory of the Union tempered by the death of the deified hero. In less than two decades after its dedication, however, the memorial became the site of demonstrations for civil rights; later years have seen anti-war, gay rights, and Tea Party demonstrations, among others. Struggles over the meanings of freedom and democracy and tolerance, the values of American civil religion, have made a site sacred to the dead into a place where the living make their own statements.

Figure 22.1 Both the Lincoln statue, which resembles the statue of Zeus in his temple at Olympus, and the inscription behind the statue drew objections at the time of their creation and dedication in 1922. Photograph by William Gardella.

As the last lines of the inscription imply, the Lincoln Memorial was intended to be a mausoleum without the actual body, a tomb to preserve memory. The inscription echoes a speech that the Athenian leader Pericles gave at the services honoring the dead from the first battles of the Peloponnesian War. Pericles said that those dead Athenians had "the noblest of all tombs," not simply where their remains were buried, but also a "memorial of them, graven not on stone but in the hearts of men." Both Henry Bacon, the architect of the Lincoln memorial, and Royal Cortissoz, the art critic and friend of Bacon's who wrote the inscription, would surely have read this speech. Just as Pericles eventually built the Parthenon, the temple of Athena, on the same Acropolis where the war dead were remembered, and later Christian churches housed the tombs of bishops and the relics of saints, so the Lincoln Memorial and its surroundings have come to blend the atmospheres of temple and mausoleum.

A section of the National Mall devoted to death has grown up around the Lincoln Memorial. Just to the north and east of the memorial, on Lincoln's left hand, lies the Vietnam Veterans Memorial with its list of the dead, and across the Potomac to the south and west is Arlington National Cemetery. A few hundred

Figure 22.2 Entering the Lincoln Memorial in *Mr. Smith Goes to Washington* (1936), actor James Stewart reflects the impact of the Lincoln statue. Behind him, the National Mall stretches for a mile over the Reflecting Pool to the Washington Monument. Columbia Pictures/Photofest. Photograph by Irving Lippman. © Columbia Pictures.

yards from Lincoln's right hand stand the Korean War Veterans Memorial and the statue of another slain hero, Dr. Martin Luther King.

While Christian churches often associate saints, political leaders, and divine powers while still differentiating between the three, Greek and Roman temples and mausoleums directly conflated divine and political authority, and the Lincoln Memorial follows this pattern. Bacon and many other artists and architects of his generation—the decades in which the United States acquired its first colonies—belonged to a movement known as Ecole des Beaux Arts Classicism, after the Paris school where many of them trained, and they believed in decorating American cities along Greek and Roman lines. As Daniel Chester French, the sculptor of the Lincoln statue, said, "the Greeks alone were able to express in their buildings, monuments, and statues the highest attributes and the greatest beauty known to man." The 30-foot statue of Lincoln in the memorial resembles the statue of Zeus from his temple at Olympia (which was destroyed), in several ways: the subject is seated but enormous, looks straight out from a throne-like chair, and extends one foot. Blending the shape and approximate size of the temple at Olympia with Roman models, Bacon gave the Lincoln Memorial a Roman flat roof, an opening on one of the long sides rather than the narrow end, and a structure of three chambers inside. Here he followed the pattern of the Temple of Concord in Rome, built by the Emperor Augustus to celebrate the end of Rome's civil wars. On the arms of Lincoln's chair are carved fasces, or bundles of rods bound together, like those that were carried before the consuls of Rome and that also appear on each side of the Speaker's chair in the House of Representatives, where presidents give the State of the Union address each year.

One message of the statue is that the spirit of Lincoln always holds power. As sculptor French described his intentions, the expression of the face and body of Lincoln were meant to signify "Work over, victory his." The statue faces the Capitol and watches, in the manner of a divine ancestor.

Although all commentators have recognized the force of the memorial, many have disapproved. According to Frank Lloyd Wright (following the sentiments of his mentor, Louis Sullivan), it was "depravity" to erect "a Greek temple as a fitting memorial to Abraham Lincoln." Gutzon Borglum, who would later carve the heads of Mount Rushmore, petitioned the Lincoln Memorial Commission to discard ancient models for a three-sided enclosure with friezes depicting Lincoln's life and the Civil War. "In heaven's name, in Abraham Lincoln's name, don't ask the American people to associate a Greek temple with the first great American," Borglum wrote. He mocked Bacon's design as "a colonnade, torn from the pages of little Greece." According to critic Lewis Mumford, the Lincoln Memorial conveys "not the living beauty of our American past, but the mortuary air of archaeology." Mumford asked, "Who lives in that shrine, I wonder—Lincoln, or the men who conceived it: the leader who beheld the mournful victory of the Civil War, or the generation that took pleasure in the mean triumph of the Spanish-American exploit, and placed the imperial standard in the Philippines and the Caribbean?" Decades after the memorial was built, two members of the Commission of Fine Arts that oversaw the plan were still trying to have the inscription behind the statue, which one of them denigrated as "that poor, cheap, sentimental, erroneous, disfiguring inscription," removed, primarily because they thought it incorrectly called the memorial a temple.

Such disagreements extended a long history of conflict that culminated in the memorial's dedication in 1922, almost sixty years after Lincoln's death. Congress had established a Lincoln Memorial Commission in 1867. That commission had planned for a bronze complex of statues as tall as the Statue of Liberty to be built near the Capitol, with Lincoln at the top and many Union generals and scenes of war on lower levels, but the planning and fund-raising for such a monument collapsed with the end of Reconstruction in 1876. With Congress evenly balanced between South and North, Democrats and Republicans, no consensus could be reached on how to remember Lincoln. After

1896, when Republicans behind William McKinley took control of the White House and both branches of Congress, serious attempts to complete a memorial began again, but disputes between progressive and conservative wings of the Republican Party broke out. Some progressives, backed by automobile industry interests, wanted a Lincoln Highway between Washington and Gettysburg, Pennsylvania. The heirs of Abolitionist Republicans clung to the 1867 dream of a memorial that would stress the Civil War and commemorate the victory of North over South. Ultimately, the most conservative Republicans, working through an art and culture establishment linked to Northeastern money, carried the day. Senator James McMillan of Michigan brought Daniel Burnham, the architect who had enshrined classicism at the 1893 Columbian Exposition in Chicago, into a project to revive Pierre L'Enfant's original concept of a National Mall for Washington, and the Lincoln Memorial became the western anchor of their plans. With former President William Howard Taft as chair of the Lincoln Memorial Commission, the conservative side of the Republican Party kept control of the project.

The resulting building stood primarily for national power and unity. Thirty-six massive columns, each 44 feet high, represented every state—including those that attempted to secede—of the Union in Lincoln's day, and there were no scenes of war. At the dedication, President Warren Harding explicitly denied that Lincoln led the nation to war to eliminate slavery, and the single African-American speaker (Robert Russa Moton, the successor of Booker T. Washington as head of the Tuskegee Institute) sat with the other speakers before the ceremony, but retreated to a segregated area across the street after delivering his address.

Despite the conservative forces that drove its design, the monument quickly began to provide a setting for prophetic moments in American civil religion. In 1939, when the Daughters of the American Revolution denied opera singer Marian Anderson the use of their theater in Constitution Hall for a concert in Washington because of her race, the administration of Franklin Delano Roosevelt offered her the Lincoln Memorial, and the concert turned into a dramatic demonstration for racial equality. Twenty years later, in 1959, Martin Luther King, Jr., ran a civil rights protest from the foot of the memorial steps. In 1963, at the peak of the movement that resulted in the Civil Rights Act and the Voting Rights Act and ended legal segregation, King gave his most famous speech, the "I Have a Dream" address, before hundreds of thousands of people as he stood atop the steps, with Lincoln at his back. The Vietnam War brought many protests at the memorial, including one in 1970 that saw President Richard Nixon visit the students who were occupying the memorial at midnight. When Vietnam War veterans sought a site on the National Mall for their non-triumphal memorial, the neighborhood of Lincoln appealed to them as the natural place. Although it was built by those who wished to celebrate national unity and power, the Lincoln Memorial has come to stand for justice for those who feel unrepresented, from gays and lesbians in 1979 to Louis Farrakhan's Million Man March of 1995 to Tea Party partisans in 2010.

A radical potential does exist in the original design, because the texts of Lincoln's two greatest speeches, the Gettysburg Address and the Second Inaugural, are engraved on the walls in the chambers on each side of the statue. As the chapters on those speeches indicate, their themes of sacrifice, democracy, equality, repentance, and submission to divine judgment challenge all images of national or imperial triumph. Above the speeches are two murals painted by Jules Guerin: one above the Gettysburg Address in which an angel liberates slaves, and the other above the Second Inaugural, in which an angel brings together North and South. If the murals were more visible, their theme of angelic intervention might blunt the impact of Lincoln's words, but their position and lighting mean that few notice them. For most visitors, the experience of the Lincoln Memorial consists of confronting Lincoln, reading the speeches or parts of the speeches, and turning to Lincoln again.

Visitors may also browse in the small souvenir store, which was not opened until 1968 but which reported profits of about $1.4 million in 2005. The impulse to acquire some object at sacred sites is as old as the practice of pilgrimage itself. An unobtrusive presence, the store does not disturb the solemn atmosphere created by the statue and the words, but it does offer a place for visitors to recover their sense of normality, to decompress.

This need to decompress results from the intense reflections on death and violence that are often inspired by the Lincoln Memorial, through the brooding expression of the statue and the words of the two speeches. Just as the Civil War added a cult of the dead to the American civil religion, beginning with the cemetery at Gettysburg and extending to Arlington National Cemetery and Memorial Day, so the Lincoln Memorial marks a special aspect of that cult, the tradition of turning presidents into sacrificial martyrs. Though Lincoln was the first to be killed in office, he was followed by James Garfield, William McKinley, and John F. Kennedy, and there were serious attempts to kill Franklin Roosevelt, Gerald Ford, and Ronald Reagan, who was gravely wounded. No other economically advanced nation has such a record of violence associated with its leaders. British and Japanese prime ministers, Soviet premiers and Russian presidents, French and German and Israeli leaders have rarely been targeted. American presidents, and even candidates for president, live in routine danger, and the Lincoln Memorial is associated with that fact. The funeral processions of President Kennedy and of presidential candidate Robert F. Kennedy paused at the memorial on their way to Arlington National Cemetery.

To understand this deadly pattern, it may help to recall the fasces that form the arms of Lincoln's chair. Such bundles of rods were carried before Roman consuls and emperors. Among the great civilizations of world history, only the Romans established a similar record of killing and trying to kill their leaders. In both Rome and the United States, the form of government itself remained stable, despite the chronic violence directed at the chief. In contrast to America, however, the assassinations of Roman emperors were usually committed by people who wanted to become emperor themselves or to replace the emperor with someone they favored. American assassins seem bent on making a gesture, as John Wilkes Booth did when he leaped to the stage after shooting Lincoln and shouted, "*Sic semper tyrannis*" ("Thus ever to tyrants").

In their aftermath, assaults on American presidents enter the realm of religion. For citizens observing and reflecting on these assaults, the president becomes a sacrificial victim who stands for the nation. The overarching message of the Lincoln Memorial—expressed through the form of the building, the details of the statue, the inscription and the speeches carved into the walls, and even in the ways that the building has been used—is that American civil religion demands that freedom and democracy must be protected and advanced, even at the cost of death. But such a death may confer immortality.

SOURCES

Boime, Albert, *The Unveiling of the National Icons: A Plea for Patriotic Iconoclasm in a Nationalist Era* (Cambridge and New York: Cambridge University Press, 1998).

Meyer, Jeffrey F., *Myths in Stone: Religious Dimensions of Washington, D.C.* (Berkeley and Los Angeles: University of California Press, 2001).

Miller, Char Roone, "Neither Palace nor Temple nor Tomb": The Lincoln Memorial in the Age of Commercial Reappropriation" in Michael E. Geisler, ed., *National Symbols, Fractured Identities: Contesting the National Narrative* (Lebanon, NH: Middlebury College Press, 2005).

Thomas, Christopher A., *The Lincoln Memorial and American Life* (Princeton and Cambridge: Princeton University Press, 2002).

23

Mount Rushmore in the Black Hills

Mount Rushmore is the largest, most awe-inspiring, and most hotly contested monument of American civil religion. Carved into a 500-foot-high mountain in the Black Hills, which are themselves holy to many Indians, the heads of George Washington, Thomas Jefferson, Theodore Roosevelt, and Abraham Lincoln stand about 60 feet high and 365 feet across. Intended to express the triumphs of white men on this land, or what its sculptor Gutzon Borglum called "our race's secret and sacred dreaming," Mount Rushmore has been inevitably associated, through the presidents who are its subjects, with the values of personal freedom and political democracy. It has also come to reflect the American value of cultural tolerance, both because Borglum had a complex relationship with Indians, and because the Indians who live around Mount Rushmore participated in its creation and have marked their own history at nearby sites, like Greasy Grass (Little Bighorn) and Wounded Knee, with cooperation from the National Park Service. Still, though held sacred by many, Mount Rushmore is often seen as an example of idolatry or arrogance, a desecration of nature and of Indian land, and it has sometimes been occupied or used in protest.

Gutzom Borglum wanted to immortalize the sacred history of the United States, but his work interrupted a longer history. Centuries before the faces were carved, Lakota Indians knew Mount Rushmore as "Six Grandfathers," or *Tunkasila Sakpe*. The mountain stands near the middle of the Black Hills, about 15 miles from Wind Cave, which some Lakota regard as the place where their ancestors emerged from the earth. While this mountain and the whole Black Hills area are seen by the Lakota as holy and powerful, they were never the site of a permanent settlement for this nomadic people. Too rugged and too wooded to support the massive herds of buffalo that roamed the Great Plains, the Black Hills were used for healing rituals, special hunts, and vision quests. The Six Grandfathers are spirits of the four horizontal directions revealed by the sun and the compass, along with the heavens above and the earth below. According to Black Elk, the Lakota holy man who lived from the days of Crazy Horse and Sitting Bull into the time when the mountain was carved, and whose visions

Figure 23.1 This photograph of *Tunkasila Sakpe* (Six Grandfathers), the mountain holy to the Lakota, shows the shapes of granite that inspired sculptor Gutzom Borglum. National Park Service.

appear in the book *Black Elk Speaks*, these grandfathers gave him his mission. In pictures of the mountain before the carving, distinct outcroppings of granite can be seen along its flat peak, suggesting how the association between this mountain and the grandfather spirits may have arisen (see Figure 23.1).

The fact that one of the most dramatic sites of American civil religion was created by removing half a million tons of granite from the Six Grandfathers, using dynamite and jackhammers to cut as deep as 180 feet into the mountain, can be seen as proof of the negative relations of American civil religion both to Native American religions and to nature. Yet, those relations are not unambiguously negative. Black Elk himself prayed for protection for all those who worked on the monument, and many Lakota have taken part in dedication ceremonies at the site. Practitioners of Lakota religion might see some spiritual influence of Lakota participation in the fact that, during fourteen years of blasting and dangling from the cliff by about four hundred workers, no one was killed or seriously injured. It could also be said that, through the carving of the mountain that white Americans came to call Mount Rushmore (naming it for a New York lawyer who visited the site and gave an early, small donation to the project), the United States made a sacred place of Native Americans into one of its own sacred sites.

Figure 23.2 Whether Mount Rushmore is seen as a desecration or a sacred site, its power is undeniable. From left to right, George Washington, Thomas Jefferson, Theodore Roosevelt, and Abraham Lincoln. National Park Service.

Arguably, it was the natural power of the mountain that caused the artist Gutzon Borglum to choose it. The sculptor always said that the faces of his heroes were there before he released them (Figure 23.2).

The practice of carving mountains did not begin with the United States. In Egypt, Pharaoh Rameses II had a temple to the goddess Hathor carved into the side of a mountain at Abu Simbel more than 3,000 years ago. Ancient Persian kings carved their tombs into mountains, and in India there are huge cave temples to Vishnu and to the Buddha. Perhaps the closest predecessor to Mount Rushmore was the unrealized proposal of Deinocrates, architect to Alexander the Great, to carve an image of the conqueror into the side of Mount Athos, the island of Alexander's birth.

Just as that project would have deified Alexander, who was said to be the son of Zeus, so the figures on Mount Rushmore show how it can plausibly be said that American civil religion has made its heroes into gods. There are other such places, most notably the memorials in Washington, D.C., to Presidents Washington, Lincoln, and Jefferson, and the memorial to Martin Luther King, Jr. Unlike the creators of those memorials, however, Borglum was quite frank about aiming to represent divinity. He wrote and spoke a great deal about the philosophy behind his monument, including the statement that the faces of the heroes should express "a serenity, a nobility, a power that reflects the gods who inspired them and suggests the gods they have become." For Borglum, these gods were not just individual deities, but also an organized pantheon that worked in succession through American history. The artist's title for the Mount Rushmore Memorial is "The Founding, Preservation, and Expansion of the United States." Washington and Lincoln, at each end of the series, represent Founding and Preservation, while Jefferson and Roosevelt represent Expansion. Borglum wanted to leave an image of American history marching across the mountain. He also wanted, excavated to a depth of 70 feet behind Lincoln, a Hall of Records to identify the heroes and their deeds. In 1998, some documents were placed in the unfinished hall.

The monument was first dedicated in 1925, just thirty-five years after the slaughter of hundreds of Lakota at Wounded Knee, the massacre that ended the war between the US government and the Lakota. It was fifty-one years after the discovery of gold in the Black Hills led white Americans to begin mining in the area, despite a treaty granting it to the Lakota. It was forty-nine years after the battle of Greasy Grass or Little Bighorn, the slaughter of hundreds of US cavalry commonly called Custer's Last Stand—an event that writer Jesse Larner calls "the Alamo, the *Maine*, the Pearl Harbor, the World Trade Center of its day"—a moment that galvanized white resolve to remove these Indians from the Plains and from their sacred Black Hills. Mount Rushmore stands only about 15 miles from Custer State Park, the site of the battle, and about 50 miles from Wounded Knee.

Although Gutzon Borglum was not born in the Black Hills, he was a child of the West when it was still Indian country, born in Idaho in 1867. This was one year before the Lakota and the other nations in the group that white Americans called the Sioux were granted ownership of the Black Hills and much other territory for "all time" in the Fort Laramie Treaty, which ended a war with the United States that the Sioux had won. Later in life, Borglum claimed that his father knew great Lakota chiefs like Red Cloud, and that as a child, he himself had met and been blessed by the legendary Lakota medicine man Crow Dog. While he was working at Rushmore in the winter of 1931, he saw that the Lakota were starving and organized a campaign that delivered 65 cattle, 100 sheep, two railroad cars full of clothing, and 5,000 army blankets to the Pine Ridge reservation. In return, he was invited to come to the reservation and to be received into the tribe, with the gift of a full-length headdress and the name *Inyan Wanblee*, or "Stone Eagle." He admired the Lakota, calling them "the Romans among the red men...that great war-like race." In a speech on NBC radio in 1934, he urged that Indians be allowed to live "without interference by the white man," and promised the Indians a statue of one of their chiefs like those at Mount Rushmore, "if the Great Spirit gives me life."

Gutzon's father Jens (Anglicized to James) was an immigrant from Denmark and a convert to Mormonism who had two wives. As an adult, Gutzon never mentioned his Mormon background, perhaps because his family left the church when he was so young (about four) that he knew nothing about it, or perhaps because to be the child of Mormons and polygamists seemed a matter of shame. Still, the adult Gutzon Borglum gave voice to the concept of men becoming gods, which is basic to Mormon theology. Other Mormon ideas—such as the expectations that the continent of North America, especially the center of that continent, has a special destiny in the history of salvation, and that the white settlers of America have an important role in realizing that destiny—also informed Borglum's work at Mount Rushmore.

Filling in Borglum's silences, biographers now say that his father seems to have given up his Mormonism before he moved to Omaha, Nebraska, where Gutzon's mother Christina was passed off as a servant. James then moved to St. Louis, where he studied medicine. Christina at some point left the family, never to see her sons again.

After James Borglum acquired his medical diploma, which at the time involved no certification by any professional organization or government regulator, he moved west again, to the town of Fremont west of Omaha. James changed his religious affiliation to Theosophy, and then to Roman Catholicism. He sent Gutzon to a prep school run by Jesuits, and it was there that the child's talent for drawing was first discovered. In 1884, the Borglums moved to Los Angeles, and Gutzon became a painter of frescoes for people's homes. At twenty-two, he married his painting teacher, Elizabeth James Putnam, who was forty. Biographers have speculated that he was still seeking the mother he had lost.

Meanwhile, another older woman had entered Borglum's life: Jessie Frémont, the sixty-four-year-old wife of General John C. Frémont, explorer of California and founder of the California Republic. Borglum's portrait of her husband pleased her so much that she urged him to study in Europe and wrote letters to friends who would buy his paintings to help finance the trip. One letter went to Theodore Roosevelt, then the police commissioner of New York City, who became Borglum's friend. The deep agreement between Theodore Roosevelt and Gutzon Borglum on the meaning of the West, the destiny of white Americans, and the direction of history resulted in Roosevelt being elevated to equivalence with Washington, Jefferson, and Lincoln on Mount Rushmore.

In England, Borglum studied painting, but it was Paris that really shaped his later life. He took classes at the École des Beaux Arts and spent hours in the Paris museums. Above all other influences was that of Auguste Rodin, the Romantic sculptor of *The Thinker*, *The Kiss*, and many other highly dramatic pieces. Because of Rodin's example, Borglum returned to America as a sculptor, not a painter. Rodin's recommendation letters helped Borglum as his career in sculpture took off in New York.

Between 1901 and 1911, Borglum gained recognition as a major American sculptor. His most successful works included a massive bust of Lincoln (40 inches tall, in 375 pounds of marble) that Lincoln's son Robert called the best likeness of his father, and which sat for many years in the Capitol Rotunda and is now displayed in the Capitol Crypt. Borglum carved the marble for that bust himself, with no clay model and no assistance, contrary to the usual practice of modern sculptors.

The Mount Rushmore project grew directly from Borglum's early success, and later failure, in building a monument to the Confederacy in Georgia. Impressed with Borglum's bust of Lincoln, the Daughters of the Confederacy asked him to make an even larger bust of Robert E. Lee for the top of Stone Mountain, the 1,700-foot granite dome near Atlanta where the Ku Klux Klan was reborn in 1915. Borglum surveyed the scene, told the Daughters that a bust of Lee on the top of the mountain would be as unimpressive as "a postage stamp on a barn door," and began to plan to carve one whole side of the mountain itself. He made plaster models for figures of Lee, Stonewall Jackson, and Confederate President Jefferson Davis, who were to be followed by troops in a gigantic bas relief, and actually carved the figure of Lee into the mountain, learning as he went the technique of using dynamite in sculpting. In January 1924, Borglum hosted a fried chicken lunch for many guests, including three Southern governors, who reached their tables by a three-hundred-foot stairway from the top of the Stone Mountain to Robert E. Lee's shoulder, about a quarter-mile from the ground below. When the figure of Lee was unveiled, it made such a sensation that as many as two thousand people a day began to come to Stone Mountain.

Meanwhile, in South Dakota, a state historian named Doane Robinson heard about Stone Mountain and began to consider how to draw tourists by carving mountains in the Black Hills. He wrote to Borglum in August 1924, asking if the artist might do something to commemorate the history of the West. Robinson wanted a regional theme, featuring local heroes including the Lakota chief Red Cloud. But Borglum already had dreams of a monument for the United States in the center of the country, and he agreed to come up to South Dakota in September to pursue ideas that did not include any Indians. It was on this trip that he chose the site of Mount Rushmore.

Back at Stone Mountain, things began to go badly. Fund-raising was a chronic problem, as it proved to be at Mount Rushmore. Ultimately, Borglum was fired. He then destroyed the models he had made for Stone Mountain, after which he had to flee Georgia. Borglum's likeness of Robert E. Lee was blasted off the mountain, which was not completed until 1970. Although Stone Mountain did become the largest bas relief in the world, it has never attained the status of Mount Rushmore.

The first of many dedication ceremonies at Mount Rushmore took place before 3,000 people on October 1, 1925. After a dance by a Lakota named Black Horse and six other Indians, Borglum asked Black Horse to preside over the rest of the ceremony. Flags of Britain, Spain, and France were raised and lowered on the mountain, accompanied by the firing of salutes by soldiers from Fort Meade and a thirty-piece band playing national anthems, honoring the previous European claimants. There was a moment of silence in which Black Horse was asked to stand alone on the mountain, with what thoughts we do not know. As a finale for the ceremony, the American flag was raised, a band played "The Star Spangled Banner," and the soldiers fired a final volley. Among the speakers who then addressed the crowd, Borglum struck a religious note: "The hand of Providence is seen decreeing that a national memorial shall be erected," he said. He also challenged those present to join him there in a year, when he predicted that the figure of Washington would be complete.

As at Stone Mountain, slow fund-raising led to slow progress and to the need for another dedication. It was August 1927 before there were roads to the site so that President Calvin Coolidge could come, as part of his summer vacation in the Black Hills, and see Gutzon Borglum dangle from the cliff and make the first six holes for the carving of George Washington's head. On that occasion, Coolidge gave a speech that surprised people with its passion. "We have come here to dedicate a corner stone that was laid by the hand of the Almighty," he said.

For Coolidge, Mount Rushmore represented four specific values. He associated Washington with independence, Jefferson with self-government, Lincoln with freedom, and Roosevelt with economic justice. He called the whole project "a national shrine to which future generations will repair to declare their continuing allegiance" to those values. In the controversy over whether to include Theodore Roosevelt on the mountain, Coolidge had been a warm supporter, saying that Roosevelt was the first president who did anything to protect the working man.

President Coolidge's visit to Mount Rushmore exposed him to another value, cultural tolerance. Before leaving South Dakota, he went to Pine Ridge Reservation and accepted induction into the Sioux Nation as Chief *Wanbli Tokaha*, or Leading Eagle. At that ceremony Henry Standing Bear, a friend of Gutzon Borglum's and frequent participant in ceremonies at Mount Rushmore, called upon Coolidge to succeed Sitting Bull, Spotted Tail, and Red Cloud "as our new High Chief, to take up their leadership and fulfill the same duty call from which they never did shrink, a duty to protect and help the weak." Since Henry Standing Bear gave this speech in the Lakota language, it is not clear whether Coolidge understood, but he may have been given the translation, which was published in the *Black Hills Engineer*.

With support from Coolidge, who signed a bill giving the Mount Rushmore project $250,000 just before he left office in 1929, Borglum now made the first of his great triumphs on the mountain, the head of George Washington. He had a giant egg-shaped section of granite blasted away with dynamite, then went to work on a face that translated the expression from Houdon's statue of Washington, done from life in 1784. Apparently, the French sculptor was struck by how Washington looked when he was dismissing from Mount Vernon a man who had tried to sell horses that Washington believed to be stolen. The mouth, in particular, is very severe and controlled, the sign of a patriarch accustomed to command. On July 4, 1930, the Washington head was dedicated at another ceremony, with the face of Jefferson already beginning to appear to its right.

A six-year epic then began, in which the head of Jefferson was found to be placed on an inadequate area of granite and had to be moved to Washington's left, with most of a face blasted off the rock to the right after eighteen months of work. As a side benefit of this disaster, the head of Washington now emerged from the mountain so that it could be seen in profile from both sides, as well as from the front. Lack of money slowed the process of carving Jefferson again, until Senator Peter Norbeck of South Dakota managed, while dying of cancer in 1934, to get a bill passed to appropriate another $200,000 for the project. A large piece of feldspar, a soft mineral, appeared in Jefferson's lip and had to be patched with a mixture of linseed oil, lead, and granite dust that Borglum developed. Jefferson's head had to be tilted upward to take advantage of the best granite. Still, Borglum managed to create what one writer, John Taliaferro, has called "the best, most expressive bit of carving on the mountain." He was trying to depict Jefferson at age thirty-three, when he wrote the Declaration of Independence, even though Jefferson's place on the memorial was largely based, in Borglum's mind, on his having bought the land on which Mount Rushmore stood, as part of the Louisiana Purchase. At any rate, the Jefferson of Mount Rushmore was left with an expression that has been described as "bemused," youthful, and hopeful, as opposed to the severity of Washington.

Politics also became involved at this stage. Until the 1928 election, Borglum had always been a Republican of the Theodore Roosevelt wing, and Theodore Roosevelt called Jefferson "the most incompetent chief executive we ever had." In the Republican ascendancy during the seven decades between Lincoln and Franklin Roosevelt, Jefferson's reputation suffered in comparison with that of Alexander Hamilton, his great Federalist rival. As a slaveholder and connoisseur of wines, a man of dubious morality and religion, Jefferson did not suit the age of Prohibition. Still, he was one of those whom Borglum called "the Empire Builders" in a note on the memorial, and when the nation slid into Depression in 1929, Democratic concern for the common man seemed appropriate. Borglum publicly endorsed Theodore Roosevelt's cousin Franklin against Herbert

Hoover with a few weeks left in the 1932 presidential campaign. "I believe that a Rooseveltian national consciousness alone will save this republic," he said. When Borglum was finally ready to dedicate the Jefferson head, on August 30, 1936, President Franklin Roosevelt came to the event.

Though Roosevelt's presence was in part an accident—he was already in the area reviewing the West on what was called "the drought tour," attempting to lift the spirits of people affected by the Dust Bowl—Borglum did manage to use the occasion to get a speech from FDR and a commitment for more funds. Roosevelt said that he had never, until then, understood the "permanent importance" of what Borglum was doing on Mount Rushmore. The monument moved him to meditate on what "Americans ten thousand years from now" would think about his generation. Facing the imminent threats of fascism in Germany, Italy, and Spain, of military dictatorship in Japan, and of Stalinist communism in the Soviet Union, FDR said that Mount Rushmore could be "an inspiration for the continuance of the democratic republican form of government, not only in our own beloved country, but, we hope, throughout the world." To Franklin Roosevelt, Mount Rushmore stood for the value of political democracy.

On the day before the 1936 unveiling of Jefferson's head, the man called Black Elk (or Nicholas Black Elk, because he was a baptized Catholic as well as a Lakota shaman) gave a half-hour prayer on Mount Rushmore. He asked for the safety of Borglum and the men on the mountain, who were beginning their most intensive period of work. He prayed to the *Tunkasila*, the six grandfathers of the mountain, and asked that the greatness of the men sculpted on the memorial would be carried on "through changes in nations and races." No one was sure of what Black Elk meant by those words, though Gutzon Borglum probably had an idea.

Like his mentor Theodore Roosevelt, Borglum often contemplated the end of the civilization he represented. He was simultaneously nationalist and universal, indomitable and fatalistic. He wanted to serve the United States, but he wanted even more to make a monument that would endure for all time. At the 1930 unveiling of George Washington, a geologist and former president of the South Dakota School of Mines, Cleophas C. O'Harra, answered the question of how long it might last. "One hundred years? Yes. One thousand years? Yes. A hundred thousand years? In all likelihood, yes. A half million years? Possibly so, nobody knows. The time at any rate will be long, far longer than we can readily comprehend. And this will doubtless abundantly suffice."

Borglum wanted to insure that his monument would be understood, even if the civilization that made it had passed away. To that end, he had made part of the plan passed by Congress in 1929 an "entablature," or a 500-word summary of US history, to be carved into the rock, or alternatively stored in the Hall of Records. President Calvin Coolidge was first enlisted to write this summary, but he withdrew from the task when Borglum insisted on editing his words. Ultimately, the text of the summary was made the subject of a contest for college scholarships funded by the Hearst newspapers, and the winning essay was a pedestrian listing of events that Borglum wanted to include, from the Declaration of Independence to the building of the Panama Canal. It was inscribed on a bronze plaque that was mounted in 1975 at the Borglum View Terrace of the memorial, on the site of Borglum's studio.

The young Nebraskan who wrote the essay, William Andrew Burkett, did provide a few rhetorical flourishes. His essay began, "Almighty God, from this pulpit of stone the American people render thanksgiving and praise for the new era of civilization brought forth upon this continent." It ended with a sentiment fitting for 1934: "Holding no fear of the economic and political, chaotic clouds hovering over the earth, the consecrated Americans dedicate this nation before God, to exalt righteousness and to maintain mankind's constituted liberties so long as the earth shall endure." According to this text, Mount Rushmore stood primarily for the value of freedom, or "constituted liberties."

The late 1930s saw the Mount Rushmore project rise to the center of national consciousness. As some historians have noted, just as World War I made the Statue of Liberty into a national icon, the decade of Depression and buildup to war elevated Mount Rushmore. Federal money now made construction go more quickly. The Lincoln head was dedicated on September 17, 1937, to celebrate the one hundred fiftieth anniversary of the Constitution, and the Theodore Roosevelt head on July 2, 1939. People marveled at the realism of Lincoln's beard, the delicate effect that suggested Roosevelt's glasses, and the lifelike quality that all eight of the eyes acquired from the play of light off the two-foot granite columns that protrude from the center of each pupil. There was a bill introduced in Congress in 1937, with the support of Eleanor Roosevelt, to add the head of Susan B. Anthony to the memorial, but it was thwarted by a rider on an appropriation bill that required all money to be spent on the four figures already begun. During the Roosevelt dedication, the whole memorial was lit at night for the first time.

According to the plan, carving was to continue until the figures had clothing and arms down to the waist, with one of Washington's hands on a sword and Jefferson's right hand on Washington's arm, while Lincoln held the lapel of his coat. Work continued until 1941, when Congress cut off funding, because of the need to give priority to preparations for war. Borglum died on March 6, 1941, of complications from what was thought to be minor surgery. His son Lincoln was asked to supervise completion of the tops of the heads, which he did by October 31, five weeks before Pearl Harbor and the entrance of the United States into World War II.

The decades between Pearl Harbor and 1970 were relatively uneventful for Mount Rushmore and the Black Hills. In 1959, film director Alfred Hitchcock set the climax of a spy thriller, *North by Northwest*, on Rushmore, including a vividly staged, fake shooting "witnessed" by the four heads watching through the window of a beautiful modern visitors' center, built in 1958, and a communist villain falling to his death from Lincoln's nose. Apart from a National Park Service complaint that Hitchcock had broken an agreement that he would avoid violence near the monument, the film raised no controversy. The 1970s were another story.

Taking part in the general trend toward ethnic pride and militant protest, the American Indian Movement (AIM) was gaining momentum in the late 1960s. It had already claimed Alcatraz Island in San Francisco Bay in 1969, and on August 24, 1970, about 150 AIM demonstrators protested at Mount Rushmore, demanding the return of 100,000 acres taken from the Pine Ridge Reservation for a gunnery range during World War II. They camped on the mountain until mid-September, accommodated by the Park Service, which was told to help them, and they left when nighttime temperatures began to fall below freezing. On June 4, 1971, they returned to a camp above the heads, carrying cans of red paint to pour on the faces, but this time they were removed within two days by National Park Police, National Guardsmen, FBI agents, and local police. Meanwhile, the rest of the Black Hills area saw more serious violence, including a two-month standoff between Indians and the FBI at Wounded Knee in 1973, and the shooting deaths of two FBI agents and one Indian demonstrator in 1975. Violence came to Mount Rushmore on the day after those shootings, when a bomb destroyed eleven of the eight-foot windows in the Visitors' Center. July 3, 1975, saw an FBI SWAT team rappelling out of a helicopter onto George Washington's head, "just to make sure everybody knew we were there," and camping out over the holiday.

In 1980, a lawsuit by the Lakota that had been working its way through the courts since 1929 was finally decided, with an eight-to-one vote of the Supreme Court that said Congress had failed to make "a good faith effort" to give what the Constitution demands, "just compensation" for taking private property for public use. The Court assessed the debt owed to the Indians for the Black Hills at $106 million. But days after that decision, a Lakota attorney named Mario Gonzalez, raised on the Pine Ridge reservation, filed a series of suits alleging that the the Black Hills were taken not for public but for private use, with the land turned over to miners, loggers, and other private individuals, and that it still belonged to the Sioux Nation under the terms of the Fort Laramie Treaty of 1868. He demanded $11 billion in compensation from the federal government and $6 billion from the Homestake Mining Company, the gold mine that had launched the Hearst fortune, as well as title to all federal and Homestake Mine property. Although the suits have not succeeded, they have kept the government from identifying Indians to pay, and the original $106 million set aside for payment has now grown to about $800 million, which the tribal government has still refused to accept.

Several changes in the direction of multiculturalism have occurred in the Black Hills since the 1970s. The Custer Memorial was renamed the Little Bighorn National Monument under a law signed by President George H. W. Bush on December 10, 1991. Until then, the memorial had honored only the fallen of the Seventh Cavalry, but now, as the National Park Service says, it marks the place where "two divergent cultures clashed in a life or death struggle." A sunken, circular Indian Memorial, which appears from the outside as only a mound on the prairie, was dedicated in 2003 to commemorate the Sioux, Cheyenne, Arapaho, Crow, and Arikara Indians who fought at Greasy Grass to defend their families and to preserve their way of life. According to the *Rapid City Journal* and other local sources, far more Indian events than events celebrating Custer and the Seventh Cavalry are scheduled each year to mark the anniversary of the battle, on June 25. Elsewhere in the Black Hills, multiculturalism won another small victory in the 1990s when the Park Service established a "voluntary ban" on rock climbing at a famous butte called *Mata Tipila*, "the lodge of the bear," during the month of June when Indian ceremonies are held there.

Meanwhile, another monument that many regard as a desecration has emerged in the Black Hills. A man named Korczak Ziolkowski, a Polish-American who had done a larger than life bust of Ignace Paderewski for the 1939 New York World's Fair, worked for a few weeks on Mount Rushmore before Gutzon Borglum fired him. In 1946, Ziolkowski bought a mountain in South Dakota, ten miles from Mount Rushmore, and announced his intention to carve it into a likeness of Crazy Horse, mounted and pointing straight ahead, that would be 500 feet tall and 600 feet wide—ten times the size of Mount Rushmore. Ziolkowski brought two survivors of the fight with Custer to the dedication of the mountain on June 4, 1948, and one of them said that the statue he designed looked nothing like Crazy Horse, who had a thin straight nose, as opposed to the wide, pug nose of the Indian on the statue. But the sculptor was undeterred. Even though he died in 1982, and was buried at the bottom of his mountain, work slowly continues on the colossal sculpture, and visitors come by the thousands and pay admission that supports the continuing work. Some Indians have endorsed the project, but others see it as a provocation that will bring the spirit of Crazy Horse back for vengeance.

In 2001, author John Taliaferro interviewed Charlotte Black Elk, a lawyer and activist and granddaughter of Black Elk. He had to pay her a lawyer's fee, $325 an hour, for the talk. She predicted that no new law would be needed for the Lakota to get the Black Hills back, because "South Dakota is a state of old white women and young Indians," and the young Indians were studying forestry and business and would "be ready when they have to manage those resources." About Mount Rushmore and the Crazy Horse memorial, she was more apocalyptic. "The earth will cleanse herself. We've already had earthquakes in the Black Hills...they could level Mount Rushmore and Crazy Horse. Right now nature is only smacking mosquitoes. One day she's going to pull out the Raid."

If Mother Nature does attack Mount Rushmore, she will find the National Park Service trying to repair the damage, and perhaps perpetuating the monument into a virtual eternity. In 2009, the Park Service contracted with a California firm called CyArk to make a 3-D laser record that would provide "the data needed to repair or rebuild the monument in case it is ever damaged by an attack, an earthquake or some other calamity." The 3-D file will also enable people distant from the site to have models of the monument that "they can touch and feel and see and maybe even walk around." This effort seemed especially important after eleven Greenpeace demonstrators were arrested, in July 2009, for draping an enormous banner, featuring a picture of President Barack Obama and the words, "America Honors Leaders, Not Politicians. Stop Global Warming," over Lincoln's head. As Navrit Singh, the director of interpretation and education for the Park Service at Mount Rushmore reflected, "Say it was something more than a banner, something more malicious. We would have the ability [because of the 3-D laser record] to go back and do repairs."

Repairs and cleaning go on continually at Mount Rushmore, which was rather amazingly described by the BBC as a "fragile structure" in an article about a proposal to add Ronald Reagan's face to the mountain in 1999. For the fifty years between 1941 and 1991, Park Service employees used Borglum's own recipe of linseed oil, lead, and granite dust to fill in cracks, but this has since been found too susceptible to temperature change and replaced with a silicone compound. Although the Park Service website continues to repeat the idea that "erosion" will take as little as one inch of granite from Washington's nose every 10,000 years, the fact that about twenty different blocks of granite meet within the four faces inspires less confidence. Were it not for the cleaning the Park Service does, nature would allow moss and lichen to grow on the granite faces, and eventually trees would grow in the cracks. Even without catastrophe, the faces would gradually soften back into the mountain. The heads at Mount Rushmore may remain perfectly intact only a century or so longer than adherents of American civil religion continue to regard them as worthy of constant cleaning and preservation. If an earthquake or a bomb shook them apart, would we actually reconstruct them, even now?

In the meantime, the meaning of Mount Rushmore has already been changed from an expression of the triumph of white men to that of a site for reflection on American history. Because Mount Rushmore is in the Black Hills, it is surrounded by sites that teach cultural tolerance and by Indians who are demanding that their culture be respected. The message of Mount Rushmore will continue to be changed by the changing attitudes of white and Indian Americans toward the land of the Black Hills, toward each other, and toward their ancestors.

SOURCES

Borglum, Lincoln, *Mount Rushmore: Heritage of America* (Las Vegas: KC Publications, 1977).
Campo, Juan Eduardo, "American Pilgrimage Landscapes," *Annals of the American Academy of Political and Social Science* 558 (July 1998), 40–56.
Glass, Matthew, "Producing Patriotic Inspiration at Mount Rushmore," *Journal of the American Academy of Religion* 62, no. 2 (Summer 1994), 265–283.
Larner, Jesse, *Mount Rushmore: An Icon Reconsidered* (New York: Thunder's Mouth Press/Nation Books, 2002).
Schama, Simon, *Landscape and Memory* (New York: Alfred A. Knopf, 1995).
Taliaferro, John, *Great White Fathers: The Story of the Obsessive Quest to Create Mount Rushmore* (New York: Public Affairs, 2002).

24

God Bless America

God bless America,
Land that I love.
Stand beside her, and guide her
Thru the night with a light from above.
From the mountains, to the prairies,
To the oceans, white with foam,
God bless America,
My home sweet home.

This deceptively simple, powerful song is both loved and hated because it expresses a religious attitude toward the United States. The song was first written by Irving Berlin in 1918, during the first World War, then revised and reissued in 1938 as a plea for peace while a greater war loomed. Since then, it has become deeply embedded in American civil religion. Its opening phrase, or a longer variant on that phrase ("God bless the United States of America"), is the almost-mandatory ending for presidential speeches.

Over the decades, the song has been associated strongly with American hope for victory in World War II, with reactions against anti-war protests in the Vietnam era, and with expressions of solidarity after the terrorist attacks of September 11, 2001. It has been sung at the seventh inning of many baseball games in the post–9/11 era. In the presidential campaign of 2008, a video that showed candidate Barack Obama's former pastor, Jeremiah Wright, inverting the opening phrase ("God Bless America? No, no, no God damn America, that's in the Bible for killing innocent people") went viral and nearly cost the future president his nomination.

Though the phrase "God Bless America" preceded the song, the song gave that phrase its central place in the national discourse. A recent researcher, Sheryl Kaskowitz, has counted fifteen appearances of the phrase in the *New York Times* between 1858 and 1938, but hundreds immediately after the song appeared. Because of the song, the phrase "God Bless America" has become one of the most popular and concise expressions of adherence to American civil religion, a prayer suitable for printing on auto magnets.

Behind "God Bless America" stands the epic American story of Irving Berlin. Born Israel Beilin in 1888, he told a biographer that his earliest memory was lying beside a road, wrapped in a blanket, while his home was burned in a pogrom. The family came to America on September 13, 1893, passing the Statue of Liberty, which was then still a new fixture in the harbor, next to Ellis Island. The Beilin family had their name changed to Baline as they were registered as residents of the United States. Israel Baline apprenticed to his father, who worked as a cantor, a singer who accompanied Jewish prayer in synagogues, but his training was cut short at age twelve, when his father died. Then everyone in the family went to work, with Israel selling newspapers. Shortly after his bar mitzvah at thirteen, he concluded that his earnings did not equal the drag that he placed on the family finances and he left, sleeping on the streets or in flophouses, until he landed a job as a singing waiter in a Bowery bar. As a waiter he published his first song, "Marie from Sunny Italy," in 1907. The song appeared over the name "I. Berlin," apparently reflecting what had happened to "Baline" on the Bowery, and Israel decided that he preferred "Irving." For the song, he earned 32 cents in royalties.

His big break came in 1911, when Berlin published "Alexander's Ragtime Band," which quickly sold a million copies of sheet music in the United States and another million abroad, more than any popular song had ever sold. At that moment, ragtime music was associated with black musicians and cities and was seen by many as leading American youth astray. This song by a white composer, with a lyric referring to "the best band in the land," asked everyone to "come on along," and mentioned Stephen Foster's "Swanee River." It made the new music seem safer. Berlin used the proceeds to return to his family, moving his mother from the Lower East Side to an apartment in the Bronx, where he went every Friday for Sabbath dinners until she died in 1922.

During World War I, which the United States did not enter until 1917, Irving Berlin decided to become a US citizen. He was drafted in 1918, at the age of thirty, and was assigned for basic training to an Army camp in Yaphank, New York. There he convinced the commanding officers that a stage show featuring soldiers could raise money for the Army (a Navy show featuring sailors had already succeeded). The resulting revue, called *Yip Yip Yaphank*, had a brief run in New York. "God Bless America" was written as the finale, but others didn't like it, and Berlin was convinced to shelve the song.

The 1920s and 1930s were incredibly successful decades for Irving Berlin. He opened his own theater on Broadway and became a leading composer for movie musicals. *Time* magazine put Berlin on its cover in 1934. At the point when Kate Smith asked him for a patriotic song as a finale for her Armistice Day (November 11) show in 1938, Berlin stood at the top of the popular music world.

In May of that same year, Berlin had been in England, negotiating overseas rights for his music, at the moment when Adolf Hitler and Neville Chamberlain were meeting in Munich. Impressed with the danger of war, Berlin was already trying to write a song about peace, with the hope of influencing public opinion, when Smith's agent called looking for a patriotic number. He began a song called "Thanks America," and another called "Let's Talk about Liberty," which he later said turned into a lecture. Then he remembered "God Bless America" and asked his secretary to find it in his enormous files of rejected songs. He made two crucial changes to the lyrics. In 1918, the prayer asked God to "guide her, to the right with a light from above," but by 1938 the meaning of "to the right" had acquired a fascist connotation, so Berlin substituted "thru the night." Second, the World War I song asked God to make America "victorious on land and foam," but Berlin now wanted peace. At first, he developed a geographically specific line: "From the green fields, of Virginia, to the gold fields, out in Nome," which appeared in Kate Smith's first performance, but which Berlin quickly changed to "From the mountains, to the prairies, to the oceans, white with foam." Possibly this change reflected Berlin's experiences of mountain climbing and fishing trips, which he had come to love during the 1920s and 1930s.

At any rate, "God Bless America" gave the country a simple affirmation. It resembled "America the Beautiful," the patriotic hymn by Katherine Lee Bates, in celebrating nature. It was a peace song, and not only because it never referenced a war. The introductory lyrics, which are rarely performed today, contrasted American peace, freedom, and beauty with "storm clouds" overseas. In 1938, the third line of this lyric was decisively non-interventionist: "Let us all be grateful, that we're far from there." Before the sheet music went on sale, in February 1939, Berlin had changed that line to a reference to America: "Let us all be grateful for a land so fair." The final form of the song expressed the values of peace, freedom, and a solidarity made possible by tolerance.

> While the storm clouds gather, far across the sea,
> Let us swear allegiance to a land that's free.
> Let us all be grateful for a land so fair,
> As we raise our voices in a solemn prayer.

Of course, the highlight was the chorus, the actual prayer, beginning with "God bless America, land that I love."

The reaction to Kate Smith's first performance in 1938 was electric: listeners immediately called the studio to ask where they could get sheet music or recordings of the song. Irving Berlin left his Tin Pan Alley office, where he typically worked well into the night, and went to the studio to take part in the second live broadcast of the show that Smith did for the West Coast. There were calls in Congress to make "God Bless America" the national anthem, and both the Republican and Democratic parties had the song performed at their conventions in 1940. In response, Berlin opposed any change in the national anthem. He also donated all royalties from his song to a fund that he established, called the God Bless America Fund, which still holds the copyright, "to benefit America's youth," and which has contributed more than 10 million dollars over the decades to the Boy Scouts and Girl Scouts. The song had become an institution.

At the same time, there were critics, such as Dr. Edgar Franklin Romig, pastor of the West End Collegiate Reformed Church in New York, who complained that the song made patriotism into a "specious substitute for religion." Folk singer Woody Guthrie wrote "This Land Is Your Land" as a leftist alternative, after a trip across the country on which "God Bless America" seemed to be playing whenever he heard a radio. There was criticism from anti-Semites that a Jewish immigrant had written a song that was being sung at Memorial Day celebrations and ship launchings alongside "The Star-Spangled Banner." According to Cleve Sallendar, a writer for an American Nazi newspaper, "God Bless America" reflected "the 'How Glad I Am' attitude of the refugee horde," rather than the solemn sentiments of "real" Americans who had suffered for their country.

The message of the song actually reflected the deep appreciation that Irving Berlin had for the values of American civil religion, particularly freedom, peace, and tolerance. According to Herbert Bayard Swope, appointed by Berlin as the first trustee of the God Bless America Foundation, Berlin chose to donate royalties to the Scouts because "the completely nonsectarian work of the Boy Scouts and Girl Scouts is calculated to best promote unity of mind and patriotism, two sentiments that are inherent in the song itself." From his first days in the United States, Irving Berlin had opened himself to religious assimilation, going as a child to the apartment of a neighbor to celebrate Christmas. One daughter later recalled that the Berlin family always celebrated Christmas, not as a Christian but as an American holiday. His eldest daughter, Mary Ellin, wrote in a biography that no other singer, even Kate Smith, could sing "God Bless America" with quite the conviction that Irving Berlin himself gave to it. Evidence of this can be found on YouTube, where many have viewed Berlin's performance of the song on television's *Ed Sullivan Show* to celebrate his eightieth birthday, in 1968.

When the United States entered World War II, Berlin found a way to use "God Bless America" to support the war effort of the United States around the world. He was fifty-four years old, far beyond the age for normal military service, but he took part in the war effort as a very active non-combatant. At the request of the War Department, he created an all soldier-revue, *This Is the Army*, which played on Broadway, across America, was made into a movie, and toured the European and Pacific war theaters. One of the first numbers in the show, an evocation of the days of peace now integrated into an affirmation of war, was "God Bless America." The show opened on July 4, 1942, with a cast that included black soldiers, which made that cast the first integrated unit of the American army. Berlin himself sang a song in the show and traveled with *This Is the Army* to North Africa and Italy, where infantry fresh from action made up the audience. It ran in Rome, then went to the Pacific, and ultimately was performed before 2 million service personnel. Meanwhile, a film version (starring Lieutenant Ronald Reagan) was made in 1943. Kate Smith recreated her 1938 broadcast of "God Bless America" for the movie. Besides entertaining troops, *This Is the Army* raised 9 million dollars for the families of those killed in military service. After the war, Irving Berlin was given a Presidential Medal of Merit, an event that he called "the biggest emotional experience of my life."

The postwar career of "God Bless America" was conjoined for decades with that of Kate Smith. Although Bing Crosby and Gene Autry also recorded the song, Smith's 1939 recording remained the standard. She also performed it on the *Ed Sullivan Show* in 1957, and during the 1970s at several Philadelphia Flyers hockey games. The Flyers had adopted the practice of playing "God Bless America" before their games, supposedly because their management found that the crowd was less rowdy when they did. In 1978, a Vietnam movie called *The Deer Hunter*, which won the Academy Award for Best Picture, ended with a funeral at which the survivors sang "God Bless America."

With the terrorist attacks on the World Trade Center in New York and the Pentagon on September 11, 2001, "God Bless America" embarked on a new career. Canadian singer Celine Dion made an emblematic recording at a benefit concert for victims of the attacks. When major league baseball resumed its season after the attacks, Commissioner Bud Selig requested that teams have a performance or play a recording of "God Bless America" at the break between the visitors' and the home team halves of the seventh inning, as part of a ritual in which fans were asked to stand and to remove their hats to "honor America" and those serving in the military. After 2002, the practice was less universal, but most teams have continued to do it on Saturdays and Sundays, and the New York Yankees perform this ritual, generally with Kate Smith's recording, at every home game.

Some controversies have arisen from this practice. In 2003, Carlos Delgado, a first baseman for the Toronto Blue Jays, expressed his dissent from the invasion of Iraq by refusing to stand for the ritual, instead leaving the field for the locker room, an act that earned him intense boos, particularly in New York. Years later, Delgado was traded to the New York Mets, after which he agreed to stand for "God Bless America." In 2009, the New York Yankees paid $10,000 to settle a lawsuit by one customer who attempted to go to the men's room during the ritual, was stopped by a security guard, and then was thrown out of Yankee

Stadium when he continued his attempt to reach the lavatory. The Yankees had a policy, which they have since modified, of enforcing no movement during the playing of "God Bless America." Sheryl Kaskowitz has noted that surveys show large majorities of baseball fans in favor of dropping "God Bless America" from the seventh-inning stretch. Even if that change happens soon, however, "God Bless America" will have held this place for more than ten years.

Although militancy and a will to enforce conformity have become associated with "God Bless America," the song retains an undeniable gentleness, seeking blessings on "my home sweet home." The rhythm and melody are powerful, with rising notes and repeated intervals, and they can have a strident effect, but the lyrics are peaceful. This combination of militancy and sweetness expresses a central element of American civil religion. Like ancient Rome, the United States fights its wars in the name of peace, extending its military borders for thousands of miles for the sake of defense. The genius of Irving Berlin also integrated the tradition of a blessing, which is the central form of Jewish prayer, into the lyric. Berlin gave American civil religion something it had previously lacked: its own prayer.

SOURCES

Barrett, Mary Ellin, *Irving Berlin: A Daughter's Memoir* (New York: Simon & Schuster, 1994).
Freedland, Michael, *A Salute to Irving Berlin* (Santa Barbara, CA: ABC-Clio, 1986).
Furia, Philip, *Irving Berlin: A Life in Song* (New York: Schirmer Books, 1998).
Greene, Bob, "Irving Berlin's Gift of 'God Bless America,'" CNN.com, December 12, 2011 (accessed June 8, 2012).
Jablonski, Edward, *Irving Berlin: American Troubadour* (New York: Henry Holt and Company, 1999).
Kaskowitz, Sheryl Renee, *God Bless America: The Surprising History of an Iconic Song* (New York: Oxford University Press, 2013).
Kimball, Robert, and Linda Emmet, eds., *The Complete Lyrics of Irving Berlin* (New York: Alfred A. Knopf, 2001).
Sears, Benjamin, ed., *The Irving Berlin Reader* (New York: Oxford University Press, 2012).

25

This Land Is Your Land

This land is your land, this land is my land,
From California to the New York island;
From the redwood forest to the Gulf Stream waters,
This land was made for you and me.

As I was walking that ribbon of highway,
I saw above me that endless skyway.
I saw below me that golden valley.
This land was made for you and me.

I've roamed and rambled, and I followed my footsteps
To the sparkling sands of her diamond deserts;
And all around me a voice was sounding:
"This land was made for you and me."

When the sun comes shining and I was strolling,
And the wheat fields waving and the dust clouds rolling,
As the fog was lifting, a voice was chanting,
"This land was made for you and me."

"This Land Is Your Land" was written as a response to "God Bless America," and it has become another alternative national anthem, especially popular in schools. Woody Guthrie wrote the first version of the song on February 23, 1940, in a cheap New York hotel room after a trip by car, bus, and hitched rides across the country from California through Oklahoma and Pittsburgh. During that trip, Guthrie said, he heard Irving Berlin's hit every time he stopped at a diner or a bar or turned on the radio. To the folk singer named Woodrow Wilson Guthrie, who had come of age in the Dust Bowl and Depression and worked as a columnist and cartoonist for the communist *People's World* newspaper, Berlin's sunny vision of America sounded incomplete. Guthrie wanted to affirm the nation, but also wanted to call on common people to take it back.

"This Land Is Your Land" reinforces the values of freedom, democracy, and tolerance in American civil religion. Concentrating on people, "you and me," rather than the abstract "America" of "God Bless America" or the sacrament of the flag in "The Star-Spangled Banner," the lyrics celebrate the geography of America, not in itself, but as "your land" and "my land," the heritage of all Americans. The words speak from the perspective of a "road man," as Guthrie called himself, a wanderer enjoying freedom who saw the landscape not from a mountain peak, as Katherine Lee Bates had in "America the Beautiful," but from a dusty road, walking across deserts and next to fields. Immersed in this landscape, the song evokes a mystical voice that sounds from "all around" and "chants" the claim that the land belongs to all of us. Though the lyrics sung today do not mention God, the history of the song reveals that this voice is surely divine.

In the song's first version, each verse ended not with "This land was made for you and me," but with "God blessed America for me." Guthrie was an intensely but unconventionally religious man, who, like Irving Berlin, expressed his faith mainly through his songs. The 1940 version of "This Land Is Your Land" had two verses that were not published until the 1970s. One recalled encountering a "great high wall" with the words "private property" on one side but nothing written on the other. Here the ending of "God blessed America for me" confirmed the traveler's right to roam the land as a right given by God, in spite of any claim of private property. A second verse pictured a line of people who "stood there hungry" waiting for a relief office to open, and ended with the singer wondering whether God had really "blessed America" for him.

These verses came fourth and sixth in the handwritten version that is now in the Woody Guthrie Archives. In 1944, Guthrie changed the last line of all verses of the song to "This land is made for you and me." He used the song as the theme for his weekly radio show on WNEW New York from December 1944 to February 1945. On the radio, he dropped the two verses mentioned above, but added another verse that mentioned a "freedom highway" where no one could stop him or make him turn back, expressing his sense of struggle and of hope.

The chain of events that caused what some have called the "protest verses" of "This Land Is Your Land" to fall into disuse and nearly disappear began with Guthrie's recording of the song in 1951. For that record he sang only the four better-known verses (quoted at the start of the chapter). In the anti-communist atmosphere of the McCarthy era and the Cold War, when singers like Guthrie's friend Pete Seeger were blacklisted, there was little demand for songs that criticized private property or pictured hungry Americans standing on line for relief.

Singers from Bing Crosby to Harry Belafonte, Mitch Miller, the Kingston Trio, Loretta Lynn, Connie Francis, Jay and the Americans, Country Joe and the Fish, Peter, Paul and Mary, the Mormon Tabernacle Choir, and Bruce Springsteen, among others, have recorded "This Land Is Your Land," but no one sang all of the verses. Woody Guthrie's son Arlo tells a story about going to a progressive grammar school in 1955 and finding to his embarrassment that all the other children knew his father's song, but he did not. By then, the elder Guthrie was spending most of his time in the hospital, stricken by the neuromuscular disease that would eventually kill him, but in one of his times at home he responded to his son's request to learn the song by taking Arlo into the backyard of their apartment building and, barely able to strum his guitar, teaching him how to play and sing "This Land Is Your Land," including the protest verses. According to Arlo, Woody was afraid that if his son didn't learn those verses, no one would remember them.

Amid the tumult of the 1960s and 1970s, more people recalled the protest verses. They were performed at a Hollywood Bowl memorial concert for Woody Guthrie in 1970. In 1972 Guthrie's publisher, Ludlow Music, brought out *A Tribute to Woody Guthrie* that included all verses of the song.

Unlike "God Bless America," "This Land Is Your Land" has never made the top of the Hit Parade or the Billboard Top Forty, nor even had a signature recording like Kate Smith's version of Irving Berlin's song. "This Land Is Your Land" has become a pervasive presence in American life through two channels: the movement of folk music that began in the 1930s and the schools. On March 13, 1975, it was used as the opening song for the first annual Music in Our Schools Day, with millions of children in public schools simultaneously singing "This Land Is Your Land" and watching others sing it on live television. The song's patriotism, its freedom from reference to God, its limited vocal range (only one octave, as opposed to "God Bless America" and "The Star-Spangled Banner"), and the peaceful, progressive message of its better-known verses have made it appeal to teachers.

The extremely simple melody of "This Land Is Your Land," which some have said derives from a Baptist hymn or from the popular song "You Are My Sunshine," has proven amenable to use by folksingers writing verses to serve new causes and by comedians. As early as 1959, Dave Van Ronk and Richard Ellington published a parody, "This Land Is Their Land," which sang of landlords and bosses and concluded, "This land is not for you and me." In 1973, a compilation called "Folksinger's Wordbook" included a new verse about Vietnam. The "land" of that verse, Vietnam, "isn't my land," but instead is "meant for the V.C.," or Viet Cong.

The most famous use of "This Land Is Your Land" in parody came during the 2004 presidential campaign, when brothers Evan and Greg Spiridellis created a cartoon of President George W. Bush and Senator John Kerry singing many verses with the refrain of "This land will surely vote for me" on their JibJab website. The video was viewed by more than a million people on all continents, including Antarctica and the International Space Station, in 24 hours. Ludlow Music sued the brothers over their very public and profitable use of the song, but reached a settlement when the Spiridellis contended that it had passed into the public domain in 1973.

On the other hand, most new verses for "This Land Is Your Land" by folksingers have remained true to the spirit of the original song, extending its message of freedom and tolerance to new topics and continuing Woody Guthrie's effort to repair the nation through song. In 1971, Pete Seeger published a verse on poverty. Seeger pictured a man working "as hard as you're able" wondering whether it was "truth or fable" that the land was made for you and me. Seeger also included an ecological verse, written by Jerry J. Smith, that listed fountains, tin, plastic, and "crowded freeways" among things added to the land made for you and me. Country Joe McDonald had already gone further into ecology with two verses on his album, *Thinking of Woody Guthrie*, from 1969. McDonald's version recalled hearing "the Redwoods falling, and the loggers calling," and later mentioned that "[t]he smog kept rolling, the populations growing."

One night in June 1968, when Pete Seeger was taking part in a sing-along on the National Mall, where the Poor People's Campaign organized by Martin Luther King, Jr., had pitched tents they called Resurrection City, he witnessed an objection to "This Land Is Your Land" that resulted in a new verse extending the message of the song. Chief Henry Crow Dog of the Lakota Sioux approached the man leading the singing, poked a finger into his chest and said, "Hey... It belongs to me!" Stunned, the singer asked whether the Indian wanted the song to stop. Then the Lakota man smiled and said, "No it's okay... *As long as we are all down here together to get something done.*" In response to this, they added another verse, written by a man named Cappy Israel, complaining that the land "once was my land" until it "was stole by you from me."

Scholar Mark Allan Jackson, a biographer of Woody Guthrie, has pointed out that the meaning of a song depends on the context in which it is sung. "This Land Is Your Land" can sound conservative if it is sung (as it was) by the overwhelmingly white, male delegates to the Republican Convention of 1960 that nominated Richard Nixon, and liberal if it is sung (as it also was) by the Democrats who had just heard George McGovern's acceptance speech at their convention in 1972. When Loretta Lynn sang it for an advertisement for the National Wildlife Federation, with images of forests and deserts and wheat fields showing on the screen, the song carried an ecological message, even without any additional verses.

Other nations have adopted "This Land Is Your Land" into their own civil religions. A Canadian group called The Travellers recorded a version in 1955 that celebrates land "From the Arctic Circle to the Great Lakes waters." In Sweden, Wales, and Israel, the words have been translated and adapted, and English versions with adapted geographical references have been recorded in Ireland, the US Virgin Islands, the Bahamas, and Namibia. When Arlo Guthrie sang "This Land Is Your Land" at the Tanglewood campus of the Boston Symphony Orchestra on July 18, 2010, he reported seeing a performance by Chinese schoolchildren in English, with no change in the references to American places. Guthrie reflected that when the Chinese sing, "From California to the New York island," they imagine a journey west from California, over China and back to the United States, that circles the entire world.

Such universal appeal shows that Woody Guthrie succeeded in expanding American civil religion. When he changed "God blessed America for me" to "This land was made for you and me," Guthrie eliminated all limits on who could identify with his song. Believers in God could still see an implication in the statement that the land "was made," but non-theists did not have to think of God. Americans could use the geographic references to locate themselves without ever saying the word "America." People of other nations could plug in their own geography and participate in the very American values of liberty, democracy, and tolerance that inspired the song. Alongside the Declaration of Independence and later the Disney parks, "This Land Is Your Land" proved by the turn of the twenty-first century to be one of the most exportable expressions of American civil religion.

SOURCES

Jackson, Mark Allan, "Is This Song Your Song Anymore?: Revisioning Woody Guthrie's *This Land Is Your Land*," American Music 20, no. 3 (Autumn 2002), 249–276.
Klein, Joe, *Woody Guthrie: A Life* (New York: Alfred A. Knopf, 1980).
Partridge, Elizabeth, *This Land Was Made for You and Me: The Life and Songs of Woody Guthrie* (New York: Viking, 2002).

26

The Four Freedoms

The four freedoms—freedom of speech, freedom of worship, freedom from want, and freedom from fear—were first set forth by President Franklin D. Roosevelt in his State of the Union address on January 6, 1941, as the United States hesitated on the brink of World War II. After the United States entered the war in the wake of the December 7, 1941, Japanese attack on Pearl Harbor, the four freedoms became war aims for the United States and its allies, the new United Nations. In the spring of 1943, Norman Rockwell turned the four freedoms into paintings that were reproduced in the millions to sell war bonds. The ideal of spreading these freedoms throughout the world became part of an era of internationalism in American history. In 2012, a Four Freedoms Park opened in New York City, within sight of the United Nations headquarters.

Still, the place of the four freedoms in American civil religion has never been secure. Freedom in the negative sense, the absence of restraint, is an original value of American civil religion, but what freedom means in positive terms is not so clear. Here are the words of Roosevelt's original statement from 1941:

> In the future days, which we seek to make secure, we look forward to a world founded upon four essential human freedoms.
>
> The first is freedom of speech and expression—everywhere in the world.
>
> The second is freedom of every person to worship God in his own way—everywhere in the world.
>
> The third is freedom from want—which, translated into world terms, means economic understandings which will secure to every nation a healthy peacetime life for its inhabitants—everywhere in the world.
>
> The fourth is freedom from fear—which, translated into world terms, means a worldwide reduction of armaments to such a point and in such a thorough fashion that no nation will be in a position to commit an act of physical aggression against any neighbor—anywhere in the world.

That is no vision of a distant millennium. It is a definite basis for a kind of world attainable in our own time and generation. That kind of world is the very antithesis of the so-called new order of tyranny which the dictators seek to create with the crash of a bomb.

By articulating the four freedoms, Roosevelt attempted to expand the original value of freedom in American civil religion beyond the negative concept of an absence of restraints into the positive presence of well-being and security. This did not appeal to all Americans. After Norman Rockwell produced his iconic images of freedom from want and freedom from fear, the artist received a letter that called those two freedoms "utopian promises so popular with all dictators... that if the people will give up their independence and do what the government tells them, the government will take care of them." The values of economic and physical security are important to Americans, but they have not been raised to a level of sacredness equal to that of individual liberty, political democracy, world peace, and cultural tolerance as central values of American civil religion.

But Roosevelt did succeed in extending the reach of American civil religion to the entire world. With the repeated phrase, "everywhere in the world"—a phrase that the president vocally emphasized, underlining the radicalism of what he proposed to Congress—Roosevelt securely established the concept of American responsibility to secure world peace. The value of world peace in American civil religion went back to Puritan dreams of the millennium and of America's role in promoting that era of peace. World peace appeared at the end of Lincoln's Second Inaugural ("to do all which may achieve and cherish a just, and a lasting peace, among ourselves, and with all nations"), and in the dreams and actions of presidents like Theodore Roosevelt and Woodrow Wilson. Despite some disillusionment following World War I and the failures of the League of Nations, most Americans of the 1920s and 1930s believed that the United States should use its influence to bring about world peace. Although many in 1941 (and later) did not agree that the American government had the responsibility to ensure freedom from want, and many in January 1941 did not want the United States to send armies against Germany and Japan, even those with limited views of what the United States could or should do agreed that America could no longer regard wars between major powers with indifference. Those who questioned the four freedoms or worked to keep the United States out of World War II, including German sympathizers and Republican isolationists, still agreed with Roosevelt that the United States had a responsibility to seek world peace.

For example, almost seven months after the 1941 State of the Union address, on June 25, the isolationist Republican senator Robert A. Taft of Ohio spoke to the nation on CBS radio. Germany had begun its invasion of the Soviet Union on June 22. The Germans had met with great early success, and many in the United States wondered whether it was now time for America to intervene, but Taft said no, primarily because of the moral effects of war. "No one can deny the desirability of spreading democratic principles," said Senator Taft, but at the same time he warned that "the forcing of any special brand of freedom and democracy on a people by brute force of war" amounted to "a denial of those very democratic principles which we are striving to advance." Taft compared the mission of spreading the four freedoms by war to the aim of making "the world safe for democracy" in World War I, and even to the Crusades and the Spanish Inquisition, which had attempted to bring Christianity by force to "infidels who preferred to believe in other gods." He argued that the United States lacked the power "to carry through the moral principles implied in the four-freedoms theory," unless we were prepared to face a war in Europe "for years to come," a war which would involve "tremendous losses." If we were not prepared for a long war, "[i]t is futile to bluster about the kind of freedoms we will impose everywhere in the world," Taft said.

Instead, Taft hoped for a quick peace, perhaps by the end of 1941. He speculated that "the Russo-German war may perhaps be the solution of the present problems of the world," lessening German pressure on Britain, and he urged President Roosevelt to explore the possibilities of peace while continuing and expanding American aid to Britain. We should aid Britain because "by and large, they do have the same ideals as we ourselves," Taft argued. Besides, the defeat of Britain "would mean an unsettled world, with the greatest hazard to the peace and prosperity of the entire world." For Taft, supporting world peace was "a wholly sufficient reason" to aid Britain "without any spreading of the four freedoms anywhere else in the world."

Six months after Taft's call for peace, and eleven months after Roosevelt's 1941 State of the Union address, the Japanese attack on Pearl Harbor brought the United States into the war. British prime minister Winston Churchill arrived at the White House in secret on December 21, two weeks after Pearl Harbor, and stayed until January 14, 1942, in an event that came to be called the Arcadia Conference. During that visit, Roosevelt coined the phrase "United Nations" as a name for the alliance of nations who agreed to fight the Axis powers (Germany, Italy, and Japan) to the end, not accepting any separate peace or settlement short of victory. Churchill's term for these nations had been "Grand Alliance," but the name "United Nations" had a more peaceful connotation and made a more universal claim. The number of those nations quickly grew to twenty-six. In August 1942, the US Office of War Information published a sixteen-page pamphlet called "The United Nations Fight for the Four Freedoms," with a preface by President Roosevelt and essays by Max Lerner, Malcolm Cowley, and Reinhold Niebuhr.

That pamphlet responded to a sense that the four freedoms and the United Nations had not captured the imagination of the United States. In the summer of 1942, the Office of War Information had made a study that indicated that only about a third of the American people had any knowledge of the four freedoms, and only 2 percent could name all four. There was a need for explicit war aims because of the widespread belief that World War I had been a failure. The war to "make the world safe for democracy," in President Woodrow Wilson's phrase, had instead produced an era of dictatorship in Italy, Germany, Spain, Japan, and the Soviet Union. Before Pearl Harbor, great majorities of Americans had told pollsters that the United States should not become involved in any future war in Europe. This number had reached as high as 95 percent in 1936. After the United States was really engaged in war, the need for national unity became acute, and unity required a common vision of what the nation was fighting for.

As the most popular visual artist in the United States and as a deep believer in the American people, illustrator Norman Rockwell wanted to contribute to that common vision. In 1942, when he was awakened on a spring morning at three A.M. by the inspiration to paint the four freedoms, Rockwell had already been a prosperous artist for more than two decades, painting covers for *The Saturday Evening Post* magazine and calendars for the Boy Scouts of America. His style of realistic illustration, focusing on human figures in poses that told a story, often with strong elements of humor, nostalgia, and sentiment, appealed to a mass audience. Twice Rockwell had gone to Paris to study more abstract, impressionist, and expressionist styles, but he had not succeeded in becoming a different painter and returned to his own, largely self-taught approach. During World War I, in which Rockwell had joined the Navy, he did posters for the armed forces that stressed camaraderie, for example soldiers singing around a campfire. Like most Americans, Rockwell now found that image of war unrealistic. Early in 1942, he had already produced one World War II poster, featuring a machine-gunner with a ripped uniform and a nearly empty gun, to advertise sales of War Bonds. But Rockwell wanted to reach for a more profound message about the meaning of this war. The idea that woke him at three A.M., and led him to ride his bicycle to wake a neighboring artist in his little Vermont village to talk about it, was to make the four freedoms more concrete by using the only subject of his art, ordinary Americans doing everyday things, to illustrate what the four freedoms were in practice.

Freedom of speech (Figure 26.1) was his first definite idea. Rockwell attended the town meetings that governed his community, and he recalled one at which a man named Jim Edgerton had stood up to speak against a plan to build a new school. No one at the meeting had agreed with him, but they allowed him to say what he thought. "That's it, there it is. Freedom of speech," Rockwell said to himself. As a model for the speaker he hired not Jim Edgerton but Carl Hess,

Figure 26.1 A town meeting, at which a man stood alone to speak against a plan to build a new school, gave Norman Rockwell the inspiration for this illustration of freedom of speech. Printed by permission of the Norman Rockwell Family Agency. Book Rights Copyright © 1943 The Norman Family Entities. Photograph from the National Archives.

a gas station owner from his neighborhood who had a "noble head," and went to work.

The idea of illustrating freedom from want with a Thanksgiving dinner (Figure 26.2) came quickly, and freedom from fear (Figure 26.3) reminded Rockwell of an idea he had first thought of during the London blitz of 1940, a picture showing an American couple tucking their children into bed while the father held a newspaper with a headline about bombing. The concept for *Freedom of Worship* (Figure 26.4) proved to be a false start, but Rockwell soon made a sketch. In this first version, it featured a barber shop with clergy of several faiths. After only a few days, Rockwell had four full-size (four feet by three feet) color sketches. He took the sketches to Washington in the company of his artist neighbor, Mead Schaeffer, who also had ideas for war posters. Although Rockwell and Schaeffer were both so well known that they got to see officials in various branches of the War Department (now the Department of Defense), they found no takers for their ideas. One man insulted them by saying that in the last war, they had hired illustrators to do war bond posters, but now they were using no one but "fine arts men, real artists." He offered Rockwell the job of illustrating a manual of calisthenics for the Marine Corps.

On the way back from Washington to Vermont, Rockwell stopped at the offices of *The Saturday Evening Post* in Philadelphia, where he showed his

Figure 26.2 After Thanksgiving, Rockwell said that the painting of freedom from want was the only instance in this career when he ate his model. Rockwell criticized his own painting for emphasizing American prosperity, but critics have praised its composition and its use of white on white color. Printed by permission of the Norman Rockwell Family Agency. Book Rights Copyright © 1943 The Norman Family Entities. Photograph from the National Archives.

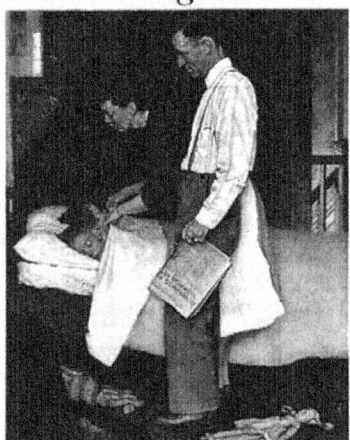

Figure 26.3 This idea for a painting came to Rockwell when he was reading about the London blitz in 1940, long before President Roosevelt announced the four freedoms. Although Rockwell immediately connected the image to freedom from fear, he regretted that the picture might seem smug. Printed by permission of the Norman Rockwell Family Agency. Book Rights Copyright © 1943 The Norman Family Entities. Photograph from the National Archives.

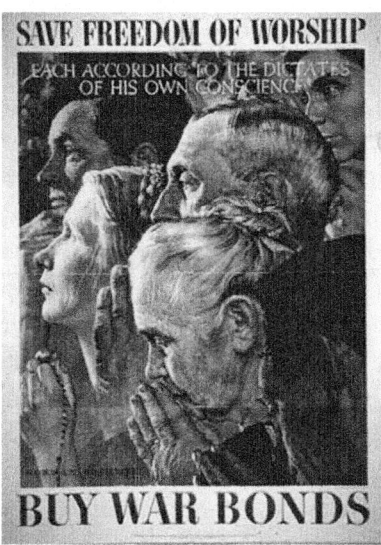

Figure 26.4 Freedom of Worship, sometimes called *Freedom of Religion*, was Rockwell's favorite of the pictures, and the one on which he worked longest, with a false start involving clergy in a barbershop. Printed by permission of the Norman Rockwell Family Agency. Book Rights Copyright © 1943 The Norman Family Entities. Photograph from the National Archives.

sketches for the four freedoms to the new editor of the magazine, Ben Hibbs, a young man he had never met. Hibbs loved the idea and wanted to run the four freedoms pictures on four consecutive covers of the magazine. He told Rockwell to drop all of his other cover projects and work on these. The artist predicted that the task of turning the sketches into paintings would take about two months.

It actually took Rockwell six months, during which he worked so hard that he lost fifteen pounds from an already thin frame, to complete the pictures. While he usually did illustrations of stories and conferred with editors about what they wanted for magazine covers, this was a pure concept of his own, and sometimes it seemed too large for him. He reflected that painting the four freedoms was a commission worthy of Michelangelo, and that he was not Michelangelo.

Freedom of Speech was painted four different times, always with Carl Hess as the speaker, but in four different compositions. There was one panoramic scene with more listeners, rejected by Rockwell because it lacked focus, and another with the viewer looking down as if from a balcony at the speaker, who stood with his mouth closed. The one that the artist found acceptable has great coherence and power, but has also been criticized for looking too reverential. Everyone who looks at the speaker seems approving, and Hess himself is looking up as though at a vision. At the extreme left corner, Rockwell painted half of his own head with an observing eye, as though he was taking one last look at his neighbors in the town meeting, assuring himself that he was finally done.

Freedom of Worship gave Rockwell the most trouble, again going through four versions, but this time with entirely different characters as well as compositions. The first version, with several clergy together in a barber shop, met criticism from people of the different faiths who objected that the clergy were stereotypes. In the final painting, which became Rockwell's favorite in the four freedoms series, a focus on the heads and hands of people at prayer provided a serious tone, as did the almost uniform golden color. The words printed across the top in capitals, "EACH ACCORDING TO THE DICTATES OF HIS OWN CONSCIENCE," came to Rockwell's mind from no obvious source. Concerned about copyright, he sent his models and friends off to search for the words. He recalled that he had read these words "somewhere," and they appear in the "Principles of Worship" by Mormon prophet Joseph Smith, but a more likely source would be the Vermont state constitution, where the clause "That all persons have a natural and unalienable right, to worship Almighty God, according to the dictates of their own consciences" occurs in Chapter 1, Article 3. The model holding the rosary beads, a neighbor of Rockwell's named Rose Hoyt, was not a Roman Catholic and so did not pray the rosary, but Rockwell asked her permission to use her image in that way.

Not everyone has shared Rockwell's appreciation for *Freedom of Worship*. Shortly after the picture appeared, on *The Saturday Evening Post* cover of February 27, 1943, the artist received a letter from T. C. Upham, general director of the Cape Theater of Cape May, New Jersey, that rejected the picture in its entirety. Upham objected that the people were too old, that they all looked "foreign," that they all seemed poor and worn, that no one was praying with his eyes closed, that they all faced in the same direction "like cattle or sheep," that they all were portrayed in the same dull color (although some people wear their most colorful clothes to church), and that the caption about conscience was "ill chosen," because Catholics try not to follow their own consciences but the teachings of the Church. Rockwell replied to Upham that he was sorry, but he had tried to express what he felt about freedom of worship, "which I believe is all anybody can do." In one Rockwell biography, the art critic Christopher Finch concluded that the design of *Freedom of Worship* was not sufficiently concrete. Unlike the other pictures in the series, Finch contended, *Freedom of Worship* does not depict any definite scene, and so "the image is rather weak," resulting in the effect of "a painted slogan."

Rockwell was a harsh critic of his own work, and he was least satisfied with *Freedom from Want* and *Freedom from Fear*. He used the actual Thanksgiving turkey from the Rockwell dinner on Thanksgiving, 1942, in *Freedom from Want*, and often said that this was the only instance in which he ate the model for a picture. Today, it is probably the best remembered of the series. What Rockwell found distasteful on reflection was that the size of the turkey sent a message of American excess, which he feared would be offensive to Europeans who were starving under wartime conditions. Rockwell made a similar criticism of *Freedom from Fear*, saying that there was something too smug about the image of an American couple tucking in their children as the father held a newspaper with a headline about bombing elsewhere.

Meanwhile, other critics, including Christopher Finch, have said that *Freedom from Want* and *Freedom from Fear* are the best of the four paintings. In the Thanksgiving scene, Rockwell's use of white on white has been praised, and *Freedom from Fear* has been compared to the work of Vermeer as a single image that encapsulates an entire philosophy of life. Rockwell's meticulous realism was evident in *Freedom from Fear* in the newspaper, which he painted from the model of a mock headline that he ordered to be printed by his local newspaper, the *Bennington Banner*.

Whatever the artistic merits or demerits of the four freedoms pictures, there can be no doubt that the public loved them. After *The Saturday Evening Post* published them, beginning on February 20, 1943, and ending on March 13, more than 25,000 people immediately ordered color reproductions. The Office of War Information eventually printed 4 million sets of posters, many of which were given to buyers of war bonds, while others were used to advertise war bond sales. For the rest of the war years, the pictures were everywhere: in railroad stations, poolrooms, hotels, post offices, churches and synagogues. An old enemy of Rose Hoyt, the Vermont model holding the rosary beads in *Freedom of Worship*, triumphantly asked whether Rose was satisfied now that her picture was hanging in every bar in the country. Between April 26, 1943, and May 8, 1944, the original paintings went on a national tour, appearing at department stores from Washington, D.C., to Philadelphia, New York, Boston, Buffalo, Rochester, Pittsburgh, Detroit, Cleveland, Chicago, St. Louis, New Orleans, Dallas, Los Angeles, Portland, and Denver. Entertainers, politicians, and intellectuals came to these shows and gave speeches and performances. A "Four Freedoms Symphony" inspired by the paintings was composed by Robert Russell Bennett and performed on a national broadcast from Radio City in New York. By the time the tour was over, more than 1.2 million people, or about one in 100 Americans, had come to the shows, and $133 million in war bonds had been sold.

Such popularity came at the cost of some change of emphasis. When Roosevelt declared the four freedoms, he was calling for the international recognition of human rights, repeating the ringing phrase, "everywhere in the world." But Norman Rockwell made Americans love the four freedoms by making the freedoms American. Freedom of speech meant a town meeting; freedom of worship meant their neighbors at prayer; freedom from want meant their

Thanksgiving turkey; and freedom from fear meant American parents tucking in their children, with the danger of bombs represented by a newspaper headline. The freedoms were our possessions as Americans, freedoms we were fighting to defend, not necessarily to export. When the pictures were made into war bond posters, the words added at the top and the bottom emphasized that point. "SAVE FREEDOM OF SPEECH," the poster said above the scene from the town meeting. Above the Thanksgiving scene were the words, "OURS...to fight for," with "FREEDOM FROM WANT" below.

Other artists illustrated the four freedoms with goddesses (Roosevelt suggested angels facing in four directions) and grand scenes, but Rockwell focused them on local and personal images. His paintings had an underlying message not of war—not even triumphant war—but of peace in a context of family and local life. Like all of Rockwell's art, his paintings of the four freedoms suggested the universal by means of a sharp focus on the particular.

The international mission of the United States to spread the four freedoms was financed in part by Rockwell's pictures, and the aim of spreading the four freedoms passed into the mainstream of American politics. It is arguable that the final outcome of World War II, including the Marshall Plan, the Cold War that ended in 1991, and the NATO intervention in Bosnia in the 1990s, did bring the four freedoms to all of Europe. A direct line surely connected Roosevelt's four freedoms to President John F. Kennedy's pledges to "bear any burden" to expand liberty, to eradicate world poverty, and to place nuclear weapons under "the absolute control of all nations" in his Inaugural Address of 1961. "If a free nation cannot help the many who are poor, it cannot save the few who are rich," Kennedy said, and he was referring to the United States and to all of the world's poor. Kennedy also spoke strongly of the United Nations, describing it with the phrase, "our last best hope," which Lincoln had used for the United States, and promising "to strengthen its shield of the new and the weak—and to enlarge the area in which its writ may run."

This kind of thinking about the connections of world peace, prosperity, and freedom had not begun with Franklin Roosevelt, but with many writers and theorists who had been led by the Depression and the rise of fascism to see such connections. In the wake of the French surrender to the Nazis in the summer of 1940, a *New York Post* columnist named Samuel Grafton had been inspired by his reading of the British press to write that "Hitlerism" could be defeated "in the world forever by establishing minimum standards of housing, food, education, and medical care, along with free speech, free press, and free worship." Similar reasoning led the United States and Great Britain to issue a document called the Atlantic Charter in winter of 1942. In that same year in England, Sir William Beveridge produced a report on social welfare for the British government that also linked individual security from hunger and destitution to international security and peace. After the war, as Britain introduced its National Health System and the United States helped its veterans to enlarge the middle class with the G.I. Bill, British and American governments drawn from all political parties tried to put the four freedoms into practice. Looking back on the occasion of an annual Atlantic Charter conference in 1991, economist John Kenneth Galbraith argued that one of the four freedoms, freedom from want, was the foundation for all the others.

The four freedoms continued to provoke critics. In the fall of 1990, as 240,000 American soldiers prepared to fight to enforce a United Nations resolution to dislodge Saddam Hussein's Iraqi Army from Kuwait in the first Gulf War, *Boston Globe* columnist Ellen Goodman drew a negative comparison between the United States military of World War II and that of her own time. "When the president [George H. W. Bush] talks about defending 'our way of life' we don't visualize four freedoms, but great tankers of oil," she lamented. In December 2005, as Americans fought the second war in Iraq, cartoonist Ward Sutton produced a parody of Rockwell's four freedoms in *The Nation* magazine. Sutton's cartoons were called *Freedom to Suppress Free Speech, Freedom of Mandatory Prayer, Freedom to Supersize It,* and *Freedom to Be Fearful.*

The original four freedoms had nevertheless become established as touchstones of American civil religion, among the central definitions of what freedom meant, even though all four of these goals were not shared by all. Simple statements of the four freedoms were engraved in capital letters, one above the other, on one wall of the Franklin Delano Roosevelt Memorial, which opened in 1997, after decades of work, on the National Mall in Washington. In his acceptance speech for the 2009 Nobel Peace Prize, President Barack Obama said that "Just peace includes not only civil and political rights—it must encompass economic security and opportunity. For true peace is not just freedom from fear, but freedom from want." In New York City, an island long called Welfare Island was renamed Roosevelt Island in the early 1970s, when architect Louis Kahn successfully campaigned for it as the site for a Four Freedoms Memorial. Kahn's death delayed the project, but construction of the memorial began in 2010, and it reached completion in 2012. As Americans of the twenty-first century considered how to respond to the Arab Spring revolts against dictators who had long been recipients of our military aid, the conclusion of Franklin Roosevelt's State of the Union Address of 1941 seemed particularly relevant once more. These were the words that immediately followed Roosevelt's proclamation of the four freedoms:

> Since the beginning of our American history we have been engaged in change, in a perpetual, peaceful revolution, a revolution which goes on steadily, quietly, adjusting itself to changing conditions without the

concentration camp or the quicklime in the ditch. The world order which we seek is the cooperation of free countries, working together in a friendly, civilized society.

This nation has placed its destiny in the heads and hearts of its millions of free men and women, and its faith in freedom under the guidance of God. Freedom means the supremacy of human rights everywhere. Our support goes to those who struggle to gain those rights and keep them. Our strength is our unity of purpose.

To that high concept there can be no end save victory.

Sadly, the president who called for "the supremacy of human rights everywhere" would later sign orders to send innocent Japanese-Americans and Italian-Americans to internment camps. Nevertheless, the four freedoms and the moment of American history that produced them added a dimension of internationalism to American civil religion. The four freedoms represented a durable commitment to the value of world peace.

Although all four freedoms have never attained universal acceptance in the United States, they were institutionalized in the United Nations. This war alliance became an organization dedicated to maintaining world peace immediately after the war ended. In a process led by Eleanor Roosevelt, who was not only Franklin Roosevelt's widow but also the first US ambassador to the United Nations, the United Nations passed a Universal Declaration of Human Rights that included the four freedoms in its Preamble. The United Nations helped to create Israel in 1948 and fought communism in Korea in the early 1950s. Beginning with the Suez Crisis of 1956, the United Nations has deployed sixty-nine peacekeeping operations around the world, with sixteen ongoing operations in 2013. Through the four freedoms and United Nations, American civil religion began, at least for a time, to merge with a civil religion of the world.

SOURCES

Borgwardt, Elizabeth, "FDR's Four Freedoms as a Human Rights Instrument," *OAH Magazine of History*, April 2008, pp. 8–13.

Finch, Christopher, *Norman Rockwell's America* (New York: Harry N. Abrams, 1975).

Galbraith, John Kenneth, "Finding Freedom in a World of Poverty," *The Guardian* (London), August 27, 1991.

Glendon, Mary Ann, *A World Made New: Eleanor Roosevelt and the Universal Declaration of Human Rights* (New York: Random House, 2001).

Goodman, Ellen, "Americans Are Becoming World's Mercenaries," *St. Petersburg Times*, November 20, 1990.

Hennessey, Maureen Hart, "The Four Freedoms," in Maureen Hart Hennessey and Anne Knutson, eds., *Norman Rockwell: Pictures for the American People* (New York: Harry N. Abrams, 1999).

Marling, Karal Ann, *Norman Rockwell* (New York: Harry N. Abrams, 1997).

Murray, Stuart, and James McCabe, *Norman Rockwell's Four Freedoms: Images That Inspire a Nation* (Stockbridge, MA: Berkshire House, 1993).

Posner, Michael H., "The Four Freedoms Turn 70: Address to the American Society of International Law, March 24, 2011," www.state.gov/g/drl/rls/rm/2011/159195.htm.

Sutton, Ward, "The Four Freedoms, 2005," *The Nation*, December 5, 2005, p. 10.

Taft, Robert A., "Russian and the Four Freedoms: The Russian War Has Weakened Every Argument for Intervention," Columbia Broadcasting System, June 25, 1941. Reprinted in *Vital Speeches of the Day, 1941*.

United States. Office of War Information. *The United Nations Fight for the Four Freedoms* (Washington: US Government Printing Office, 1942)

Walton, Donald, *A Rockwell Portrait: An Intimate Biography* (Kansas City: Sheed Andrews and McMeel, 1978).

27

Iwo Jima: The Picture, the Monuments, and the Battle

Joe Rosenthal's *Old Glory Goes Up on Mt. Suribachi* (Figure 27.1) froze a violent battle into a sacred moment. It captured the extension of American civil religion from commitments to liberty and democracy to a commitment to world peace. One of the most reproduced photographs in history, it served as model for the largest bronze sculpture in the world, the 78-foot statuary group at the Marine Corps Memorial near Arlington National Cemetery (Figure 27.2), which in turn has been reproduced at the Marine base on Parris Island, in a Connecticut park, and in many other places. A re-enactment of the event ended one of John Wayne's most successful war movies, *Sands of Iwo Jima* (1949). Clint Eastwood's *Flags of Our Fathers* (2006) dramatized both the battle and the impact of the photo.

As many scholars have argued, religious power or charisma does not inhere in objects or people, but is bestowed by the beholders. Rosenthal's picture of Marines raising the flag caught the nation's attention when the Associated Press sent it to newspapers across the country on Sunday, February 25, 1945, along with the story that the battle for Iwo Jima had decisively turned. Part of its power arose from the novelty of instant coverage, because until Iwo Jima the Navy had delayed all news from the Pacific for at least a week.

The photo turned into an icon during what might be called a series of revival meetings in American civil religion in the spring of 1945. These events were the rallies of a war bond drive that toured cities across the country. The rallies featured the three surviving flag raisers from the photograph, sculptures based on the photo, and re-enactments of the flag raising. That drive sold $26 billion (far exceeding its goal of $14 billion) in bonds, or more than $150 from every man, woman, and child in the United States, in less than two months. Like the religious revivals of the 1740s and the 1830s, or the more recent campaigns of Billy Graham, that bond drive was carefully planned and the crowds psychologically prepared. The Mt. Suribachi photo was a useful symbol of victory, and before the drive was done, the photo had acquired a power of its own.

Figure 27.1 Joe Rosenthal's miraculous (not staged) photo of the second flag raising on Iwo Jima featured (from left, in front) Ira Hayes, Franklin Sousley, John Bradley, and Harlon Block. In back are Michael Strank and René Gagnon. The battle had not ended: Sousley, Block, and Strank all died on Iwo Jima. AP Photo/Joe Rosenthal.

Among its more specific effects, the photo has inspired initiation rituals and advertisements for the Marine Corps. Marines now get their Eagle, Globe, and Anchor insignias only after completing an exercise called "the Crucible," which concludes at Camp Pendleton (one of two sites for Marine basic training) with the climbing of an artificial mountain and the raising of a flag on the top. At Parris Island, Marine recruits receive their insignias before a sculpture based on the Rosenthal photo. Since 2002, some Marine Corps television advertisements have featured a recruit climbing a cliff on which is projected a moving image of the flag raising, while others have ended with an image of the flag raising in the Marine Corps Memorial.

At the Marine Corps Memorial, the giant sculpture based on the photo has become a sacred site. The sculpture rises from a base where the names of all Marine engagements since 1775 are inscribed in gold. The location of the memorial next to Arlington National Cemetery gives it the solemnity of a monument for the dead. At the dedication of the memorial in 1954, then Vice President Richard M. Nixon said that the statue pointed to "something more" than the heroism of six men or even the whole history of the Marines. According to Nixon, it represented "the hopes and dreams of all Americans," and in some sense, "America itself." To the extent that Nixon was correct, the image of the

Figure 27.2 In the Marine Corps War Memorial near Arlington National Cemetery in Washington, D.C., Felix de Weldon created the largest bronze sculpture in the world. He brought the figures from Rosenthal's photo into a tighter mass and gave the men determined faces. The image has become a metaphor for all united effort. Photograph by William Gardella.

flag being raised on Mt. Suribachi stands as one of the purest icons of the civil religion, an evocation of spiritual force arising from the nation directly, without reference to God.

Although images may not have inherent religious power, the specific aspects of images enable them to direct power in particular directions, with particular emotional effects and messages. In the case of Rosenthal's photo, the positioning and dynamics of the figures continues a tradition of heroic war imagery dating back to Roman triumphal arches, and, before that, to Egyptian battle scenes sculpted into friezes at Karnak. More immediate predecessors are the historic paintings of the eighteenth and early nineteenth centuries, such as Benjamin West's *Death of Wolfe* (1771) or *Liberty Leading the People* (1830) by Eugene Delacroix. Rosenthal's picture shares with all of these predecessors the compositional element of massed figures implying motion by leaning at a common angle, so that the harmony of the figures brings order out of the chaos of battle.

All of these heroic images also imply victory over death. This victory comes only through intense struggle. On February 27, 1945, two days after the photo appeared, the *Times-Union* of Rochester, New York, reviewed it in a story, titled

"Art from Life in Defiance of Death," that compared the composition of *Old Glory Goes Up* to Leonardo da Vinci's *Last Supper* because of the way that the photo's action moves along a horizontal but refers the viewer's attention to the empty space above the center. Where Leonardo used Christ to mark this aspiration to transcendence, Joe Rosenthal used the flag.

Unlike most war memorials of the past, Rosenthal's photo has been recognized as profoundly democratic. The six men (two of them hardly visible) are nearly anonymous, backs bent and faces obscured by helmets and raised arms. Instead of a glorious general riding a horse into battle, or even the Egyptian cavalry or chariots crushing their enemies, this photograph celebrates ordinary infantry. The men in the picture are also working together, each doing his part in the struggle to do one thing, to raise the flag, which itself stands for democracy.

Because *Old Glory Goes Up on Mt. Suribachi* is a photograph, it can claim to represent reality in a way that no painting or sculpture can. Although the image became an icon and eventually a painting, a postage stamp, and a sculpture in many forms, its entrance into the realm of symbol and myth did not destroy its claim to authenticity, but made that claim more urgent. If it were revealed that the Marines never did exactly what the photograph shows, or that the event had been staged and the figures arranged, the power of the image would be at least damaged, if not lost.

Challenges to the picture's authenticity arose almost immediately, because Rosenthal had captured the second flag raising on Iwo Jima, not the first. Since Mt. Suribachi—a dormant volcano, about 600 feet high—dominated the island, all plans for the invasion focused on taking it, and those plans always included a flag raising at the earliest possible moment. The hope was to maintain the morale of the Marines and to give the home audience in the United States a sign of victory. On the fourth day of the battle, enough of Suribachi had been cleared so that Colonel Chandler Johnson could order Lieutenant Harold Schrier and his platoon to take a flag to the top. Resistance broke out as soon as the flag went up, however, and Schrier's platoon had to deal with snipers, hand grenades, and a Japanese officer who charged the Marines with a samurai sword. Meanwhile, the flag did have positive effects on American morale. Sailors of the invasion fleet cheered, and Marines fighting elsewhere on Iwo Jima saw that one objective had been reached. On a landing craft en route to the island, Secretary of the Navy James Forrestal told Marine General Holland Smith that the flag guaranteed that there would be a Marine Corps for the next five hundred years.

Only hours later, however, after the firefight on Suribachi was over, Colonel Johnson decided that a new flag was needed. The first flag was too small (54 by 24 inches) to be seen all over the island, and he had a larger, 96 by 56 inch flag that had been rescued from Pearl Harbor. Johnson gave the new flag to Private First Class René Gagnon, who was going to the top of the mountain with four other

Marines to string telephone wire. Photographer Joe Rosenthal of the AP and two other photographers went with them to record the action and the view from Suribachi, just as Marine photographer Louis Lowery had gone with Schrier's men. Lowery had already taken good photographs of the first flag raising.

Although there were charges later that Rosenthal posed the Marines who raised the second flag, the accounts of those on the scene indicate that this did not happen. The pole holding the second flag was raised at the same moment as the first was lowered. Rosenthal chose an angle that allowed him to focus only on the second flag, but another picture shows both flags in motion and no evidence of posing. There was a strong wind, the pole and the flag were heavy, and the five Marines needed help from a Navy corpsman, John H. Bradley, to hold the pole. Rosenthal caught the struggle of the six men for 1/400th of a second with his Speed Graphic camera. Then he asked everyone to pose for a celebration shot, waving their helmets in the air, and took other pictures of the scene. He sent the film to be processed without having seen the pictures, in an envelope that said it contained images of Marines on Mt. Suribachi who "hoist the Stars and Stripes, signaling the capture of this key position."

As soon as Associated Press photo editor John Bodkin saw the printed photo he exclaimed "Here's one for all time!" and sent it immediately to AP headquarters. Newspapers found themselves printing special editions to meet the demand for more copies. Sculptor Felix de Weldon, who eventually created the statues for the bond drive, the Marine War Memorial, Parris Island, and many other locations, began to make statues based on the picture almost as soon as he saw it.

Struck by the picture and by the immediate sensation it caused, President Franklin Delano Roosevelt (just weeks before his death) ordered that the men from the picture be sent home for the bond drive that would begin in May. Besides René Gagnon, the five Marines were Sergeant Mike Strank, Private First Class Franklin R. Sousley, Corporal Harlon Block, and Private Ira Hayes. By the time the order to send them home reached the Pacific, Strank, Sousley, and Block had all been killed on Iwo Jima, and the Navy corpsman in the photo, John H. Bradley, was in the hospital with shrapnel wounds in his legs. Gagnon, Hayes, and Bradley went home, met President Truman, and performed in the bond drive, raising the flag again and again all over the United States. Four years later they turned up in *Sands of Iwo Jima*, facing the camera, taking the flag from John Wayne, and raising it. They were the most honored guests at the dedication of the Marine Corps Memorial in 1954. At that ceremony, Harold Schrier (still in the Marines, and now a major) and photographer Louis Lowery, along with James R. Michaels and Charles W. Lindberg, who had raised the first flag, were seated at the back of the crowd and received no recognition.

Although there was little or no deception involved in the story of the photograph—except for the initially mistaken identification of the man on the far right, Corporal Harlon Block, as Sargeant Henry Hanson, which Private Ira Hayes was ordered to keep quiet during the bond drive—the public relations campaign masked incredible human costs. Iwo Jima was a terrible battle, in which the Marines suffered more than 6,000 dead and 20,000 injured in forty days. Even survivors like John H. Bradley bore emotional scars; Bradley's wife said that he cried in his sleep for four years.

Ira Hayes, a Pima Indian, never fully recovered. During the bond drive, he began to drink so heavily that he was arrested several times, and he was sent back to the Pacific from Chicago, not even allowed to see his family in Arizona. Hayes frequently recalled that his company had arrived on Iwo Jima with 250 men and left six weeks later with 27. Unable to hold a job, he died at 32, having apparently choked on his own vomit after passing out, in 1955. Hayes was then honored with three funerals—one on the Pima reservation, one at the Arizona statehouse, and one in Arlington National Cemetery, near the monument. Before the battle, Hayes had visited his home on a furlough and given a speech, predicting that "some fine things are going to come out of this war," and especially that "[w]hite men are going to understand Indians; and Indians will understand white men." The toll of Iwo Jima meant that the white men Hayes had met, "some of the best buddies anybody ever had," were almost all dead.

In some ways, the making of an icon from the Iwo Jima photograph claimed the surviving raisers of the second flag as the battle's last victims, because their private lives were largely sacrificed to the picture. René Gagnon, who died in 1978, always responded to requests for appearances, but complained that he was treated as a hero for a day or two and then forgotten as he struggled to hold menial jobs. John H. Bradley succeeded in his plan to run a funeral parlor in his hometown, but frequently had to hide to preserve his privacy. Asked whether he would have helped to raise the flag if he had known about the picture and the consequences, Bradley said no. Meanwhile, Charles W. Lindberg worked for years to win recognition for the raising of the first flag. The legislature of his native state of Minnesota passed a resolution honoring him in 1995, and a medal was struck representing the photo by Louis Lowery. When Lindberg died in June 2007, his funeral received national television coverage and participation from the Marines.

Revisionist views of the battle and its heritage included a movie, *The Outsider* (1961), in which Tony Curtis played Ira Hayes, but the film proved too pessimistic to have much audience appeal. Military historians have pointed out that inter-service rivalry between the Army, Navy, and Marines made the American death toll higher than it might have been. As the rival Pacific campaigns led by General Douglas Mac Arthur and Admiral Chester Nimitz competed for resources, Iwo Jima emerged as a compromise target that both the Navy and the Army Air Force could support. The Marine request for ten days of naval bombardment before the invasion was cut to eight and then to three as commanders argued over where ships should be used. Since the Marines were then fighting for their continued existence as an independent unit, it has been suggested that they could not resist the push for an invasion that should never have occurred. The new strategy that Japanese general Tadamichi Kuribayashi devised for defense—to allow the landing, but to dig deep tunnels and bunkers that enabled 20,000 defenders to hold out and resist 70,000 invaders for forty days, on an island four miles long—may have helped to convince President Truman that an invasion of Japan would be too costly, and so led to the decision to use the atomic bomb on Hiroshima and Nagasaki.

In 2006, director Clint Eastwood produced two movies about Iwo Jima—*Flags of Our Fathers*, telling the story of the battle and the flag raisers from the American side, and *Letters from Iwo Jima*, based on a cache of letters from the Japanese commander that had only been discovered in 2005. These films spoke to millions, won numerous awards (*Letters from Iwo Jima* was nominated for Best Picture), and formed part of a larger story of contact between the American and Japanese civil religions. In 1995, on the fiftieth anniversary of the battle, eight hundred American survivors joined many Japanese veterans to hold a reunion and ceremonies on the island.

On Iwo Jima, the cultures of the United States and Japan, perhaps more widely separated in geography and in values than any other technologically advanced civilizations on earth, came into intimate contact. The flag raising on Iwo Jima meant a great deal to the Japanese because Iwo Jima was the first American conquest of Japanese soil; the island had been legally governed as part of Tokyo, although that city was seven hundred miles away. When the Americans discovered that 150 Japanese in caves below Suribachi had blown themselves up with hand grenades rather than be captured, and when they found that the Japanese sometimes tortured and mutilated American captives, they were confronted with attitudes toward war that seemed profoundly alien and evil. For many Americans, the battle for Iwo Jima was a key moment in an encounter with Japan that transformed World War II into a crusade, a war to spread a superior American civil religion around the world, before the full discoveries of Nazi and Stalinist war crimes were known.

As Joe Rosenthal's photograph became translated into monuments, other artists changed the character of the image. Sculptor Felix de Weldon, the creator of the Marine Corps Memorial, had been mesmerized by the photograph from the first moment that he saw it, but he was not content to reproduce it exactly. He tightened the relations between the figures, narrowed the spacing, and tilted the elbow of Harlon Block up into a sharper angle, to give the whole group of men more energy as they thrust the flagpole into the ground and carried Old Glory into the air. When Iwo Jima veteran George Gentile built a memorial in

Connecticut, he hired a Hungarian sculptor, Joseph Petrovics, who was trained in the norms of socialist realism. Petrovics tightened the figures from the photo still further, into a single mass. Critics have suggested that the Marine Corps War Memorial echoes Nazi and Soviet totalitarian art in its glorification of male strength and solidarity, and the same could be said of the Iwo Jima Memorial Monument in Connecticut.

The calm but heroically determined faces of the Marines in the Washington memorial contrast with the faceless bodies of the Rosenthal photo. The anonymous Marines of the photo express democracy, but the heroes of the Memorial generate a more triumphal effect. Although dedicated to fallen Marines, the Marine Corps War Memorial is also a victory monument. The procession of golden names of battles around the base, which extended only to Korea when the monument was dedicated in 1954, now includes Lebanon (twice), Panama, and Somalia, and will soon extend to Afghanistan and Iraq. Plenty of room remains for more engagements to be recorded in gold.

Meanwhile, the classical proportions of Rosenthal's photo have kept it open to many appropriations. Cartoonists and painters have used it again and again, from an editorial cartoon ridiculing a Supreme Court decision on flag burning to a mural showing United Farm Workers raising their flag. The African nation of Kenya took the Iwo Jima photo as a model for its Uhuru (Freedom) National Monument, in which a group raises a flag with the message, "People of Africa, Now All Together."

The photograph of US Marines raising a flag on Iwo Jima has become both an element of American civil religion and a universal symbol of united effort. Decades after the battle and the photograph, another effect has become apparent. This raising of an American flag on what had been soil of another sovereign nation signified a commitment to values beyond freedom and democracy within the United States. After Pearl Harbor, and especially after Iwo Jima, American civil religion would include a central commitment to world peace.

SOURCES

Boime, Albert, *The Unveiling of the National Icons: A Plea for Patriotic Iconoclasm in a Nationalist Era* (Cambridge and New York: Cambridge University Press, 1998).
Bradley, James, with Ron Powers, *Flags of Our Fathers* (New York: Bantam, 2000).
Burrell, James S., *The Ghosts of Iwo Jima* (College Station, TX: Texas A&M University Press, 2006).
Gallo, Bill, "Back to Iwo Jima: News Editor Says New WWII Movie Is Painfully Realistic," *New York Daily News*, October 20, 2006, and "The Score: Clint Gets It Only Part Right with Iwo Films," *New York Daily News*, December 31, 2006.
Marling, Karal Ann, and John Wettenthal, *Iwo Jima: Monuments, Memories, and the American Hero* (Cambridge, MA: Harvard University Press, 1991).

28

Disney Parks

Seventy percent of Americans have visited Disneyland in California or Walt Disney World in Florida. Every year, about as many tourists enter these two parks as visit Washington, D.C. Disney also exports its parks: Tokyo Disneyland draws as many visitors as the original. Disneyland Paris now exceeds the Eiffel Tower in yearly visitors, a Hong Kong Disneyland opened in 2005, and a Shanghai Disneyland is in the works. From parades on a late-Victorian Main Street to the *It's a Small World* ride in Fantasyland to the permanent world's fair of the Epcot Center, the Disney Parks create a global version of American civil religion, a version that both celebrates cultural tolerance and holds dreams and wishes sacred.

Because the guests (always called guests, never mere customers) at a Disney park are entirely surrounded by fictional worlds, the messages of the parks are inescapable. To walk through the parks feels like walking onstage during a Broadway musical, not only without disrupting the performance but while being integrated into it. At one moment a plaza or street contains only ordinary pedestrians, and at the next an announcer introduces an event and the area fills with "cast members," some of them famous cartoon characters and some from fairy tales that Disney made into movies, while singing and dancing breaks out. "Come and share the exciting adventure / Of Disney dreams come true," says a typical song, and resistance becomes impossible. How not to smile when Tigger from Winnie the Pooh walks up and waves at you, or even shakes your hand? Mickey Mouse rides by on a float or dances with Minnie and urges everyone to believe in their dreams. Donald Duck dissents for a moment, but even he is converted. Every night there are fireworks, and one of the shows (called "Wishes") includes Tinker Bell flying across the sky, spreading pixie dust on the crowds, and Jiminy Cricket urging everyone to wish together to deliver Sleeping Beauty from the Wicked Witch. Characters and stories mix into a seamless whole.

Each of the five Disney parks centers on an area originally called "Main Street U.S.A.," modeled on Walt Disney's childhood hometown of Marceline, Missouri, in the years before World War I. Main Street runs from a town square to the plaza in front of Cinderella's Castle, from which regions like Fanatasyland,

Adventureland, and Tomorrowland branch out. In Tokyo, Main Street is called the "World Bazaar," but it looks essentially the same, and the Hong Kong Disneyland is proud to claim that its Main Street exactly duplicates the one in California. Main Street is the first place that Disney guests encounter and the last place they walk through before leaving. It features a City Hall information hub, a bakery, a working barber shop, a firehouse with antique equipment, a museum of photography and animation, a movie theater that continuously runs the oldest Disney cartoons, a newsstand with no newspapers (but filled with souvenirs and tourist needs), and clothing and jewelry stores. All of the storefronts are built at eight-tenths of normal size, with upper stories even smaller, so that people seem larger than life, while costumed cast members become huge. On the streets, pedestrians share space with horse-drawn trolleys, "horseless carriages," and antique buses that make quaint "put-put" sounds.

Critics charge that Main Street is basically a shopping mall. As Umberto Eco writes, "The Main Street facades are presented to us as toy houses and invite us to enter them, but their interior is always a disguised supermarket, where you buy obsessively, believing that you are still playing." Travel guides warn that the shops will be crowded at the end of the day, as people seek souvenirs. Often the functions of market and museum are mixed, as displays of old cameras or drawings from the history of animation share space with recordings and cameras for sale.

The most important events on Main Street sell ideas, or at least use ideas to sell products, and take place outside the shops. These are the frequent parades of Disney characters and floats. Several times every day and once or twice at night (with spectacular visual effects), parades make their way down Main Street and end in its town square. Some of these parades have patriotic messages. For example, at the end of the "Family Fun Day Parade" at Walt Disney World, in which volunteer guest families march alongside costumed characters like Snow White, Goofy, or Chip and Dale, a twelve-piece band and a recorded group of singers perform a "Red, White, and Blue Patriotic Finale" including "I'm a Yankee Doodle Dandy" and "It's a Grand Old Flag."

Such specifically American finales do not happen in Japan, France, and China. Allowing for cultural differences, Disney puts on different parades in those parks, mixing English with other languages. But holidays like Christmas, Halloween, and the Western New Year produce special parades in all of the parks, and all of the parades happen in Disney's American hometown. They also always celebrate the sacredness of wishes, dreams, and imagination. Although the Mickey Mouse who leads parades in Tokyo Disneyland wears a Japanese man's kimono, some of his words in English are the same as in Florida: "Believing in your dreams is swell! Gosh, everyone can imagine!" And the America presented in all of these parks is a good place for dreams: a harmless, innocent place, with brick streets and wooden storefronts, populated by friendly chipmunks, ducks, and mice. Even the anachronistic movie theater and cartoons, neither of which would have existed until the late 1920s and early 1930s, tell stories of animals and plants, farm life and steamboats. Walt Disney used a nostalgic version of small-town America to promote hope from the beginning of his career. Today, the parks built on Disney's heritage share that American hope with Europe and Asia.

Two places in Florida's Walt Disney World use nostalgia and hope to teach a specific reverence for America: the Hall of Presidents in the Magic Kingdom and the American Adventure in Epcot's World Showcase. In both of these attractions, a combination of film, music, and what Disney calls "audioanimatronic" figures—the moving, speaking robots that first appeared at the New York World's Fair in 1964 and that take various animal and human forms to entertain passengers on Disney rides—are used to re-create American history. The Hall of Presidents has recently abandoned a narrative about racial issues and the Constitution to focus more closely on presidential leadership, while the American Adventure makes a more general survey of American history.

The Hall of Presidents grew directly from Disney's fascination with Abraham Lincoln. In 1903, Walt Disney's father Elias moved his family near Kansas City, Missouri, to escape the dangers of Chicago. It was a place where Lincoln epitomized American virtue, at least for people from the North like the Disneys. The conflict over slavery that brought on the Civil War had centered on that region, where John Brown had first killed slaveholders. All of the Republican presidents through William McKinley, who was assassinated in 1901 (the year Walt Disney was born), had been officers in the Union army, and Civil War veterans dominated the Memorial Day observances that Disney saw every May.

As living memory of Lincoln disappeared and technology improved in the 1950s, Disney became obsessed with the idea of bringing Lincoln back. He and his team of "Imagineers" worked for the state of Illinois to create an audioanimatronic Lincoln for the New York World's Fair of 1964. In the show "Great Moments with Mr. Lincoln," first at the Fair and later at Disneyland (where it ran until 2005), the Lincoln robot rose from its chair, took a step forward, and delivered a speech that was strikingly aggressive. Re-enacting an address of Lincoln's from 1838, the figure of Lincoln boasted that "All the armies of Europe, Asia, and Africa combined could not, by force, take a drink from the Ohio or make a track on the Blue Ridge." What prevented this was not the American military, but "the spirit that prizes liberty as the heritage of all men." If that is destroyed, Lincoln warned, the United States could destroy itself. "As a nation of free men, we must live through all time, or die by suicide." That suicide would not take place, the speech concluded, because God had not created humanity to live and die in futility, but "for immortality." American freedom was part of God's plan of salvation.

The Lincoln show provoked strong reactions. Protesting the "phony reverence and pomposity" with which Disney had surrounded the Lincoln figure in 1968, critic Richard Schickel asked, "Are we really supposed to revere this ridiculous contraption, this weird agglomeration of wires and plastic...?" He contrasted Disney's life-size replica to the massive statue of the Lincoln Memorial and concluded that "art is not imitation." Schickel saw the Memorial as an invitation to genuine religious experience, a reflection on the mysteries of the human spirit, while the audioanimatronic Lincoln offered itself as an idol and reminded viewers that Lincoln was only a man. According to Disney himself, on the other hand, the audioanimatronic figures he was making for his parks combined all the arts, from sculpture and painting to theater and motion pictures, and the highest use of technology was to bring human history to life.

This disagreement reflected themes that have recurred throughout the history of religions. Disney's reverence for and devotion to Lincoln were undoubtedly sincere, even if they produced something that Schickel and others saw as a "horror" and led them to respond in the manner of prophets confronting idols. Iconoclasts had also found fault with the Lincoln Memorial and before that with Michelangelo's Christ in the *Last Judgment* and with the statues in St. Peter's Basilica. The attempt to draw hard distinctions between true and false religious experience, idolatry and worship, goes back to the Second Commandment in the law of Moses.

When Walt Disney died in December 1966, the Disney company was already producing Walt Disney World in Florida. In that new Magic Kingdom, "Great Moments with Mr. Lincoln" became the Hall of Presidents, one of the central features of Liberty Square. A visitor walking from Main Street into the circular court around Cinderella's Castle has only to walk a few yards to enter a district celebrating the political birth and history of the United States. As the text on a plaque at the entrance reads:

> Past this gateway stirs a new nation waiting to be born. Thirteen separate colonies have banded together to declare their independence from the bands of tyranny. It is a time when silversmiths put away their tools and march to the drums of a revolution, a time when gentlemen planters leave their farms to become generals, a time when tradesmen leave the safety of their homes to become heroes. Welcome to Liberty Square!

A building with a golden "1787" (for the year when the Constitution was ratified) emblazoned over its central doorway houses the Hall of Presidents. Inside the front doors is a large, semicircular foyer for crowds awaiting the show, which repeats every half-hour. On the rug in this foyer is the presidential seal—the only authorized reproduction of that seal on any architectural feature outside the White House. Glass cases display presidential memorabilia, such as a pair of Lincoln's driving gloves, monogrammed cowboy boots from George W. Bush, and a letter written by Harry Truman to his wife Bess on their twenty-ninth anniversary. In a 2009 makeover, several dresses worn by First Ladies were added. Large portraits of several presidents hang on the walls. The choice of these presidents seems to depend on some combination of great historical prominence and terms of office in living memory, with the notable exclusions of Lyndon Johnson and Richard Nixon.

The show itself begins with a trip through US history told in colorful paintings projected on several large screens, accompanied by narration and a soundtrack. Over the decades since the Hall of Presidents opened in 1971, this show has undergone three major changes. For the first twenty-two years it included many details of conflict in American history. It spent considerable time on the crisis of the Union, including excerpts from the Lincoln-Douglas debates and the Civil War, and celebrated inventors like Thomas Edison and Henry Ford. After 1993, a shortened script written and narrated by Maya Angelou focused on slavery and equal rights, using some of the same paintings and audio but leaping from Reconstruction to the astronauts. Beginning in 2009, Morgan Freeman has become the narrator, and the story has been completely rewritten and focused on the presidents. Washington's decision to refuse kingship, Andrew Jackson's identification with the common people, and Theodore Roosevelt's populism in attacking corporate trusts are offered as evidence of the importance of having a leader who is also "one of us." From Theodore Roosevelt the narration moves to Franklin Roosevelt, then to John F. Kennedy, telling the stories of surmounting the Depression and World War II and beginning a new age of civic activism. For a few seconds each, Lyndon Johnson, Bill Clinton, and George W. Bush are shown comforting Americans after the tragedies of Kennedy's assassination, the Oklahoma City bombing, and the World Trade Center attack.

All three versions of the show have come to the same climax, a moment when the screens are retracted, a presidential seal is projected on a curtain, and the narrator says, "Ladies and gentlemen, the Presidents of the United States," whereupon the curtain parts to reveal forty-three (as of 2013) life-sized audio-animatronic figures on the stage. Each president is introduced in order of succession, although they are not standing or sitting in that order; a spotlight rests on each briefly as his name is intoned, and the figure makes a slight nod of the head in acknowledgment. Meanwhile, those not spotlighted may fidget, and some presidents appear to say a word or two to each other. Lincoln and Washington are seated near the front, with Lincoln at the center. Before Barack Obama, all of the audioanimatronic presidents were sculpted by Blaine Gibson, a man described as a "Disney legend" who began to work for the company in 1939 and came out of retirement to complete the second President Bush in 2001. In 2009, Valerie Edwards, the daughter of a Disney animator and a protégé of Gibson, took over for the Obama head.

What happens once the presidents are introduced also changed dramatically in 2009. For decades Lincoln gave a long speech, followed by a speech from the current president. Between 1971 and 1993, Lincoln gave the Lyceum address from 1838, about American being invulnerable to foreign armies but endangered if it lost its faith in liberty. This reflected the mood of a nation that saw itself as embattled by communist enemies of freedom. From 1993 until 2009, the Lincoln figure gave a fictional speech about America's future, a compilation by historian Eric Foner from passages in several speeches of Lincoln. But now Lincoln delivers the Gettysburg Address during the review of history, before the other presidents appear on stage. Now after the introductions, George Washington gets up from his chair and takes his first speaking role at a Disney park. Washington says that he had no greater moment of apprehension than when he took the oath of office as president, but that he knows that the American dream will endure as long as that oath is faithfully executed. Morgan Freeman then introduces Barack Obama, who recites the oath, then gives a speech about the dream enduring as long as children awake with the knowledge that they can aspire to anything.

At times, the speech by the serving president has been very political. In his first year, George W. Bush gave a speech about tax cuts, though he later moved to a more generic evocation of the future. Bill Clinton, the first president to record the speech in his own voice, said that there was no problem in the world that could not be cured by the ideals America represents, and looked forward "to a day when those principles extended beyond our borders will have circled the globe." Now the Hall of Presidents may have reached a lasting equilibrium, focusing on the presidents as citizens who fulfill their duty.

Less political evocations of America also occur in the Magic Kingdom. Beyond Liberty Square lies Frontierland, a celebration of the American West. A feature called "The Rivers of America" connects the two regions, and guests may ride between them on a paddle-wheel riverboat. On the other side of the park, Tomorrowland invokes American history with another show that began at the General Electric pavilion in the 1964 World's Fair, a Carousel of Progress in which guests ride on a revolving bank of seats to visit a family in a series of kitchens from the last century.

The most elaborate Disney vision of America unfolds before guests at the American Adventure, in the park called Epcot (Experimental Prototype

Community of Tomorrow), which was the last great dream of Walt Disney before his death. Originally intended as a planned city for twenty thousand people, Epcot evolved by the time it opened, in 1982, into a kind of permanent World's Fair, celebrating science, industry, progress, and multiculturalism. One of the two main divisions of Epcot is the World Showcase, a set of eleven national pavilions and courtyards grouped around a lake. Walking from the Epcot main entrance and proceeding around the lake from West to East, guests encounter Mexico, Norway, China, Germany, Italy, The American Adventure, Japan, Morocco, France, the United Kingdom, and Canada. Each area is staffed by citizens of the nations, and corporations from these countries have heavily invested in the shops, restaurants, and educational features. For The American Adventure, the corporate sponsors are Coca-Cola and American Express.

Before or after the show in The American Adventure, guests may be entertained by the Voices of Liberty, an a capella choir in eighteenth-century dresses, wigs, and knickers that performs several times a day in an oval vestibule. On the walls of the vestibule hang large paintings by Disney artists working in a style reminiscent of Norman Rockwell, without Rockwell's humor but adding a touch of socialist realism, depicting American scenes that begin with Indians showing Puritans how to plant corn and continue through covered wagons crossing a river to immigrants arriving in New York to workers building skyscrapers and airplanes to rockets taking off. Other rooms off the vestibule display memorabilia from a disparate group of American figures, including baseball player Jackie Robinson, union leader Cesar Chavez, and Nez Perce war leader Chief Joseph. In a gift shop nearby, guests can buy dolls of the presidents that recite dozens of short passages from their speeches.

Human audioanimatronics have their greatest triumph on the stage of the American Adventure Theater, where the half-hour review of American history is hosted by moving and walking versions of Benjamin Franklin and Mark Twain. The journey through history starts with paintings of the Mayflower, then leaps to colonial protests over British taxation and then to the Revolution. Franklin climbs stairs to visit an audioanimatronic Thomas Jefferson who is struggling over the Declaration of Independence. An upbeat song about "the liberty trail" intervenes, and the scene shifts to Valley Forge. Robotic soldiers complain about the cold, but the figure of George Washington can be seen in the background sharing their hardship. The Revolution concludes with triumph for what Franklin calls "an entire nation of dreamers and doers."

Now the focus shifts to Mark Twain (who would probably have been enraged to see himself used in this setting), and his figure takes over as guide. An audioanimatronic Frederick Douglass appears, remarking that "along Mark Twain's beloved Mississippi, I hear the rattle of chains and the crack of the whip." The show moves to a family at Matthew Brady's studio, having a photograph taken to mark the mother's birthday while two of her sons argue about slavery. The folk song "Two Brothers" is sung—"Two brothers on their way, one wore blue, the other gray"—and the single dead body of a Confederate soldier appears on the screen. Twain announces that, with the Civil War over, "[i]t seems there was a new dawn coming."

Suddenly, Chief Joseph of the Nez Perce, the last great war leader of the Plains Indians, rises from the stage. "Enough! Enough of your words," he says. "Let your new dawn lead to the final sunset on my people's suffering." Chief Joseph repeats the famous lines associated with him, "From where the sun now stands, I will fight no more forever;" but before saying these words, he asks that all should be brothers, with one government and one country, using words that Chief Joseph never said. Mark Twain says that Chief Joseph reminds Americans of "our long, painful journey to the frontiers of human liberty."

Cultural critic Stephen Fjellman dismissed the fictional Twain's statement as meaningless words, "a ritual incantation that denies the truth of the history to which it has just alluded." Though there is undeniable truth in this critique, and the real Mark Twain would almost certainly not have replied to Chief Joseph with the words Disney has given his electronic double, there is another kind of meaning being expressed here. The whole show in The American Adventure flows in a rhythm that has been called the "Disney sine curve" of ups and downs along a rising trajectory of history. Every success is followed by a failure, every advance by a retreat or at least a challenge. But every challenge is met, and every retreat gives rise to a new advance. An optimistic faith underlies the whole story. Almost certainly, this faith began with Walt Disney himself, but it also connects with the view of history implicit in American civil religion, which teaches that personal freedom, political democracy, world peace, and cultural tolerance will prevail despite all challenges.

In the American Adventure, the celebration of the nation's centennial in 1876 comes next, and we see the electronic figure of Susan B. Anthony speaking for women's rights. Alexander Graham Bell and Andrew Carnegie appear. Technical progress is invoked by film showing early zippers, trolley cars, vacuum cleaners, and airplanes.

Then the scene shifts to a mountain top, where Teddy Roosevelt and John Muir have a dialogue. Roosevelt calls the scene "bully beautiful" but regrets that "timber thieves" threaten it. John Muir tells Roosevelt that he must put the giant Sequoias into a national park, despite the hunger of the growing nation for lumber, so that Americans may leave something grand to their children.

With the national park system secured, Twain says that Americans were "thrust into the role of a world leader and into the war to end all wars." Film of Eddie Rickenbacker flying his fighter plane and of Charles Lindbergh crossing the Atlantic intervenes. Next comes the 1929 stock market crash and the

Depression. A scene rises to the stage that includes a gas station and robotic men singing "Brother, Can You Spare a Dime?" Franklin Delano Roosevelt announces that "the only thing we have to fear is fear itself." Then comedian Will Rogers walks to center stage, twirling a lariat as the real Rogers sometimes did, and points out that "We're the only nation in the world that waits until we're *in* the war before we start getting ready for it." A recording plays of FDR intoning that on December 7, 1941, "a day that will live in infamy," the United States was attacked by the empire of Japan.

The gas station sinks into the stage and is replaced by an airplane factory in which Rosie the Riveter, copied from the famous poster, is working on a wing. Frank Sinatra's music plays in the background while Rosie converses with another worker, hoping that the boys will soon come home. The scene goes dark, preparing us for a climax.

A flying eagle appears on the screen as a song with the repeated refrain, "America, spread your golden wings, soar on freedom's winds, 'cross the sky," plays in the background. Film clips include General Douglas MacArthur, Eleanor Roosevelt, Walt Disney himself, Marilyn Monroe, Albert Einstein, Jonas Salk, Frank Sinatra, Louis Armstrong, and Elvis Presley—all evoking the immediate postwar era. Now the song is punctuated by the Kennedy inauguration, and the famous line "Ask not what your country can do for you" rings out in Kennedy's voice. The casket of Kennedy rolling through the street appears, and is followed (anachronistically, since the 1963 march happened while JFK was still alive) by Martin Luther King's "I Have a Dream" speech at the Lincoln Memorial. Then the song and the film resume with Vietnam War protesters, Cesar Chavez leading union drives among farm workers, Gloria Steinem as an icon of feminism, and Ryan White, the child AIDS victim of Indiana, with a placard reading "STOP AIDS" behind him. The Vietnam Veterans Memorial appears, and then firemen raising an American flag amid the rubble of the World Trade Center on 9/11. The Statue of Liberty appears with fireworks exploding around it.

Three-dimensional drama returns with Franklin and Twain, now standing in the small cage around the torch of the Statue of Liberty. Franklin asks Twain what he thinks of the American story, and the writer answers that the Founding Fathers "never dreamed of an America like this." Twain then quotes John Steinbeck to warn that success, plenty, and comforts have often destroyed "dynamic people." He seems pessimistic. Liberty can be relied on to counter this threat, answers Franklin. If we give everyone a chance, he assures Twain and the audience, "The American Adventure will continue for a long, long time."

Although the American Adventure show is far longer and more inclusive than the version of American history at the Hall of Presidents, it can still be accused of favoring an imperial agenda. Chief Joseph appears only to surrender. No questions are raised about the carnage of wars, the atomic bombs dropped on Japan, or whether the United States should station military forces in about half of the world's nations.

There are remarkable contrasts between The American Adventure and the presentations at the China and France pavilions. Both China and France feature the geographical and cultural aspects of their countries without any triumphal, historical narrative. In fact, the position of The American Adventure at the center of the arc of nations around the World Showcase Lagoon and the American self-presentation both imply that among nations, the United States stands at the center and leads all others.

On the other hand, Walt Disney World and its duplicates in Japan, France, and Hong Kong do have a multicultural message that stems from Walt Disney himself. Disney's contributions to the 1964 New York World's Fair, alongside "Great Moments with Mr. Lincoln" and the General Electric "Carousel of Progress," included the Pepsi-Cola pavilion, which featured "It's A Small World—A Tribute to UNICEF." This ride continues as part of Fantasyland in all versions of the Magic Kingdom today. Guests sit in boats and glide past audioanimatronic children (297 in the original show) with variously colored faces, gathered in signature scenes like the Eiffel Tower, the Taj Mahal, and the windmills of Holland, wearing colorful native costumes, nodding and blinking and dancing as they sing (in various languages) an infinitely catchy tune. Most people who have been exposed to the song cannot help but recall the English chorus: "It's a small world after all" three times, followed by "It's a small, small world." Most do not notice that the sweetness of the chorus, the childish voices, and the tune mask some poignant verses, such as "It's a world of laughter, a world of tears / It's a world of hopes, it's a world of fear."

One of the men who wrote these lyrics (Robert B. Sherman, who worked with his brother Richard M. Sherman as a Disney staff songwriter and who also wrote the music for *Mary Poppins*) had led the half-squad of American soldiers that accidentally found the German concentration camp at Dachau, hours after the Germans left. In 1964, when the Berlin Wall was only a few years old and before the word "multicultural" was commonly known, the message that "It's time we're aware / It's a small world after all" was not a cliché. According to Robert Sherman, who argues that no other song is constantly played in five places in the world, "It's a Small World" has now for decades been the most constantly performed song on earth. In the California, Florida, Tokyo, Paris, and Hong Kong Magic Kingdoms where the ride continues today, the costumes, the words of the song in various languages, and the dances of the children are frequently updated. Commentator Douglas Brode has written that the Disney show at the Pepsi pavilion at the World's Fair introduced diversity and multiculturalism as values before the words existed.

Many experts, including the leadership of the Southern Baptist Convention, have noticed that Disney's promotion of tolerance extends to gays. Gay Days at the Disney parks began as a guerrilla raid in 1978, when a group called the Los Angeles Bar and Restaurant Association held a private party at Disneyland without disclosing that it was a gay organization. Disorder ensued, involving public displays of affection and the attempts of Disney security to prevent them. Since then, relations between Disney parks and the gay community have settled into peaceful patterns. In the 1990s, regular benefits for AIDS research took place at Disney World and Disneyland. The first weekend of June is unofficially understood as Gay Pride weekend in the parks. Though this is not an official event, Disney World in Orlando sells special red t-shirts, rainbow mugs, and rainbow-colored Mickey Mouse figures for the occasion. Gay Days at Disney have become prominent enough to draw reviews from gay writers and travel sites and protests from evangelical Christian and conservative political groups. The reputation of the Disney company for nondiscrimination against gays led Southern Baptists—the largest Protestant denomination in the United States—to run a boycott of Disney in 1997. The appeal of the parks proved so great that the effort failed.

At Epcot in Walt Disney World, expressions of multiculturalism, tolerance, and globalism are elaborate and corporate. The signature building of Epcot is a sphere about eighteen stories high called Spaceship Earth, a dodecahedron made of 11,324 aluminum triangles that seems to float in the air, gleaming white. People take the *Spaceship Earth* ride inside the sphere. Beginning in 1982 with an original text by Ray Bradbury and narration by Walter Cronkite, the show has told the story of communication from the dawn of human civilization in caves, through Egyptian hieroglyphics, Roman roads, Jewish rabbis, Muslim scholars, Christian monks, and Renaissance artists to printing, newspapers, radio, television, and computers. When the vehicles carrying guests reach the top of the dome, the guests confront an image of earth seen from space and journey into a future that concludes with new means of communication. The corporate partners with Disney for *Spaceship Earth*—first Bell, then AT&T, and since 2005 Siemens—have always had communications and electronic products to sell.

Every night at Epcot ends with a trip through more ancient history, an outdoor display called "IllumiNations: Reflections of Earth." A massive globe, covered in computer-controlled lights, is floated on the World Showcase Lagoon, and pictures showing the evolution of continents and civilizations play across its surface as fireworks and lasers light the sky. A song, "We Go On," tells guests that they live in a time when they can "touch tomorrow" and "take the future by the hand." At the climax, the globe opens like a flower and explodes with white fireworks.

When Disney's messages are added together, it becomes clear that the Disney parks are teaching a system of commitments to certain symbols, words, and behavioral norms that amounts to a religion. Walt Disney disliked organized religion, which had played an oppressive role in his childhood, but he believed in belief. While there is no church in the Magic Kingdom, even on Main Street, the whole place presents itself as a sacred site. There must be no litter, no bad language, no violence, no unhappiness. Employees are cast members who are always onstage, drawing guests into rituals. The God of Abrahamic tradition is invoked only by historic figures like Lincoln. Instead, magical beings like Tinker Bell and Mickey Mouse abound, and many shows imply that such beings might help ordinary people. The attitude toward these characters, from Lincoln and Will Rogers to Mary Poppins and Peter Pan and Disney's own Goofy and Donald Duck, expresses what I have called "trans-theism," the provisional acceptance of many gods with an implied, underlying oneness.

The parks do have one central symbol. Before Walt Disney died, he tried to convince his brother Roy to make an audioanimatronic figure of himself and put it on a pedestal in Disneyland. Although Roy did not install a robot Walt, all five Magic Kingdoms include a statue called *Partners*, designed and sculpted by Blaine Gibson, in which a life-sized Disney and Mickey Mouse hold hands, at the center of the plaza in front of Cinderella's Castle (Figure 28.1). Both Walt Disney and Mickey are Trickster figures, magical builders of culture rather than

Figure 28.1 *Partners*, the statue of Walt Disney and Mickey Mouse by Blaine Gibson, stands at the end of Main Street and in front of Cinderella's Castle. Photograph by Herb Leibacher, WDWmemories.com.

ruling deities, and the Disney religion centers on Tricksters rather than on a high God.

The classical religious theme of immortality appears repeatedly at Disney parks. Mickey Mouse has not made a feature film since the 1940s, but at the parks he seems as young as ever. Here are Benjamin Franklin and Mark Twain, not dead but walking around on stage and commenting on American history up to the present. As the announcer for the "Great Moments with Mr. Lincoln" show proclaimed for fifty years at Disneyland, "We pay tribute here, not to a man who lived a century ago, but to an individual who lives today." After Walt Disney's death, rumors persisted that he had frozen his body for resuscitation at some later date. Roy Disney boasted that Walt had left the company with a ten-year plan, and in fact Walt Disney World and the subsequent parks, not to mention the movies and television networks, have maintained a remarkable continuity. It may seem improbable that people will still throng to these parks centuries from now, but such approaches to immortality are not impossible if the Disney system continues to renew itself. Japanese Buddhists have maintained a park at Nara, with a huge wooden temple, tame deer, and museums displaying artifacts from around the world, since the 700s.

At the opening of the first Disneyland on July 17, 1955—a televised event, hosted by Art Linkletter, Robert Cummings, and Ronald Reagan—Walt Disney said this:

> To all who come to this happy place: Welcome. Disneyland is your land. Here, age relives fond memories of the past, and here youth may savor the challenge and promise of the future. Disneyland is dedicated to the ideals, the dreams, and the hard facts that have created America, with the hope that it will be a source of joy and inspiration to the world.

In these four sentences, Disney defined his new world as America's heir and successor. Disney parks grow out of America, but go beyond America to the future of the world. Though the Disney parks make use of American civil religion, and the parks in the United States are sacred places within American civil religion, people in Japan, France, and Hong Kong do not need to become Americans to enter Disney's vision. In Disney's parks, the facts of American history have become symbols and rituals of hope for increasing personal freedom, world peace, and cultural tolerance.

An edge of prophetic insight into injustice can sometimes be felt in the parks, but it is always blunted by sentimental celebrations. Meanwhile, any revolutionary actions or demonstrations are kept at bay by the price of admission and the rules set by the Disney corporation. But such limits are not unique to Disney. All sacred sites have rituals to evoke sentiments, standards for admission, and rules of behavior. The function of sacred places is less to enable prophets to find new visions and more to express and to secure what has already been seen. If prophets do obtain tickets to the Disney parks, at least they can observe without fear, in a place that sometimes tries to represent all of history and to respect all cultures. In much of the world and in parts of the United States, this continues to be a revolutionary freedom.

SOURCES

Birnbaum Guides, *Walt Disney World 2008: Expert Advice from the Inside Source* (New York: Disney Enterprises, 2007).

Brode, Douglas, *Multiculturalism and the Mouse: Race and Sex in Disney Entertainment* (Austin: University of Texas Press, 2005).

Budd, Mike, and Max H. Kirsch, eds., *Rethinking Disney: Private Control, Public Dimensions* (Middletown, CT: Wesleyan University Press, 2005.

Clarke, Sara K., "'Rainbow Mickey'" Souvenirs Come Out for Gay Days," Orlando Sentinel, May 30, 2013.

Fjellman, Stephen M., *Vinyl Leaves: Walt Disney World and America* (Boulder, CO: Westview Press, 1992).

Gabler, Neal, *Walt Disney: The Triumph of the American Imagination* (New York: Alfred A. Knopf, 2006).

Schickel, Richard, *The Disney Version: The Life, Times, Art and Commerce of Walt Disney* (New York: Simon and Schuster, 1968).

Wasko, Janet, *Understanding Disney: The Manufacture of Fantasy* (Cambridge, UK: Polity, 2001).

29

The Kennedy Inaugural

John F. Kennedy was president for only a thousand days, but on his first day as president he set a new course for the nation. Kennedy's inaugural address began a new era in American civil religion. Kennedy applied the values of personal freedom and political democracy to the entire world. The transformation that Kennedy wrought on January 20, 1961, was comparable to that produced by the two greatest speeches of Abraham Lincoln. Just as Lincoln connected personal freedom with political democracy, demanding "a new birth of freedom" so that "government of the people, by the people, and for the people" could survive, so Kennedy connected freedom and democracy with world peace.

In January 1961, it was not yet clear whether the nation would rally behind Kennedy. He had been elected by the narrowest of margins, with widespread suspicions of voter fraud in Chicago. The opening of his inaugural address sought to bring the country together by linking his presidency with the whole history of the United States, while at the same time declaring that America stood at a moment of transformation.

> We observe today not a victory of party but a celebration of freedom—symbolizing an end as well as a beginning—signifying renewal as well as change. For I have sworn before you and Almighty God the same solemn oath our forebears prescribed nearly a century and three-quarters ago.
>
> The world is very different now. For man holds in his mortal hands the power to abolish all forms of human poverty and all forms of human life. And yet the same revolutionary beliefs for which our forebears fought are still at issue around the globe—the belief that the rights of man come not from the generosity of the state but from the hand of God.

When sociologist (and Episcopalian lay preacher) Robert Bellah made his case for considering American civil religion as seriously as any other religion, the opening of Kennedy's speech was his central example. Bellah pointed out that the two uses of God in these first paragraphs were not merely conventional rhetoric, but proof that civil religion had its own claim to transcendent values. As Bellah argued, Kennedy was not speaking as a Roman Catholic or even as a Christian but simply as a believer in God, and he made the inauguration a religious event by placing himself, the American people, and the Constitution under God. Kennedy's assertion that human rights come from God meant that for him no state could ever become so absolute as to legitimately deny those rights. Bellah said that this appeal to God against the state has always been the most revolutionary aspect of American civil religion.

Certainly the sacredness of freedom, of individual liberty against state or collective control, is the first value of American civil religion, and that value has often been affirmed by reference to God. But Kennedy went well beyond this in his next paragraphs, which are inscribed in granite at his tomb in Arlington Cemetery. Here Kennedy transformed the value of freedom for Americans into an American commitment to a worldwide mission that must itself be seen as religious. World peace was already a value of American civil religion, especially since Pearl Harbor, but Kennedy argued that freedom could not survive in America unless it triumphed in the world.

> We dare not forget today that we are the heirs of that first revolution. Let the word go forth from this time and place, to friend and foe alike, that the torch has been passed to a new generation of Americans—born in this century, tempered by war, disciplined by a hard and bitter peace, proud of our ancient heritage—and unwilling to witness or permit the slow undoing of those human rights to which this nation has always been committed, and to which we are committed today at home and around the world.
>
> Let every nation know, whether it wishes us well or ill, that we shall pay any price, bear any burden, meet any hardship, support any friend, oppose any foe to assure the survival and the success of liberty.

For five decades and more, the United States has been living out this commitment. Beginning with the Bay of Pigs and the subsequent Cuban missile crisis, continuing through Vietnam, onward to interventions in Somalia, Haiti, and Bosnia, and most recently in Iraq and Afghanistan—the United States has attempted, by military means, to spread the gospel of liberty.

Before Kennedy, American policy toward foreign threats to liberty was containment, not victory. After World War II, the United States seemed content to pursue its own interests abroad. Such interests might demand armed interventions, as in central America, or covert actions, as in Iran, or even a large-scale war, as in Korea, but the intention to make the whole world free, much less unified in a free world order, was not the driving force of US policy. But since Kennedy's inaugural address, whether policy was being made by realists such as President Nixon and Henry Kissinger or idealists like Presidents Carter, Reagan, and George W. Bush, Americans have found it impossible to put down the torch that Kennedy raised.

In Kennedy's speech, the old commitment of American civil religion to the sacredness of freedom developed into commitments to promote democracy in specific ways. Kennedy's vision of a world both free and at peace was dramatically egalitarian. His statements about economic development aid and international government under the United Nations would soon become too radical for any American politician.

> This much we pledge—and more.
>
> To those old allies whose cultural and spiritual origins we share, we pledge the loyalty of faithful friends. United, there is little we cannot do in a host of cooperative ventures. Divided, there is little we can do—for we dare not meet a powerful challenge at odds and split asunder.
>
> To those new states whom we welcome to the ranks of the free, we pledge our word that one form of colonial control shall not have passed away merely to be replaced by a far more iron tyranny. We shall not always expect to find them supporting our view. But we shall always hope to find them strongly supporting their own freedom—and to remember that, in the past, those who foolishly sought power by riding the back of the tiger ended up inside.
>
> To those peoples in the huts and villages of half the globe struggling to break the bonds of mass misery, we pledge our best efforts to help them help themselves, for whatever period is required—not because the Communists may be doing it, not because we seek their votes, but because it is right. If a free society cannot help the many who are poor, it cannot save the few who are rich.
>
> To our sister republics south of our border, we offer a special pledge—to convert our good words into good deeds—in a new alliance for progress—to assist free men and free governments in casting off the chains of poverty. But this peaceful revolution of hope cannot become the prey of hostile powers. Let all our neighbors know that we shall join with them to oppose aggression or subversion anywhere in the Americas. And let every other power know that this Hemisphere intends to remain the master of its own house.
>
> To that world assembly of sovereign states, the United Nations, our last best hope in an age where the instruments of war have far outpaced

the instruments of peace, we renew our pledge of support—to prevent it from becoming merely a forum for invective—to strengthen its shield of the new and the weak—and to enlarge the area in which its writ may run.

Speaking of the United Nations as having a "writ," or legal jurisdiction, would seem dangerously internationalist today. Calling the UN the "last best hope" for the world gave it the status that Lincoln had assigned to the United States. Meanwhile, by promising to help the poor of the whole world "for whatever period is required" and to partner with all nations of the Americas in "casting off the chains of poverty," Kennedy took on a global commitment even more vast than his pledge to spread liberty.

In Kennedy's view, America stood at a unique moment in history, when "all forms of human poverty and all forms of human life" could both be abolished. American vision and American effort could make the difference between a world plunged into the chaos of a final war or a world that emerged into the sunlight of peace and freedom. Such a dichotomy of fear and hope had been growing since the late 1940s. Part of the reason for this was technological. The advent of a nuclear age led to people building all-electric homes, with the expectation that electricity would soon be so cheap that no one would meter it, but the nuclear age also meant the building of enormous stockpiles of nuclear weapons and new ways to deliver them.

The most important source of this sense of crisis in 1961 was the growing influence of an ideology, communism, that was often spoken and written about as a religion in itself, and that seemed to espouse values—equality rather than freedom, control by Party leaders rather than democracy—that directly contradicted American civil religion. Since World War II, communist political parties had come to power in Eastern and Central Europe, China, North Korea, North Vietnam, and Cuba. Communism was powerful in South Asia, Africa, and Latin America. Many in the United States felt encircled and embattled, fearing that the "free world" was losing the Cold War to nations more insidious than the dictatorships of the 1930s and 1940s. Nikita Khrushchev, the leader of the Soviet Union, was encouraging communist revolutions everywhere in the world. In the longest section of his inaugural address, Kennedy addressed the nation's enemies with a transformative message.

> Finally, to those nations who would make themselves our adversary, we offer not a pledge but a request: that both sides begin anew the quest for peace, before the dark powers of destruction unleashed by science engulf all humanity in planned or accidental self-destruction.

We dare not tempt them with weakness. For only when our arms are sufficient beyond doubt can we be certain beyond doubt that they will never be employed.

But neither can two great and powerful groups of nations take comfort from our present course—both sides overburdened by the cost of modern weapons, both rightly alarmed by the steady spread of the deadly atom, yet both racing to alter that uncertain balance of terror that stays the hand of mankind's final war.

So let us begin anew—remembering on both sides that civility is not a sign of weakness, and sincerity is always subject to proof. Let us never negotiate out of fear. But let us never fear to negotiate.

Let both sides explore what problems unite us instead of belaboring those problems which divide us.

Let both sides, for the first time, formulate serious and precise proposals for the inspection and control of arms—and bring the absolute power to destroy other nations under the absolute control of all nations.

Let both sides seek to invoke the wonders of science instead of its terrors. Together let us explore the stars, conquer the deserts, eradicate disease, tap the ocean depths and encourage the arts and commerce.

Let both sides unite to heed in all corners of the earth the command of Isaiah—to "undo the heavy burdens...(and) let the oppressed go free."

And if a beach-head of cooperation may push back the jungle of suspicion, let both sides join in creating a new endeavor, not a new balance of power, but a new world of law, where the strong are just and the weak secure and the peace preserved.

Rather than fighting about economic and political theory or practice, Kennedy argued, the free world and the communist world could learn to cooperate in arms control, technological development, cultural exchange, and trade. He twice affirmed international government, with balanced phrases evoking an ideal world where nuclear arms were placed "under the absolute control of all nations" and humanity inhabited "a new world of law." And these ideals proved not entirely impractical.

Over the thousand days of the Kennedy administration, a Nuclear Test Ban Treaty was negotiated. News stories that the Americans or the Soviets had just detonated a 50-megaton or 100-megaton bomb, spreading strontium-90 into the milk supply, ceased to appear. A cultural thaw between the United States and the Soviet Union under Khrushchev accelerated artistic exchange. Before the 1960s were over, Kennedy's old opponent Richard Nixon would be negotiating enormous sales of wheat to the Soviets and pursuing a policy of *détente*. From the 1970s to the present, Americans and Soviets, and then Russians, have often cooperated in space exploration. Although "a new world of law" has not emerged, more international courts are now functioning than ever before. The commitments of Kennedy's inaugural have not been without result. The next section of the address invited all humanity to take part in the battle to avoid war and to create an earthly paradise.

> All this will not be finished in the first one hundred days. Nor will it be finished in the first one thousand days, nor in the life of this Administration, nor even perhaps in our lifetime on this planet. But let us begin.
>
> In your hands, my fellow citizens, more than mine, will rest the final success or failure of our course. Since this country was founded, each generation of Americans has been summoned to give testimony to its national loyalty. The graves of young Americans who answered the call to service surround the globe.
>
> Now the trumpet summons us again—not as a call to bear arms, though arms we need—not as a call to battle, though embattled we are—but a call to bear the burden of a long twilight struggle, year in and year out, "rejoicing in hope, patient in tribulation"—a struggle against the common enemies of man: tyranny, poverty, disease, and war itself.
>
> Can we forge against these enemies a grand and global alliance, North and South, East and West, that can assure a more fruitful life for all mankind? Will you join in that historic effort?
>
> In the long history of the world, only a few generations have been granted the role of defending freedom in its hour of maximum danger. I do not shrink from this responsibility—I welcome it. I do not believe that any of us would exchange places with any other people or any other generation. The energy, the faith, the devotion which we bring to this endeavor will light our country and all who serve it—and the glow from that fire can truly light the world.

At this distance, it can seem remarkable that Kennedy called January 20, 1961, the "hour of maximum danger" for freedom. No armies like those of the Persian Empire, or of Rome or of Hitler, were on the march. In fact, the United States was at peace in January 1961. Although the Soviets had launched Sputnik in 1957 and threatened to rule the world from space, and both sides possessed weapons that might "abolish all forms of human life," no particular crisis was taking place on Inauguration Day. Yet, the assumption that this was the hour of maximum danger for freedom was real and widespread. In a sense, that belief proved a self-fulfilling prophecy. The confrontation in October 1962 between the United States and the Soviet Union over Soviet missiles in Cuba nearly brought about the apocalyptic war that Kennedy feared. By a narrow margin, the hope expressed in the Kennedy inaugural that the whole world could work together for peace prevailed over the conviction (certainly shared by Kennedy) that communism posed the ultimate threat to freedom.

Kennedy's affirmation that American energy, faith, and devotion could start a fire that would "truly light the world" brought to a climax his theme of an American mission to lead the world to freedom. The language of faith and devotion and the symbolic power of fire marked these words as religious. They affirmed a non-rational commitment strong enough to hold life together. Once again, Kennedy's call to Americans transcended nationalism, but here transcendence required no invocation of God. In the concluding paragraphs, Kennedy did mention God for a third time, but now only to dismiss Him.

> And so, my fellow Americans: ask not what your country can do for you—ask what you can do for your country.
> My fellow citizens of the world: ask not what America will do for you, but what together we can do for the freedom of man.
> Finally, whether you are citizens of America or citizens of the world, ask of us here the same high standards of strength and sacrifice which we ask of you. With a good conscience our only sure reward, with history the final judge of our deeds, let us go forth to lead the land we love, asking His blessing and His help, but knowing that here on earth God's work must truly be our own.

This passage had poetic or musical power that derived from its rhythms. Its ultimate messages were acceptance of the need for sacrifice and exhortation to continued effort, as at the end of Lincoln's Second Inaugural. While mentioning God, Kennedy also followed Lincoln in claiming no knowledge of God's will. Good conscience became our only sure guide. That philosophical stance brings to mind the fact that Kennedy had considered an academic career before his eldest brother's death in World War II led to his inheritance of his father's political ambitions. Besides a good conscience, the speech here offered the thrill of sharing in a universal, human effort.

The "Ask not" phrase was not Kennedy's, but was borrowed from George St. John, the headmaster of the Choate preparatory school from 1908 to 1947, who had nearly expelled the young John Kennedy for his disrespectful attitude. In many speeches, St. John told Choate students to ask not what their school could do for them, but what they could do for their school. One can only wonder what St. John thought when he heard his lines repeated in the inaugural address.

Presumably he was proud, noticing that Kennedy had indeed learned something at Choate.

Reactions to this inaugural address were overwhelmingly positive. "God, I'd like to be able to do what that boy did there," Senator Barry Goldwater said immediately after hearing the speech. Polling placed the president's approval rating at almost 75 percent after the inauguration. There was also international impact: Pope Paul VI reportedly read and reread the speech and sought to reinforce its themes in the encyclical letter that inspired Roman Catholic liberation theology, *Populorum Progressio* (1967). The inaugural address of a forty-three-year-old man, the second son in a family that had risen from the status of Irish immigrants fleeing the potato famine to produce an ambassador to the United Kingdom in two generations and a president in three, quickly attained canonical status in American civil religion.

Like Lincoln's great speeches, Kennedy's inaugural was written from the perspective of a speaker who stood between opposing camps, and so could sympathize with both. Lincoln was raised in Ohio, southern Indiana, and southern Illinois, with slave states just over the border and a white population partly drawn from the South. Intellectually, Lincoln lived on the border between the rationalism of Tom Paine and Thomas Jefferson and the evangelical Protestantism of his parents and his culture.

Kennedy came from Irish and Roman Catholic roots but had an education that was culturally Yankee and Protestant, both at Choate and at Harvard. At his inauguration, Richard Cardinal Cushing, the Catholic archbishop of Boston, offered the invocation, and Robert Frost—the poet of New England Protestantism, who had hailed Kennedy as the heir of the Puritan sense of responsibility—recited his poem "For John F. Kennedy, His Inauguration." Because of Kennedy's Irish ancestry, he felt sympathy for nations breaking free from European empires, the greatest of which was the same British Empire that had ruled Ireland. At the same time, his education gave him a sense of an American national mission that descended from Anglo-American Puritans. Kennedy claimed the Puritan John Winthrop, author of the "City on a Hill" speech, as a political ancestor. For three years as an undergraduate he had lived in Winthrop House, eating every day in front of a portrait of John Winthrop.

On economic issues, Kennedy's Roman Catholic heritage made him more open to arguments for collective action in favor of economic justice than most Protestant politicians. Though the Catholic leadership of Kennedy's day was firmly anti-communist, the church had long responded to communism by teaching its own social doctrines that supported state action in favor of the poor. With regard to the conflict with communism, Kennedy tried to stand in the center, between the extreme anti-communism of his father and some in his family, who had inclined toward sympathy with fascism before the war and later toward

McCarthyism, and the liberal wing of the Democratic Party that included Eleanor Roosevelt, Hubert Humphrey, and Adlai Stevenson, all of whom had opposed his nomination for president.

Catholicism also linked Kennedy to a tradition of internationalism. The Roman Catholic Church has affirmed world government and international law ever since its birth in the Roman Empire. In the twentieth century, popes became great supporters of the League of Nations and the United Nations.

Another source of the attempt to unify the world in the inaugural was Kennedy's speechwriter, a thirty-two-year-old lawyer named Theodore Chaikin Sorensen. The son of Christian Sorensen, who served as a Republican attorney general of Nebraska, and Annis Chaikin, a social worker, Sorensen called himself "a Danish Russian Jewish Unitarian." Inheriting a commitment to pacifism from his mother, he registered with his draft board as a conscientious objector when he turned eighteen. On the other hand, the memory of two Republican presidents shaped much of his early life. He was named for Theodore Roosevelt and lived the first twenty-three years of his life in Lincoln, Nebraska, where he often visited a statue of Lincoln near the State House and read the text of the Gettysburg Address that was inscribed there. Sorensen lived in Lincoln through college and law school, then left for Washington and got a job in the office of Senator John F. Kennedy.

There has probably been no relationship between a president and a speechwriter closer than that between Kennedy and Sorensen. After working together on the Pulitzer Prize–winning book *Profiles in Courage* in 1956, the two men traveled together to all fifty states over the next few years, sometimes accompanied by no one else, as Kennedy made the speeches and the connections that would win him the Democratic nomination in 1960. Sorensen came to know Kennedy's voice, his rhythms, and his message extraordinarily well. For the inaugural, Sorensen and Kennedy worked together for months, beginning immediately after the election. They solicited suggestions and drafts from many people, but Kennedy specifically directed Sorensen to study Lincoln's great speeches and to model his work after them. Though critics sometimes charged that Sorensen really wrote the Kennedy inaugural, Sorensen himself always insisted that Kennedy took an active role in the writing at every point of the long process and made all final decisions.

At the end of his pathbreaking article, Robert Bellah used Kennedy's inaugural to raise questions about the future of civil religion. Bellah feared that the mission to spread freedom was blinding Americans to the shortcomings of the governments we supported in Vietnam and elsewhere. He wondered whether, in an age when the consensus belief in God was weakening, Kennedy's use of God in the address could be sustained. On the other hand, it also worried Bellah to think that an open agnostic or atheist might never be able to be elected or to function as president. He quoted Senator J. William Fulbright's famous speech of April 28, 1966, on the danger posed to American ideals not by loss of faith but by "the arrogance of power." Finally, Bellah asked what would happen to American civil religion if the world ever really developed an international government.

If the words of the Kennedy inaugural are taken seriously enough, all of Bellah's questions can be answered by the text. In the address, those new governments "whom we welcome to the ranks of the free" and to whom we offer help are addressed as equals, not bullied or expected to follow our lead in all things. Though God is invoked, an atheist or a non-theistic Buddhist could take comfort from the closing assertion that "here on earth God's work must truly be our own." As with Lincoln, Kennedy's biblical quotation (from Romans 12:12, "rejoicing in hope, patient in tribulation") and his biblical ideas and tone serve a worldview that goes beyond belief in God to present history itself as the revelation of truth. With regard to international government, Kennedy four times affirms the need for one. This inaugural address was entirely devoted to foreign policy, and it called on Americans to believe that the American values of personal freedom, political democracy, world peace, and cultural tolerance could be extended to the world.

Because the Kennedy inaugural began a new era in American foreign policy, it can be difficult to read today without recalling all of the failures and all of the costs of that era. There is some justification for blaming the speech for mistakes made by the United States in Cuba, Vietnam, Iraq, and Afghanistan. Yet it should also be remembered that Kennedy was killed about as early in the era he began as Lincoln was in the era of Reconstruction. Kennedy's inaugural stands as a sacred text that shows how inspiring, profound, and globally inclusive American civil religion can be. Whether the United States ever lives up to the standard it set remains to be seen.

SOURCES

Bellah, Robert, "Civil Religion in America," *Daedalus* 96, no. 1 (Winter 1967), 1–21.
Clarke, Thurston, *Ask Not: The Inauguration of John F. Kennedy and the Speech That Changed America* (New York: Henry Holt and Company, 2004).
Dallek, Robert, *An Unfinished Life: John F. Kennedy, 1917–1963* (Boston: Little, Brown, and Company, 2003).
Sorenson, Theodore, *Kennedy* (New York: Harper & Row, 1965).
Schlesinger, Robert, *White House Ghosts: Presidents and Their Speechwriters* (New York: Simon & Schuster, 2008).
Tofel, Richard J., *Sounding the Trumpet: The Making of John F. Kennedy's Inaugural Address* (Chicago: Ivan R. Dee, 2005).
Weiner, Tim, "Theodore Sorensen, 82, Kennedy Counselor, Dies," *New York Times*, October 31, 2010.

30

King's Speeches: The Mall (1963) and Memphis (1968)

Without holding any political office or fighting in any war, the Reverend Doctor Martin Luther King, Jr., has attained the status of a saint in American civil religion. King has a memorial next to the memorials for Abraham Lincoln, Franklin Roosevelt, and the veterans of Vietnam and Korea on the Mall in Washington, where, on August 28, 1963, King gathered 250,000 people and gave the crucial speech at an event that changed the nation. According to John Lewis, a civil rights leader who also spoke that day, the King speech was "the finest hour in American history." Plans for that march on Washington provoked President Kennedy to propose the Civil Rights Bill that passed in 1964. Dr. King is now the only American who has a federal holiday named for him. He is truly *the* saint of American civil religion. Arguably, he did more than anyone to turn the values of freedom and democracy into realities.

Saints are often people with difficult messages, who have come to be remembered within a soft halo of sentiment, and King is no exception. He is now inseparable from his most famous phrase, "I have a dream." But in 1963, as the nation marked one hundred years since the Emancipation Proclamation, King was not simply a dreamer. He stood at the Lincoln Memorial and reminded the nation of how little progress had been made. "Five score years ago," he began, with a deliberate echo of the Gettysburg Address. Then he continued to argue that in the hundred years after Emancipation, which was the "joyous daybreak to end the long night of their captivity," little or nothing good had happened to the former slaves.

> But one hundred years later, the Negro still is not free. One hundred years later, the life of the Negro is still sadly crippled by the manacles of segregation and the chains of discrimination. One hundred years later, the Negro lives on an island of poverty in the midst of a vast ocean of material prosperity. One hundred years later, the Negro is still

languished in the corners of American society and finds himself an exile in his own land.

King's observation was undeniably true. Legal segregation of restaurants, hotels, beaches, bathrooms, and drinking fountains was enforced across the South, where most African-Americans lived in 1963. Although the Supreme Court had held school segregation unconstitutional in 1954, little had actually changed. Few of the descendants of slaves in the South could vote or serve on juries, let alone hold public office. One Mississippi county had 7,250 black people of voting age but only one black voter, a man who had registered in 1892. In the North, segregation was not maintained by formal laws but by the practices of banks and real estate agents, who kept whites and blacks in separate neighborhoods and therefore in separate schools. The incomes of black men averaged half those of white men.

King then employed the metaphor of a "bad check," one of the themes he had considered for days as the master metaphor in framing the speech.

> And so we've come here today to dramatize a shameful condition. In a sense we've come to our nation's capital to cash a check. When the architects of our republic wrote the magnificent words of the Constitution and the Declaration of Independence, they were signing a promissory note to which every American was to fall heir. This note was a promise that all men—yes, black men as well as white men—would be guaranteed the unalienable rights of life, liberty, and the pursuit of happiness.
>
> It is obvious today that America has defaulted on this promissory note insofar as her citizens of color are concerned. Instead of honoring this sacred obligation, America has given the Negro people a bad check; a check which has come back marked "insufficient funds."

Here King spoke the only line that evoked laughter from the crowd: "But we refuse to believe that the bank of justice is bankrupt." He went on with his prepared text, one he had been rewriting for several days, still making notes and corrections even as the earlier speeches were given. He reminded the audience of "the fierce urgency of now." The rhythms of his language, rolling out through the instrument of his great baritone voice, built to the speech's first climax:

> Now is the time to make real the promises of democracy. Now is the time to rise from the dark and desolate valley of segregation to the sunlit path of racial justice. Now is the time to lift our nation from the quicksands of racial injustice to the solid rock of brotherhood. Now is the time to make justice a reality for all of God's children.

King then warned the nation in general—the rally was being televised nationally and was aimed primarily at Congress and the president—not to hope "that the Negro needed to blow off steam and will now be content." There would be "neither rest nor tranquility in America," Dr. King said, until equal rights became a reality. "Whirlwinds of revolt" would continue to blow until "the bright day of justice emerges."

But for his fellow demonstrators he had another message, a reminder of the nonviolent and even loving character of the civil rights movement. In Birmingham, Alabama, a few months earlier, the movement had won a great victory when demonstrators, many of them children, had allowed themselves to be beaten with clubs, bitten by police dogs, and taken to prison without resistance, all on national television. The crowd on the Mall was dignified and quiet, filled with men wearing jackets and ties and women in dresses, despite the August heat. Many had been marching all over the South, but for many others, perhaps for a majority, it was their first protest. It was also an integrated crowd, by most estimates about 25 percent white.

Both King and the government he was trying to influence were constantly fearful of violence. Tens of thousands of police, National Guard, and regular army troops were ready to act if disorder broke out. President Kennedy was watching on television, and his brother Robert, the attorney general, controlled a switch that was set to cut off power to the speaker's microphone and to play a recording of the spiritual, *He's Got the Whole World in His Hands*, sung by Mahalia Jackson, over the public address system. Standing at the center of this tension, Martin Luther King recommended trust:

> Let us not seek to satisfy our thirst for freedom by drinking from the cup of bitterness and hatred. We must forever conduct our struggle on the high plane of dignity and discipline. We must not allow our creative protest to degenerate into physical violence. Again and again we must rise to the majestic heights of meeting physical force with soul force. The marvelous new militancy which has engulfed the Negro community must not lead us to a distrust of all white people, for many of our white brothers, as evidenced by their presence here today, have come to realize that their destiny is tied up with our destiny and they have come to realize that their freedom is inextricably bound to our freedom. We cannot walk alone.

Now King moved back to building emotional power, with a passage that answered the rhetorical question, "When will you be satisfied?" The answer moved from vivid examples of daily life under segregation to biblical language, the command of God as spoken by the ancient prophet Amos.

We can never be satisfied as long as the Negro is the victim of the unspeakable horrors of police brutality. We can never be satisfied as long as our bodies, heavy with the fatigue of travel, cannot gain lodging in the motels of the highways and the hotels of the cities. We cannot be satisfied as long as the Negro's basic mobility is from a smaller ghetto to a larger one. We can never be satisfied as long as our children are stripped of their selfhood and robbed of their dignity by signs stating "for whites only." We cannot be satisfied as long as a Negro in Mississippi cannot vote and a Negro in New York believes he has nothing for which to vote. No, no, we are not satisfied, and we will not be satisfied until justice rolls down like waters and righteousness like a mighty stream.

Building on the crowd's reaction that greeted this climax, King decided to skip ahead in his text, past several paragraphs centered on work for "strong civil rights legislation in this session of Congress." He came back to the text to urge his hearers, some of whom had come to Washington "fresh from narrow jail cells," to keep up their work with the faith "that unearned suffering is redemptive." According to some witnesses, Mahalia Jackson, who was on the podium, began to urge King to "tell them about the dream," remembering a set piece from some of his speeches that was not in the text. Whether he heard Jackson or not, King's sense of the crowd's emotions led him to add the verbal equivalent of a musical cadenza, a long solo about the dream followed by a variation on a hymn, that made this speech into the event it became. He was using themes that he had used before, but never to such effect.

I say to you today, my friends, so even though we face the difficulties of today and tomorrow, I still have a dream. It is a dream deeply rooted in the American dream.

This phrase "the American dream" had first appeared in print in the work of James Truslow Adams, who wrote in his 1931 book, *Epic of America*, about "a dream of social order in which each man and each woman shall be able to attain to the fullest stature of which they are innately capable." Later, the phrase came to be identified with material success and even specifically with home ownership, but that was not its original meaning. King clearly connected the phrase, as Adams had, with the philosophy of natural rights expressed in the Declaration of Independence.

I have a dream that one day this nation will rise up and live out the true meaning of its creed: We hold these truths to be self-evident, that all men are created equal.

Here was the revolutionary creed, first written by the conflicted slave owner Jefferson and cited as the central American "proposition" by Lincoln at Gettysburg. King was using the most basic sacred text of American civil religion to challenge the actual practices of the United States. In this, he was following the tradition of the Hebrew prophets, who constantly used the terms of the original covenant with God to challenge the practices of Israel and Judah in their days.

> I have a dream that one day on the red hills of Georgia, the sons of former slaves and the sons of former slave-owners will be able to sit down together at the table of brotherhood.
> I have a dream that one day even the state of Mississippi, a state sweltering with the heat of injustice, sweltering with the heat of oppression, will be transformed into an oasis of freedom and justice.
> I have a dream that my four little children will some day live in a nation where they will not be judged by the color of their skin but by the content of their character. I have a dream today!

It is difficult now, half a century after legal segregation by race ended, to appreciate how revolutionary it was in 1963 to suggest that skin color would not be a primary characteristic by which to categorize people. The idea of color-blind human relations was indeed a dream. It would soon be challenged by Black Power separatists and by advocates of Affirmative Action and other forms of identity politics. At the moment when King spoke, there was no Affirmative Action except for such examples as the admission of children of alumni at prestigious colleges. Labor unions sometimes acted "affirmatively" in allowing children of members to join and so blocking access to blacks. For Martin Luther King, the ultimate goal was always integration, and through integration reaching a stage where skin color no longer determined anything.

> I have a dream that one day, down in Alabama, with its vicious racists, with its governor having his lips dripping with the words of interposition and nullification, one day, right there in Alabama, little black boys and black girls will be able to join hands with little white boys and white girls as sisters and brothers. I have a dream today!

Here the hopeful, optimistic tone of the speech was broken by a disturbing image. The governor of Alabama, George Wallace, lately elected on a platform of "segregation forever" and standing in the door of the University of Alabama to prevent integration, was pictured with his "lips dripping" monstrously. But at the next moment came the image of children joining hands. King's voice soared, paradoxically, upward on the word "down," and lovingly caressed the syllables of

"Alabama, with its vicious racists." Then his rhythm accelerated over the "little black boys and black girls" who would "join hands with little white boys and white girls as sisters and brothers." The "I have a dream today!" came as an exclamation point, a rhythmic stop that led naturally to the next paragraph.

> I have a dream that one day every valley shall be exalted and every hill and mountain shall be made low, the rough places will be made plain, and the crooked places will be made straight and the glory of the Lord shall be revealed and all flesh shall see it together. This is our hope. This is the faith that I go back to the South with.

This paraphrase of Isaiah 40:4–5 introduced a millennial note. From this point to the end of the speech, King described a transformation of the very landscape of America by the divine force of freedom. At first, freedom would work through the struggles of civil rights activists, but then it would burst forth and ring from every hill. For two sentences, King returned to his text:

> With this faith we will be able to hew out of the mountain of despair a stone of hope. With this faith we will be able to transform the jangling discords of our nation into a beautiful symphony of brotherhood.

Moving back into improvisation, King built a rhythm while describing the work to come. He then introduced a line from the hymn "America," which he had heard Archibald J. Carey, an African Methodist Episcopal pastor and attorney, use as a refrain in his speech at the 1952 Republican National Convention. Though King himself had used this refrain in other speeches, he had not planned to do so here. The music of the speech was beginning to carry him toward a climax.

> With this faith we will be able to work together, to pray together, to struggle together, to go to jail together, to stand up for freedom together, knowing that we will be free one day. This will be the day—this will be the day—when all of God's children will be able to sing with new meaning: "My country 'tis of thee; sweet land of liberty; of thee I sing; land where my fathers died, land of the pilgrim's pride; from every mountain side, let freedom ring!" And if America is to be a great nation, this must become true.

Now King invoked the land itself. Only rarely has a dimension of geomancy, an animistic attitude toward the land, appeared in American civil religion. Holy places like Gettysburg are not holy because of their natural qualities but because of history. While the Grand Canyon inspires reactions in many visitors that can be called religious, these responses do not attach to the nation but to the canyon itself, and sometimes to God through the sense of confronting a divine power that made the canyon. In the closing paragraphs of his speech, however, King linked the American landscape directly to the holiness of freedom, the first value of American civil religion. He used the mountains to invoke freedom for the whole nation, North and South.

> And so let freedom ring from the prodigious hilltops of New Hampshire. Let freedom ring from the mighty mountains of New York. Let freedom ring from the heightening Alleghenies of Pennsylvania. Let freedom ring from the snow-capped Rockies of Colorado. Let freedom ring from the curvaceous slopes of California.
> But not only that. Let freedom ring from Stone Mountain of Georgia. Let freedom ring from Lookout Mountain of Tennessee. Let freedom ring from every hill and molehill of Mississippi, from every mountainside, let freedom ring.

Still improvising, with an accelerating rhythm and rising volume, King drove to the climax of his last written line, which quoted a spiritual. As he spoke, he raised his right hand as if in benediction, bestowing the blessing of freedom on the crowd. The image was millennial unity, a unification of the nation by a single spirit.

> And when this happens, when we allow freedom to ring, when we let it ring from every village and every hamlet, from every state and every city, we will be able to speed up that day when all of God's children—black men and white men, Jews and Gentiles, Protestants and Catholics—will be able to join hands and sing in the words of the old Negro spiritual, "Free at last, free at last, thank God Almighty, we are free at last."

Watching on television in the White House, President Kennedy turned to an aide and said, "That guy is really good." Watching from a reclining chair in Hot Springs, Arkansas, the seventeen-year-old Bill Clinton "wept like a baby all the way through it." But there were also naysayers. One man, who preferred the NAACP slogan "Freedom now," cried out, "Fuck that dream, Martin! Now, now, goddamit, now." Anne Moody, a CORE worker from Mississippi, recalled "thinking that in Canton we never had time to sleep, much less dream." Under arrest in Louisiana, activist James Farmer watched the speech on television and cried, but later saw King's dream as the "beginning of the end of the civil rights movement" because it did not speak to the poor of the Northern cities. Malcolm X called the whole March on Washington a "Farce on Washington" that served the Kennedy administration.

Even though those who criticized the speech and dismissed the march had their points, there can be no doubt that the "I Have a Dream" speech immediately entered the canon of American civil religion and remained there. It entered the canon not so much as a text but as a performance, replayed on anniversaries and in classrooms. It became the defining act of "Saint" Martin Luther King. *Time* magazine named King its Man of the Year for 1963, and in 1964 he won the Nobel Peace Prize. And the momentum from that speech and that march led, with the additional force provided by President Kennedy's death and President Johnson's legislative skill and courage, to the passage of the Civil Rights Act of 1964 and the Voting Rights Act of 1965, which over time transformed the nation.

King reached sainthood not just because of that speech, however, but also through the more traditional route of martyrdom. His martyrdom began years before he was shot on April 4, 1968. Beginning in 1956, when he was first elected to head the boycott of segregated buses in Montgomery, Alabama, until he was killed, King was jailed twenty times and seriously assaulted four times. During those same years, he traveled more than 6 million miles and gave more than 2,500 speeches. In 1963 alone, King traveled 275,000 miles and gave more than 350 speeches. A Pulitzer Prize–winning book on King's work was titled *Bearing the Cross*. King bore the cross of leadership for a movement that divided not only the nation but also his own people. In 1959, at a book signing in New York, he was stabbed in the chest by a black woman and almost killed, saved only by an emergency operation.

On the night before he was murdered, King gave a speech that is less well-known but theologically more profound than "I Have a Dream." A reflection on history and on King's own life, the Memphis speech (sometimes called by one of its last lines, "I've Been to the Mountaintop") expressed a view of salvation history from within one branch of American civil religion. Though the view of history found here is specific and limited, it is also revelatory, and the ending of the Memphis speech retains permanent power. Speaking of longevity and death, just hours before he was shot, King's voice left behind a mystical affirmation that still rings in the air.

The Memphis speech came about by accident, at a difficult time. In the years since the March on Washington, King had become more marginalized and controversial. Attempting to use the technique of mass demonstrations to promote housing desegregation in the North proved ineffective and frightening to some white liberals. The call for "Black Power" rang out from young leaders like Stokely Carmichael, drowning out King's calls for freedom, justice, and reconciliation. The Black Panthers urged black people to arm themselves; the Nation of Islam called for a separate homeland; the cities of the North burned with riots every summer; and the war in Vietnam grew larger and more deadly, killing as many Americans in two months of 1968 as were killed in the first six years of the Iraq war that started in 2003. When Martin Luther King continued to preach nonviolence and the goal of integration, he lost support from many young black followers. When he decided to oppose the Vietnam war, he lost support from many white moderates and Democrats, including President Lyndon Johnson.

Yet King was still working as hard as ever, campaigning for peace and economic justice and planning a Poor People's March on Washington. When sanitation workers, almost all black, called an illegal strike in Memphis because they were paid so little they were eligible for welfare and yet were denied the right to organize a union, King was asked to help. Insufficiently trained in nonviolence, some of those participating in demonstrations staged a small riot, breaking windows and making national headlines, losing sympathy for their cause and damaging King's reputation. The city obtained an injunction against all demonstrations for ten days, and King decided to defy it. On the evening of April 3, the strikers were holding a meeting to prepare for the next day's action. Ralph Abernathy, King's closest friend and assistant, went to address this meeting and found that the two thousand people who had turned out were disappointed not to see King, who was resting in his motel room. Abernathy called King, and without a prepared address King responded to the demand for yet another speech.

Wind and rain lashed the windows of the Mason Temple (not a Masonic Temple but a large Pentecostal church) where the crowd was gathered. King thanked Abernathy for his long introduction, called him "the best friend I have in the world," and said he was "delighted" to see such a crowd "in spite of a storm warning," by which he meant both the weather and the injunction against the next day's march. Then he launched into a recapitulation of world history, with the intention of showing how important this moment was.

> Something is happening in Memphis; something is happening in our world. And you know, if I were standing at the beginning of time, with the possibility of taking a kind of general and panoramic view of the whole of human history up to now, and the Almighty said to me, "Martin Luther King, which age would you like to live in?" I would take my mental flight by Egypt and I would watch God's children in their magnificent trek from the dark dungeons of Egypt through, or rather across the Red Sea, through the wilderness on toward the Promised Land. And in spite of its magnificence, I wouldn't stop there.
>
> I would move on by Greece and take my mind to Mount Olympus. And I would see Plato, Aristotle, Socrates, Euripides and Aristophanes assembled around the Parthenon. And I would watch them around the

Parthenon as they discussed the great and eternal issues of reality. But I wouldn't stop there.

I would go on, even to the great heyday of the Roman Empire. And I would see developments around there, through various emperors and leaders. But I wouldn't stop there.

I would even come up to the day of the Renaissance, and get a quick picture of all that the Renaissance did for the cultural and aesthetic life of man. But I wouldn't stop there.

I would even go by the way that the man for whom I am named had his habitat. And I would watch Martin Luther as he tacked his ninety-five theses on the door at the church of Wittenberg. But I wouldn't stop there.

I would come on up even to 1863, and watch a vacillating President by the name of Abraham Lincoln finally come to the conclusion that he had to sign the Emancipation Proclamation. But I wouldn't stop there.

I would even come up to the early thirties, and see a man grappling with the problems of the bankruptcy of his nation. And come with an eloquent cry that "We have nothing to fear but fear itself." But I wouldn't stop there.

Strangely enough, I would turn to the Almighty, and say, "If you allow me to live just a few years in the second half of the 20th century, I will be happy."

Here was a vision of breathtaking scope, what amounted to a history of freedom. It was profoundly biblical and Protestant. King cited nothing from medieval or Roman Catholic history and nothing from Islam, though he had been dealing with Catholics and Black Muslims for years. From American civil religion, King claimed Abraham Lincoln and Franklin Roosevelt, but for now he left out the Founding Fathers, perhaps because the American Revolution did not free the slaves. He would return to them later.

Turning to the present, where King and his audience were both mired in a difficult struggle, facing a losing battle against the law and public opinion, Martin Luther King offered a deeply rooted hope. He connected the American drive for civil rights, and American civil religion, to the drive for freedom in the formerly colonized world. King had been to India and learned from people who had worked with Mahatma Gandhi. He connected both the tactic and the ideal of nonviolence to world history. Finally, he linked the situation of the descendants of slaves in America to that of "colored peoples" everywhere, and gave the resolution of their problems an apocalyptic dimension. His vision of hope began with an explanation of why he would ask God to let him live in the twentieth century.

Now that's a strange statement to make, because the world is all messed up. The nation is sick. Trouble is in the land; confusion all around. That's a strange statement. But I know, somehow, that only when it is dark enough can you see the stars. And I see God working in this period of the twentieth century in a way that men, in some strange way, are responding.

Something is happening in our world. The masses of people are rising up. And wherever they are assembled today, whether they are in Johannesburg, South Africa; Nairobi, Kenya; Accra, Ghana; New York City; Atlanta, Georgia; Jackson, Mississippi; or Memphis, Tennessee—the cry is always the same: "We want to be free."

And another reason that I'm happy to live in this period is that we have been forced to a point where we are going to have to grapple with the problems that men have been trying to grapple with through history, but the demands didn't force them to do it. Survival demands that we grapple with them. Men, for years now, have been talking about war and peace. But now, no longer can they just talk about it. It is no longer a choice between violence and nonviolence in this world; it's nonviolence or nonexistence. That is where we are today.

And also in the human rights revolution, if something isn't done, and done in a hurry, to bring the colored peoples of the world out of their long years of poverty, their long years of hurt and neglect, the whole world is doomed. Now, I'm just happy that God has allowed me to live in this period to see what is unfolding. And I'm happy that He's allowed me to be in Memphis.

At this point, King became very specific. He descended from the lofty plane of world history to urge nonviolence and to praise particular ministers. He called for participation in a boycott against Coca Cola, Sealtest milk, and Wonder Bread. He recommended the use of black insurance companies, one particular bank, and local savings and loan associations.

As he stressed the practical, King's poetry slackened, until he regained a higher plane through another "set piece" from earlier speeches. He told the story of how he had nearly been killed in 1959. Andrew Young recalled that King often told this story when he was thinking about death. For more than a decade at this point, death threats had been a continual presence in the life of Martin Luther King. Threats of death from whites were supplanted, however, by King's memory of the time that he was really almost killed, by a black woman. Not every black person thought that the position of blacks in America would be improved by a campaign of civil disobedience. In 1959 some blacks thought, like some whites, that "civil disobedience" was only a mask for criminal behavior; that maintaining civility was more important than standing for a principle; and that change would more readily come through gradual acceptance than through abrupt, perhaps legally forced, integration. King recounted how one woman had expressed her disagreement:

> You know, several years ago, I was in New York City autographing the first book that I had written. And while sitting there autographing books, a demented black woman came up. The only question I heard from her was, "Are you Martin Luther King?" And I was looking down writing, and I said, "Yes." And the next minute I felt something beating on my chest. Before I knew it I had been stabbed by this demented woman. I was rushed to Harlem Hospital. It was a dark Saturday afternoon. And that blade had gone through, and the X-rays revealed that the tip of the blade was on the edge of my aorta, the main artery. And once that's punctured, you're drowned in your own blood—that's the end of you.

Then King told the story of his recovery. It began with how the *New York Times* had reported on the next day that if he had sneezed, he would have died. While recuperating in the hospital, he received many telegrams and letters. Two came from the president and vice president, one from the governor of New York, but the only one he remembered was from a girl in the ninth grade at White Plains High School, who said she wanted to mention that she was a "white girl," and that she was "so happy that you didn't sneeze." King went from here to say that he was also happy that he had not sneezed, because if he had he would have missed what began in 1960, "when students all over the South started sitting-in at lunch counters."

This was a crucial moment in the civil rights movement. Nothing important had happened since the integration of Montgomery's buses in 1957, but now black college students, well-dressed and smiling, began to sit in at legally segregated lunch counters in Southern cities. Viscerally emotional reactions ensued. Waitresses dropped trays and cried. People sat in stony silence, waiting until the offending protesters were handcuffed and taken off to jail. These events began to move the conscience of the nation, and they moved King here to recall his own allegiance to American civil religion.

> And I knew that as they were sitting in, they were really standing up for the best in the American dream, and taking the whole nation back to those great wells of democracy which were dug deep by the Founding Fathers in the Declaration of Independence and the Constitution.

While King could criticize the United States, no one spoke more fervently of American civil religion. Before King became a saint, he was a prophet of civil religion, recalling the American people to their covenant just as the biblical prophets had recalled Israel. As commentator Julius Lester wrote, King believed in America "as if he were one of the signers of the Constitution," and King loved America "as if he had sewn the first flag." By evoking the clean-cut, college-student sit-ins of 1960, King was asserting here in the darkness of 1968 that Lincoln's emancipation was still real, and that the America of the Founding Fathers was really the heir of Israel in the divine history, the biblical history of freedom. America had proven herself by producing these black college students, who were ready to take the nation back to its wells of democracy. The successes of the civil rights movement followed in quick succession.

> If I had sneezed, I wouldn't have been around here in 1961, when we decided to take a ride for freedom and ended segregation in inter-state travel. If I had sneezed, I wouldn't have been around here in 1962, when Negroes in Albany, Georgia, decided to straighten their backs up. And whenever men and women straighten their backs up, they are going somewhere, because a man can't ride your back unless it is bent. If I had sneezed—if I had sneezed I wouldn't have been here in 1963, when the black people of Birmingham, Alabama, aroused the conscience of this nation, and brought into being the Civil Rights Bill. If I had sneezed, I wouldn't have had a chance later that year, in August, to try to tell America about a dream that I had.

But the narrative trailed off at this point, with a lack of years and specifics from 1964 until 1968. These were the years when progress flagged, as the Vietnam War heated up and Black Power and violent separatist ideologies seemed more plausible than nonviolent efforts toward integration. King came back to the present struggle. "If I had sneezed, I wouldn't have been in Memphis to see a community rally around those brothers and sisters who are suffering." Groping a little in his rhythm, King said for the first time that "Now, it doesn't matter, now. It really doesn't matter what happens now." He recounted how on his trip from Atlanta, the airplane had been guarded all night and delayed in its takeoff because, as the pilot explained, "we have Dr. Martin Luther King on the plane," and everything had to be checked very carefully. Then he came into Memphis, where people began to talk about the threats "from some of our sick white brothers." He was aware, but he was not afraid.

> Well, I don't know what will happen now. We've got some difficult days ahead. But it really doesn't matter with me now, because I've been to the mountaintop. And I don't mind. Like anybody, I would like to live a long life. Longevity has its place. But I'm not concerned about that now.

I just want to do God's will. And He's allowed me to go up to the mountain. And I've looked over. And I've seen the Promised Land. I may not get there with you. But I want you to know tonight, that we, as a people, will get to the Promised Land! And I'm so happy, tonight. I'm not worried about anything. I'm not fearing any man! Mine eyes have seen the glory of the coming of the Lord!

Those words, ending with a quotation from "The Battle Hymn of the Republic," were Dr. Martin Luther King's last public statement. A little more than twelve hours later, he was dead, shot on the balcony of his motel room in Memphis at thirty-nine years of age. Lincoln had not expressed such a comprehensive vision until he was fifty-six, when he gave his Second Inaugural Address.

For Martin Luther King, Jr., there was no ultimate distinction between biblical religion and American civil religion. Both belonged to the history of freedom. King's central value was freedom, not simply in the negative sense of freedom from constraints but also in the positive sense of freedom to pursue a community of peace and cultural tolerance. He preached that the history of freedom that began in the Bible would find its consummation in America, when freedom rang from the mountains and transformed the land. Although the enemies of freedom might kill its prophets, heroes, and saints—men like Jesus and Abraham Lincoln—the cause of freedom would finally triumph. Free people working together would create what Jesus called the kingdom of God, what the Constitution called "a more perfect union," and what King called the Promised Land, or sometimes "the beloved community."

This is not to say that King saw no flaws in America. On April 4, 1967, exactly a year before his death, King said that the war in Vietnam was only "a symptom of a far deeper malady within the American spirit." He prophetically warned that the organization he was then addressing, Clergy and Laymen Concerned about Vietnam, would be succeeded by organizations concerned about many other wars in the future. He reminded his audience in New York's Riverside Church that the United States was on the wrong side of a world revolution, not only in Vietnam but in many nations, motivated by "the need to maintain social stability for our investments." Quoting John F. Kennedy, he warned that "[t]hose who make peaceful revolution impossible will make violent revolution inevitable." In order to return to the right side of history, America required "a radical revolution of values." Americans needed to see communism as "a judgment against our failure to make democracy real and follow through on the revolutions we initiated." King was not certain that this would happen, but he still hoped. Despite the strength of what he called "the giant triplets of racism, extreme materialism, and militarism," he believed that America could be transformed by unconditional love.

As the United States went through this transformation, it would bring into being a world of freedom, democracy, peace, and tolerance. King was a saint of American civil religion who cared deeply about the whole world. In his address on Vietnam, he described the doctrine that love is the ultimate reality as a "Hindu-Muslim-Christian-Jewish-Buddhist belief." He saw his own mission, the mission of the Christian church, and the mission of the United States as the redemption of the world.

SOURCES

Abernathy, Ralph David, *And the Walls Came Tumbling Down* (New York: Harper & Row, 1988).
Garrow, David J., *Bearing the Cross: Martin Luther King, Jr., and the Southern Christian Leadership Conference* (New York: William Morrow and Company, 1986).
Hanson, Drew D., *The Dream: Martin Luther King Jr., and the Speech That Inspired a Nation* (New York: HarperCollins, 2003).
Sundquist, Eric J., *King's Dream* (New York: Oxford University Press, 2009).

31

Vietnam Veterans Memorial

Unlike most war memorials, the Vietnam Veterans Memorial does not glorify war. It is also an example of the increasing tendency of American civil religion to create sacred space and to induce reverence without any reference to God. Juxtaposed on the National Mall between the temple of the Lincoln Memorial, where Lincoln himself appears divine and the words carved on the walls refer to God, and the obelisk of the Washington Monument, where sheer verticality points to heaven and the words *Laus Deo* ("Praise God") are carved at the top, the Vietnam Veterans Memorial clings to the earth and remembers the dead. Ancient Romans would recognize the monuments to Lincoln and Washington, but they would not understand the Vietnam memorial.

Despite its unconventional nature, the Vietnam Veterans Memorial connects with three of the basic values of American civil religion. By listing each of the American dead from the Vietnam War, with no distinctions of rank or any other kind between them, the memorial stands for democracy and for cultural tolerance. By omitting any heroic gesture to commemorate war, the memorial makes a strong statement for peace.

Americans react to and use what everyone calls "the Wall" in ways that reveal how a place can be sacred yet contested, and how sacred places can incorporate the profane. Since before the Vietnam Veterans Memorial opened in 1982, the Wall designed by Maya Lin has drawn praise and blame both from Left and Right. Some who supported the memorial protested the design, then came to accept the real monument. Some who continued to protest forced the construction, in 1984, of a memorial featuring statues of soldiers that Maya Lin called a "moustache" defacing her work. Conservative critics have called the Wall a "black gash of shame" a "wailing wall for anti-draft protesters" and a "tribute to Jane Fonda." Radicals have accused the Wall of effacing the reality of war, the crimes of American leaders and soldiers, and the deaths of Vietnamese. Meanwhile, visitors come at the rate of about 4 million a year, sometimes as many as twenty thousand per day. In a practice that began unexpectedly, tens of thousands of these visitors leave items: not just flags and flowers and medals and letters, but beer cans and cigarettes, motorcycles and storm doors, high-heeled shoes and cowboy boots, money in many amounts, playing cards and fishing gear and golf clubs. The Wall is among the most frequently visited memorials in the United States, and certainly among those the one that evoke the most intense emotions in the broadest variety of people.

The Wall came into being through the work of Jan C. Scruggs, a former infantryman wounded and decorated in Vietnam, who was working for the Veterans Administration and dreamed up the idea of a memorial after seeing *The Deer Hunter* (1978), a movie about Vietnam veterans. Recruiting other veterans, Scruggs organized the Vietnam Veterans Memorial Fund, which obtained Congressional passage of a bill setting aside two acres of the National Mall to commemorate the dead from Vietnam. Billionaire H. Ross Perot contributed seed money; an Alexandria, Virginia, radio station raised $256,000 over one weekend; and thousands of veterans contributed in memory of dead friends at the rate of twenty dollars per name. Congress demanded that the design be approved by the secretary of the interior, the National Commission of Fine Arts, and the National Capital Planning Commission; the Fund placed the choice of a design in the hands of eight professional jurors. All proposals were required to be sensitive to the site, reflective and contemplative in character, to include the names of all dead and missing Americans from Vietnam, and to make no statement about the political justification of the war. By March 31, 1981, the deadline for proposals, 1,421 entries had arrived. In an aircraft hangar at Andrews Air Force Base, they were hung from frames that stretched more than a mile. The unanimous selection of the jury, which made their choice without knowing the names of those submitting, was the design of twenty-one-year-old undergraduate Maya Ying Lin, the daughter of immigrants from China who had created her design as part of a course at Yale College.

Though controversy ensued, to a point at which President Ronald Reagan's secretary of the interior, James Watt, would not accept the design unless a more conventional statue was also commissioned, the Wall attracted fervent adherents from the moment that panels began to be brought to the site. People wanted to touch the names, to leave letters and objects, while construction went on. A Navy pilot had a Purple Heart won by his dead brother covered by concrete in the foundation. At the dedication of the Wall on November 13, 1982 (the Saturday after Veterans Day), 15,000 Vietnam veterans held a delayed homecoming parade, while 150,000 watched.

Simplicity, size, and a design that requires interaction account for much of the impact of the Wall. Because the Wall follows a depression in the landscape, visitors do not see it until they come close. The memorial actually consists of two walls, each almost the length of a football field (246 feet), made of seventy panels of polished black granite, which join in a broad "V" of about 125 degrees.

Lin has said that she was trying to suggest a circle. The panels at each end of the Wall are only one foot high, but they gradually rise, while the path that curves along the Wall slopes down, until at the vertex where the walls join the panels stand more than ten feet tall. At each end of the wall is carved a date—1959 at the east, toward the Washington Monument, and 1975 at the west, toward the Lincoln Memorial—marking the beginning and end of American combat deaths in Vietnam. Names of the dead carved into the granite are listed chronologically and alphabetically within a single day; the location of particular names can be found in large alphabetical books. The two tallest panels at the center, each bearing 137 lines with five names each, or a total of 1,370 dead, represent some of the 2,350 who died in the month of May, 1968. From that lowest point, where the names looming overhead seem overwhelming, the path gradually rises toward the West. As they walk or stand before the Wall, visitors see their own reflections, as well as the clouds and the Mall behind them, on the brightly polished granite. The reflection creates depth and induces a sense of inclusion with the dead or of standing at a door between life and death. Lin deliberately made the names touchable, and the taking of rubbings is not only allowed but encouraged by the National Park Service, which provides paper and stepladders on request. The sheer number of names, stretched over almost 500 feet, demands solemnity. A total of 58,272 names were etched on the Wall by 2012, including some listed as missing rather than dead. Space remains in case more casualties are discovered, as they seem to be every year.

The statue of three servicemen that stands 120 feet from the wall, with a flag behind it, is the work of sculptor Frederick Hart, who placed third in the original competition. Though Maya Lin complained that the statue defaced her work, it could also be said that it deserves a place among the thousands of artifacts that bear testimony to the power of the Wall. Hart intended his soldiers to appear stunned by the "ocean" of the Wall that they are facing; they are not heroic, but very young and very realistically portrayed, down to small details of weapons and uniforms. The statue is not elevated but at eye level to visitors; its location means that those who come to the Wall may choose to notice it or not. Even Lin eventually said that the statue contributed to the truth of the memorial, by showing how unresolved the United States remained about the war in Vietnam.

The same sense of uncertainty can be seen in the inscriptions that were added to the wall itself before and after the list of names. The first of these messages, which were not intended by Lin, appears near the date "1959" and announces that the names "are inscribed in the order they were taken from us," while the second, next to the date "1975," says that "Our nation honors the courage, sacrifice and devotion to duty and country of its Vietnam veterans," and that "[t]his memorial was built with private contributions from the American people." The first inscription stresses loss, and the second stresses dedication, willing sacrifice,

Figure 31.1 In 1993, eleven years after the Wall was dedicated and nine years after the installation of Frederick Hart's sculpture of soldiers, this sculpture by Glenna Goodacre honoring Vietnam nurses was unveiled. It attracts mementos as powerfully as the Wall itself. Photograph by William Gardella.

and gift. Considering these inscriptions and the addition of the flag and Hart's statue, it seems that Lin's original concept was too powerful for many people to bear without mediation. The Vietnam Veterans Memorial succeeded so well in expressing loss that it provoked demands for expressions of survival or recovery.

After the statue of male soldiers was erected, pressure began to build for a memorial to women. More than 10,000 women served in Vietnam, but only eight, all military nurses, died and so have their names inscribed on the Wall. In 1993, the Vietnam Women's Memorial Project succeeded in placing a statue by Glenna Goodacre, of three women assisting a wounded male soldier, three hundred feet from the Wall (Figure 31.1). Some visitors leave items near the statue of the nurses, as they do at the Wall itself.

The emotional unease and need to connect that many feel around the Wall is typical of behavior at sites that are called holy. According to Rudolf Otto, one of the first modern scholars to study religion as a phenomenon, the experience that humans call "the holy" is a complex emotional mix that includes awe, fear, fascination, and a sense of personal connection with ethical consequences. Architects of religious sites attempt to evoke holiness in many ways, ranging from darkness and massive scale to realistic portrayals of gods and saints to extreme brightness and stark simplicity. As a piece of design, the Wall evokes the holy in the same manner as chapels built according to the modernist architectural school of Frank Lloyd Wright and others. Hewn like a tombstone from granite, the appropriate material, it makes minimal gestures of meaning, subordinates form to the functional needs of visitors to a memorial, and follows the landscape on which it is built. It does not soften its message by invoking any spiritual inheritance from Greek, Roman, Egyptian, or medieval systems of symbol or belief, but stands uncompromisingly within its own time. The Wall can also be understood as a continuation and culmination of a tendency to produce a sense of holiness by conjuring an enormous number of ghosts, including all names of the dead as individuals, that began with the Union Army cemetery at Gettysburg and continued in many cemeteries and memorials to World War I.

The behavior of Americans at the Wall has included ways of relating to the holy that deny modernist simplicity and individuality. While Protestants since Martin Luther and Jews since biblical times have rejected attempts to speak or transact business with the dead, visitors to the Wall drink beers with their lost comrades, leave letters and pictures, give gifts, and abandon personal items. Such uses of material things to commune with the dead can be seen in the cultures of Latin America and in graveyards of African-Americans in the South, where anthropologists have sometimes failed to recognize graves under the seashells, clocks, dishes, eyeglasses, flashlights, and other objects left by mourners. The non-perishable items left at the Wall are being collected every day, catalogued and stored in an enormous Park Service warehouse in suburban Maryland, where they constitute a record of America's attempt to come to terms with the unresolved questions of Vietnam. From the standpoint of the history of religions, they add a new chapter to the long history of objects connecting the living and the dead that includes Egyptian and Viking funerals and the relics of saints. Some of these items will eventually be displayed in an underground Vietnam Veterans Memorial Visitors' Center near the Wall. That Center, authorized by Congress in 2003, will be another site of controversy over the meaning of Vietnam and has been criticized as another attempt to blunt or to cope with the Wall's stark expression of loss.

The Wall has reached out to shape American culture. Direct effects have included a Moving Wall, a half-scale replica that traveled through the nation in the 1980s and now rests, with items left at it, in a Moving Wall Museum in Santa Fe, New Mexico. The Internet includes a Virtual Wall, which maintains data on each person listed on the Wall in partnership with the Library of Congress, and other websites listing events both in Washington and at Santa Fe.

On Christmas Eve of 1982, less than two months after the Wall was opened, members of organizations dedicated to bringing home prisoners of war and those listed as missing in action began a vigil at the Wall that continues in 2013. On long tables under tents, they sell t-shirts, black POW/MIA flags, and bracelets with names of the missing, among many other things. Though Jan Scruggs, the veteran whose activism founded the memorial, has scorned those who keep the vigil as "Kmart on the Mall" their activism helped to force the investigation that sent Senators John McCain and John Kerry to Vietnam to bring back remains of the dead. Through the "Rambo" movies and other television shows involving prisoners of war in the 1980s, the American soldier in Vietnam was redefined, moving from aggressor to victim. The black POW/MIA flag with the words "You are not forgotten" still flies in front of town halls and post offices all over the United States, decades after the last helicopter lifted off from the American Embassy in Saigon.

Like the Vietnam War itself, the Vietnam Veterans Memorial moved the civil religion of the United States beyond its previous cultural limits. As a non-theistic sacred space, the Wall gave the civil religion new ways to express solidarity, to live with unresolved differences, and to deal with grief. By mourning rather than celebrating war, the Wall demonstrated a religious commitment to peace. As the next chapter shows, the Wall also gave rise to a whole new generation of memorials on the National Mall.

SOURCES

Fish, Lydia, *The Last Firebase: A Guide to the Vietnam Veterans Memorial* (Shippensburg, PA: White Mane Publishing, 1987).

Hixson, Walter L., ed., *Historical Memory and Representations of the Vietnam War* (New York and London: Garland Publishing, 2000).

Haines, Harry W., "Disputing the Wreckage: Ideological Struggle at the Vietnam Veterans Memorial," *Vietnam Generation I* (1989): 141–156.

Hass, Kristin Ann, *Carried to the Wall: American Memory and the Vietnam Veterans Memorial* (Berkeley: University of California Press, 1998).

Parsons, Gerald, *Perspectives on Civil Religion* (Aldershot, UK: The Open University, 2002).

Savage, Kirk, *Monument Wars: Washington, D.C., the National Mall, and the Transformation of the Memorial Landscape* (Berkeley: University of California Press, 2009).

Wagner-Pacifici, Robin, and Barry Schwartz, "The Vietnam Veterans Memorial: Commemorating a Difficult Past," *American Journal of Sociology* 97 (1991), 376–420.

32

Transforming the National Mall

In American civil religion, the National Mall (Figure 32.1) is the most sacred space. It has functioned as a theater of democracy, where people gather to protest and to celebrate. Sacred space gives people a sense of connection with something unchanging, and the Mall has done this even as it has been transformed, from a commons with slave pens and markets into a forested park, then into a classical space, and now into a setting that enshrines the American values of freedom, democracy, peace, and tolerance. Since 1900, and especially since 1982, monuments and activities on the Mall have developed in distinctly more democratic and multicultural directions. Conflict continues over decisions about which monuments to include, about how they should be designed, and about how the Mall should be both secured from attack and used for free expression.

The original Mall is the swath of grass, as broad as fifteen of the adjoining streets, lined by art galleries and museums, that stretches 1.2 miles from the steps of the Capitol to the Washington Monument. Since the early 1900s, the Mall has continued for almost another mile to the Lincoln Memorial. That newer space, which is sometimes called West Potomac Park, includes the reflecting pool and sites like the World War II Memorial, the Vietnam Veterans Memorial, and the Korean War Veterans Memorial, with the memorials to Thomas Jefferson, Martin Luther King, and Franklin Roosevelt at its margins.

The story of the Mall began with Pierre Charles L'Enfant, the Franco-American designer who laid out plans for the capital city. In L'Enfant's plan, the Capitol building stood at the center of a network of streets, with a north-south grid and diagonal avenues. The Mall ran from the Capitol straight to the west, forming the base of a right triangle. The monument that L'Enfant planned for George Washington (not completed until 1888) was to stand at the right angle where the baseline of the Mall connected with another broad park that ran north to the White House, with Pennsylvania Avenue as the diagonal side of the triangle. For L'Enfant, the Mall was an American version of the Champs Élysées, the central avenue of Paris. But while the Champs Élysées has become known primarily for shopping and dining, with an occasional military parade or national celebration,

Figure 32.1 From the Capitol to the Washington Monument, the original length of the Mall, is 1.2 miles, and the extension to the Lincoln Memorial, in the background here, brings the length of the Mall to 2.2 miles. Since 2004, the National Museum of the American Indian has filled the lot to the left of the Capitol. National Park Service.

the Mall turned into something more governmental and less commercial, less gorgeous and more populist.

There were many years before the Civil War when slave pens stood on the Mall, to the shock and disgust of European visitors. After the slaves were freed, there were many slovenly years when cattle grazed near the unfinished Washington Monument and the city's railroad station stood on the mall. In the middle of the nineteenth century, a landscape architect named Andrew Jackson Downing planted seven gardens and many trees on the Mall, to make a series of nature parks that influenced the design of Central Park in New York City. The original building of the Smithsonian Institution, a corporation charged with the diffusion of knowledge, was begun in 1847, and the Washington Monument in 1848, but for decades the Smithsonian remained an isolated brick castle and the monument a short, broken chimney of marble. When Jacob Coxey's "army" of the unemployed marched on Washington in 1894, they held their demonstration on Pennsylvania Avenue, not the Mall.

A turning point came in 1901, when Senator James McMillan of Michigan, then chair of the Senate Committee on the District of Columbia, led the committee to create a Senate Park Commission. The Commission brought in Daniel H. Burnham, the designer of the White City of the 1893 Columbian Exposition in Chicago, to redesign the Mall. Intending to finally give the Mall the grandeur that L'Enfant had envisioned, the Commission cleared away Downing's gardens and trees, moved the railroad yards to their present position in Union Station (a building that Burnham designed), and extended the Mall seven-tenths of a mile to the west, where the Lincoln Memorial was eventually built. During this process, some bemoaned the wholesale destruction of trees. Scholar Kirk Savage has described the result of the Commission's work as the transformation of the Mall from a specific place with its own character into a neutral space that would serve as a setting for buildings, monuments, and ideological statements.

Demanding only neoclassical buildings, with none approaching the height of the Capitol or the Washington Monument, the Commission strongly influenced the design of all construction around the Mall, Capitol Hill, and the Federal Triangle north of the Mall until the 1970s. As discussed in Chapter 22 on the Lincoln Memorial, despite protests against the dominance of classical architecture, the plan and the standards of the Commission prevailed. Buildings like the headquarters of the Department of Agriculture (1908), the National Museum of Natural History (1911), the Freer Gallery of Art (1923), and the National Gallery of Art (1941) framed the mall in rows of marble columns and mammoth facades.

Even within a classical framework, however, democratic changes began. The memorial for Ulysses S. Grant, virtually the only known statue by Henry Merwin Shrady (1871–1922), did place the general in a classical setting, on a horse atop a tall pedestal facing outward from the western steps of the Capitol, but departed from heroic conventions in several ways. Grant looks worn, with his hat pulled low on his head and his coat wrapped as though against a storm. Common soldiers are honored in bronze reliefs and sculptural groups on each side of the general. In one group, men and horses struggle to pull a cannon through the mud, while in the other, cavalry horses and riders charge with visible strain. One man is dying, falling forward with his horse.

In the same year (1922) that the Grant Memorial was dedicated, the Lincoln Memorial was opened to the public. It is also classical, but not entirely so. Though Lincoln's building was modeled on a Temple of Zeus, and his chair has Roman fasces, a symbol of executive power, on both arms, the expression on Lincoln's face is pensive and burdened, rather than commanding or triumphant. Sculptor Gutzon Borglum, who carved a more heroic Lincoln in a bust for the Capitol Rotunda and later on Mount Rushmore, complained that the sculptor of the memorial, Daniel Chester French, had made Lincoln look like a Sunday School teacher. Nevertheless, the reaction to this memorial has been so reverential that it could be called the greatest temple of American civil religion.

The first monument for a Democratic president to be erected on the Mall, the Thomas Jefferson Memorial, also provoked the first democratic protests against a monument. Seeking to preserve the cherry trees on the site, which the city of Tokyo, Japan, had given to Washington in 1912, female protesters chained themselves to 171 trees. President Franklin Roosevelt, who was the moving force for building a memorial to Jefferson, waited the protestors out, then went ahead with construction. Roosevelt also had trees removed from the shore of the Tidal Basin, just south of the Washington Monument, so that he could see Jefferson's 19-foot statue from the South Lawn of the White House. That view remains unobstructed today. Dedicated on the two hundredth anniversary of Jefferson's birth, April 13, 1943, this replica of the Roman Pantheon was the last classically designed memorial on the Mall. It was also the last new memorial of any kind until 1982, when the Vietnam Veterans Memorial began three decades of rapid memorial construction.

During the mid-twentieth century, the character of the Mall still hung in the balance. In 1917, a set of "temporary" structures were erected between the site of the Lincoln Memorial and the Washington Monument, to accommodate military and civilian staff needed for World War I. These wooden buildings were not removed until 1971, on the orders of President Nixon. Nixon had plans made for a three-story parking garage under the Mall, and for a Ferris wheel and a carousel on the surface, but these plans were not fulfilled. In the 1960s, a new director of the Smithsonian Institution, S. Dillon Ripley, called the Mall "Forest Lawn on the Potomac," comparing it to a California cemetery famous for its monuments to the dead, and sought to enliven the space by initiating the Smithsonian Folklife Festivals in 1967. Every summer since then, the Mall has filled with tents and activities celebrating various cultures for two weeks. At first, the programs featured individual state exhibitions, but they have also involved Native Americans from the beginning, and recent festivals have included national exhibits from Korea, France, India, Tibet, Senegal, and Haiti. Each festival showcases three or four different cultures.

Meanwhile, the center of gravity for political demonstrations had definitely shifted from Pennsylvania Avenue to the Mall. The Mall was the site of the historic gathering for civil rights in 1963, when Dr. Martin Luther King, Jr., gave his "I Have a Dream" speech, in front of the Lincoln Memorial. There were precedents for that use of the Lincoln Memorial, by singer Marian Anderson in 1939 and by King and others in 1957. After King was assassinated in 1968, a few thousand representatives of the Poor People's Campaign came to the Mall and camped out near the Lincoln Memorial for more than a month. The first Earth Day, on April 22, 1970, included a rally at the Washington Monument. In 1971, Vietnam Veterans Against the War brought half a million protesters to the Mall for five days of demonstrations.

In the realm of architecture, the authority of the McMillan Plan came under attack. One leader of this attack was sociologist Daniel Patrick Moynihan, who was serving as assistant to the secretary of labor in 1962, when that department, in cooperation with others, produced a memo called "Report to the President by the Ad Hoc Committee on Federal Office Space." The report recommended a "building spree," and attempted to insure that new buildings did not copy neoclassical style. Instead, new federal buildings should reflect the "finest contemporary" norms of architecture. President Kennedy accepted the report. In 1994, the General Services Administration produced a video, *Architecture & Democracy*, that extolled the results, but not all observers have been thrilled. On the Mall, the departure from classicism resulted in buildings such as the Behring Center for the National Museum of American History (1964), the Hirschorn Museum and Sculpture Garden (1974), and the National Air and Space Museum (1976). The American Institute of Architects (AIA) Guide to Washington calls the Behring Center a "giant closet" with an "infamous warren" of rooms in its interior. The Guide also recalls that the Hirschorn Museum has been called a "glorified bunker." Others have criticized all three of these buildings for combining classical proportions and shapes with modernist austerity, sacrificing the strengths of both styles.

The new buildings did contribute to the trend toward democratization of the Mall's sacred space. While the National Air and Space Museum was not intended to be a sacred site like the Lincoln Memorial, it draws 9 million visitors each year, which makes it the most popular museum in the world. All of those 9 million leave the displays of aircraft and space capsules to enter a space where they can turn right and see the Capitol dome or left and see the Washington Monument. They have been drawn into the monumental core of American civil religion. As for the National Museum of American History, though it has been described as a trivial place that displays props from television shows, old typewriters, and light bulbs, it also exhibits what is left of Old Glory, the three-story flag that flew over Fort McHenry and inspired "The Star-Spangled Banner." There are certainly visitors who respond to the gowns of First Ladies and the cardigan sweater worn by Mr. Rogers as objects that are sacred in some sense, like the relics of saints. Scholars such as Catherine Albanese may be correct to classify such relics as belonging to a cultural religion, but here the relics of culture are brought into civil religion by their location on the Mall.

During the 1980s and 1990s, popular appropriation of the Mall accelerated. Vietnam veterans marched on the Mall to their new memorial in 1982, and other groups lobbied for and obtained monuments. Popular actions on the Mall included displays of the AIDS quilt, a community art project in which thousands of panels, each measuring 6 by 3 feet, were made to represent people who died in the epidemic caused by the human immunodeficiency virus (HIV). The AIDS quilt was displayed on the Mall in 1987, 1988, 1989, 1992, and 1996. In the 1996 display, the quilt arrived in ten train cars and was unfolded by a thousand people. It covered the entire space between the Capitol and the Washington Monument grounds, in effect absorbing the original Mall into itself. A spokesman for the Names Project, the group that created the quilt, said that the Mall was one of the few spaces in urban America that could still accommodate the quilt. It was also arguably the most meaningful place where the quilt could be displayed. In July 2012, an updated version of the AIDS quilt returned to the Mall for the Folklife Festival and remained for weeks afterward.

In 1995, the famed March on Washington of 1963 was surpassed in numbers, if not in influence, by the Million Man March, an event organized by Minister Louis Farrakhan of the Nation of Islam. Estimates of the crowd drawn to the Mall varied widely, but even the lowest estimate of 400,000 exceeded the 250,000 who had heard Dr. King's 1963 speech in person. The messages of the march, that black men should register to vote, work hard at their jobs, invest in black businesses, avoid drugs and violence, care for their families, and let God into their lives, combined values of American civil religion with those of Christianity and Islam. Almost exactly two years after the Million Man March, in October 1997, about a million white evangelicals who called themselves Promise Keepers gathered on the Mall. They echoed the Million Man March in their commitment to family and morality, though with more emphasis on organized religion. This rally showed what one modern scholar has observed, that the aim of marching on Washington has changed from affecting government policy to affirming personal belief.

On January 20, 2009, when President Obama was inaugurated, the Mall played its greatest role to date as a setting for the rituals of political democracy. For the first time in history, the entire length of the Mall, including West Potomac Park, was filled by a crowd (estimated at 1.5 million people). The celebration had begun two nights before, with a concert by many artists before 400,000 at the Lincoln Memorial. In contrast, the 2005 inauguration of President George W. Bush drew about 100,000. Crowds at the 2001 Bush inaugural had been held down by rain and cold weather.

The crowds for both Obama and Bush gathered on the Mall among many memorials that did not exist when the last great throng, the 1.2 million who turned out for President Lyndon Johnson in 1965, appeared at a presidential inauguration. They also passed through, and were sometimes stopped and frustrated by, security measures unknown on the Mall in the past. A paradoxical situation in which increasing participation and a flourishing of democratic symbols collide with restrictions on access and increasing regimentation of experience, both in the name of security and in the interests of promulgating certain messages, has become characteristic of the memorials built on the Mall since the 1980s.

This began with the Vietnam Veterans Memorial, which was a response to democratic demand. In the midst of the struggle to express and to control the meaning of Vietnam, veterans of Korea and of World War II began to ask why their wars were forgotten. Congress granted land on the southeast side of Lincoln, across the Mall from the Vietnam Memorial, to a group of Korean veterans, on condition that the veterans raise the money for their memorial. The Korean War Veterans Memorial was completed and dedicated in 1995, designed by a group from Pennsylvania State University who won a competition but withdrew before construction because of disagreements. Continuing the new tradition of realistic, non-heroic statues, the memorial consists primarily of nineteen slightly larger than life bronze soldiers, walking as though on patrol over difficult terrain. Across a walkway from this bronze platoon is a black granite wall etched with more than 2,500 images of faces and pictures from Korea. Stone markers at ground level list the numbers of the dead, not only American but also allied and Korean. Though the AIA Guide expresses an architect's opinion that this memorial "inadvertently trivializes the subject matter," it seems effective for most who visit. Few do, because the Korean War has always lived in obscurity.

In the years between the building of memorials for the wars in Vietnam and Korea, a less American subject attained a memorial on the Mall. The United States Holocaust Memorial Museum broke new ground in the civil religion when it opened in 1993. It was designed to be a sacred site, on the block next to the Washington Monument grounds, yet it did not commemorate something American. Many questioned the appropriateness of building a Holocaust Museum in Washington, which at the time lacked a memorial to Native Americans and still lacks a memorial to African-American slavery. One commentator compared the creation of a Holocaust memorial in Washington to establishing a memorial museum about American slavery in Berlin.

Despite these arguments, the United States Holocaust Memorial Museum gained its place on the Mall. It was paid for by privately raised funds, but the project was initiated by the Carter administration in 1978, at a moment when President Carter was under attack for his approach to relations between Arabs and Jews in the Middle East. The government donated the site, a disused set of buildings that had been occupied by the Department of Agriculture.

The design competition passed over modernist and classical proposals to settle on a very inward-turning concept by architect James Inigo Freed, a Jew who was born in Germany in 1930 and who rode streetcars all night with his father to escape violence on *Kristallnacht* in 1938. Within Freed's design there was space on three stories for narrating the Holocaust and two three-story spaces for a Hall of Remembrance, where visitors enter, and a Hall of Witness, where they go after experiencing the exhibits. Controversy broke out over the lack of windows in the two Halls, where the walls included spaces shaped like windows that were bricked up or reduced to small slits. This was an important choice on a site where full windows could have revealed fairly close views of the Washington

Monument and the Jefferson Memorial and distant views of the Capitol and the Lincoln Memorial. According to one member of the commission supervising the museum, Diane Wolf, Freed was wrong in "blocking those symbols of America." But the architect insisted that he did not want museum visitors to have a clear look at the icons of American democracy. Inside the museum, he wanted people to experience "a world of shifted values unlike anything they have ever perceived." Still, he left the possibility that the monuments on the Mall could be partially glimpsed from the stairs on some levels of the main exhibit, "because those are the things that save you." He also replaced the brick that closed the windows with limestone, so that some of his original use of brick to evoke ghetto walls and barracks at Auschwitz was sacrificed in the interest of harmonizing with the rest of the Mall.

Inside the museum, there are few compromises. Speakers blare with the sounds of Hitler's speeches and of Nazi boots on parade; pictures of the slaughtered inhabitants of a village line a chimney for two stories. Visitors walk through a cattle car that was used to bring Jews from the Warsaw Ghetto to the gas chambers at Treblinka. To protect children, some of the worst videos of medical experiments and of Lithuanians beating Jews to death with clubs are projected inside four-foot enclosures and are viewed by looking down. A room filled with shoes of those killed at Majdanek fills the nostrils with the smell of old leather. To help visitors identify with the experience, they are given passports that tell the story of one person who lived through those times, detailing where that person was at each stage of the exhibit and how he or she survived or died. The intention throughout is to remove visitors from American space, from the space of the Mall outside, then lead them back through the Hall of Witness into a state of mind altered by what they have seen and heard and smelled and touched. Explicitly named as both a memorial and a museum, the site combines these very different functions. It aims to provoke religious experience, through confrontation with absolute evil and then with good and with responsibility, and also to educate by providing facts.

The United States Holocaust Memorial Museum is well integrated with American civil religion. The entrance features a quotation from George Washington's letter to the Jewish congregation at Newport, Rhode Island, assuring those Jews that the government of the United States "gives to bigotry no sanction, to persecution no assistance," along with words from the Declaration of Independence affirming the "unalienable rights" of humanity. Inside the Hall of Remembrance, quotes from presidents Carter, Reagan, and George H. W. Bush appear on the walls. The first image of the Holocaust that visitors encounter in the main exhibit is a picture, taken by American soldiers, of the bodies of Holocaust victims, accompanied by words from General Eisenhower about the discovery of the camps. According to columnist George Will, it belonged in the capital of the United States because "no other nation has broader, greater responsibilities in the world," and no other nation had more need of "an antidote to our innocence." Raul Hilberg, an Austrian-born Jew who became the leading American historian of the Holocaust and a member of the commission appointed by President Carter, said that the memorial museum "rewrites the ground rules about what Americans should be concerned about" and brings the Holocaust into "the fabric of our national memory." There is no doubt that the United States Holocaust Memorial Museum both introduces an international presence to the Mall and expands the scope of American civil religion to include the world.

More recently dedicated sacred sites on the Mall, such as the Franklin Delano Roosevelt Memorial (1997), the World War II Memorial (2004), and the National Museum of the American Indian (2004), have continued this trend toward bringing the world to Washington. Each of these memorials appeared during the decades when the United States began to regard itself as the sole custodian of world order. In different ways, they made some of the major themes in the American view of what world order should be into sacred memories, ideas embodied at sacred sites.

This trend toward making American ideas into elements of a global civil religion, enshrined on the Mall in Washington, is nowhere more evident than at the Franklin Delano Roosevelt Memorial (Figure 32.2), which ranges across 7.5 acres along the shore of the Tidal Basin, between the Korean War Veterans Memorial and the Jefferson Memorial. For example, one of the many granite walls of this complex of outdoor rooms displays, in all capitals, one beneath the other, FDR's "Four Freedoms": "FREEDOM OF SPEECH / FREEDOM OF WORSHIP / FREEDOM FROM WANT / FREEDOM FROM FEAR." In his 1941 State of the Union address, Roosevelt said that he sought to secure each of these freedoms "everywhere in the world." The culminating image of Roosevelt in the memorial is a larger-than-life statue of him seated in a chair, gazing upward. Behind him (and Fala, his terrier) are the words, "THEY (WHO) SEEK TO ESTABLISH SYSTEMS OF GOVERNMENT BASED ON THE REGIMENTATION OF ALL HUMAN BEINGS BY A HANDFUL OF INDIVIDUAL RULERS...CALL THIS A NEW ORDER. IT IS NOT NEW AND IT IS NOT ORDER." Again, American ideals are extended to the world.

First authorized by Congress in 1955, the Roosevelt Memorial was forty-two years in the making. Roosevelt had actually discussed a memorial during his third term, as he was fighting to have the memorial for Jefferson built, and said that he would be happy with a slab of stone no larger than his desk, with the words "In Memory of Franklin Delano Roosevelt," just off the Mall in front of the National Archives building. Such a stone was dedicated on the twentieth anniversary of his death through the efforts of some surviving associates of FDR.

Figure 32.2 The breadline statues in the Franklin Delano Roosevelt Memorial, by sculptor George Segal, fulfilled the guidelines given by the memorial's designer, Lawrence Halprin, who forbade any abstract or expressionist sculpture. Photograph by William Gardella.

But the nation was not satisfied, and the commission that Congress appointed hired several designers to produce something larger, worthy of a space between Lincoln and Jefferson. Two modernist attempts were submitted but rejected, in part by Roosevelt's surviving family. The second failed attempt was by the renowned designer Marcel Breuer. It was Breuer's student Lawrence Halprin, an old socialist, World War II veteran, and landscape architect, who finally succeeded in getting approval for a design in 1976—twenty-one years before the memorial finally opened.

Though Halprin's design was not classical, it was not modernist or abstract either. He planned four rooms without ceilings, defined by granite walls and waterfalls, representing the four terms of Roosevelt's presidency. To populate these rooms he hired several sculptors to make bronze statues and reliefs, drawing from a store of photographs and newsreel images from the Roosevelt presidency. Halprin forbade the sculptors to create anything abstract. One of the most striking sculptural groups, by George Segal, was a line of life-sized men in a breadline. Another sculpture showed a single man sitting on a kitchen chair, head and body bent next to a large radio, presumably listening to one of FDR's "fireside chats." As Halprin said, he wanted to make "a tribute not only to one man, but to the people of the United States who went through this. It is a memorial to democracy."

A low point in the history of the project came in 1979, when the Department of the Interior withdrew its support for the monument. Interior Secretary Cecil Andrus cited the projected cost of $50 million and suggested a grove of trees instead. In response, Halprin eliminated 500 feet of granite walls, an interpretive center, and several fountains from his original plan, cutting the cost in half. Still the project languished without funds until Florida congressman Claude Pepper, who had known Roosevelt and who chaired the memorial commission, left the bed where he lay dying of cancer to make a final appearance in the House of Representatives to plead for the memorial. When President George H. W. Bush visited him in the hospital a few days later, Pepper pressed his point again, and the money was finally appropriated, with a groundbreaking ceremony in 1991 and construction beginning in 1994.

Two major sources of controversy dogged the memorial, even after it was completed. First was the treatment of Eleanor Roosevelt, who was the most prominent First Lady of all time. Eleanor Roosevelt wrote a regular newspaper column, visited coal miners and African-American communities, and generally served as the eyes, ears, and conscience of the American government during her husband's presidency. After his death, she became the first US Ambassador to the United Nations and an architect of the UN Declaration of Universal Human Rights. Yet, this was Franklin Roosevelt's memorial, and how to deal with Eleanor was a serious question. It was resolved with a life-sized statue in her own niche, apart from any representation of FDR, with the seal of the United Nations behind her and the words "THE STRUCTURE OF WORLD PEACE CANNOT BE THE WORK OF ONE MAN, OR ONE PARTY, OR ONE NATION…IT MUST BE A PEACE THAT RESTS ON THE COOPERATIVE EFFORT OF THE WHOLE WORLD" inscribed on the granite beside her. The fact that these words came from one of his speeches, rather than from one of her many writings or speeches, has troubled some critics, and so has what they see as her marginalization in the memorial. On the other hand, many find her presence inspiring and the UN emblem behind her fitting. In the gift shop, pictures of the Eleanor statue outsell all other items. Whatever the critical verdict on the Roosevelt memorial's treatment of Eleanor, it cannot be doubted that the way she is presented strengthens the position of world peace as a central value of American civil religion.

A more vehement and more famous controversy sprang up because none of the statues or reliefs in the original memorial showed FDR in a wheelchair or on crutches, despite the fact that he was stricken by polio in 1921 and was unable to walk throughout his presidency. Using thick leg braces, strong aides who would hold him by the arms, an order to the press not to reveal his condition in a photograph or otherwise, and wearing long cloaks to cover his wheelchair, Roosevelt concealed the extent of his disability from the American public. But when the memorial was built in the 1990s, Americans who could not walk were demanding equal rights, and for many those rights included equal representation in history. President Clinton urged Congress to authorize another statue, the National Organization on Disability raised another $1.5 million, and a statue of Roosevelt clearly in a wheelchair was added to the forecourt of the memorial. Though this disturbed some critics, who complained of historical revisionism or political correctness, the process showed what high values American civil religion places on democracy and cultural tolerance. The realistic statue represented the inclusiveness that is an aspect of multiculturalism.

When the Roosevelt Memorial opened in 1997, it included the only references to World War II on the National Mall, with a few exceptions such as some warplanes in the Air and Space Museum or the soldiers in the Holocaust Memorial Museum. In the Roosevelt Museum, the mention of war was not only indirect but negative. The third room, representing Roosevelt's third term, had scattered blocks of granite suggesting rubble carved with the words, "I hate war." Some commentators complained that the memorial's emphasis on this quote distorted the record of the vigorous war leader Roosevelt. At any rate, neither this nor the warplanes in Air and Space nor the depictions of the US Army in the Holocaust Memorial Museum could be considered an adequate acknowledgment of the American military effort in World War II.

The long neglect of memorials for World War II grew out of bitter history. After World War I, once regarded as the war that would end all wars, many local and specialized monuments were quickly built in Washington and in cities and towns across the nation. A classical dome still stands on the Mall, near the FDR Memorial, commemorating those from the District of Columbia who served in World War I. A magnificent Nike, or angel of victory, cast by Daniel Chester French, soars on a 65-foot pillar in front of the Old Executive Office Building, near the White House, in honor of the Army's First Division from World War I. But soon after these monuments appeared, it became clear that the promise of an end to war would not be fulfilled. Pacifism, dreams of disarmament, and the League of Nations yielded to fascism and the Great Depression, and the World War that provoked those earlier monuments began to seem futile. That verdict of futility seemed to be confirmed when the United States became engaged in another and greater World War.

In the years after World War II, the Cold War between the United States and its allies and the Soviet Union and the communist bloc began almost immediately. The Korean War broke out only five years after World War II ended. Both sides began to test nuclear weapons as statements of strength, and in America the moment of triumph yielded to an age of anxiety. All over the Soviet and Eastern

European world, heroic monuments to the victory of World War II proliferated, both because the threat of fascist victory had so nearly been realized and survival itself had been a triumph, and also because the Soviet government wanted to inspire resistance to the new Western threat. In the United States, there was much less sense than in the Soviet Union that this was a time to celebrate anything at all. After China went communist, in 1948, and what Churchill called the "iron curtain" divided East from West in Europe, there was a broad consensus that the victory in World War II had yielded only the "hard and bitter peace" and the "long twilight struggle" that the decorated World War II veteran John F. Kennedy spoke of in his 1960 Inaugural Address. The building of memorials for World War II seemed increasingly irrelevant.

The experience of Vietnam and the Veterans Memorial changed that. By 1982, when the Vietnam Veterans Memorial was dedicated, it was clear that World War II had set world politics into a pattern that remained stable for decades. In February 1987, a veteran of the Battle of the Bulge named Roger Durbin challenged his Congressional representative, Marcy Kaptur, with the question, "How come there's no memorial to World War II in Washington?" Representative Kaptur referred him to the Iwo Jima statue. Durbin replied that the Iwo Jima statue was not a World War II but a Marine Corps memorial, and Kaptur later discovered that he was correct. Before 1987 ended, Kaptur submitted a bill for a World War II memorial, and the bill passed and was signed into law in 1993.

Once again, the primary impetus and support for a war memorial came from veterans, not from government. Out of almost $200 million raised for the memorial, only $16 million came from the federal government. Large donations were made by the American Legion and the Veterans of Foreign Wars. Individuals such as Tom Hanks, the star of *Saving Private Ryan* (1998), a film about D-Day, Senator Bob Dole, a highly decorated and seriously wounded World War II veteran, and Frederick W. Smith, CEO of the Federal Express Corporation and a former Marine officer, led fund-raising campaigns.

A site on the Rainbow Pool, a somewhat neglected fountain between the Reflecting Pool in front of the Lincoln Memorial and the grounds of the Washington Monument, was chosen in 1995 by a committee that combined the American Battle Monuments Commission and a special group, the Memorial Advisory Board, appointed for this purpose by President Clinton. After a competition limited to experienced architects, a design by Friedrich St. Florian was chosen in 1997. Born in Austria in 1932, St. Florian came to the United States in 1961 and became a citizen in 1973.

St. Florian's concept provoked fierce criticism that delayed the completion of the memorial and changed its design. His original design included a museum and projected a memorial with a much higher profile than the one that was dedicated in 2004 (Figure 32.3). Organized under the title of the National Coalition

Figure 32.3 The overall design of the World War II Memorial is organized by the two theaters of the war and by states. Critics have called the design, by Austrian-born architect Friedrich St. Florian, overly classical and even fascistic. Groups of veterans are often photographed next to the pillars for their states. National Park Service.

to Save Our Mall, opponents succeeded in lowering the entire site, so that the view between the Lincoln Memorial and the Washington Monument remained unobstructed, and in eliminating the museum. Even after the changes, the bitterest critics continued to suggest that the memorial reminded them of the Nuremberg stadium built for Nazi rallies by Albert Speer. In the 2006 guide of the American Institute of Architects, the memorial is criticized for its "stiff classicism" and "lack of compelling gestures," and the guide concludes that the overall impression "is not so much fascist as it is merely generic." Kirk Savage has written that the changes forced on St. Florian preserved sightlines on the Mall, but also eliminated some aspects of the original design, such as tall but broken columns and imposing berms around the pool, that expressed the cost of war, leaving only triumphal elements intact. Among positive critics, Judith DiMaio predicted that "future generations" would absorb the memorial into "their Washington experience," and that it would be "greatly loved."

The memorial features fifty-six columns, one for each state and territory of the United States, decorated with bronze wreaths and linked by bronze ropes, with two domed entrances or *baldochinos* marking the Atlantic and Pacific theaters of war (Figure 32.4). To represent the details of the struggle, twenty-four bas-reliefs based on wartime photographs (twelve for the Atlantic and twelve for the Pacific) were created by sculptor Ray Kaskey and installed on two walls.

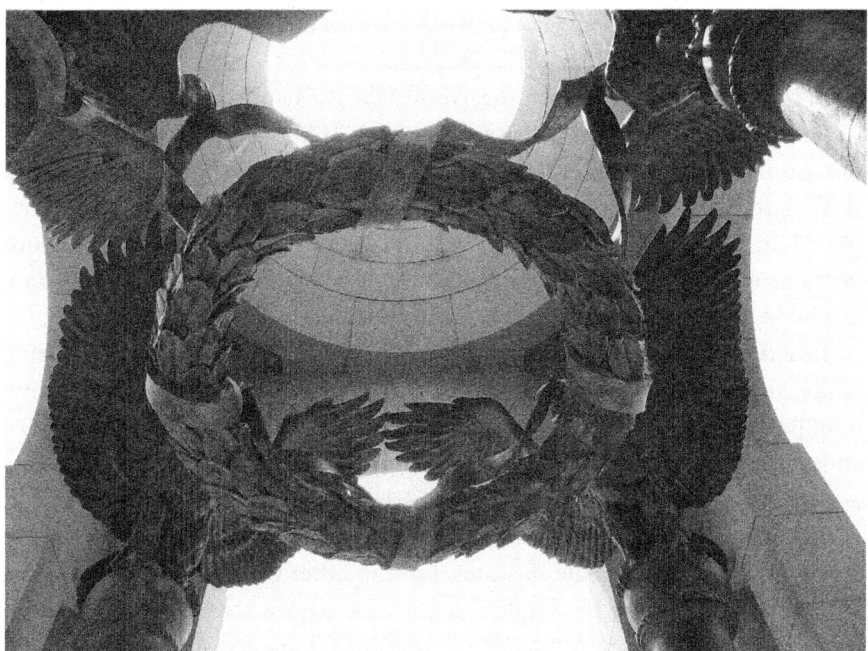

Figure 32.4 Eagles and wreaths decorate the insides of the *baldochinos* of the World War II Memorial. Photograph by William Gardella.

A field of 400 gold stars, under the inscription "HERE WE MARK THE PRICE OF FREEDOM," stands for the 400,000 American military dead, recalling the gold stars that once appeared on the homes of families who had lost sons (and sometimes daughters) during the war. Some have speculated that the bronze bas-reliefs and the field of gold stars will come to mean more, as specific reminders of the war, as time goes on.

There can be no doubt that the World War II Memorial has already become a place that evokes feelings of reverence and extends those feelings to sites around the world. The severity of the granite and the wreaths, suggesting funerals, enforce solemnity. There are also ten quotations, from sources such as President Roosevelt, Generals Eisenhower and MacArthur, and President Truman, engraved in capitals on the granite walls. One in particular, from General (and later Secretary of State) George C. Marshall, directly expresses hope that the American flag would be recognized in the whole world: "WE ARE DETERMINED THAT BEFORE THE SUN SETS ON THIS TERRIBLE STRUGGLE OUR FLAG WILL BE RECOGNIZED THROUGHOUT THE WORLD AS A SYMBOL OF FREEDOM ON THE ONE HAND AND OF OVERWHELMING FORCE ON THE OTHER." During the war years, filmmaker Frank Capra projected these words across the screen, in front of an

American flag, at the opening of each of a series of films that he made for the US government under the title of *Why We Fight*.

In the same year, 2004, that the World War II Memorial was dedicated, the National Museum of the American Indian (NMAI) opened in a prime location on the original Mall, just southwest of the Capitol. Where the World War II Memorial offered granite and bronze and stern declarations, the NMAI presented orange sandstone walls that softly curved over flowing water. The moods of these two new sacred places could not be more different, but both have extended American civil religion to realms beyond the United States.

Like the United States Holocaust Memorial Museum, the National Museum of the American Indian serves both as a memorial and as an educational institution. Both places also represent a gesture of reparation for genocide. The NMAI adds to these functions those of an art museum and a cultural center, coordinating and publicizing contemporary Native American events and programs beyond its walls. Critics of the new museum often focus on a lack of cohesion that may arise inevitably from its disparate missions. On the other hand, the inchoate nature of the NMAI must also be counted among its strengths. A visitor can stand one block from the west front of the Capitol, where the dome, the steps, and the Grant Memorial appear at their most imposing, and walk half a block into a place that aspires to contain all of Indian Country, today and yesterday and tomorrow, in North and South America. The first peoples of both Americas have finally found a place of their own on the most central ground of American civil religion.

The roots of this new institution go back to an American magnate, George Gustav Heye (pronounced "High"), who lived from 1874 to 1957. The son of a German immigrant who struck it rich in oil, Heye graduated from Columbia University as an electrical engineer and went to work on a railroad construction job in Arizona, where he admired and purchased a Navajo deerskin shirt. Early in the twentieth century, he made his own fortune as an investment banker and began to collect Native American objects in vast quantities. Through the 1920s and even into the Depression years, Heye financed archaeological digs, not only in the West but in Guatemala and Ecuador, bought entire private collections, and traveled to Europe to buy objects and collections that had crossed the Atlantic in colonial times. He collected with no regard to artistic merit or rarity, seeking even the most ordinary of objects in an effort to document the lives of cultures that he, like most Americans of his day, was convinced were disappearing. In 1922, Heye opened some of his collection to the public as the Heye Foundation Museum of the American Indian, at 155th Street and Broadway in Manhattan, with a larger collection available to professionals at a research center in the Bronx.

When Heye died in 1957, the Museum had already entered into a period of decline that would eventually require it to redefine itself. It was located in a poor neighborhood, unconnected with any academic institution, and increasingly subject to cultural pressures for the restoration of items deemed sacred by Native Americans. Heye himself had restored a medicine bundle to the Hidatsa of North Dakota, in an attempt to end a drought, in 1938, and received membership in the Hidatsa nation in return, though it later appeared that he had kept back some of the most unique contents of the bundle. In 1989, the board of the Heye Foundation agreed with the Smithsonian Institution to use its collection to establish a National Museum of the American Indian, with one center in New York, one in the District of Columbia, and a facility for storage and research in Maryland. Within the Smithsonian, the National American Museum of the American Indian became a semi-autonomous body with its own governing board reporting to the Smithsonian trustees. A 1989 Congressional statute mandated that this board have twenty-three original members, at least seven of whom were Native American, with the minimum number of Native Americans increasing to twelve (or a majority) as the initial terms of board members expired.

Under these auspices, the NMAI evolved quickly into a center of living Native American culture. A Canadian architect named Doug Cardinal, with a heritage from Blackfoot, Mohawk, and Ojibwa as well as European ancestors, was hired to design the Washington building. Although Cardinal later resigned over disagreements with the board, his attempt to create an Indian space is generally believed (even by the museum's harshest critics) to have succeeded. He worked from a document called *The Way of the People*, based on interviews in more than fifteen locations from Alaska to Albuquerque to Philadelphia. Interior highlights of the building include an enormous central "Potomac," from the same Algonquian word for meeting place that has attached to the Potomac River. An exhibit on "Our Universes" takes up one floor with illustrations of cosmologies and rituals for the year from eight different nations, while another floor on "Our Lives" presents up-to-date histories of eight others. Changing exhibits in the art gallery feature Native American artists. Even the cafeteria forms an integral part of the museum, offering dishes from each of five different regions of the Americas.

At the opening of the museum, critics in the press (particularly the *Washington Post* and the *New York Times*) expressed disappointment. They liked the building, but found the displays chaotic, lamented the lack of historical narrative, and called the presence of two gift shops and the relatively expensive café overly commercial. Defenders of the museum have noted that the people who have contributed to its creation have not wanted to practice anthropology or history, but to celebrate their cultures. The museum's defenders have also pointed out that the quality of goods in the gift shops and food in the café exceeds that in any other site on the Mall, so that the gift shops and café function as legitimate parts of the museum. There is no doubt that the National Museum of the American Indian is a great popular success, that the crowds in it are visibly more diverse in ethnic origin than those elsewhere on the Mall, and that it has added a new element of recognition for Native Americans to the value of cultural tolerance in American civil religion.

The power and frequency of controversies over the future of the National Mall is one of the best illustrations of how vigorous American civil religion has become during the late twentieth and early twenty-first centuries. The last twenty years have seen two new projects—the Martin Luther King Jr. National Memorial and the National Museum of African American History and Culture—struggle toward completion. The memorial and the museum have given new energy to continuing questions, such as who decides what goes onto the Mall; how much more can be located there before the Mall becomes too crowded to be solemn, or to be useful for public gatherings; and how much security should influence the design of spaces that aim to be both sacred and public.

A movement for a King memorial on the Mall began with George H. Sealey, Jr., a retired Army major and member of the Alpha Phi Alpha fraternity, an organization of African-American professionals. It took two years before Alpha Phi Alpha endorsed the project, and another twelve before Congress passed a law allowing a location on the Mall. In December 1999, the National Capital Planning Commission approved a four-acre site next to the Franklin Roosevelt Memorial, forming part of a line of memorials extending southeast from the Lincoln Memorial through the Korean War Veterans Memorial and on to the memorials to King, Roosevelt, and Jefferson. After a design competition, in September 2000 a proposal by the ROMA group of San Francisco was approved. The design features a massive granite entrance, a rough stone split in the center so that visitors can walk through, called the "Rock of Despair." Within the semicircular space of the memorial itself, walls display fourteen quotations from Dr. King, selected from his speeches and writings by a "council of historians" that included John Hope Franklin, Henry Louis Gates, Cornel West, and Maya Angelou. At the center of the space formed by the walls and the shore of the Tidal Basin, visitors come to a "Stone of Hope," another massive (30 feet high) piece of granite, from one side of which emerges a likeness of Dr. King, standing with his arms folded in a posture based on a photograph taken by Bob Fitch in King's Atlanta office in 1966. The statue was designed by Lei Yixin, a Chinese sculptor who has made massive images of Mao Zedong.

Controversy over this memorial has focused on the statue (Figure 32.5). For some, it has looked too confrontational and grim, while others have called it an example of the heroic style of socialist realism. Still others have said that Lei Yixin has made King look Chinese, or objected that a statue of Martin Luther King on the National Mall should not have been made in China. In response to requests by the executive architect for the memorial, Ed Jackson, Jr., and the United States Commission on Fine Arts, the sculptor smoothed out the furrows

Figure 32.5 The Martin Luther King Memorial faces the memorial for Thomas Jefferson and stands within sight of the Washington Monument. The Lincoln Memorial is a few hundred yards behind King's statue, though that view is obscured by trees. Photograph by the author.

in King's brow, gave his mouth a slightly softer look, and removed a pen that King had been holding in his left hand, the result of Lei's being sent a reversed image of the Fitch photograph. Though Jackson agreed with those seeking change, he supported the power of Lei's concept, saying that the statue "will take your breath away."

By the fall of 2009, the costs of the proposed memorial had almost doubled since its approval by Congress, but fund-raising had kept pace, with all but $10 million of the $120 million cost covered by private funds. In an unusual expense, the King family had been paid $800,000 for the use of King's words and image. All approvals had been obtained except for a building permit from the National Park Service.

But here arose a concern typical of the new condition of the Mall: security. In response to the National Park Service's fear of terror attacks on monuments, architect Jackson included sixteen bollards, heavy posts designed to stop vehicles laden with explosives, on the two pathways leading to the memorial entrance. The US Commission on Fine Arts and the National Capital Planning Commission both rejected the bollards, saying that the restrictive atmosphere created by these barriers would contradict King's messages of freedom and hope.

In part through direct intervention by two members of President Obama's cabinet, Secretary of the Interior Ken Salazar (who oversees the Park Service) and Secretary of Education Arne Duncan, the security plan was eventually relaxed so that the memorial could be entered from three sides.

When the King Memorial finally opened, in the late summer of 2011, it was greeted with serious criticism. Writing in the *New York Times*, Edward Rothstein said that the statue turned "the minister into a warrior or a ruler," as if the sculptor had been trying too hard to match the others on the Mall. Five months after the opening, Secretary Salazar announced that the words on one side of the statue, which condensed a passage from one of King's speeches and distorted its meaning, would be corrected, despite the difficulties of changing words that are literally carved in stone. Those words were erased in 2013. Meanwhile, visitors to the site seemed very impressed.

The power of the King Memorial arises partly from the site, which critics usually do not mention. The King statue faces the Jefferson Memorial, and visitors have a clear view of that building across the water of the Tidal Basin. There is beauty, irony, and direct power in this position of the descendent of slaves, facing the monument to the man who wrote that all were created equal and yet held more than two hundred slaves. Over the King statue's left shoulder looms the white obelisk of the Washington Monument, seeming much closer than it is because of its height and the low site of the King Memorial. Though the Lincoln Memorial is not visible from the King site, Park Service guides remind visitors that Lincoln sits just to the northwest through some trees. The setting could not be more fitting, and the simplicity of the monument uses the setting to its full advantage. A small waterfall at the entrance dampens any sound from outside, turning the area around the statue into an island of peace. Though King's expression is stern, it is a real expression, and the sternness avoids sentimentality. It may remind visitors that in his life, King was a man who had enough courage to make the powerful feel insecure.

Throughout the Mall, the Park Service has in recent years made security a higher and higher priority. The Visitors' Centers at the Capitol and the White House have become substitutes for visiting the buildings themselves, except for those who have made special appointments through elected officials. There are proposals to establish an underground approach for visitors to the Washington Monument and to dig a Vietnam Veterans Memorial Visitors' Center into the earth just northwest of Maya Lin's Wall, in part to create space for historic displays but also to screen visitors. The closing of parking lots near the Jefferson Memorial and the Washington Monument have left visitors facing longer walks, and metal detectors and the closing of many streets to vehicles have clogged both pedestrian and vehicular traffic. According to a former Park Service official, John Parsons, the ideal would be to eliminate private vehicles on streets around the

Mall altogether. "Nobody drives through Disneyland," Parsons said. "They're not allowed. And we've got the better theme park." In some Park Service visions of the future, which can be seen in maps on the agency's website, Mall visitors would not simply wander onto the Mall, even on foot, but enter at specific points and go from attraction to attraction on Tourmobile buses. Presumably, demonstrations and rallies could still take place, but the participants would be carefully screened.

Against this vision of control, the National Coalition to Save Our Mall, a group organized to fight the creation of the World War II Memorial in 1997, has proposed an expansion of the Mall to the southeast and across the Potomac. The guiding spirit of that group, American University professor Judy Scott Feldman, has supported expansion in the expectation that pressure to create new monuments for new interest groups, other heroes, and future wars will increase. Similar demands are expected by the National Capital Planning Commission, which has issued the (probably alarmist) estimate that if recent trends continue, fifty new memorials will be added to the Mall by the middle of the twenty-first century. Though Congress passed a law declaring the Mall "a substantially completed work of civic art" in 2003, and declaring a moratorium on further construction, that law included an exception for the Vietnam Veterans Memorial Visitors' Center, and Congress has ignored its own moratorium by authorizing other buildings. Feldman's group would like Mall expansion to be planned by a new version of the McMillan Commission.

Dangers of chaos and overcrowding loom alongside those of restricted access and regimentation, yet for now a delicate balance persists. On a day with bad weather or overcrowding, the Mall can feel both messy and restrictive, and some aspects of its museums and monuments can seem both trivial and ponderous or pretentious. More often, however, the recent additions to the Mall do succeed both in evoking the sacred and in presenting the new emphases of American civil religion.

Perhaps the best example is the National Museum of African American History and Culture, supported by former President George W. Bush, authorized by Congress in 2003, and scheduled for completion in 2015 on a site across the road from the Washington Monument and next to the United States Holocaust Memorial Museum. On the Smithsonian website, an animation shows the plans for the museum growing from the inside out to four stories, with the top three clad in bronze porous enough to let in natural light. Designed by David Adjaye, an English architect born in Tanzania, this building will offer a dramatic contrast with the Holocaust Memorial Museum's limitation of sightlines to other monuments. Here special windows called "lenses" will focus on and frame the White House, the Lincoln Memorial, the Capitol, the National Archives building, the Jefferson Memorial, and the Washington Monument to bring them into the building. The open interior, several stories high, will be lined with exhibits of African-American history. A replica slave ship will hang in the middle of the space. Along with the Martin Luther King Memorial, this museum should help to integrate the journeys from Africa and up from slavery into American sacred history, adding to the multiculturalism of civil religion.

In contrast to the smooth progress on an African-American Museum, a planned Eisenhower Memorial, on a four-acre site just behind the National Air and Space Museum with a direct sightline to the Capitol, has run into serious disagreements. Designed by Frank Gehry, the most famous living architect, the projected memorial is an outdoor space involving ten round stone columns, each eighty feet tall, holding tapestries of stainless steel that evoke the landscape of President Dwight Eisenhower's Kansas home. There would also be statues, standing on piles of stone blocks, representing Eisenhower as a general and as president and as a young man surveying the scene. Though the Memorial site was approved in 2005, opposition from the Eisenhower family to Gehry's design (not unlike the opposition of Franklin Roosevelt's family to the design of Marcel Breuer) has led to delay, and the project spent 2013 in limbo, awaiting further action by both the National Capitol Planning Commission and the US Commission on Fine Arts.

In 1902, when the McMillan Commission unveiled its plan to expand the Mall on landfill into the Potomac, people objected to the enormous cost of that project. Some said that the Mall was complete and should not be enlarged. Charles Moore, who served as Senator McMillan's secretary and editor of the Commission report, replied that the Mall could never be finished because if it were, "the nation itself would be finished, destined only for stagnation and decay." The recent history of the Mall has made Moore's words seem prophetic.

SOURCES

Barber, Lucy G., *Marching on Washington: The Forging of an American Political Tradition* (Berkeley: University of California Press, 2002).

Buckley, Christopher, *Washington Schlepped Here: Walking in the Nation's Capital* (New York: Crown Publishers, 2003).

Campbell, Robert, "Pressing Pause, for Cause, on the Eisenhower Memorial," *Boston Globe*, October 13, 2012.

Chidester, David, and Edward T. Linenthal, eds., *American Sacred Space* (Bloomington: Indiana University Press, 1995).

Dillon, David, *The Franklin Delano Roosevelt Memorial Designed by Lawrence Halprin* (Washington, DC: Spacemaker Press, 1998).

Ferguson, Andrew, "The Mess on the Mall," *The Weekly Standard* 10, no. 45 (August 22, 2005).

Glazer, Nathan, and Cynthia R. Field, eds., *The National Mall: Rethinking the Nation's Monumental Core* (Baltimore, MD: Johns Hopkins Press, 2008).

Lonetree, Amy, and Amanda J. Cobb, eds., *The National Museum of the American Indian: Critical Conversations* (Lincoln: University of Nebraska Press, 2008).

Moeller, G. Martin, *American Institute of Architects Guide to the Architecture of Washington, D.C.* (4th ed., Baltimore, MD: Johns Hopkins University Press, 2006).

Rothstein, Edward, "A Mirror of Greatness, Blurred," *New York Times*, August 25, 2011.

Savage, Kirk, *Monument Wars: Washington, D.C., the National Mall, and the Transformation of the Memorial Landscape* (Berkeley: University of California Press, 2009).

33

Ground Zero, Martyrdom, and Empire

When the terrorist group known as al-Qaeda, or "The Base," attacked the United States on September 11, 2001, the attack not only killed thousands of Americans but also threatened the values of American civil religion. The value of personal freedom was confronted by a government claiming rights to unlimited surveillance and indefinite detention. Political democracy was challenged by the American need to find allies among despotic governments. While avowing that it still pursued world peace, the United States claimed a right to wage preemptive war to defeat the terrorists. Cultural tolerance sometimes yielded to a general suspicion of Arabs, or Muslims, or anyone from the Middle East, South Asia, or Africa.

And yet, in another sense, the event called "9/11" and the reactions it provoked were not new. Freedom, democracy, peace, and tolerance could still be asserted as antidotes to the poison of the terrorists. A very aggressive response could be justified by the need to create a sphere of order in which these values could flourish. This pattern of attack and response had occurred before.

Four incidents of martyrdom had already become part of American history as the United States expanded. First came the Alamo in 1836; then Custer's Last Stand in 1876; next the sinking of the battleship *Maine* in 1898; and then Pearl Harbor in 1941. Each of these events created a sacred place and marked a step in the emergence of an imperial version of American civil religion. The September 11 attacks began another step.

Remembering the Alamo, Americans took Mexico City in 1848 and then seized vast areas of the Southwest and California. Remembering Custer, Americans forgot the Fort Laramie Treaty of 1868 and took the northern Great Plains, including the Black Hills, from the Sioux. Remembering the *Maine*, Americans took Cuba, Puerto Rico, Hawaii, Guam, and the Philippines from Spain. Remembering Pearl Harbor, Americans took partial military control of Asia and Europe. Remembering 9/11, Americans removed governments and occupied territory in Iraq and Afghanistan. As of 2013, the United States still had 33,000 troops in Japan and 28,000 in Korea and ships on patrol in the Atlantic and Pacific, as well as about 50,000 troops in Germany, 90,000 in Afghanistan, and large fleets in the Mediterranean and in the Persian Gulf. In each case, an attack on Americans had been seen as justification for a massive response that ended with the United States increasing its sphere of military control.

These events also added an American corollary to traditional "just war" theory. Ever since Augustine, the first Christian theorist of just war, who lived in the Roman Empire, most Christians have believed that war may be justified to defend the innocent against an aggressor. The history of American civil religion has added the justification of preventing any repetition of the attack by a response large enough to entirely change the situation. The United States has acquired its empire under a theory of self-defense and of consent by client nations. In the new imperial context, the values of personal freedom and political democracy have continued, though of course with some alterations, while the values of world peace and cultural tolerance have grown much more important.

Though the concept of a democratic empire is somewhat self-contradictory, commemorations of the Alamo, the Custer battlefield, the *Maine*, Pearl Harbor, and 9/11 each added to the democratic character of American civil religion. Before the Alamo, American war heroes had an aristocratic aura. George Washington, the first venerated ancestor of American civil religion, was revered for his calm and detachment, his integrity and judgment. But the heroes of the Alamo—189 men who died after resisting a force of 4,000 for thirteen days, led by the famed frontiersman Davy Crockett, the dashing and somewhat disreputable Jim Bowie, and the young Colonel Travis—belonged to an age of passion, emotion, and showmanship. Similarly, George Armstrong Custer had been last in his class at West Point but proved a courageous and colorful leader in the Civil War. Custer was the "boy general" who held off J.E.B. Stuart's cavalry at Gettysburg, and a man who cultivated celebrity with his long blond hair and buckskin uniforms. At the site of Custer's Last Stand are 249 marble markers for soldiers of all ranks. Such a democracy of the dead is even more pronounced in the cases of the *Maine* and Pearl Harbor. The 165 (out of 266) sailors killed in the *Maine* explosion who were brought to Arlington National Cemetery lie buried together, facing a mast from their ship. At Pearl Harbor, many of the 1,117 sailors who died on the battleship *Arizona* have been left together in the wreckage, with a monument over the place, where they are regarded as equal martyrs to the cause of freedom. The 9/11 sites—at Ground Zero in New York, at the Pentagon in Washington, and at Shanksville, Pennsylvania—included egalitarian lists of all the dead. As one negative result of the increasingly democratic conditions of war, the 9/11 monuments listed many more civilian than military martyrs.

In each case of martyrdom, the political effects began immediately, but the creation of a shrine took years or decades. The Alamo, Little Bighorn (or as the Indians call it, Greasy Grass), the *Maine* memorials in Cuba and at Arlington Cemetery, and Pearl Harbor have all come to resolution. Issues surrounding the memorials for 9/11, particularly at Ground Zero in New York City, have not been completely resolved, although much progress has been made.

"Remember the Alamo!" was the battle cry of General Sam Houston at the Battle of San Jacinto just weeks after the Alamo defenders died, and General Santa Anna conceded Texan independence immediately following San Jacinto. At the fiftieth anniversary of the Alamo's fall, however, in 1886, the Alamo site was a neglected ruin that witnessed no ceremonies, and by 1900 it was dominated by a commercial warehouse. The Daughters of the Republic of Texas, a private group of women claiming descent from those who lived in Texas before 1836, fought for decades to restore and to preserve the site. They did not succeed in clearing away the warehouse and restoring the two surviving buildings from the battle, the chapel and a barracks, until the 1930s. Elaborate ceremonies marked the centennial of the Alamo in 1936, and a 60-foot cenotaph was erected in 1939. Only during the 1950s, after Walt Disney's new television show featured a three-part series on the life of Davy Crockett that caused a national sensation, did the Alamo become a truly national shrine. In recent times, it has drawn between 2 and 3 million visitors a year, from all over the nation and the world, as opposed to the hundreds of thousands it drew, mostly from Texas, in the years before Disney.

Multiculturalism has lately transformed the content of commemorations at the Alamo. At first, the trend expressed itself in hostility to the old tale of white heroism. On March 3, 1968, the *New York Times* editorialized that "gallant men died needlessly in that old mission" and that the war they began "reflects little credit on the United States." Throughout the 1980s, culminating in Jeff Long's *Duel of Eagles* in 1991, scholars from the new school of Western history cast the Alamo defenders as partisans of slavery and profit-seeking invaders. Meanwhile, Mexicans and Mexican-Americans demanded recognition of their roles fighting on both sides in the battle of 1836. By 1994, the dust was settling, and the Daughters of the Republic of Texas began to run "Bravo at the Alamo," a celebration of folk cultures of all kinds. Beginning in the late 1990s, the March 6th anniversary has opened with prayers in English and Spanish and featured re-enactors wearing Mexican uniforms as well as the garb of the American West, with a script that recognizes "two great peoples" who met and gave their lives in a heroic struggle that made the Alamo "sacred ground."

At the site of Custer's Last Stand, the change has been even more dramatic. News of the death of Custer with all of his command led the nation of 1876 to act immediately against all Indians of the Plains who had not yet moved to reservations. Disregarding a treaty that gave the Lakota the Black Hills and enough land to hunt what buffalo were left, the United States used its army to clear the whole area for white settlement. In 1890, this Indian war reached its anti-climax with the slaughter of Ghost Dancers by Custer's old regiment, the Seventh Cavalry, at Wounded Knee. Marble markers had by then already appeared on the hill near the Little Bighorn River where Custer and his troops had died, but the history of the shrine was only beginning.

Gradually, starting with the friendship between Buffalo Bill Cody and Tatanka Iyotanka (Sitting Bull), one of the Lakota leaders who had defeated Custer, it began to be recognized that Indians were Americans. They gained the right to vote by an act of Congress in 1924. Civil rights movements of the 1960s and 1970s led to further laws, such as the Indian Civil Rights Act (1968) and the American Indian Religious Freedom Act (1978), and to organizations promoting cultural awareness among Native Americans. One such organization, the American Indian Movement (AIM), occupied the town of Wounded Knee for seventy-one days in 1973, provoking a battle with the US government that ended with one FBI agent, one US Marshal, and two Indians dead. Throughout the 1970s and 1980s, members of AIM and other Native Americans pressured the National Park Service to change the story that it told about Custer and the Lakota. By 1990, the centennial of the Wounded Knee massacre brought new attention to the historical sites around the Black Hills, including the Custer site, which Indians called Greasy Grass. In 1991, President George H. W. Bush signed legislation changing the name of the site from the Custer Battlefield National Monument to the Little Bighorn Battlefield National Monument, and National Park Service guides began to include the standpoints of Indians in their account of the battle. Under the leadership of the first Native American director of the site, red granite monuments for fallen Indians appeared among the cavalry's white marble stones. An artistic memorial for the Indians who fought at Greasy Grass was dedicated in 2003. That memorial was designed by a committee of Native Americans and featured a circle of stones with pictographs and ghostly black wire outlines of three Indian warriors and a woman, based on the drawings of Cheyenne warrior White Bird, who fought in the battle.

The least resolved site of imperial civil religion is in Cuba. When the battleship *Maine* entered Havana harbor in January 1898, it was on a mission of diplomatic influence or intimidation. Cuban revolutionaries were fighting for independence from Spain, and the Spanish government was formulating plans to grant autonomy, but conservative elements in the Spanish military were resisting. By showing the American flag, President McKinley hoped to support the rebels and to pressure the Spanish. But twenty days after the *Maine* arrived, on the night of February 15, an explosion tore the ship in two, sinking it and killing 265 American sailors. Investigations in March concluded that there were two explosions, first from an external mine and then from the powder magazine of the ship itself. The call to "Remember the *Maine*" went out across headlines in the American press, and by April the United States was at war with Spain. Three months later, what Theodore Roosevelt called a "splendid little war" was won, and the United States had become a power in the Caribbean and the Pacific.

Shrines appeared both in Cuba and Washington. Arlington National Cemetery was then in the midst of its expansion from a site for Union dead from the Civil War to its current national status. By 1899, coffins containing 163 of the sailors who died on the *Maine* were interred together at Arlington. A design competition for a memorial was held in 1912, and by 1915 a site including one of the masts from the ship was built. The *Maine* memorial was one of the first large shrines at Arlington. Meanwhile, in Havana, a 40-foot granite monument, with two columns supporting an eagle and two of the biggest guns from the *Maine* at the base, was dedicated in 1925 and rebuilt after a hurricane in 1928. The Castro revolution of 1959 resulted in the removal of the eagle, but the granite towers, the guns, and the plaque listing the dead remain. The other lasting result of the *Maine* being destroyed in Cuba is the American base at Guantanamo Bay.

The Spanish War made America a Pacific power, and that contributed to tension between the United States and Japan. As noted in Chapter 3 on Jamestown, some feared war with Japan in 1907 when President Theodore Roosevelt sent a Great White Fleet including sixteen battleships from the Norfolk naval base on a cruise around the world, partly to show that we intended to keep Hawaii and the Philippines. But war did not come then, and relations between the two nations sometimes went smoothly. When Roosevelt sent the Great White Fleet, he had already won the Nobel Peace Prize for brokering a treaty that ended the war between Russia and Japan in 1905. In 1914, a Japanese professor presented the Alamo with a stone monument inscribed with a poem. The gift was inspired by the professor's perception of a resemblance between the willingness of the Alamo's defenders to fight until death and the traditional values of Japanese warrior heroes. Such friendly gestures grew more difficult as the United States reacted against immigration and responded to world events in the aftermath of World War I and the communist revolution in Russia. The restriction of immigration to the United States in 1924, when Congress established national quotas and placed an absolute prohibition on all Asian immigrants, led some in Japan to predict an eventual war. As Japan took on the role of the defender of Asia against Western imperialism, tension increased. Japan had already colonized Korea in 1910. A critical point was reached after the Japanese invasion of Manchuria in 1931 and American embargoes of raw materials going to Japan in 1940 and 1941.

On December 7, 1941, the day that President Franklin Roosevelt told Congress would "live in infamy," Japanese airplanes and ships attacked the American Pacific Fleet at Pearl Harbor, killing 2,403 Americans. The Japanese attack also sank or severely damaged eight battleships and thirteen other ships, while destroying or damaging more than 300 airplanes. Fortunately for the United States, the two aircraft carriers stationed at Pearl Harbor were both at sea when the attack came, and the Japanese did little damage to the repair facilities of the naval base.

As in the cases of the Alamo, Little Bighorn, and the *Maine*, the American military response to Pearl Harbor was quick and overwhelming. On the day of the attack, bandleader Sammy Kaye wrote a song with the lines, "Let's remember Pearl Harbor, as we did the Alamo," that was released eight days later and became an immediate hit. Most of the nation had been against becoming involved in war with Japan and its allies in Germany and Italy, but the attack united Americans in favor of war. Just seven months later, at the Battle of Midway between June 4 and June 7, 1942, four of the Japanese aircraft carriers that had attacked Pearl Harbor were sunk by American airplanes. By August 1945, Japan surrendered unconditionally, and in 1947 the United States imposed a "peace constitution" on Japan that sought to guarantee individual liberty and political democracy—the most basic values of American civil religion—while committing Japan to maintaining no armed forces and to renouncing its government's right to wage war.

Years passed before Pearl Harbor had a monument to mark what had happened there. The USS *Arizona*, a battleship that has never been raised or repaired, and in which the bodies of 1,177 crewmen (almost half of the total who died in the attack) still remain, provided the base for this memorial. In 1950, the admiral commanding Pearl Harbor ordered a flagpole set up over the sunken ship. A memorial was approved by Congress and President Eisenhower in 1958 and completed in 1962. At first, architect Alfred Preis (a native of Austria who was imprisoned by the United States on Sand Island during the war) wanted a building with underwater portholes to allow visitors to see the ship clearly, but the Navy found this distasteful and insisted on its original concept, a bridge-like structure that would soar over the ship without touching it. The *Arizona* is still visible through the water below the memorial building, and drops of oil still rise to the surface from the wreck every day. More than a million people come to the site every year, dropping flowers and leis into the water and reading the names of the dead inscribed in the marble of the memorial building's walls. More than seventy years have now passed since the *Arizona* sank under Japanese torpedoes and bombs, and few survive who recall that day, but the beauty of the memorial, the setting in the harbor, the presence of the dead, and the lasting effects of the event make it likely that the site will continue to draw pilgrims. Many comment on the large numbers of Japanese who come to Pearl Harbor, and the Park Service presentation at the memorial is notably evenhanded, praising Admiral Yamamoto both for opposing the attack and for executing it with precision.

In December 2008, the administration of President George W. Bush took a step beyond changing the presentation at Pearl Harbor when it integrated that site into what is now called the World War II Valor in the Pacific National Monument. The monument now commemorates Pearl Harbor and the defense of the Aleutian Islands in Alaska, while it also recalls the internment of American citizens of Japanese ancestry in the United States. The larger monument consists of nine sites, five in Hawaii, three in Alaska, and one at the former site of the Tule Lake Segregation Center in California, where Japanese-Americans were imprisoned during the war. As part of this new monument, the National Park Service also created an extensive account of the American occupation of Japan that can be found through the monument's website.

The multicultural developments at the sites of the Alamo, Custer's Last Stand, and Pearl Harbor can be seen as part of an increasing acknowledgment on the part of Americans that the United States may be an empire as well as a nation. By definition, empires (as opposed to nations) are always multicultural. The United States has included many cultures since its colonial prehistory, but it has never come to terms with its status as an empire. That issue became more acute throughout the twentieth century. The question of American empire and the related issue of multiculturalism came to a new crisis in the decade following the attacks of September 11, 2001.

Conceived as an extension of the British Empire but born in revolt against Britain, the United States has always had an ambivalent relationship with the word and the idea of empire. During the nineteenth century, American speakers and writers like Senator Daniel Webster and President John Tyler had no qualms about calling the United States an empire, but they were referring only to the North American continent. Overseas expansion in the Spanish-American War brought out both imperialists and anti-imperialists in the American establishment. After World War I, Woodrow Wilson's dream of world peace rejected empires in favor of national self-determination and international organizations, particularly the League of Nations, but a majority in America disliked that form of international involvement and opted instead for isolationism. After World War II, the United States led the way in founding a United Nations that welcomed former European colonies to its General Assembly. The concept of empire then quietly lost any sense of legitimacy on the grounds of cultural superiority. Explicit opposition to empire appeared in the communist charge that American resistance to communist (and usually nationalist) insurgencies was based on "imperialism." That charge baffled most Americans, who saw their government's interventions in nations like Iran, Guatemala, Lebanon, Nicaragua, the Dominican Republic, and Vietnam as attempts to defend liberty and democracy from communist aggression.

The fall of the Soviet Union and the end of the Cold War seemed to justify this American attitude. In the 1990s, military interventions in Iraq, Somalia, and Bosnia continued to be seen by many as defenses of the values of personal freedom, political democracy, world peace, and multicultural tolerance. Two theorists of the Left, Michael Hardt and Antonio Negri, published a book called *Empire* in the year 2000 that put forth the theory that an unacknowledged world government already existed. Within that government, the United States and other Security Council members enforced order as an executive branch, multinational corporations and regional powers decided policy as a senatorial class, and international organizations like churches and Amnesty International postponed revolt by mitigating conditions for the world's plebians. Presciently, Hardt and Negri identified al-Qaeda as the first postmodern revolutionary group challenging this empire.

On September 11, 2001, members of al-Qaeda hijacked four large airliners. They flew two into the Twin Towers of the World Trade Center in New York, causing each of these 110-story buildings to fall within hours, killing 2,752 people. They crashed a third into the Pentagon, the headquarters of the US Defense Department in Washington, killing 125 people in that building and 59 passengers on the plane. The fourth plane, which may have been intended to hit the Capitol or the White House, crashed in a field in Shanksville, Pennsylvania, apparently because the passengers on that flight heard about the fate of the earlier planes and fought the hijackers. The most lasting physical impact of the attacks was a wound the size of sixteen football fields in New York City, next to Wall Street, the financial center of the nation. For more than ten years, that wound remained open. The scene of destruction was immediately called Ground Zero by broadcast journalists, who borrowed the phrase from the terminology of nuclear war.

Like the Alamo, Custer's Last Stand, the *Maine*, and Pearl Harbor, the attacks of September 11, 2001, shook the nation. All of those earlier attacks took place on or beyond the borders of US territory. No comparable act of destruction by a foreign enemy at a central site had happened since the British burned the White House in the War of 1812. Many Americans responded, as Americans had responded in the past, by affirming their values with new energy.

Immediately after the attacks of 2001, explanations of why the terrorists hated the United States focused on the values of American civil religion. The terrorists hated our personal freedom and feared that the people of their nations would demand their own liberty, along with political democracy. While Americans valued cultural diversity, members of al-Qaeda and the Taliban rulers of Afghanistan did not. The United States went to war to defend freedom, democracy, and tolerance. We would inevitably win, and our victory would re-establish world peace. "Freedom is on the march," President George W. Bush repeatedly declared.

But the march of freedom depended on extending American military domination. Within months, in 2001, the government of Afghanistan was deposed, and at the start of the 2010 decade, the United States had about 200,000 troops and hundreds of bases in Afghanistan and Iraq, supported by fleets of ships and bases throughout the Middle East and Central Asia. The pattern—laid down after the Alamo, Custer, the *Maine,* and Pearl Harbor—of an attack followed by a lasting expansion of American influence seemed evident. Much discussion of American empire, both in positive and negative terms, took place for years before and after the invasion of Iraq in 2003.

Among the first effects of 9/11 on the practice of American civil religion was a dramatic increase in the intensity and extent of the cult of the flag. Flags were suddenly everywhere, displayed in disregard of the formalities of the Flag Code and of tradition. According to Annin & Company, the largest flag manufacturer in the nation, more flags were sold in the ten days following September 11, 2001, than in the entire year 2000. Wal-Mart stores sold 118,000 flags on one of those days. At this writing, flags still hang all day and night on many highway bridges. Though the flag mania has subsided, some effects look permanent. A return to the rules that would have prevented exposure of the flag to bad weather or flying the flag at night is unlikely. Also, the flag has come to seem less of a partisan, conservative symbol than it had been. In the presidential campaigns of 2008 and 2012, Democratic candidates like Barack Obama felt just as much pressure as Republicans to wear flag pins.

Other religious responses to the attack appeared at Ground Zero. People quickly began to leave signs, photographs of the missing, and objects like flowers and dolls along the fences and walls that marked the edge of the disaster area. This leaving of objects resembled what visitors to the Vietnam Veterans Memorial did when that wall was dedicated in 1982 and what African-Americans in the South have done for centuries on gravesites. Meanwhile, firefighters removing human remains created a ritual as they placed the remains into coffins covered by American flags and walked them out, pausing to take off their helmets, to line up the coffins, to have a moment of silence, and to pick up and drop handfuls of dirt before moving the coffins off the site. Even the phrase "Ground Zero" itself quickly took on an aura as the name of a sacred place. These spontaneous responses added to what scholar Paul Christopher Johnson has called organic civil religion, which Johnson contrasts to the instrumental civil religion sponsored by official agencies.

When planning began for creating an official memorial at Ground Zero, basic disagreements emerged. Some argued that the Twin Towers should be rebuilt exactly as they were. Others, especially some survivors of those who died in the attack, pleaded that the entire area should be regarded as a graveyard and turned into a memorial park. A competition was held for designs to rebuild, while incorporating space for a memorial, and in February 2003 a panel, including Maya Lin, chose the plan submitted by architect Daniel Libeskind. Libeskind's concept centered on a skyscraper he named the Freedom Tower. Intended to rise 1,776 feet in height, a number that was both historically meaningful and more than 400 feet higher than the fallen towers, the design featured a 276-foot spire rising from one corner of the building and the suggestion of a spiral in the building's shape, with a vertical wind turbine occupying many of the higher floors. Deliberately echoing the shape of the Statue of Liberty, which stands nearby in the harbor, Libeskind's Freedom Tower was intended to affirm that great symbol of American civil religion.

Almost immediately, Libeskind's building was denounced as impractical. The turbine, the shape of the building, and the off-center spire were all seen as engineering nightmares. The design has been modified twice, first by Libeskind and British architect David Childs and then by Childs alone. The final design retains nothing but the total height of 1,776 feet and a tapering shape from the original. Its spire is now centered, and it has the straight walls of a standard skyscraper. Security concerns voiced by the New York Police Department in 2005 resulted in revisions that included making the first 200 feet from the ground a windowless block of steel and concrete, which led some to call the building Freedom Bunker. In 2009, the Port Authority of New York and New Jersey decided for commercial and security reasons to change the name of the building from Freedom Tower to One World Trade Center.

With regard to the memorial, another design competition was held, and in 2004 a design by Michael Arad and Peter Walker was chosen. Their proposal was called "Reflecting Absence." Its concept centered on two large square holes, 200 feet on each side (or about the same size as the towers of the World Trade Center), at the places where the Twin Towers once stood. Each square would be cut into the ground to a depth of 30 feet, with waterfalls flowing down their walls into pools (Figure 33.1). The names of those killed in all of the September 11 attacks, at the Pentagon and on the airplane that crashed in Pennsylvania as well as at Ground Zero, would be inscribed on the walls behind the waterfalls. Alongside this memorial, a museum would be constructed to house relics from the attacks, such as crushed police cars and fire trucks.

As construction progressed, some elements of the original plan were eliminated and others were challenged. Among the features dropped was an International Freedom Center to document the history of freedom. People on the political Right feared that the Freedom Center might be used to criticize the policies and actions of the United States. Conflict long raged over whether to include access to the bedrock under the World Trade Center, 70 feet below the surface, as part of the new museum, and whether to bring unidentified human remains from the attack into the museum at the lower level. New York mayor

Figure 33.1 One of the two pools, each as large as the base of one tower of the World Trade Center, at the Ground Zero Memorial. The sound of water rushing from the sides mutes noises from the streets, creating a quiet plaza. Photograph by the author.

Michael Bloomberg opposed some of the plans for the lower level as part of his effort to cut projected costs from $973 million to $530 million. Some family members of Ground Zero victims objected to having the human remains become part of what they saw as a tourist destination. Flooding of the museum in the late fall of 2012 led others to argue that all valuable items and remains should be placed at the level of the plaza.

Before the memorial park opened in September 2011, it was decided to inscribe the names of the dead on bronze parapets above the waterfalls rather than on the walls below. The water now rushes from behind each parapet in hissing jets, with a sound strong enough to dampen noises from surrounding streets, then flows toward a square hole at the center, about 50 feet on each side, where the water is slowed by a slightly raised lip so that it disappears into the blackness in separate, noiseless cascades. The movement and the sound of the water powerfully suggests that the Twin Towers and the people represented by the names are constantly falling with the water, then disappearing. The memorial opened to the public on the tenth anniversary of the attack, but the museum remained unfinished.

Steel columns and beams from the Twin Towers began to be treated as relics. In August 2009, the last column left standing by the attacks was returned to the site to be displayed in the museum. Meanwhile, many others have been cut up and shipped around the world, including several sent to fire companies in France. Twenty-five of these shipments were made in 2008. The state of Kansas received a 600-pound piece of steel that will be cut into eight pieces and displayed at eight airports. At Kennedy Airport, the Port Authority is storing 2,000 more pieces of World Trade Center steel in a special hangar with humidity control to prevent rust. Two pieces of steel in the shape of a cross that fell on September 11 and stuck into the ground were displayed for years near Ground Zero, on the outside wall of the Church of St. Peter, the oldest Roman Catholic parish in Manhattan, and they have been moved to the museum. Opposition to having a cross in the museum has led to a lawsuit, testing the symbolic limits of civil religion.

Ground Zero and the blocks around it form an unusually complex holy place. It is simultaneously a neighborhood dedicated to big business, where developers will seek to make more offices; a construction site that will probably never be entirely finished because of the dynamism of New York; and a tourist area, the oldest site of European settlement in the city, with several very old churches and a few museums. Within a short walk is Battery Park, where people line up on the landing dock for boats to the Statue of Liberty and Ellis Island. Unlike most holy places, the neighborhood has strip clubs, massage parlors, lunch counters, and bars. In June 2010, Ground Zero became more complicated when a group of American Muslims received approval by a community zoning board for their application to build an Islamic community center and mosque two blocks from where the towers fell.

Immediately called the "Ground Zero Mosque" by the conservative press and the "9/11 Victory Mosque" by some family members of victims who demonstrated against it, this project tested the value of cultural tolerance. National polls revealed that about 70 percent of Americans saw the mosque near Ground Zero as inappropriate, though large majorities also said that Muslims had the right to build there if they wished. New Yorkers were somewhat less opposed, with 52 percent against and 31 perent in favor. Mayor Bloomberg spoke out strongly in support, calling the issue "a test of our commitment to American values." Addressing those who wanted another place for the mosque to be found, Mayor Bloomberg noted that there was already a mosque within four blocks of the former World Trade Center and asked how large the "no-mosque zone" around Ground Zero should be. Bloomberg also linked his support to the character of New York City, saying that accepting the new Islamic center would help to "keep New York the most open, diverse, tolerant, and free city in the world."

Irony, farce, and political posturing alternated around the issue of the mosque in the summer of 2010. Two Egyptian-Americans, Coptic Christians who worked as reporters for a Christian TV station in California, flew across the country to take part in a rally against the mosque and found themselves in need of rescue by police from the anti-mosque crowd they had sought to join. They had been overheard speaking Arabic and were threatened with violence. President Obama gave a speech on August 12, 2010, at a Muslim gathering for Ramadan, strongly supporting the right of Muslims to build the mosque wherever they liked, even on what he called the "hallowed ground" of Ground Zero, but two days later he issued a "clarification" to the effect that he was just endorsing their right to build, not expressing a judgment on the wisdom of building in that particular place. Sarah Palin, the former Republican candidate for vice president, then challenged the president to take a position for or against the mosque itself, but he did not respond. Late in August, the pastor of a tiny Florida evangelical church, Terry Jones, became a international figure for a moment, when he threatened to hold a public burning of copies of the Quran on September 11 if the plans for the mosque were not changed. His threat touched off demonstrations in Muslim nations around the world, elicited warnings from President Obama and from General David Petraeus that such an action would endanger our troops in Iraq and Afghanistan, and provoked a personal phone call from Secretary of Defense Robert Gates before Jones called off the plan. On Fox News and at Tea Party rallies, conservatives used the mosque issue to rally support for Republicans in the 2010 elections, in which Republicans took control of the House of Representatives and increased their numbers in the Senate.

Occasionally, a writer tried to clarify the situation by pointing out facts, such as that the name "Ground Zero Mosque" was a misnomer, since the proposed building was not on but only near the area called Ground Zero and was not primarily a mosque, but a community center named Cordoba House (or at other times, Park51), which included a prayer room along with a swimming pool, auditorium, and meeting rooms. Sharif El-Gamal, the businessman who had purchased the site and sought to develop the project, repeatedly described his concept as analogous to the buildings of the YMCA, where he had learned to swim as a child. Despite all attempts at clarification and reconciliation, the projected Islamic center remained caught up in the clashes over morality and religion, sometimes called "culture wars," that have roiled US politics since the 1980s.

The potential to stand above partisan strife has always been part of American civil religion, however, and that potential remains. Once the memorial and museum at Ground Zero are both open and the One World Trade Center skyscraper is complete, the symbolism of the site will probably stabilize. At that point, an Islamic building in the neighborhood will no longer seem so threatening. As at the sites of the Alamo, Custer's Last Stand, the *Maine* memorial, and Pearl Harbor, a process taking decades will have produced a consensus. Whether that consensus includes agreement on the relation of American empire to American civil religion remains to be seen.

SOURCES

Bloomberg, Michael, "A Test of Our Commitment to American Values," *The Wall Street Journal*, August 25, 2010.

Gibson, Eric, "A Memorial We Want to Love," *The Wall Street Journal*, September 15, 2011.

Hardt, Michael, and Antonio Negri, *Empire* (Cambridge, MA: Harvard University Press, 2000).

Jasper, Joy Waldron, ed., *The USS Arizona: The Ship, the Men, the Pearl Harbor Attack, and the Symbol That Aroused America* (New York: St. Martin's Press, 2001).

Johnson, Paul Christopher, "Savage Civil Religion," NUMEN—International Review for the History of Religions 52, no. 3 (2005), 289–324.

Linenthal, Edward Tabor, *Sacred Ground: Americans and Their Battlefields* (Chicago: University of Illinois Press, 1991).

Nussbaum, Martha C., "The Case of Park51," in *The New Religious Intolerance: Overcoming the Politics of Fear in an Anxious Age* (Cambridge, MA: Harvard University Press, 2012), 188–239.

Roberts, Randy, and James S. Olson, *A Line in the Sand: The Alamo in Blood and Memory* (New York: The Free Press, 2001).

34

Conflict, Consensus, and the Future

The values of freedom, democracy, peace, and tolerance emerged over the phases of American civil religion outlined in Chapter 1 and described in the other chapters of this book. From the colonial phase through the classical, continental, sacrificial (Civil War), imperial, global, and multicultural periods, these four values continued to develop. Often freedom, democracy, peace, and tolerance have won out through conflict with conditions that contradicted these values. In an age of surveillance, voter suppression or manipulation, war, and xenophobia, a survey of this pattern may give hope. Such a survey of conflicts over values may also provide a sense of direction.

To begin the survey with freedom, the Constitution that declared in its preamble the intention to "secure the blessings of liberty" also protected slavery, and the ensuing struggle to free the slaves and their descendants has shaped the nation's history. Though Article IV of that same Constitution gives the federal government the power to protect "republican" state governments against invasions or anti-democratic revolutions, federal and state governments long limited political democracy by race and sex. The relations between personal freedom, political democracy, and wealth are still hotly contested.

Peace with all nations was announced as our goal by Washington and Lincoln, but to secure world peace many wars and military actions have seemed necessary. The United States has sought peace by waging wars against the Barbary pirates, against Great Britain, against Mexico, against Native Americans, against the Confederacy, against Spain, twice against Germany, against Japan, and against North Korea and Communist China. American military forces have intervened (sometimes repeatedly) in places like the Soviet Union (during the 1920s), Nicaragua, the Dominican Republic, Cuba, Vietnam, Panama, Lebanon, Somalia, the former Yugoslavia, Iraq, and Afghanistan.

Some of this fighting for peace was done in the name of another value, cultural tolerance. At the foundations of Jamestown, Plymouth, and New Amsterdam, cultural tolerance was a critical American value, helping those settlements to survive and prosper, but Native Americans were soon driven away and Africans enslaved in those places. Today, Ellis Island celebrates cultural tolerance, but it began as a place for screening immigrants and sending undesirables back home. Regulating immigration still tests the limits of cultural tolerance in America.

Sometimes conflict increases cultural tolerance. The United States became more connected to the world in many ways as a result of the long conflict that began at Ground Zero. People from 80 nations, including 130 Israelis, more than 250 citizens of India, and hundreds of British, died in the September 11 attacks. About 60 Muslims, from many nations, died in the attacks, excluding the 19 terrorists who carried them out. In Paris, the French newspaper *Le Monde* carried the headline "We Are All Americans Now," and Italians carried signs that said the same thing to the home port of the US Navy's Sixth Fleet in Naples. Orchestras played "The Star-Spangled Banner" in front of Buckingham Palace in London and at the Brandenburg Gate in Berlin. The North Atlantic Treaty Organization, the military alliance set up to face the Soviet Union during the Cold War, for the first time invoked the clause in its treaty that obligated members to fight in defense of any member that was attacked. As one result, NATO troops—including Poles, Danes, Spaniards, Italians, Germans, Canadians, and others—fought for more than a decade alongside Americans and British in Afghanistan, and some served for a time in Iraq. Beyond NATO, soldiers from more than 40 nations from as far away as South Korea and New Zealand have joined with forces from the United States in the fighting and rebuilding in Afghanistan.

On the negative side, the attacks of September 11, 2001, also led to Palestinians celebrating in the streets of East Jerusalem and to images of the celebrations being shown in America. Some Americans attacked mosques in the United States. Two Sikh brothers, both American citizens, were killed in separate incidents because they were wearing turbans and were mistaken for Muslims. The US invasion of Iraq in 2003 brought millions of protesters into the streets of Europe. Though Spain sent troops to Iraq, a terror attack in Madrid in 2004 led to a change of government and the withdrawal of Spanish troops. News of American abuse of Iraqi prisoners in Abu Ghraib prison, of torture at many secret sites, and of drone airplanes that often killed civilians made American rhetoric about freedom, democracy, peace, and tolerance seem hypocritical to many, among both enemies and allies. British support for the American wars contributed to the fall of the British Labour government in 2010. Still, the new British government maintained troops in Afghanistan.

American civil religion showed its capacity to reach a consensus beyond the attacks of September 11 when the United States elected Barack Hussein Obama, whose father was a black African and a Muslim, as president. In the prologue of Obama's 2006 campaign book, *The Audacity of Hope*, the future president recalled a meeting that took place in late September 2001, with a media consultant who had been urging him to run for statewide office in Illinois. Looking at a newspaper with a picture of Osama bin Laden on the front page, the consultant expressed regret for the apparent death of Obama's political hopes. "You can't change your name," the consultant said. And it is a name that might not be believed in a work of fiction. "Barack" comes from the root that means "Blessed" in Semitic languages, such as Arabic and Hebrew. In Jewish services of worship, no word is more often repeated than "Baruch," as in "Blessed be God, ruler of the universe." The middle name of "Hussein," from an Arabic word meaning "handsome" or "beautiful," a name which has sometimes been used as a weapon against President Obama, comes from the grandson of the Prophet Muhammad. That Hussein died a martyr in 680, and is revered by all Muslims and regarded as an ancestor of the messianic leader of the future by Shi'ites. Finally, "Obama" derives from the president's grandfather, who adopted it when he became a Muslim. Meaning "one who bends" (or performs Islamic prayer) in the language of the Luo tribe of Kenya, it is a name commonly taken by converts to Islam. The name of Barack Hussein Obama, then, might be translated into English as "the blessed, beautiful, messianic leader who prays." That a biracial man with this name would be elected president seven years after the September 11 attacks, and elected while carrying states like Virginia, Indiana, and North Carolina as well as the Democratic base, was about as close to a miracle as anything in the realm of civil religion could be. Without the financial crisis of September 2008, the election of Obama might not have happened, at least as such a landslide, but for whatever reason, it did occur. Obama's reelection in 2012 showed that 2008 had not been a fluke, but a real sign of cultural change.

During the 2008 campaign, issues of race, religion, and civil religion became explicitly intertwined. The pastor of the Baptist church that Obama attended in Chicago, the Rev. Dr. Jeremiah Wright, had for decades been an exponent of Afrocentric theology, emphasizing the virtues of African culture and condemning white racism and oppression. In the midst of the spring presidential primaries, a video was uploaded on YouTube that showed Dr. Wright vigorously preaching, "God bless America? No, God *damn* America," at least when America sins, as he charged that the United States often did. Candidate Obama responded to the furor by giving a lengthy, nationally televised speech on race in America, in which he said that he could no more disown Dr. Wright than his own white grandmother, who had also held some racist views. Soon after, however, Wright gave his own speech on the issue, calling Obama a "politician" and emphasizing what he saw as basic emotional and cultural differences between Africans and whites. Obama then did disown Wright in effect, by resigning from his church.

Obama's election dramatically extended American civil religion's relations with the world. That extension began with Obama's background in Kenya and Indonesia, but continued through his actions. In July 2008, he became the first presidential candidate to hold a campaign rally abroad, speaking to a huge crowd in Germany and hurting his poll numbers in the United States. In its issue covering the election result, the German magazine *Der Spiegel* carried on its cover a picture of Obama with the headline, *Die Weltpresident*, or "the World President." The Nobel Prize Committee gave President Obama its 2009 Peace Prize, a gesture that seemed unaccountable except as an expression of the world's astonishment at his achievement in being elected. Without doing anything else, he had already become a transformative figure for the nation and the world.

Accepting the Nobel Peace Prize, President Obama gave a speech defending the wars that he had inherited and that his administration continued to fight. The persistence of these wars demonstrated that the attacks of September 11 had not been entirely overcome. As the wars continued, they contributed to a trend within American civil religion toward religious nationalism, a trend that ran counter to the international development represented by Obama.

One small symptom of the nationalistic narrowing of civil religion is the now-obligatory ending of nearly all presidential speeches (or at least all domestic presidential speeches) with the words "God bless the United States of America." Adding this last line would have undermined the messages of the Kennedy Inaugural and of Lincoln's Second Inaugural, both of which emphasized human work and divine judgment. Meanwhile, the National Mall in Washington is increasingly used for very partisan rallies, led by figures like Glenn Beck and Jon Stewart, who do not even pretend to address the whole nation. Tea Party rallies to "take back our country," dating from 2010, and Occupy encampments that began in 2011 both implied that the nation had somehow been lost, or that a real American civil religion needed to be reasserted against a heretical form. There are times when it seems that no political or cultural leader can be heard by all Americans.

Meanwhile, an object accessible to all American citizens, the United States passport, was redesigned in 2007 in a manner that both reflected the culture wars and demonstrated a continuing capacity to come to consensus. Literally named "American Icon" by the Department of State, the new passport has rich imagery and messaging on each of its 28 pages. Pictures range from the Liberty Bell to bison and eagles and from Mount Rushmore to a totem pole, concluding with the Earth seen from the Moon on the inside of the back cover. Even the most functional pages have pictures or inspirational quotes. On pages six and seven, for example, above some closely printed advice on travel security, registering with US embassies, and dual citizenship, stands a quote from Daniel Webster: "The principle of free government adheres to the American soil. It is bedded in it, immovable as its mountains."

The new passports seem jingoistic or coercively patriotic to some, but great care was taken to make them multicultural. One quotation comes from a Mohawk (a native nation in New York State and Canada) thanksgiving ritual and gives thanks to (not for) all animals, saying that animals have "many things to teach us as people." This quote appears above two very non-Mohawk Native American images, a totem pole from the Pacific Northwest and a buffalo from the Great Plains, and that enhances the multicultural lesson. Another quote, printed over two pictures of the Statue of Liberty, could have been taken from many speeches given by President George W. Bush to justify the War on Terror: "The cause of freedom is not the cause of a race or sect, a party or a class—it is the cause of humankind, the very birthright of humanity." These words actually came from the writings of Anna Julia Cooper (1858–1964), who was born in slavery and who became the fourth African-American woman to earn a doctorate, a Ph.D. in history from the University of Pennsylvania. The quote facing the picture of the Earth and the Moon came from Ellison S. Onizuka, the first Asian-American astronaut, who died in the explosion on launch of the Challenger space shuttle in 1986. George Washington and Martin Luther King, Jr., are quoted on the pages of the passport, as are the Declaration of Independence, the national anthem, the Gettysburg Address, and the Kennedy Inaugural. The new passport represents, for good or for ill, a time capsule version of the official consensus on American civil religion as it stood in 2007.

Among the forces tending to create a consensus version of American civil religion that continues to expand its vision, none is so important as the National Park Service. The armed forces were the first priesthood of civil religion, guarding the flag and the Tomb of the Unknown Soldier and Arlington Cemetery, but the National Park Service has become another category of clergy with a more universal field of action. Founded in 1916 under President Woodrow Wilson, the Park Service is most often identified with natural sites like Yellowstone and the Grand Canyon. Since March 1933, an order of President Franklin Roosevelt has given the Park Service responsibility for the whole array of historical sites and memorials owned by the federal government. As custodian of the Capitol and many other sites on the Mall, as well as of the Liberty Bell and Independence Hall, Gettysburg, the site of Custer's Last Stand, Pearl Harbor, Jamestown, much of Boston's Freedom Trail, Ellis Island, and many other sites, the National Park Service has shown itself open to listening to what constituents of the sites want and to constantly revising its historical narrative. Under the slogan of "civic engagement," the Park Service has consulted competing groups, often consciously trying to promote what one of its historians has called a "post-ethnic society." In a sense, just because the Park Service has sought to tell an accurate story of the conflicts that shaped these places, it has become dedicated to promulgating the value of cultural tolerance. Where once critics speaking for Native Americans, African-Americans, and Europeans from the East and South of Europe felt neglected by the Park Service and marginalized in its version of civil religion, now such complaints come primarily from white conservatives.

For example, in 2004, an organization called the Traditional Values Coalition demanded and got changes in the eight-minute video about the Lincoln Memorial that the Park Service had been showing for a decade. The video's emphasis on civil rights marches and gay rights demonstrations seemed leftist to them, and the Park Service added four minutes of events like presidential visits and the Gulf War victory parade of 1991. Gerald Baker, a Hidatsa Indian and Park Service employee who was the first Native American superintendent of Mount Rushmore, received death threats because of his efforts to include Native American exhibits at that site, but he was not deterred. The display around the Liberty Bell brought complaints in 2007 from Stephen Warshawsky, who wrote that the exhibit implied that the bell had "little relevance to a middle-class white male." Nevertheless, the Park Service went on working with those who sought to memorialize the presidential slave quarters that stood near the Liberty Bell exhibit, and this memorial opened in 2010. At Pearl Harbor, some visitors find the narrative in the Park Service presentation too evenhanded, particularly in its praise of Admiral Yamamoto. A 2010 conference at Pearl Harbor on the Pacific war that the Park Service co-sponsored (with the East-West Center of the University of Hawaii and the National Endowment for the Humanities) was denounced by some participants and by correspondents for Fox News as anti-American.

In November 2010, the Park Service unveiled a comprehensive response to the Traditional Values Coalition's critique of its video on the Lincoln Memorial. It opened an interactive website about the Lincoln Memorial that demonstrated remarkable intensity of emotion and inclusiveness. The site featured personal talks about aspects of the memorial by a dozen Park Service interpreters who spoke from their own experience. One interpreter from Tennessee said that after a childhood and education in which Lincoln was never presented as a hero, she at first felt as if she was in a hostile atmosphere when she worked in the memorial. Reading the text of the Second Inaugural that is inscribed on the south wall, she thought that Lincoln was blaming the South. After she accepted a Park Service assignment to work on the interpretation of the speech, however, she came to understand what Lincoln wanted and to regard him as a friend.

The Park Service does not always seek to broaden American civil religion, however. With regard to the Mall in Washington, its directors have sought restrictions on access that might prevent or severely curtail the use of the Mall for political demonstrations. Simply by fulfilling functions like designing visitors' centers at historic places, writing narratives for interpreters, and running websites associated with historic places, the National Park Service naturally tends to establish a consensus that may harden into orthodoxy. Orthodoxy may have some good effects. There is hope that the ongoing conflicts over sites like Plymouth Rock and the Ground Zero memorial and museum will find a permanent settlement, and a reliable source of funding, under the Park Service.

Partly because of the efforts of the Park Service, American civil religion has developed its orthodoxy more rapidly than many other religions. Religions normally take centuries to emerge and to coalesce. Three centuries after Jesus taught, there was still no organization that could be called Christianity, or even a recognized set of Christian scriptures. Four thousand years of religious practice in India passed before anything called Hinduism appeared, and it took about a thousand years of Israelite history to produce the beginnings of Judaism. But less than two and a half centuries after the foundation of the United States, there is an American civil religion with two central scriptures, the Declaration of Independence and the Constitution. This religion also includes many comments on these scriptures in words that are themselves seen as sacred, such as the Gettysburg Address and the speeches of Martin Luther King. It has a vivid set of images, beginning with the flag, and dozens of officially presented sacred places, most recently Ground Zero. There are deities—Washington and Jefferson and Lincoln, Franklin Roosevelt and Martin Luther King—at least in the sense of spirits who are invoked and whose shrines are visited. Finally, there are caretakers or clergy—the Park Service, some members of the armed services, and many public officials, especially the president on some occasions—who guard and interpret the civil religion, holding its ceremonies and marking its holidays.

More than one scholar has questioned the reality of American civil religion. As long ago as 1975, Robert Bellah in *The Broken Covenant* pronounced American civil religion an "empty shell" because of the misguided war and defeat in Vietnam and the betrayals of trust by President Nixon. Decades of military intervention (President Reagan and Lebanon, Grenada, Iran-Contra) and non-intervention (President Clinton and Rwanda) led to further questions about whether religious values have any real effect on national policy. In the first Gulf War of 1991, President George H. W. Bush acted to drive Iraq from Kuwait with support from the United Nations, but against the votes of almost all Democrats in the Senate. He faced the charge of fighting a war for oil.

More recently, other writers have predicted the fate of American civil religion by judging it as a worthy or unworthy successor of earlier forms. In *Are We Rome? The Fall of an Empire and the Fate of America* (2007), Cullen Murphy drew negative conclusions from the parallels between the United States and ancient Rome. Just as Rome closed in on itself and lost its way, Murphy warned, so might America. Murphy's book provoked the response of a positive comparison, *Empires of Trust: How Rome Built—and America Is Building—a New World* (2008) from Thomas F. Madden, a specialist in Roman history. Relating American civil religion to the Abrahamic religions, Harold Bloom drew negative conclusions in *The American Religion: The Emergence of the Post-Christian Nation* (1992), and David Gelernter advanced a positive view in *Americanism: The Fourth Great Western Religion* (2007). The British heritage has also been brought to bear, usually by people who hope the American empire will endure. In *God and Gold: Britain, America, and the Making of the Modern World* (2007), Walter Russell Mead argued that the United States inherited from the Dutch and the British a "world system" of free trade and power justified by opposition to a tyrannical Antichrist. Mead offered a broader perspective on the Anglo-American empire with a militantly Protestant spirit that Kevin Phillips had already presented in *The Cousins' Wars* (1998).

Some consolation for those who fear that American civil religion will disappear can be found in the fate of these predecessors. None of them have really disappeared, nor have their characteristic values. Perhaps Rome emptied itself of meaning by betraying its own ideals; perhaps early Christianity became dissolved in a world of converts and politics; perhaps Great Britain fell into weakness because of two World Wars and bankruptcy brought on by imperial overstretch. But as many have noticed, the Roman Catholic Church sits like a ghost on the ruins of the empire, and the capitol of the United States bears an unmistakable Roman stamp. While the spirit of Christ has always proved hard to isolate, Christian faith and the Christian worldview have never grown with more vigor than they are showing today in Africa or Asia. The British Empire may be gone, but the Commonwealth still links fifty-four nations. Scores of nations have Parliaments that resemble the one in London, and the language of English and its literature continue to spread across the globe. As the military and economic power of the United States fades in relation to those of other nations, the values of American civil religion will remain.

One of the basic differences among commentators on American civil religion is whether or not the spread of capitalism forms part of the mission of that religion. Besides historians like Walter Russell Mead, some theorists have offered specific economic arguments. Charles Maier, the author of *Among Empires: American Ascendancy and Its Predecessors* (2006), saw methods of production, patterns of consumption, and control of credit as crucial factors in the history of the British Empire and as continuing factors in our own. There is even one American college, Grove City College in Pennsylvania, that was founded in 1876 with a mission to spread democracy and free enterprise to the world, along with a conservative brand of Presbyterianism.

But whatever economic ideals and economic incentives have driven American advocates of empire, it should be remembered that American presidents have talked about liberty and democracy and peace, not about property and trade, when sending troops abroad. Those who have seen economic motives working beneath all rhetoric, and those who have proclaimed that economic freedom is the most important aspect of the freedom that Americans hold sacred, certainly have their points. On the other hand, while free enterprise has been an important American value, the duty to spread free enterprise has never attracted support equal to the support for personal freedom, political democracy, world peace, and cultural tolerance as part of the consensus of American civil religion. Many leaders, including John Winthrop, both Theodore and Franklin Delano Roosevelt, John F. Kennedy, and Martin Luther King, as well as songs like "America the Beautiful" and "This Land Is Your Land," have criticized the unbridled seeking of wealth while affirming American civil religion.

Similar arguments have been made regarding violence. On one hand, many writers have noticed the violence of American history and culture, and some have argued that American violence has religious roots, or that violence is a basic value of American civil religion. The first perspective informs *Empire of Sacrifice: The Religious Origins of American Violence* (2010), by Jon Pahl, and the second argument is made by Gary Laderman in his *American Civil Religion* (2012). Though no one can deny that violence has played a large role in US history, however, the value of violence is more questionable. Leaders who send American military forces into the world always do so in the name of peace, not of war or conquest. Although "The Star Spangled Banner" is filled with warlike imagery, many prefer the words of "God Bless America," "America the Beautiful," and "This Land Is Your Land," all of which celebrate peace. Violence always raises religious issues, because violence causes death and leads to reflections on immortality, but violence has not become an explicit American value on the level of peaceful life in a "home sweet home." Nor has American concern for peace been without result. Since the founding of the United Nations—an American invention, the creation of Franklin and Eleanor Roosevelt—there has been no outbreak of the limitless wars between major powers that dominated the first half of the twentieth century and marked all centuries since the Renaissance.

During 2012, two books testified to the continuing strength of an American consensus. Stephen Prothero, a professor and writer for the general public, published *The American Bible*, an anthology of important American texts with historical reactions and commentary, organized according to types of biblical literature into sections with titles such as Genesis, Prophets, and Epistles. This approach implied the existence of a canon of sacred texts in American civil religion, while making room for dissenters among the commentators. In a more scholarly vein, Andrew Preston published a magisterial study called *Sword of the Spirit, Shield of Faith*, which ran through the history of American foreign policy from the Puritans through the Nobel acceptance speech of Barack Obama, detailing how religious convictions have influenced that policy at every step.

This book has attempted to provide something more basic: an outline and guide to American civil religion, including its sacred places and symbolic dimensions as well as its texts and values. Both for good and for ill, American civil religion is now a concrete reality and a vital force, one of the most influential religions in the world. It is also one of the religions most open to change.

In 1967, when Robert Bellah still affirmed American civil religion, he wrote that it would not remain vital unless it incorporated international imagery. Bellah was right about that, and what he hoped for then has happened. Since Bellah wrote his seminal piece, American civil religion has become much more international, generating new sites like Disney's Epcot Center, Ellis Island, the United States Holocaust Memorial Museum, and the National Museum of the American Indian. Americans have elected an embodiment of internationalism in the person of President Obama. Whatever verdict historians or the vagaries of American politics pass on Obama's legacy, Obama will always stand as a symbol of internationalism and cultural tolerance.

Meanwhile, there are signs that the values of American civil religion are becoming more prevalent everywhere. The last six decades of the twentieth century saw the fall of many fascist and communist dictatorships, and of colonial and military regimes. Since the 1990s, many new democratic governments have appeared in Latin America and Asia and Africa. With the Arab Spring and the continuing growth of communications, it seems possible that the values of personal liberty, political democracy, world peace, and cultural tolerance may come to be held sacred across the globe. If history turns in that direction, American civil religion will have contributed to a civil religion of the world.

SOURCES

Bellah, Robert N., *The Broken Covenant: American Civil Religion in Time of Trial* (New York: Seabury Press, 1975)

Bloom, Harold, *The American Religion: The Emergence of the Post-Christian Nation* (New York: Simon & Schuster, 1992).

Gelernter, David, *Americanism: The Fourth Great Western Religion* (New York: Doubleday, 2007).

Laderman, Gary, *American Civil Religion* (Minneapolis, MN: Fortress Press, 2012).

Linenthal, Edward T., "The National Park Service and Civic Engagement," *The Public Historian*, Vol. 28, No. 1 (Winter 2006), 123-129.

Mackintosh, Barry, *Interpretation in the National Park Service: A Historical Perspective* (Washington, DC: National Park Service, History Division, 1986).

Madden, Thomas F., *Empires of Trust: How Rome Built—and America Is Building—a New World* (New York: Dutton, 2008).

Maier, Charles S., *Among Empires: American Ascendancy and Its Predecessors* (Cambridge, MA: Harvard University Press, 2006).

Mead, Walter Russell, *God and Gold: Britain, America, and the Making of the Modern World* (New York: Knopf, 2007).

Murphy, Cullen, *Are We Rome? The Fall of an Empire and the Fate of America* (Boston: Houghton Mifflin, 2007).

Pahl, Jon, *Empire of Sacrifice: The Religious Origins of American Violence* (New York: NYU Press, 2010).

Phillips, Kevin, *The Cousins' Wars: Religion, Politics, Civil Warfare, and the Triumph of Anglo-America* (New York: Basic Books, 1998).

Preston, Andrew, *Sword of the Spirit, Shield of Faith: Religion in American War and Diplomacy* (New York: Alfred A. Knopf, 2012).

Prothero, Stephen, *The American Bible: How Our Words Unite, Divide, and Define a Nation* (New York: HarperCollins, 2012).

CPSIA information can be obtained
at www.ICGtesting.com
Printed in the USA
BVOW09s1249230617
487555BV00004B/5/P